EDWARD ELGAR: MUSIC AND LITERATURE

Elgar in 1929: Marconi photograph

Edward Elgar: Music and Literature

Edited by
RAYMOND MONK

Scolar Press

Published by
SCOLAR PRESS
Gower House
Croft Road
Aldershot
Hants GU11 3HR
England

Ashgate Publishing Company
Old Post Road
Brookfield
Vermont 05036
USA

British Library Cataloguing in Publication Data and Library of Congress Cataloging-in-Publication data are available.

ISBN 0 85967 937 3

Typeset in 10 point Garamond by Textflow Services Ltd. and printed in Great Britain at the University Press Cambridge

Contents

List of plates

Notes on contributors

Robert Anderson was born in India and educated at Harrow and Cambridge. Director of Music at Gordonstoun School, he was also an associate editor of *The Musical Times* and has broadcast frequently. He has conducted the St Bartholomew's Hospital Choral Society in a number of Elgar performances at the Royal Albert Hall, London. His *Elgar in Manuscript* was published in 1990 by the British Library and he is co-ordinating editor of the Elgar Complete Edition.

E. Wulstan Atkins, Elgar's godson, was born in Worcester in 1904 and educated at Shrewsbury and Christ's College, Cambridge. He later qualified as a Chartered Engineer and spent his career in engineering, but music has always been his special interest. Since 1973 he has been Chairman of the Elgar Foundation and the Elgar Birthplace Trust and is a Vice-President of the Elgar Society. He is the author of *The Elgar-Atkins Friendship*, which was published in 1984, and has broadcast frequently.

Christopher Grogan was born and educated in London. Since completing his doctorate in 1989 he has been Music Librarian of Royal Holloway and Bedford New College, University of London. He has published articles on Elgar and is currently editing the composer's *Wand of Youth* suites and *Dream Children* for Novello's Elgar Complete Edition.

Michael Kennedy, O.B.E., was born in Manchester and educated at Berkhamstead. He has been staff music critic on *The Daily Telegraph* since 1950, northern editor from 1960 to 1986 and joint chief critic from 1987. He has written biographical studies of many composers and conductors including Elgar, Walton, Britten, Boult and Barbirolli. He is author of the *Oxford Dictionary of Music* and is a Vice-President of both the Elgar Society and the Elgar Foundation.

Christopher Kent completed a Ph.D. study of Elgar's sketches at King's College, London before becoming a lecturer in music at the University of Reading. He is a member of the Editorial Board of the Elgar Complete Edition and a co-editor of several volumes of the series. His other main interest, both practical and scholarly, centres on the organ. As Secretary of The British Institute of Organ Studies (B.I.O.S.) he has published many historical articles and performs widely.

Ivor Keys, C.B.E., teacher, composer and organist. Professor of Music at Nottingham University 1954–68 and at Birmingham 1968–87 where, like Elgar, he occupied the Peyton Chair. This afforded him opportunities, not often given to one person, to propagate music by professional performance on piano and organ and as a choral and orchestral conductor. Ivor Keys is a Vice-President of the Elgar Foundation and has precious memories of Elgar's own readings at Three Choirs Festivals.

Diana McVeagh studied at the Royal College of Music. She works as a freelance reviewing for various periodicals. She was assistant editor of The Musical Times and was on the executive committee of *The New Grove Dictionary of Music and Musicians* for which she wrote the entry on Elgar. Her book *Edward Elgar: his Life and Music* (Dent) was published in 1955. She is a Vice-President of the Elgar Society and of the Royal Musical Association and was Chairman of the London Branch of the Elgar Society (1980–86).

Robert Meikle was born in Derbyshire and educated at the University of Glasgow and at Cornell University, where he took his doctorate under Donald Grout. He has taught at the Birmingham Conservatoire and at Glasgow University, and for fifteen years from 1975 he was Director of Music at Leicester University. Government cutbacks in education funding brought the teaching of music to an end at Leicester in 1991, since which time he has been a Senior Lecturer in the Music Department at the University of Birmingham. In addition to Elgar, his abiding interest is in the music of Mozart, and he has wide experience as a choral conductor.

Ronald Taylor was born in Southgate, Middlesex in 1928. For over twenty years he was a director of the booksellers Bertram Rota Ltd, and is now a consultant on rare books. He runs a specialist record business dealing in 78 rpm recordings, and was editor of the *Elgar Society Journal* from January 1977 to June 1991. He has prepared a discography of Columbia Records (with Frank Andrews) for future publication.

Brian Trowell was born in Wokingham in 1931. After leaving Cambridge where he had studied with Thurston Dart, he was Lecturer in Music at Birmingham and later at King's College, London. He was head of radio opera at the BBC from 1967–1970 and returned to King's College where he became King Edward Professor of Music in 1974. He now occupies the Heather Chair at Oxford University. Professor Trowell is an acknowledged authority on fifteenth-century English music and on opera of all periods. He has been Chairman of the Editorial Committee of *Musica Britannica* since 1984 and is a past President of the Royal Musical Association.

Percy M. Young, author, teacher, composer and organist, has spent a lifetime in music. He studied at Cambridge University and Trinity College, Dublin and is author of over fifty books including major biographies of Elgar, Sullivan, and Sir George Grove. He is a Vice-President of the Elgar Society and Editor of the Critical Edition of *The Spanish Lady* which appeared in 1990, an unfinished Elgar work with which his name will always be associated.

The Editor, Raymond Monk, is a Trustee of the Elgar Birthplace, a Director of the Elgar Foundation and a member of the National Committee of the Elgar Society. He is a Fellow of the Royal Philharmonic Society. Elgar has been an important part of his life since the age of twelve when he heard a performance of the Second Symphony and he recently inherited the Elgar Diaries which are quoted extensively in this volume.

Acknowledgements

This volume of essays, like its predecessor (*Elgar Studies*, Scolar Press, 1990), seeks to reflect many aspects of the life and work of Edward Elgar. Each essay is self-contained but the reader will discern a strong literary thread running through most of them – strong enough, I think, to justify the final choice of title for this collection. Many of the contributors to that earlier volume are again represented here, and together with others they have produced a body of original work which extends our Elgarian horizons and often successfully challenges well-established opinion.

The book has been a pleasure to compile and friendship has played an important part in its production. Without it, nothing would have been achieved and the book would have remained just an aspiration. So many thanks are due and these must first of all be extended to the contributors themselves. To Professor Brian Trowell in particular I owe an ever-increasing debt. With unconditional and unlimited trust he placed into my hands his masterly survey of 'Elgar's Use of Literature' and allowed me to use it as the centre-piece of this symposium. His generosity and kindness was matched by all other contributors and my debt to them is considerable.

There are many other individuals and organizations who have contributed handsomely to the preparation of this volume and I must especially thank: E. Wulstan Atkins for a splendid introduction which no-one else could have written; James Bennett and Christopher Bennett of the Elgar Birthplace Museum who, across the years, have provided invaluable support and warm hospitality to the contributors and myself; John Fletcher who has so patiently helped with the typescript; and Dr K. E. L. Simmons for constant encouragement and continuing advice. I am also indebted to Marion Simmons, Harry Windsor-Sharpe, Lindsay Wallace; and it is a pleasure for me to acknowledge the help provided by Ellen Keeling, Senior Editor of Scolar Press.

The drawing of Sir Edward Elgar by William Strang is reproduced by gracious permission of Her Majesty the Queen and I am indebted to the

Royal Library, Windsor Castle for help so generously provided. The British Library, National Portrait Gallery, Fitzwilliam Museum, Hulton Picture Company, and the Elgar Foundation have made available illustrative material for which I am most grateful. Thanks are also due to the Elgar Will Trust (administered by the Royal Bank of Scotland) for permission to quote from the music and writings of Edward Elgar.

All royalties from the sale of this volume will go to the Elgar Society and it is a very special pleasure for the contributors and myself to know that the Society has awarded its first Elgar Medal to Dr Jerrold Northrop Moore. Dr Moore is not directly represented in these pages but his stimulating presence can never be totally absent from any current or future evaluation of Elgar.

The articles here presented are examples of the kind of scholarly disquisition that Elgar himself enjoyed, with much valuable information tucked away in the footnotes and appendices ('Oh! the notes', Elgar wrote to Ivor Atkins).

RM
Leicester, 1992

Introduction

E. Wulstan Atkins

In 1990 Raymond Monk commissioned and edited ten essays on Elgar and his music in a volume entitled *Elgar Studies*. It was the success of this book which encouraged him to edit the further twelve essays in this volume. This is not the place to make extensive references to the earlier ten essays, all of which have added to the knowledge now readily available to Elgar lovers. Mention must, however, be made of three of them, namely Dr K.E.L. Simmons's 'Elgar and the Wonderful Stranger', Michael Kennedy's 'Some Elgar Interpreters', and Robert Anderson's 'Elgar's Magus and Projector'.

Dr Simmons, with his meticulous and detailed research, has made available, not only to the general reader but to the serious student, the most complete account of *The Starlight Express*, the reasons for its composition, its background and the personnel involved. This information adds greatly to our enjoyment when listening to the music, and is essential if one is fully to appreciate the brilliance of Elgar's writing. Up to this essay *The Starlight Express* has remained for most people the least known of Elgar's compositions. The article is of special interest to me since I was privileged to attend one of the original performances in January 1916, and I still have vivid memories of that enchanting evening.

Michael Kennedy's article is invaluable – perhaps it is not too strong to say essential – reading for anyone who desires to understand Elgar's music, and how he and other contemporary conductors interpreted it. His music is great enough to allow for many interpretations and styles of orchestral playing and conducting. Foreign conductors have shown us new approaches and other rewarding new lights on his music, but to understand fully Elgar's music it is essential to know how it was played at the time Elgar was writing. In his day the normal layout of the orchestra placed the first violins to the left of the conductor and the second violins to his right at the front of the platform, with violas central in front of the conductor and cellos and double basses on either side. This arrangement greatly enhances the interplay between the different sections, and Elgar obviously had this in mind when writing the music. Today the first and second violins are normally grouped together on the left of the conductor and the violas in front of him and the cellos and double basses on his right. Clearly Elgar's music can be played effectively with the new layout, but some conductors feel the old layout suits Elgar's writing better. Right up to his retirement Sir Adrian Boult insisted on the old orchestral layout when conducting Elgar's music, and it was interesting to listen in a recent Royal Festival Hall Elgar concert when Sir Charles Mackerras was conducting the R.P.O. and the players were placed in the old way, and how the interplay added greatly to wonderful performances of *Froissart*, the Cello Concerto and the *Enigma Variations*.

Another important difference in orchestral playing was that in Elgar's day the strings used portamento, or sliding. Today the sound is considered old-fashioned, but the L.S.O. and other orchestras then had brought the practice to a fine art and Elgar made great use of it. To hear all the strings 'sliding' in perfect synchronism was something to be remembered and which seemed to add to Elgar's music. He clearly loved the effect. I am delighted that Michael Kennedy has explained the system and how it has changed gradually to the point of disappearing. Today's playing certainly adds detail and clarity but does change the sound picture. Michael Kennedy has in his own inimitable and lucid way shown us exactly what to listen for in the many interpretations now available in recordings and in live performances and has illuminated Elgar's own recordings for younger Elgarians. This is especially important now that Elgar's own electric recordings are all shortly to be re-issued on C.D. His early acoustic recordings have already been issued on C.D. by Pearl.

Robert Anderson's 'Magus and Projector', with his unique Elgar scholarship and immense knowledge, has opened up new ground for all his readers and made available information regarding Elgar's writing of the libretto and music of *The Apostles* and *The Kingdom* not previously known even to serious scholars. If Elgar had incorporated Simon Magus in his libretto what wonderful opportunities for more dramatic music there would have been. What fascinating possibilities there might have been if Elgar's health and other circumstances had permitted him to include additional characters in his libretto. If all Elgar's ideas had developed would these choral works have been limited to three compositions, including the unwritten one that we do know about? Some of these ideas remained in Elgar's mind up to his death, and some did re-appear in *The Spanish Lady*. We can now only sadly conjecture on what might have been.

Robert Anderson's article has, however, clearly inspired some of the essays in the present volume, and these provide further information and enable us to channel those conjectures along positive lines. Both Michael Kennedy and Robert Anderson have again contributed to the present book, *Edward Elgar: Music and Literature*, where twelve articles cover even more ground than did *Elgar Studies*.

The first article in this volume is by Diana McVeagh, entitled 'A Man's Attitude to Life'. This moving study deals with the 'dark side' of Elgar's attitude to life, and compares it with that of Gerard Manley Hopkins, Tennyson and James Thomson. It shows how the artist in those days could express his innermost feelings in a way that would be difficult today. The study is characteristic of its author and expresses her very real understanding of Elgar and her deep love of poetry. Diana McVeagh's book *Edward Elgar: His Life and Music*, published in 1955 when she was a young musician, demonstrated her remarkable affinity with Elgar's music. This study confirms what many Elgarians already know, how that understanding was not only of the music but also of the man. Perhaps one of the most valuable sections of the study is that devoted to close friendship with men of similar ideas, and how natural this was in Victorian times. It is difficult for those born after the First World War to understand that for Victorians who were brought up not to show their emotions in public, it was normal for them to express these feelings in written word and in poetry, and that friendship between men could be deep and affectionate without in any way suggesting a sexual relationship. This is a study that all Elgar lovers should read, for it puts into perspective so much that has been written about Elgar's 'moods', and stresses his spirituality. It also shows us why his music brings comfort to troubled people and also his own great humanity.

No better study could have been found to start this volume.

Christopher Grogan's contribution entitled '*The Apostles*: Some Thoughts on the Early Plans', has involved extensive research and adds greatly to our knowledge. One of its most valuable features is the very clear picture it gives us of Elgar's enormous difficulties in trying to develop the libretto and the music at the same time, and how, even if inspiration temporarily fails, a composer must go on. How much easier when a composer is setting a finished libretto written by someone else who has already completed the research and produced a finished text. Another feature of great interest is the author's detailed reference to Longfellow's 'The Divine Tragedy', where some at least of Elgar's ideas came from and how much the poem influenced him.

The picture of Elgar surrounded by bibles, apocryphas, concordances and religious books about the Apostles and the early Church is already known, and indeed I was able to see this in 1926 and 1932 when Elgar was making further attempts to write the unwritten third part, 'The Last Judgement'. My father and Elgar frequently reminisced about the writing of *The Apostles* and *The Kingdom* and the development of the works week by week and section by section, and my father repeatedly pressed Elgar to complete the 'third part'. From this I assumed that Elgar had made a detailed Master Plan to which he was working. I knew that the original conception was on a much more comprehensive scale with additional characters, and I had always thought that it was illness or other compositions engagements or eye trouble that had compelled him to abandon sections of a broadly worked out libretto. Christopher Grogan has shown that far from this the plan evolved and constantly changed as Elgar worked on it textually and musically. The admirable tables and notes clearly lay out for us the position at each stage.

The only point on which I would differ from him is that I do not think he has done justice to Alice's contribution to the work. On page 21 the author tells us that the early lists are in Alice's handwriting, but suggests that Elgar would not have trusted her to provide suitable verses and quotations from the Bible and concordances for his ideas. Alice was in fact a poet and novelist in her own right, and brought up as an Anglican she would at that time have known her Bible extremely well. In addition to this she knew the Rector of Pendock, the Rev. William Samuel Symonds, very well since she studied geology with him, and no doubt visited the Rectory frequently where she would see and probably have some knowledge of his theological books. Indeed, before Elgar began to consider his libretto, she may have known the Bible better than he since Roman Catholics did not place the same emphasis on the reading of the Bible as Protestants.

The article is about *The Apostles*, and rightly therefore Christopher Grogan's research ends in 1903. I do hope, however, that he will in some later article extend his research to cover *The Kingdom* and whatever other Elgar material exists.

Ivor Keys' essay on '*The Apostles*: Elgar and Bach as Preachers', makes a fascinating comparison of the vocal scores of *The Apostles* and the Elgar-Atkins edition of the *St Matthew Passion*. He draws our attention to the division of both oratorios into scenes and the dramatic use of soloists and chorus in the two works, and then by references to Handel's *Messiah* and *Saul*, Mendelssohn's *St Paul* and *Elijah*, shows how the oratorio grew and changed since Bach's day.

In both Bach's *St Matthew Passion* and Elgar's *The Apostles* the music is so deeply felt in expressing the sacred theme and words that the listener is drawn in as a living witness to the familiar story of the Passion. In this way, as Ivor Keys suggests, the composers are preachers, though perhaps their genius might not have perceived this. Elgar told me that when writing the work he expected his listeners to feel themselves in the same time as the events taking place, and to associate with the characters and their settings and the drama that is taking place around them. At the time the work was written, when everybody, performers and audience, knew his Bible, this presented no difficulty, but today the situation is very different, and this, apart from the cost of the six soloists, accounts for the relatively few performances of *The Apostles*, compared with those of *The Dream of Gerontius*.

As explained by the author, the essay was based on a lecture, and one misses the many music examples on the piano that Ivor Keys, a brilliant pianist, gave to illustrate his lecture, but the references given in the text clearly enable one to follow his argument.

Robert Meikle's scholarly article 'The True Foundation', analysing Elgar's First and Second Symphonies, will be of the greatest interest to professional musicians, especially composers and symphonists. His study of the tonality and structure is most valuable. I would beg the ordinary reader not to glance quickly at it and decide that this is not for him. The article is very comprehensive and apart from its technicalities contains much of real value for all Elgarians and music-lovers. The section in which he deals with Brahms' influence on the Elgar Symphonies is particularly interesting. Elgar's love of these Symphonies, and especially the Third, is well known. He not only devoted one of his Birmingham lectures to this work, but he also conducted it and other Brahms works with the L.S.O.

I have a personal interest in the Symphonies. My father loved Brahms, and introduced me to the First and Fourth by playing them over to me in piano arrangements, and the performances of the L.S.O. conducted by Hermann Abendroth, issued by H.M.V., were among the first gramophone records that I bought. It was, however, Elgar who introduced me to the Third Symphony. He had the H.M.V. Krauss recording, and on several evenings he asked me to put on the records when he and my father discussed various points. Later, when Elgar learnt that I had recordings of the First and Fourth Symphonies but not the Third, he gave me a set of these records, and I bought the Second. At that time I became almost obsessed with Brahms, playing the records whenever I had the opportunity. I even played the last movement of the Fourth while I shaved. I remember that my father, though he was delighted that I loved Brahms so much, felt that this was excessive and an insult to the composer, since one could not concentrate on the music without cutting oneself.

Michael Kennedy's contribution, 'The Soul Enshrined: Elgar and his Violin Concerto', provides us, as one would expect, with a clear picture of the background to Elgar's writing of the Concerto and of the people involved in its various stages. The author shows us the influence that they had on its development, and, which is more important, he shows us how Elgar reveals himself in every section. He writes, 'As far as the music is concerned, there can be little doubt in the listener's mind that it enshrines the soul of Edward Elgar himself'.

Moving on to the question of whose soul is enshrined, Michael Kennedy draws our attention to Elgar's serious efforts to ensure that the Spanish quotation was put in such a form that would leave the 'soul' indefinite as to sex, or rather, gender. On this basis there are seven people clearly connected with the Concerto who could be possible 'souls': Elgar himself; Fritz Kreisler; W. H. (Billy) Reed; Leonora von Stosch, the wife of Sir Edgar Speyer; Helen Weaver; Alice Stuart Wortley; and Julia Worthington, nicknamed 'Pippa' by Elgar. Four of them were professional violinists and Helen a violin student. Alice Stuart Wortley was a fine musician, and Julia Worthington's claim rests on her friendship with the Elgars and the fact that some early sketches for the first movement and most of the framework of the slow movement were written while the Elgars were her guests in Careggi in 1909.

Kreisler can be eliminated, since the Concerto is openly dedicated to him, and we need not consider further Elgar himself or Billy Reed in view of Elgar's later remarks to Basil Maine, my father and others that the 'soul' was feminine, a view now generally accepted.

Of the four ladies only two have serious claims, Helen Weaver and Alice Stuart Wortley. Alice's claim is extremely strong, as fully set out by the author, and indeed the only serious doubt must be if, despite the very close understanding and extended relationship between 'Windflower' and Elgar, the friendship could have generated some of the passages in the Concerto which must have been written from a very deep personal emotional tension, such as would arise from a broken engagement. Ernest Newman and my father felt strongly that such passages could only have been written by one seared by some great personal upheaval early in life. When Elgar towards the end of his life told my father about his broken engagement to Helen in 1884 and how it had so deeply affected him all his life, my father was convinced that Helen Weaver was the unknown in the 13th Variation and in the Violin Concerto. Ernest Newman derived his firm conviction that Helen was behind *both* works from other sources.

The claims for both Helen and 'Windflower' will continue, but unless further evidence comes to light the problem is likely to remain a partially solved one. In his article Michael Kennedy has made two very interesting suggestions. The first is that Elgar may have told Alice Stuart Wortley about his broken engagement with Helen, a fascinating idea, since although there appears to be no evidence for it, I would agree that if Elgar did wish to confide in anyone then 'Windflower' would be the most likely. The second is in the author's own words:

> It is the nature of music that it can say two things at the same time, and if both Helen and Lady Mary are commemorated in the Romanza, why should not Helen and somebody else also be the 'soul' of the Concerto? The emotional burden of the Concerto is 'what might have been', and this would have applied equally to Elgar's thoughts of Helen and 'Windflower'.

Interestingly, Brian Trowell also suggests something rather similar in referring to Helen Weaver as a possible 'soul' in the Concerto. He writes:

> By 1910, I think, turning to this Alice (Windflower), Elgar may well have felt that the soul of Helen Weaver, in Lamb's words, 'looked out of her eyes with

such a reality of re-presentment, that I became in doubt which of them stood there before me'.

Elgar knew Lamb's writings well.

If one accepts Michael Kennedy's and Brian Trowell's suggestions, then a possible solution of the '5 dots' enigma could be that Elgar was thinking of both Helen and 'Windflower', or of *both* intertwined into one 'spiritual soul'.

Christopher Kent's article '*Falstaff*: Elgar's Symphonic Study' with its five Appendices and his usual meticulous scholarship, is again one which adds greatly to our knowledge of one of the few compositions in which Elgar, a keen Shakespearean, has left us his own analysis and programme. Until now the listener who did not have Elgar's descriptive analytical essay will have missed a great deal of the orchestral colour-pictures of the various characters, especially that of Sir John Falstaff himself, who is portrayed as a youthful page with Prince Henry and later as an old man rejected by his King.

Christopher Kent vividly brings the work to life while at the same time illuminating the framework and detailed planning that Elgar used to build up this remarkable composition. It also shows how Elgar incorporated sketches that were originally intended for other uncompleted works. All his life Elgar made great use of his sketchbooks in which he had jotted down musical ideas, sometimes with no idea where they would be used. He once told me that a composer should never throw away 'short musical themes and ideas'. If they were good enough to go into a sketch book they would always, perhaps years later, find a place in a composition.

I have a special interest in *Falstaff*. My father attended the London rehearsal of the work on 22 September 1913, and on the 29th Elgar posted to him from Leeds an inscribed miniature fullscore and a copy of his own essay, published in the *Musical Times* for September, for him to study before they met in Leeds for the final rehearsals and the first performance on 2 October. At some time between the rehearsals and the concert they must have discussed the work in detail, since in the score is written in red ink the references page by page to the various characters and events. I have it in front of me as I write; years later I had the benefit of reading these notes before hearing *Falstaff* for the first time. I also recall my father and Elgar talking about the work, and both regretting that it was so rarely performed. Fortunately today *Falstaff* is much better known, and is now appreciated as one of Elgar's great compositions.

Ivor Keys' second contribution to this book, '"Ghostly Stuff": The Brinkwells Music', makes fascinating reading, especially his theory that there is a huge ghost – Elgar himself as a resurrected composer – in all the Brinkwells chamber music. The author has made out a most impressive case to substantiate his theory, and it certainly opens up new fields of great interest. The theory assumes that in 1912 Elgar considered *The Music Makers* to be his last major work. I very much doubt that, for in 1913 we have *Falstaff*, admittedly under consideration for some years, and early in 1914, before the War had started, he was preparing to write another work continuing the theme of *The Apostles* and *The Kingdom*.

The letter from Elgar to Newman quoted by Ivor Keys was written on 5 January 1919, and the paragraph reads:

> Work has been interrupted by a variety of silly things but the Sonata is finished and the Quartet; your Quintet remains to be completed – the first movement is ready & I want you to hear it – it is strange music I think & I like it – but – it's ghostly stuff.

The author suggests that Elgar may have meant no more than 'spooky'. I do not personally agree, especially when Ivor Keys uses 'ghostly stuff' to apply to the other chamber music. Surely Elgar may have used the words much more in the sense of 'spiritual' (compare the German 'geistlich'), which would combine both meanings. If used in this sense it can rightly apply to all the Brinkwells music, including the Cello Concerto.

Reverting to the Piano Quintet Alice wrote in her diary on 24 August 1918, 'E. writing wonderful new music, different from anything else of his. A. calls it wood magic. So elusive & delicate.'

It is well known that Elgar, who loved walking through the woods surrounding Brinkwells, was influenced by some weird withered trees that stood alone on high ground adjacent to the road. There is a legend that these trees were the dead forms of monks from a settlement of Spanish monks nearby who had been struck dead for carrying out impious rites. This is said to account for the Spanish element in the Quintet. The fact that there never were any Spanish monks in this part of Sussex need not belittle the 'legend'. Algernon Blackwood, a friend who wrote many stories about trees, was staying with Elgar at the time he was composing the Quintet, and they daily walked on paths which passed these withered trees. I believe that it was Blackwood who discovered the weird trees with Elgar on their walks, and developed the 'legend' which so clearly influenced Elgar.

These are interesting points, but the real importance of Ivor Keys' article is his masterly analysis of the shape of each work, with their shifting harmonies and strange chromatic progressions which lead him to his feeling of 'ghostly stuff' and 'the Singer who sings no more'.

The article brings back to me one of the most satisfying performances of the Piano Quintet that I have ever heard. It was given in Birmingham University some twenty years ago, with Ivor Keys as the pianist. His love and understanding of the work was evident in his beautiful phrasing and his caressing of every detail.

Percy Young's article, 'Elgar and the Irish Dramatists', provides us with a picture of the revival of interest in the Gaelic language in Ireland at the end of the nineteenth century, and of the leading part that Edward Martyn,

William Butler Yeats and Lady Gregory were taking in this revival. Their greatest interest was to set up a theatre in Dublin (The Abbey Theatre) which would put on plays about Irish history and the legends of old Ireland. They realized that with a dying language the plays would have to be in English, but the atmosphere would be Gaelic. At an early stage Yeats drew George Moore into the picture. He was experienced in playwriting and production, and already knew Elgar's music, and he persuaded the composer to write incidental music for their joint play, *Diarmuid and Grania*. Dr Young then portrays through Moore's correspondence with Elgar how this composition developed, and how for many years after the production of the play in 1901 Moore unsuccessfully attempted to persuade Elgar to compose an opera. The picture, alas! has to be somewhat one-sided, since none of Elgar's letters to Moore has survived.

Dr Young also gives us an interesting account of the Elgar-Shaw relationship. Shaw, though Irish, never, so far as I know, wrote anything remotely connected with Gaelic folklore, but the author's widening of his subject has resulted in a very fascinating and instructive essay.

I can sympathize with Dr Young about his difficulties with the lack of Elgar letters, because in 1976, at the request of an American author who was writing about George Moore, I researched all Moore's eighteen letters and provided probable dates, from internal evidence, etc., for a number of undated letters, some only giving the day of the week. How much easier it would have been if the letters from Elgar had been available.

Christopher Grogan in his second article, 'Elgar, Streatfeild and *The Pilgrim's Progress*', has devoted much time and thought to Streatfeild, and presents us with a clear and intriguing account of one of Elgar's lesser known friends and of his interests. Elgar, however, really comes very little into the picture since it is made quite obvious that he never intended seriously to consider Streatfeild's conception of Bunyan's *Pilgrim's Progress* as suitable for musical co-operation. The lack of humour and tasteless verse, so opposite to Bunyan's subtlety, would have been completely alien to Elgar's literary values.

The article certainly gives us a balanced account of Streatfeild's own ideas of how operas should be written and his conception of a new fusion between music and speech. It is perhaps most valuable for the picture it gives of the pre-First World War plays and production, and especially of the work of Barker and Wilkinson.

Streatfeild was a friend of the Elgars since 1912, when they went to live in Hampstead and when they began going regularly to the London theatres. Streatfeild was also a great playgoer, and I suspect that it was because of this mutual interest that the friendship developed, but Streatfeild also knew Elgar's music and had a very high opinion of it, which no doubt widened their interests. Streatfeild clearly hoped that Elgar would consider providing music to go into his projected play on the *Pilgrim's Progress*, but evidently Elgar was not interested since he returned the script.

I am sure Christopher Grogan is right; that it was only Streatfeild's early death in 1919 that made Elgar feel that, for friendship's sake, he should have one more look at the script, and hence his request to the executors for its loan. On looking through it again he must have felt that it was impossible, and put it on one side. It is fortunate that it was not destroyed, since it has provided us with this opportunity of reading a fascinating article. How fortunate also that years later Vaughan Williams has given us such a magnificent *Pilgrim's Progress*, which maintains so much of the beauty of Bunyan's original work.

Robert Anderson's article, 'fyrst the noble Arthur', once again opens up for us, in a relatively unknown chapter of Elgar's composing life, a further co-operation with Laurence Binyon, a close friend of his and also of Alice. Since *The Spirit of England* Binyon had, through Alice, offered Elgar various other ideas, but these had not interested him. In 1923 however, Elgar agreed to provide the music for *Arthur*, partly no doubt because the play appealed to him, but also because he knew that it would have pleased Alice.

Elgar had some difficulty at the start in the writing of the music – his first substantial composition since Alice's death. This comes out clearly in the author's comprehensive description of the play and the music. A section of special interest to Elgarians is the detailed outline of how Elgar planned to use some of the *Arthur* music in both *The Spanish Lady* and the Third Symphony.

I can add a short personal note: On 1 January 1923, my father and I spent a half hour with Elgar at Shrub Hill station before he left for London. Elgar had been staying with his sister Pollie Grafton in Bromsgrove, and had to change trains at Worcester. He told us that Laurence Binyon had persuaded him to write the incidental music for his play, *Arthur*, and that he would need to work hard on it since the first performance was to be on 12 March. He also said that he had now definitely made up his mind that he wanted to rent a house near Worcester and would my parents look out for a house with a small garden not far from Worcester but in the country. On 8 April Elgar moved into Napleton Grange, Kempsey. On the following Sunday he invited me to accompany my father who was going to Napleton Grange for supper. This was the beginning of my many Sundays with Elgar up to his death in 1934. At the first visit I well remember Elgar telling my father about the great success of his *Arthur* incidental music, and how much he had enjoyed conducting at the Old Vic the first performance and two others. The theatre's own conductor, Charles Corri, conducted the other performances.

Brian Trowell's contribution, 'Elgar's use of Literature', is called by him an essay but this does not do justice to such a monumental work which occupies over a third of *Edward Elgar: Music and Literature*. I have been looking forward to reading Brian Trowell's essay ever since I learnt that he was writing on the subject. I owe most of the little I know of literature to my father and Elgar, both of whom had read deeply and acquired large libraries. They encouraged me to read the best classics and to get my own copies from second-hand booksellers. If my father interested me in the more conventional books, it was Elgar who drew my attention to the unusual ones – Lord Dunsany's wonderful books, *The King of Elfland's Daughter* and *The Curse of the Wise Woman*; Ernest Bramah's *The Wallet of Kai Lung*; Richard Garnett's *The Twilight of the Gods*, and other similar treasures. When I was about 20 Elgar introduced me to Boccaccio's *Decameron* and Margaret Angoulême's *The Heptameron*, Lesage's *Gil Blas* and later to Burton's translation of *The Thousand and One Nights*. I remember the last was suggested to me after we had been discussing a wireless performance of Rimsky Korsakov's *Scheherazade*, and Elgar had asked me if I knew the background to the composition.

With this in mind, I have always felt that sufficient importance has not in the past been given to the influence that Elgar's knowledge of literature must have had on his music. Now for once realization has equalled anticipation. The essay is fascinating and enthralling. One will not agree with all that the author writes, and especially with some of his conjectures, but this in no way detracts from a remarkable work. Brian Trowell sets out clearly the main purpose of his research, which may be briefly summarized: 1) Why Elgar read the books; 2) What he gained from them; 3) How he used his knowledge, especially in relation to his composing.

The Editor and the author have asked me to make detailed comments on the contribution, but to do justice to this extremely important and valuable addition to our existing Elgar literature would require another essay, which would be out of place in this book. To make casual comments would be an injustice to the author. I am accordingly confining myself to my own knowledge of some of the events in Elgar's life referred to, and to a limited extent to the last of Brian Trowell's three lines of research.

The author, I think rightly, devotes his first section to the 'Dent Affair' and he also provides in Appendix 1 the full content of the article in German as it appeared in the *Handbuch der Musikgeschichte*, with an English translation. The author's disclosure that the article had first appeared in 1924, six years before its reprint in 1930, which caused the furore, puts the whole affair, though still inexcusable, in a very different light. I can comment on this, because in 1930 I was visiting Elgar at Marl Bank with my father almost every Sunday, and naturally during these occasions they would discuss the various stages of the affair. Elgar was clearly very hurt, and indeed remained so until his death. His consolation was in the way his friends rallied together to defend him, and in particular Bernard Shaw. I remember on one of these evenings Elgar telling my father that perhaps what hurt him most was because it was a Cambridge Professor of Music who had attacked him, since it was Stanford, an earlier Professor of Music at Cambridge, who had given him his first honorary Doctorate. Had Elgar realized, which I am sure he never did, that Dent wrote the article in 1924, when he was still relatively unknown – a music critic and freelance writer – he would have allowed the matter to fade away and it would have lost its lifelong sting.

The Dent affair brought back to Elgar his bitterness over Gerald Cumberland's (C. F. Kenyon) article on himself in *Set down in Malice*, published in 1918, and referred to by Brian Trowell in his second section, 'Literary Culture in the Elgar Interviews'. During a discussion between Elgar and my father I gained the impression that by 1930 most of the offence had gone, and was only revived by the Dent article.

I gathered that in this case the main reason for Elgar's bitterness was that he felt let down by Cumberland, who, after a promise, had published certain information given to him in confidence. It was apparent that Cumberland had a high regard for Elgar's music, and that Elgar also had a good opinion of Cumberland's intellect.

Without going into detail, it seems to me that an essential part of Brian Trowell's study is the question of whether, when Elgar used quotations in his scores, from poems or other sources, he was thinking of the actual quotation itself or of the *entire* context from which it was taken. I do not think that the latter can be assumed, certainly not in every case. That Elgar, with a few exceptions, had read at some time a work from which the particular quotation is taken can be accepted, but that at the time he wrote the composition he was thinking of the entire literary article is a very different matter. He would, no doubt, have had a general idea of it, but seldom a detailed memory of other than the actual and appropriate quotation that he inscribed on his scores.

Elgar had an amazing photographic memory, of which more later, and he also told me about his scrapbook in which he jotted down 'phrases or quotations' which especially interested him when he first read them. This scrapbook is, as the author states, confirmed in a letter from Elgar to Troyte Griffith. From both these sources, memory and scrapbook, Elgar could, in most instances, go back to the full original article from which the quotation came, but in the white heat of composition would Elgar have had time or the wish to do this? I suspect that the quotation itself suited his immediate needs, though the general 'feel' of the entire work may have provided background.

I can illustrate Elgar's quite astonishing photographic memory from two instances:

One evening early in 1930 Elgar and my father were discussing the writing of *The Apostles*, and my father reminded Elgar of the electrifying effect of his having inserted 'Selah!' in a passage written between two of the weekly meetings. Elgar said that he knew that my father now knew the full meaning of 'Selah', but he doubted if he had done so at the time when he had inserted the word. My father agreed, and Elgar turned to me and asked if I knew the meaning of the word. I did not, and he was about to explain it when he stopped and told me to look it up in a dictionary which was on a shelf behind me. I took the book down and was searching for the word, when Elgar said, 'No, it is not on that page. You will find it in the middle of the right-hand column of a right-hand page'. I found it, and was about to read it out when Elgar said, 'Stop! I will tell you what it says', and he proceeded to quote the passage word for word. I recall accusing him of cheating by looking the word up before we came, but Elgar laughed and said, 'No, I have not seen that paragraph for years. Indeed, I last remember using that particular dictionary when I was in Hampstead. These books have only recently come out of storage'.

Another example occurred some months later. Elgar asked me to help him with a few words in the *Observer* Torquemada crossword puzzle. Usually he had finished the puzzle long before we went to Marl Bank, but on this occasion there were some odd gaps left, including one with an engineering clue. Naturally Elgar thought that I would guess this one easily, but I could not, and after a lot of puzzling by all of us he suddenly came up with 'Caisson', which once found was obvious. I wondered, however, how Elgar could have come across this highly technical word used in connection with compressed air working in underwater construction, such as the foundations for bridges. He explained that some months earlier he had seen the word in an article, and being unknown to him he had, following a practice started when he was a schoolboy, at once looked it up in a dictionary, and with his uncanny memory there it was for all time. This practice, I am sure, led Elgar early on to start his 'quotation scrapbook'.

Elgar once told me that at the end of the last century the London Library started sending fortnightly boxes of books on loan to their subscribers. He and Alice were founder members of this service. These loans may have been another reason for the scrapbooks, in which case Elgar may not always have had the entire works available at the time he used the quotations, and this would also account for some of his mis-quotations. In 'Elgar's Literary Scholarship' Brian Trowell draws attention to carelessness in transcribing the words in some of the songs he had set, including *Sea Pictures*. The author may well be right, and mental lapses do occur, but I wonder, if once Elgar had set the music to the passage or poem, and the music itself was complete and to his satisfaction, he was any longer vitally interested in the actual words. The fact that singers have been singing nonsense for all these years without it being noticed suggests that it is the music that really matters, as Elgar himself often said. This is to some extent confirmed by his advice to my father in his letter dated 3 March, 1908, 'Set to work on your new thing at once. Don't wait for words'.

Brian Trowell, in concluding his very keen and successful detective literary work, admits that 'to chase a speculative hare until it vanishes and then continue circling in order to try and pick up a fresh scent' has resulted in the finding of many texts and poems that Elgar may not have known in their entirety. This is a wonderful piece of writing and a delight to read.

Ronald Taylor's 'Music in the Air: Elgar and the BBC' is of special interest for all Elgar lovers. The author, with his usual thoroughness, has compiled a detailed list of performances of Elgar's music by the BBC in its different forms, from its beginning in 1922 up to 1934, the year of Elgar's death. This is of the greatest value as a record, and fills a large gap in our previous knowledge, but it also provides us with a complete list of the broadcast performances conducted by Elgar himself. This contribution can be considered alongside Jerrold Moore's comprehensive book on Elgar's gramophone recordings, *Elgar on Record*. It is sad that some of the BBC records of early performances, especially the Birmingham ones, are missing, but this in no way affects the importance of the article.

Ronald Taylor's article is much more than a record of performances. His research gives us a picture of the general public's appreciation of Elgar's music between 1922 and 1934, and broadly of their favourite compositions, though one must be careful here since many Elgar works were thought unsuitable for broadcasting for non-musical reasons – length, etc. What is clearly shown is that his music was more popular at this time than is generally appreciated.

The article has a great interest for me personally since it reminds me of many Elgar broadcasts that I listened to but had forgotten. I, with enthusiastic help from a technical friend, built my first wireless set – a simple crystal set with earphones – in 1922, and listened to the Birmingham broadcasts regularly. This was followed by an amplified crystal set with loud speaker; then, on Elgar's advice, a Marconi set, and later a very powerful special Phillips transportable, which allowed me to listen to most of the Elgar broadcasts wherever I was. When I was working in the North of England I remember picking up on earphones some of the Belfast broadcasts.

Finally, in referring to the book as a whole, I should like to congratulate Raymond Monk and all the authors on having produced what must be one of the most interesting additions to the ever growing Elgar literature.

1 'A Man's Attitude to Life'

Diana McVeagh

'A man's attitude to life': so Elgar said, about his Cello Concerto. It is one of the many striking phrases he used that everyone knows: 'There is music in the air . . .'; 'This is the best of me . . .'; I am still at heart the dreamy child . . .'. His earlier comment to Ernest Newman about *The Music Makers*: 'I am glad you like the idea of the quotations: after all art must be the man', is really another way of saying that his music reflected 'a man's attitude to life'.

It is a profound and precise remark. Not 'a man's life' nor the events in it, nor even his thoughts, but his 'attitude': his settled behaviour or manner of acting, his habitual mode of regarding anything. According to psychiatrists, it is our response to what happens to us, not the outward circumstance, that shapes our life. A parallel point can be made in purely musical terms, to show the importance of context and response. Music can marvellously well convey general emotion, but cannot be specific at all; cannot describe details, or particularities. So it was possible for Elgar to compose scraps of music for a dog, to amuse its owner, and then go on to use them in totally different contexts. They were the 'moods' – not the activities – of Dan. Dan 'triumphant (after a fight)' of 1899 can easily make the 'joy of living' opening of *In the South* in 1904. There is nothing unlikely in that. Composers are practical men and must not waste good ideas. Handel, for instance, was a notorious self borrower, and Elgar's Dan themes had not been published or performed. Another Dan example might seem shocking or irreverent to the religious: 'he muses (on the muzzling order)' of 1898 being modified to make the prayer theme in Gerontius of 1900. But in the sixteenth century the tradition of parody was well established, and Bach fitted new sacred texts to music that originally had secular ones.

Most people would accept that Elgar's attitude was that of an introspective and essentially spiritual man. He said of Gerontius that he was a 'man like us, not a priest or a saint, but a sinner . . . a worldly man though repentant'. But Gerontius, dying, reveals none of the actual vices or misdeeds of his past life, only in general terms speaks of sin and repentance. One may compare that with the dying man in Strauss's *Tod und Verklärung* who, it has wickedly been said, 'runs through his past cinematically, for its own

1

sake, and transfiguration is a sort of golden handshake in which religious feeling has no part'. Indeed, Elgar found Strauss's music 'wonderful and terrifying but somewhat cynical'.

There is an element of what appears like defiance in Elgar's character; time and time again he issued almost an invitation to people to pry into his life. Take the setting up of the 'enigma', which in itself was a double puzzle. First there was the identity of the actual people, his private friends or associates; masking their names behind initials was in itself an incentive to curiosity. The names disclosed, there remained the real 'enigma', and to this day people are still puzzling out fresh solutions for that. Then to choose to set the poem *Gerontius* was something of a challenge to a Protestant county and country. Then to use an obscure quotation in Spanish to preface the Violin Concerto, and above all, to leave the 'soul' unnamed and draw attention to the mystery with the five dots. Whatever did he expect? If he genuinely disliked people wondering about his private life, why had he not learnt his lesson from 'enigma'? To cap it all, he composed *The Music Makers*, with its allusions and references, many of which could not be fully understood by anyone who knew nothing of his past life! Has any other composer so *nearly* laid bare his sources, given so many hints, or been so provocative? Schumann, possibly? Shostakovich? Alban Berg? So often there seems to be a 'story' behind Elgar's music, all the more teasing because it is incomplete. In modern terms, it is like giving an interview to the tabloid press, then complaining that the article as printed is inaccurate or scurrilous. Either Elgar was absurdly naïve, or in a vulgar sense publicity-seeking – and no Elgarian could believe either imputation – or there was some compulsion behind his behaviour. It seems as though his inspiration was so closely bound up with his personal life, and needed such strong emotional stimulus, that his attitude to life was indeed a vital part of his creativity. No wonder that, being so subjective, he was so thin-skinned and so vulnerable; and liable to such deep depressions.

It would be possible to become impatient with Elgar's depressions, to regard his accounts of them as theatrical, exaggerated and melodramatic. But Elgar was by no means the only artist during the nineteenth century to suffer in such a way. In his time the serious intellectual debate was to do with religious belief, and with the rival claims of the Broad, High and Roman churches (a later generation was similarly concerned with aestheticism). To discover other depressives, one has only to look at the work of three poets, whose lives and outputs have links, even if tenuous, with Elgar's: Gerard Manley Hopkins, Tennyson and James Thomson.

Gerard Manley Hopkins was born in 1844, the decade before Elgar. He is admired for his seriousness, his originality, and for his renewal of spiritual energy in the poetry of his day. He is perhaps best known for 'Pied Beauty', 'Heaven-Haven', and 'The Windhover', and for the technical innovation of sprung rhythm. Like Elgar, he was a Catholic, but whereas Elgar was a cradle Catholic, Hopkins was converted. After searching his soul for two years or more, Hopkins, while still an undergraduate at Oxford, was received into the Roman Catholic Church by Newman at the Birmingham Oratory in 1866. Reading about Hopkins's decision illumines Elgar's life, for it emphasizes how far Catholics were made to feel outside the rigid English social structure of the time. Hopkins went further; in 1868 he entered the Jesuits, and later became a priest. At that time he burnt his poems, lest they interfered with his vocation (though many existed in copies with his friends). As a Jesuit, Hopkins was assigned a succession of teaching posts, at one time at Stonyhurst, another at the Birmingham Oratory School. 'Teaching is very burdensome . . . I have not much time and almost no energy', he wrote, reminding one of Elgar's 'teaching in general was to me like turning a grindstone with a dislocated shoulder'. Like Elgar, Hopkins was all his life subject to a pattern of alternating lethargy and hyperactivity and there was a noticeable correlation between his work and his health.

At the age of thirty-one Hopkins broke several years of silence as a poet and wrote *The Wreck of the Deutschland*, a long sustained religious poem comparable in daring and intensity with Newman's *Dream of Gerontius*. Both poems were written by Catholics for Catholics. Hopkins tried to have his published. He sent it to the Jesuit journal *The Month*, which ten years previously had published *Gerontius*. But it was deemed unreadable at that time; Hopkins was discouraged. His attitude to his own poetry was ambivalent and complicated. As a Jesuit, he felt he should not seek publicity. So, like most of his work, *The Deutschland* was not published during his lifetime. It was not till 1918 that his friend and fellow-poet Robert Bridges felt there was an audience for such a startling work, and included it in his edition of Hopkins's *Poems*. So Elgar could not have set it, even had he wished; but the speculation is irresistible. And the rejection of *The Deutschland* must have been as crushing for Hopkins as the poor reception of *Gerontius* was for Elgar.

In 1884 Hopkins was appointed Professor of Greek at University College, Dublin. He was overwhelmed with administration and academic work. He found examining 'very great drudgery . . . a burden which crushes me' and, like Elgar on his Birmingham appointment ('I am killed with the University'), he found giving lectures traumatic. 'As a tooth ceases aching so will my lectures intermit after tomorrow', Hopkins wrote. These five final years were the darkest of his life, when – probably during the summer of 1885 – he wrote what are known as the 'terrible sonnets', or the 'sonnets of desolation'.

The psychologist Dorothy Rowe, in her book *Choosing not Losing*, reckons that the experience of depression has never been better communicated than by Hopkins in these sonnets, and that all the medical knowledge gained in the last hundred years or more would not cause him to change one word of them. A critic has written of 'a tormented doubt . . . particularly in the late "terrible" sonnets, that produces a creative clash with the confidence of faith'.

It is instructive to compare excerpts from them with one of Elgar's more famous letters:

> O the mind, mind has mountains: cliffs of fall
> Frightful, sheer, no-man-fathomed. Hold them cheap
> May who ne'er hung there.

> I wake and feel the fell of dark, not day.
> What hours, O what black hours we have spent
> This night! what sights you, heart, saw; ways you went.

> I am gall, I am heartburn. God's most deep decree
> Bitter would have me taste: my taste was me;
> Bones built in me, flesh filled, blood brimmed the curse.

> I have worked hard for forty years & at the last Providence denies me a decent hearing of my work: so I submit – I always said God was against art & I still believe it. Any thing obscene or trivial is blessed in this world & has a reward . . . I have allowed my heart to open once – it is now shut against every religious feeling & every soft, gentle impulse for ever.

The immediate circumstances are of course quite different, Elgar's words coming from a letter to Jaeger written impulsively in October 1900 six days after the first performance of *Gerontius*. Jerrold Northrop Moore saw that première as a consummation of all Elgar's 'deepest doubts'. R. B. Martin, similarly, talks of Hopkins's expression 'of a doubt so profound that it can often find comfort only in the belief that death may not be eternal salvation but utter and welcome annihilation'. There is no question of influence, as the sonnets, though written, were unpublished in 1900. But in setting alongside each other such lines as:

> God's most deep decree Bitter would have me taste

> At the last Providence denies me a decent hearing of my work.

there can be sensed a similar bitterness and darkness. Two men, both creative artists, both having suffered the rejection of a major work, both Catholic, writing only fifteen years apart; both deeply spiritual but each subject to nervous debility and to moods of melancholy, even despair.

There is another famous letter of Elgar's about which Michael Kennedy has fairly said 'to modern eyes there seems to be an exhibitionist note'. This was Elgar's account to Jaeger in November 1903 of his reaction to the unexpected death of his dear friend Rodewald. Again there is a striking parallel. Alfred Tennyson and Arthur Hallam met as undergraduates at Trinity College, Cambridge, and so began what has been called one of the most celebrated friendships of the century. 'He was as near perfection as a mortal man can be', said Tennyson, long after Hallam's death, and the four years of their friendship was the most emotionally intense period Tennyson ever knew.

Hallam was only twenty-two when he died in Vienna on a continental tour, suddenly and without warning, of apoplexy caused by a malformation of the brain. Almost at once Tennyson began the first of the 132 lyrics that he was eventually to collect as his tribute to A. H. H., *In Memoriam*. Other poems followed, but for many years Tennyson insisted that the poems were written for 'his own relief and private satisfaction' and it was not till 1850, and after a private trial run, that *In Memoriam* was published.

There was surely another reason, again pertinent to Elgar, why Tennyson delayed publication. His recent *Poems* had been roughly received, and in 1833 an article in the *Quarterly Review* was the most sarcastic and damaging review of Tennyson's career. The hostility of the critics crushed him; again the effect must have been comparable to the *Gerontius* première for Elgar. By the time the last scathing reference appeared, Tennyson was already mourning Hallam's death. There were also financial misjudgments and subsequent worries. During the 1840s Tennyson's health was precarious. One of his friends rather charmingly described 'an hereditary tenderness of nerve'. Tennyson took several 'water cures', on one occasion under the care of Dr James Gully at Malvern. Possibly he had epilepsy, certainly he suffered from the fear of it: there is no doubt of his deep melancholia. But even in the depths he felt compelled to write his 'Elegies', as he called them. Publication of more *Poems* in 1842 and then of *The Princess* were encouraging. In 1850 the production of *In Memoriam*, written over a period of sixteen years, was a triumph.

In Memoriam is not really about Hallam, but much more about Tennyson himself, his reactions, moods and philosophy, and speculations about mortality. In the seventh lyric, he goes to Wimpole Street, to the house where Hallam had lived, and stands outside:

> Dark house, by which once more I stand
> Here in the long unlovely street,
> Doors, where my heart was used to beat
> So quickly, waiting for a hand,
>
> A hand that can be clasp'd no more -
> Behold me, for I cannot sleep,
> And like a guilty thing I creep
> At earliest morning to the door.
>
> He is not here; but far away
> The noise of life begins again,
> And ghastly through the drizzling rain
> On the bald street breaks the blank day.

Compare with that Elgar's account to Jaeger in November 1903 of his reaction to Rodewald's death. On hearing the news in Malvern Elgar rushed up to Liverpool. 'He was the dearest, kindest, *best* friend I ever had'. Then, two days later, back home at Malvern, he wrote:

> I found I could not rest so went up on Monday; did not go to the house but called at a friend's in the same street – they told me – I broke down & went out – *and it was night* to me. What I did, God knows. I know I walked for miles in strange ways – I know I had some coffee somewhere – where I cannot tell. I know I went & looked at the Exchange where he had taken me – but it was all dark, dark to me although light enough to the busy folk around . . . am now a wreck and a broken hearted man . . . I have lost my best & dearest.

Elgar's letter is certainly a mite theatrical, but the impulse behind it was obviously not unusual in his time. Also, both Elgar and Tennyson had suffered loss on loss – first, a professional setback, then the death of a close friend. If Elgar's letter and Tennyson's verses are laid out interlined, the similarity of circumstance, mood, reaction and imagery is the more striking:

> I found I could not rest so went up on Monday; did not go to the house but called at a friend in the same street

> > Dark house, by which once more I stand
> > Here in the long unlovely street

> They told me – I broke down and went out – *and it was night* to me. What I did God knows. I know I walked for miles in strange ways

> > Doors, where my heart was used to beat
> > So quickly, waiting for a hand
> > A hand that can be clasped no more -
> > Behold me, for I cannot sleep

> > And like a guilty thing I creep
> > At earliest morning to the door

> I went and looked at the exchange where he had taken me, but it was all dark, dark to me although light enough to the busy folk around

> > He is not here; but far away
> > The noise of life begins again

> Am now a wreck and a broken hearted man

> > And ghastly through the drizzling rain
> > On the bald street breaks the blank day.

The Elgars knew the poem, of course. Canon Gorton had lent them the manuscript of an article he had written about it during 1903. In 1920, staying close to Alice's grave, Elgar movingly wrote to Schuster, 'the line from *In Memoriam* comes to me – "I think my friend is richly shrined".'

Two comments on Tennyson's *In Memoriam* may also have some bearing on Elgar. T.S. Eliot said: 'It is not religious because of the quality of its faith, but because of the quality of its doubt. Its faith is a poor thing, but its doubt is a very intense experience'. Whichever of Elgar's qualities come uppermost from time to time, his celebratory optimism and splendour or his underlying sense of desolation, his music is always intense.

Then Anthony Storr, writing in 1989 about *In Memoriam* in his *Freud*:

> The Victorians were more, not less, tolerant of homosexual feelings, if not of homosexual practices, than we are. Tennyson's *In Memoriam*, his long lament over the death of his beloved friend Arthur Hallam, could not be published today except by a poet who had 'come out'; that is, who was openly and avowedly homosexual. Those who are certainly predominantly heterosexual, as was Tennyson, seem to be allowed less latitude than formerly in expressing passionate friendship involving their own sex.

Perhaps that throws some light on Elgar's friendship for Rodewald. Also it has a bearing on his feelings for Jaeger, and his expression of them in 'Nimrod'. 'Nimrod' has become elegiac by association with the Cenotaph and other solemn national events; but it was composed for a living man. Played up to its metronome mark, even to Elgar's revised, slower tempo, it is very passionate – not sexual, or erotic, but very warm. Then there is the marvellous, aching recall of it in *The Music Makers*.

Elgar's distracted experience of walking the Liverpool streets that night after Rodewald's death contributed to the great Larghetto of the Second Symphony of 1911, parts of which were sketched within six months of Rodewald's death, and in which Alice Elgar heard a 'lament for King Edward and dear Rodey in it and all human feeling'.

There is a link to another poet in that movement. Jerrold Northrop Moore has shown that at cue 74 Elgar incorporated sketches for a proposed sequel to the *Cockaigne* overture, probably to be called *The City of Dreadful Night*. The author of this, James Thomson, lived a sad and lonely life in London, suffering from insomnia and drunkenness. His long poem was published in instalments from 1874, and complete in 1880. The sunless city through which runs the River of the Suicides becomes a symbol of isolation, and the *fin de siècle* imagery feeds the nightmares of a man trying to come to terms with a godless universe. The city has been seen as a forerunner of Eliot's *The Waste Land*. The poem is deeply pessimistic, with a despairing and atheistic creed.

Cockaigne itself was composed in 1901. In October that year Ernest Newman first met Elgar, at Rodewald's house. He recalled:

I remember distinctly a dinner . . . at which Mrs Elgar tactfully steered the conversation away from the topic of suicide that had suddenly arisen; she whispered to me that Edward was always talking of making an end of himself.

Compare that with this from Thomson's *The City of Dreadful Night*:

> And now at last authentic word I bring,
> Witnessed by every dead and living thing
> Good tidings of great joy for you, for all:
> There is no God; no Fiend with names divine
> Made us and tortures us; if we must pine,
> It is to satiate no Being's gall . . .
>
> But if you would not this poor life fulfil,
> Lo, you are free to end it when you will,
> Without the fear of waking after death . . .
>
> Our shadowy congregation rested still
> As brooding on that 'End it when you will'.

In turn, compare *that* with Elgar's reply of 1913 to Nicholas Kilburn. Kilburn had written him a letter of encouragement, at the end of a winter when Elgar was physically low and depressed. Elgar talks of an 'all-foolish providence'. 'You say "we must look up?"', he retorts to Kilburn. 'To what? To whom? Why?

> The mind bold
> and independent
> The purpose free
> Must not think
> Must not hope –

Yet it seems sad that the only quotation I can find to fit my life comes from the Demons' chorus! a *fanciful* summing up!!'

In fact, the quotation is inaccurate. Elgar, writing no doubt from memory, misquoted from his own *Gerontius*. Newman's words run 'The purpose free, So we are told, Must not think To have the ascendant'. Significantly, it was Elgar who added the 'must not hope', and it surely indicates something about his frame of mind in 1913.

In both the Thomson and Elgar passages cited above there are elements of defiance, sarcasm and parody. Thomson's distortion of Luke II, 'Good tidings of great joy for you, for all: There is no God', is painful. So is Elgar's despairing addition to the Demons, 'Must not hope'. But one does not parody something that is meaningless, irrelevant or unimportant. To Thomson, Hopkins, Tennyson and Elgar, faith – whether held or abandoned – was still of supreme importance. From Eliot again: '*In Memoriam* is a poem of despair, but despair of a religious kind'.

To compare Elgar's attitude with these poets does not detract from his singularity; it is simply a way of seeing some of his more desperate moods in context with his contemporaries. It is possible to become so fascinated by Elgar's music and personality that we look at him too much as an individual, too much in isolation. It does not lessen the truth of his more despairing moods to understand that they were fairly common among sensitive, thoughtful, creative men in his time. The focus or issue then was man's relationship to God, to an afterlife, to Providence. During the 1930s it was probably pacifism; during the 1950s, the Bomb; today, perhaps pollution and the environment.

Elgar's despondency was obviously only one part of his 'attitude'. Where there are troughs, there must be peaks. In his life there was the jocular gusto, the puns, the japes; in his music, the elation and the splendour. In both can be found a big-spirited, life-enhancing character. But that he himself drew attention to the closeness between his life and his music means that his violent depressions do need consideration, and this study has concentrated on that dark side.

All the above comparisons have been made between formal finished expressions of poetic art by Hopkins, Tennyson, and Thomson on the one hand, and on the other Elgar's spontaneous private, immediate outpourings in letters. A 'composed' expression in Elgar is Judas's great aria in *The Apostles*: 'Whither shall I go from Thy spirit? . . . Our life is short and tedious . . . My hope is like dust . . . Mine end is come'. Here Elgar's raw emotions are transmuted into art, and the music sounds an authentic note of despair. It is one of his finest achievements.

2   *The Apostles*: Some Thoughts on the Early Plans

Christopher Grogan

Elgar's sketches and writings from the time of the 'Apostles' project include a substantial and wide assortment of ideas and plans relating to the proposed size and scope of the work. Yet it is generally agreed that *The Apostles* as eventually produced came about not as the result of some carefully organized and methodically followed grand design, but rather through a process of inspired, sporadic, and often simultaneous, growth of text and music which involved, as one recent writer has said, 'improvisation on the grandest scale'.[1] For all his apparent planning, the composer never in fact succeeded in completing a thorough and cogent blueprint for the project; had he done so, he might well have completed his task as commissioned for the Birmingham Festival of 1903. The following survey of some of the very first plans and of Elgar's initial work on the text may help to suggest why this blueprint was never forthcoming and to what extent its absence may have influenced the nature and success of his final achievement.

Although *The Apostles* was first promised to G. H. Johnstone of the Birmingham Festival Committee before December 1901,[2] the composer does not seem to have begun contemplating his task in any depth until the early summer of the following year. On 2 July 1902, he told Ivor Atkins that he was 'plotting GIGANTIC WORX',[3] but much of this month was occupied with a visit to Bayreuth, and it was only on the 31st that Mrs Elgar noted that her husband had begun 'to be very busy collecting material'. The diary then falls eloquently silent for a week, such gaps in the daily narrative often betokening a surge of creative activity to which the round of mundane social engagements had been obliged to give way.

According to the composer's own account, his first step was to study 'everything I can lay my hands on which bears on the subject directly or indirectly, meditating on all that I have sifted out as likely to serve my purpose'.[4] In March 1903, he told F. G. Edwards that he had been reading 'no end of books on divinity' for 'more than a year . . . in order to get thoroughly in touch with my all-absorbing subject'[5] and he clearly recognized the need for such preparation if he was to overcome the inevitable limitations resulting from his inexperience as a librettist and his shortcomings as a theological scholar. But it would be hasty to conclude that the beginnings of the creative process were quite as methodical as his words suggest; in fact, no definite chronological line may be drawn between the completion of his background research and the start of the construction of the libretto. The process by which he 'saturated his mind with biblical literature'[6] did not on the whole precede this work but was carried on simultaneously with it, and so rather than supplying the fertile bed from which the text would grow, the constant assimilation of new ideas acted more as a fertilizer, encouraging the growth of the plant beyond initial expectations and engendering the appearance also of a number of new shoots.[7]

How much study the composer had completed in advance of laying out what now appears to be the earliest extant plan of the work may then have amounted to very little. The plan itself (Table 1)[8] draws heavily on a single source only, the Revd. W. H. Pinnock's *Analysis of New Testament History*,[9] a chronological arrangement of the Gospels and the Acts of the Apostles in which each event is represented by a short synthesis of the various Scriptural accounts, separately numbered and titled and prefaced with the appropriate text references; Elgar's list, scrawled in pencil upon two large sheets of blue paper, is borrowed almost entirely from the relevant paragraph headings in Pinnock. Another seminal influence was to be Edward Robinson's *Harmony of the Four Gospels*,[10] wherein the various accounts of the incidents of Christ's life were placed alongside each other and set against an absolute chronology of the author's own devising. Elgar thereby had before him on one page all the available narrative sources for an episode such as the calling of the Apostles, and was able to choose the account most suitable for his own requirements, compile a new text based on a combination of the available versions, or simply transcribe chapter and verse for future reference, saving himself the trouble of working laboriously through the Gospels themselves.[11] The book is mentioned only once on the plan (in the bottom right hand corner of the first page), but its influence is apparent throughout until the Ascension, after which of course it ceased to be relevant.

Although lacking in both depth and detail, this first attempt at an outline of the work is in some important respects a remarkable anticipation of the finished product. Thus an Overture (corresponding to the Prologue) is followed by the calling of the disciples in Galilee ('The Calling of the Apostles'), and the Sermon on the Mount ('By the Wayside'). There is already some evidence that the composer was thinking ahead in musical terms in his contemplation of a chorus to precede the Sermon (from which

Table 1
B.L. Add. Ms. 47904B, ff.225–6

The *Apostles* (Disciples)

Overture
Disciples called (Galilee)
Matt iv 12–24

Chos.   Capernaum
Sermon on the Mount
this
Mark iii 13–19   Luke vi 12–16
(prayer orchl.)

this
Matt iv 25 – v vi vii
(Luke vi 17–49
Beatitudes
Galilee &c

? *Draught of fishes*

– *Apostles sent forth*
see Matt ix 36   Mark vi 7   Luke ix 1–16
Mary Magdalene – anointing
(Bless . . .
Suffer little children?

Harmony
Judas offers to betray   pp. 152–16
Matt xxvi 3–5 14–16 20–25   Mark xiv 10 11
Luke xxii 3–6 14–21–2
– John xiii 21–30

remorse &
Judas hangs himself

Crucifixion
resurrection

(2)

Pt. III

Mary Magdalene's acct. of the resurrection.
Mark xvi 9–11   John xx – 11–18

Journey to Emmaeus
Mark xvi 12–13
Luke xxiv 13–35

?
(Bethany) _____
Thomas incident?
John xx. 24–31

ascension

Pentecost Acts II
pt IV Ananias &c

Peter in
prison

Success of the Church
Acts xi 1–18 end.

was to grow 'The Lord Hath Chosen Them'), and of an orchestral depiction of Christ's night of prayer on the mountain. To end Part I, Elgar's thoughts turned to the incident of Christ quelling the storm on the Lake, and although this idea has been crossed out, it was later to resurface in a modified form. For the beginning of Part II, he considered the despatch of the newly chosen Apostles into the towns and villages, but subsequently rejected this in favour of a more personal treatment of individual characters in the group, an emphasis already evident in the prominence given to Mary Magdalene, whom he spontaneously associated with the sinful woman who anointed Christ's feet in the house of Simon the Pharisee;[12] her importance to the scheme is further stressed at the opening of Part III by the reference to her account of the Resurrection. Equally significant is the attention given to Judas, whose fate already dominates the scheme to the extent of pushing the Crucifixion and Resurrection to one side. So from the very beginning, Elgar's intention to concentrate on the Apostles themselves as dramatic characters, rather than on the central events of the Passion, comes strongly to the fore.

From here on the planned sequence of events becomes noticeably more vague.[13] The Journey to Emmaeus was to be called upon only indirectly, in *The Kingdom*, for a single line to be paraphrased by John:

> Did not their hearts burn within them, as he talked with them by the way?

while the 'Thomas incident' (his initial doubt in the truth of the Resurrection) was later found to be impracticable 'on account of bringing in another principal'.[14] The great events of the Ascension and Pentecost were incorporated, it is true, and a number of early sketches were also prepared for the scene of Peter's imprisonment; generally, however, Elgar does not seem at this stage to have been thinking ahead in very concrete terms, except in one important particular. Pinnock's survey ends effectively with the paragraph 'Success of the Church – Barnabas and Saul at Antioch'[15] and Elgar promptly seized upon this climax of Acts chapter 6, where the followers of Jesus were first termed Christians and the '*whole* of the *Church glorified God* for having granted to the Gentiles *repentance unto life*[16] as the perfect culmination for his own scheme; beneath this paragraph, he wrote decisively, 'end', and his list of headings concludes at the same place.

That the earliest plan we have should end thus is of some importance as it shows that Elgar originally conceived *The Apostles* as a single work only, leading to Antioch, and not as a trilogy culminating in the Last Judgement. The problem of the trilogy is of long standing and merits closer attention in this light. It has been said that Elgar embarked on such a scheme, fired by the example of Wagner's *Der Ring des Nibelungen*, as soon as he returned from Bayreuth, and that he only altered this to a single work design later in the year, upon realizing that 'the planning of a trilogy was a very large matter to settle in the time remaining before its Part I must be produced'.[17] The evidence of the above plan clearly conflicts with this version of events, however, while furthermore, the trilogy is not mentioned by Elgar in any of his correspondence with Jaeger or Littleton of Novello, or G. H. Johnstone prior to the end of November 1902, after which time it is generally acknowledged that the composer was now working on a single work in two parts, as outlined thus to Johnstone:

> It will take, roughly, two hours.
> It falls naturally into the two parts.
> I The Calling of the Apostles to the Ascension
> II The spread of the Gospel until the climax at Antioch.[18]

This plan was then itself abandoned at the end of June 1903, when Elgar realized that he would be unable to complete it for the Birmingham Festival in October. Deciding, however, that it might be finished in this form for a later date, he wrote a prefatory note to the vocal score which Novello had printed before the composer withdrew it at the last minute (presumably because he had by now begun to entertain the notion of making *The Apostles* as it stood the first part of a trilogy):

> It has long been my wish to compose an oratorio which should embody the Calling of the Apostles, their Teaching (schooling) and their Mission, culminating in the establishment of the Church among the Gentiles.
> The present work carries out the first portion of this scheme; the second remains for production on some future occasion.

These ideas are echoed in a letter to Littleton of 23 October 1903, nine days after the first performance of *The Apostles*, in which Elgar seems to be losing confidence even as he writes in the two work scheme and his mind veering towards an as yet unexpressed new concept:

> I have been thinking earnestly over 'The Apostles' & have now definitely decided that the present work must stand alone leaving the continuation of the scheme to be carried out in a work of similar proportions.
> . . .the remainder of the work, in whatever shape it may eventually take, is mine to deal with.[19]

Five days later, the trilogy idea had become formulated, and Elgar sent Littleton a 'rough description' of his intentions:

> I The Apostles (which you have).
> II A continuation as talked over with you.
> III The Church of God (or Civitas Dei)!
> Last Judgement and the next world as in Revelation; each work to be complete in itself – the one bearing on the other – roughly:

I The schooling
II The earthly result
III The result of it all in the next world.
I have the IIIrd part libretto done in one shape, but of course, when I begin
work, I shall go into Pt.II first![20]

All of Elgar's own references to the trilogy seem then to post-date the composition of *The Apostles*; on the other hand, if his own testimony is to be believed, the concept was not new when he adopted it in the late summer of 1903. He prefaced the outlining of the above scheme to Littleton with the words, 'My ideas now revert to my colossal scheme of years ago', a theme which he pursued in conversation with Rudolph de Cordova on 11 February 1904:

> It was part of my original scheme to continue *The Apostles* by a second work carrying on the establishment of the Church among the Gentiles. This, too, is to be followed by a third oratorio, in which the fruit of the whole – that is to say the end of the world and the Judgment – is to be exemplified. I however faltered at that idea, and I suggested to the directors of the Birmingham Festival to add merely a short third part to the two into which the already published work *The Apostles* is divided. But I found that to be unsatisfactory, and I have decided to revert to my original lines. There will therefore be two other oratorios.[21]

This begs the question of when the 'original lines' were first conceived, and, although it has been suggested that Elgar was thinking in terms of a 'gigantic trilogy' as early as 1899,[22] it seems equally possible, in the light of his known prevarication with Birmingham and Novello regarding the scheme, that the idea was a face-saving expedient thought up after the composer had been obliged to inform both parties at the end of June 1903 that the original design, as planned to end at Antioch, would not be completed on schedule. At the time of the earliest plan, then, Elgar's conception was of a single work to be subdivided into three parts which, allowing for the migration of the Mary Magdalene scene into Part I and the non-completion of the post-Pentecost sections, correspond closely to the final pattern of *The Apostles*, Parts I and II, and *The Kingdom*. Realising the amount of ground which would have to be covered in the third portion, however, he had by November rearranged the scheme to comprise two equal sections, taking the form outlined to Johnstone above.

Two further plans derived from Pinnock's *Analysis* survive from these initial stages. The first (Table 2)[23] involved very little labour; the composer simply looked up the word 'apostles' in the index and wrote down what he found there in the form of a list, which he headed 'plan'. By this easy expedient, he arrived at something approaching a survey of the careers of his chosen subjects as recorded in the Gospels. The second plan (Table 3)[24] – comprising a list of paragraph numbers from the book – reveals some marked developments in Elgar's thought. Originally on two pages, of which the first is now lost, it shows him having abandoned the tripartite design of Table I; the designation 'pt I' refers to the two-part structure outlined to Johnstone at the end of November. For the first time, Elgar here attempts to group the selected Gospel scenes into dramatic, and potentially musical, structures (although these are still arranged chronologically). The fate of Judas remains prominent, and a new element is introduced with Peter's denial, anticipating Elgar's juxtaposition of the dilemmas facing these two characters in Scene IV of the completed work. Emphasis is also given to the Last Supper, and while Elgar was not to set this in its original form, he did incorporate an extended Eucharistic celebration, based on words from the *Didache*, into the concluding section, as it was ultimately to prove, of *The Kingdom*. The incident of Thomas's unbelief (contained within paragraph 448) is still being considered; this was to be excluded on the practical grounds already mentioned, but the element of doubt, applying to the Apostles as a group after the Resurrection, was retained.

Table 2
B.L. Add.Ms. 47904B, f.233

> | Pinnock p.264 | | Apostles |
> |---|---|---|
> | | $\big($ plan $\big)$ | |
> | Appointed   Matt. x 1 | Mark iii 13 | Luke 6,13 |
> | Commissioned   Matt. 10.1 | 28.29 | Mark 16.15 |
> | Sent forth   Matt. 10.5 | Mark 6.7 | Luke 9.1 |
> | Power to bind | | |
> | &loose   Matt. 18.18 | John 20.23 | |
> | to perform great | | |
> | works   John 14.12 | | |
> | Witnesses of <u>resurrection</u> | Acts 1 22 | |
> | Sufferings   1 Cor 4 9 | | |
> | will be false ones   2 Cor 11 13 | | |
> | to tarry in Jerusalem until | | |
> | endued power from on High | Luke 24.49 | |
> | – – – – – – – – | | |
> | Ecclus. 39.6   When the great Lord will, we | | |
> | shall be filled with the spirit of | | |
> | understanding. | | |
> | all this chap. for a description of an ideal | | |
> | apostle. | | |

Table 3
B.L. Add. Ms. 47904B, f. 231

pt. I contd.

pinnock

349   Christ anointed. <u>Judas</u> [Christ anointed by a sinful woman (Lk. 7.37–50)]

363   [Christ foretels his death (Mt. 16.21–28; Mk. 8.31–9.1; Lk. 9.21–27)]

368   [Disciples contend for superiority (Mt. 18.1–20; Mk. 9.33–50; Lk. 9.46–50; 17.1–4)]

386   [Blesses little children (Mt. 19.13–15; Mk. 10.13–16; Lk. 18.15–17)]

416   [Infidelity of the Jews (Jn. 13.1–20)]

417   [Judas offers to betray Christ (Mt. 26.3–5; 14–16; Mk. 14.10,11; Lk. 22.3–6)]

419   [Washes the disciples' feet (Jn. 13.1–20)]

421   [Presents the cup (Lk. 22.15–18)]

422   [Institutes the Eucharist (Mt. 26.26–29; Mk. 14.22–25; Lk. 22.19–20)]

423   [The betrayer (Lk. 22.21–23; Jn. 13.21–30)]

430   [Christ before the Sanhedrin: Peter's denial (Mt. 26.57–75; Mk. 14.53–72; Lk. 22.54–71; Jn. 28.13–28)]

431   [Judas hangs himself: The potters' field bought (Mt. 27.1–10; Mk. 15.1; Lk. 23.1)]

Crucifixion [Pinnock's paragraph no. 434]

448   [Christ appears to the eleven (Jn. 20.24–31)]

453   [Christ appears at Bethany: His ascension (Mk. 16.19,20; Lk. 24.50–53; Acts 1.1–12)]

end.

From the earliest plans, then, a number of themes emerge as central to Elgar's conception; these may be summarized with reference to the four paragraph headings in Pinnock which are mentioned in all the lists thus far discussed and are also annotated in the book itself:

349 Christ anointed by a sinful woman
386 Blesses little children
417 Judas offers to betray Christ
423 The betrayer

Perhaps the most surprising inclusion here is that of the episode of the children, which stands alone in Table 1, but then becomes linked with the contention amongst the Apostles as to who should be greatest, a connection strengthened by several early jottings in Robinson's *Harmony*. Somewhat surprisingly, the link is not continued in Elgar's annotations of Pinnock, however, where the paragraphs dealing with the children are isolated while the account of the Apostles' dispute contains a cross-reference to paragraph 331, 'The disciples pluck the ears of corn'.

This is the earliest reference to the Gospel episode from which Elgar was to extract a scenario for his own proposed setting of the Contention in Scene 2; it may be dated to a time after the preparation of Table 3, and to the same period that saw the composer's decision to commence his work with the words of Isaiah – beginning 'The Spirit of the Lord is upon me' – quoted by Christ when he first preached in public at Nazareth. In the earliest plan, this text (Luke 4.18) is included after the Calling of the Apostles but then crossed out; however, in both Pinnock and Robinson, the composer has subsequently written 'begin' in a confident hand at this point. The common inspirational source for both this reinstatement and the cornfield idea would seem to have been his new, or possibly renewed, acquaintance with Longfellow's *The Divine Tragedy*, a versified account of the life of Christ which was to be decisive in the establishment of an outline for the first part of the work. Its influence is apparent both in the suggestion of texts such as the Nazareth opening[25] and in the composer's decision to merge many of his disparate ideas into larger, composite scenes. Thus, for example, Longfellow's fusion of the repentance of Mary Magdalene with Christ's calming of the storm on the water and Peter's trial of faith[26] determined Elgar to follow a similar course, and include these incidents, along with the later one of the sinful woman's anointing of Christ, at the end of the central sub-division of Part I.

Immediately prior to Christ's appearance in the synagogue at Nazareth, Longfellow had inserted a scene set 'In the Cornfields', based on the separate Gospel stories of the plucking of the ears of corn on the Sabbath by the Apostles and the calling of Nathanael from under the fig tree. The surroundings are described by Philip, and later Nathanael, in these terms:

> Onward through leagues of sun-illumined corn,
> As if through parted seas, the pathway runs,
> And crowned with sunshine as the Prince of Peace
> Walks the beloved Master leading us . . .

Both the notion of a pastoral scene depicting something of the peace and joy felt by the Apostles in Christ's company, and the larger implications of Longfellow's free treatment of the ordering of events in the Gospels, here bringing together into a single scene events recorded as having taken place at different times, seem to have appealed to Elgar's imagination. But whilst adopting the cornfield setting, he seems very quickly to have dropped any idea of dramatizing the incident which originally took place there, and instead combined the borrowing with his own ideas for linking the contention and the blessing of the children. Longfellow's placing of the cornfield story at the very start of the Ministry further led Elgar to revise his own arrangement which, based on Pinnock's chronological survey, had set the contention and children episodes between Mary Magdalene's anointing and Judas's betrayal. Taking a path between these extremes, he now found a role for his own pastoral scene as an interlude between the calling of the Apostles and the introduction of Mary Magdalene by the Sea of Galilee.

Exactly when these threads were brought together cannot be ascertained, but there is cause for reasonable conjecture suggesting a date around the middle of October 1902. Elgar was extremely busy, and away from home for long stretches, during the late summer and autumn and if, as seems reasonable to suppose, the first stretch of continuous intensive work on the libretto occurred in the relatively quiet and secluded surroundings of Craeg Lea, then the most likely period is between 11 and 24 October, after Elgar's return from Bristol and prior to his visits to London at the end of the month. Eight of these days are blank in the diary, while on the last of them, Mrs Elgar recorded that her husband was 'very busy writing'; the composer himself reported to Jaeger on the 18th that he was 'working hard & 'it' looms big'.[27]

It was on the basis of these plans, such as they were, that Elgar began the construction of the libretto for Part I. With the help of Pinnock, Robinson and Longfellow, his ideas had crystallized into a clear, if somewhat half-baked, scheme at least for the beginning of the work, whereby a Prologue, based on the Isaiah text read by Christ at Nazareth, would lead into a scene depicting the calling of the Apostles and the Sermon on the Mount, incorporating the Beatitudes. Then would come a pastoral interlude to precede the introduction of Mary Magdalene, comprising the Apostles' contention for precedence and Christ's blessing of the little children.

Partly, as later explained, to 'keep the diction the same',[28] Elgar chose to construct his text entirely from Biblical sources, an aim consistent with the compositional aesthetic which guided his approach to every aspect of the work:

> I am a follower of Sir Charles Eastlake who, in one of his art-lectures, says that 'consistency of convention' is essential in pictorial art. So in music . . . Every extended work must be coherent and consistent from beginning to end. If you adopt this formula of the deeper consistency, you will discover why certain things jar on you, if in an artistic frame of mind.[29]

To this end, he made considerable use of a Biblical concordance, a decision for which he has been much criticized, although it is difficult to see how else he might have reduced his task to manageable proportions. Even with its help, the selection of texts remained far from simple, a point he developed in conversation with F. G. Edwards:

> 'I have selected the words entirely myself.' Then you have not quarrelled with your librettist, Dr. Elgar, we venture to interpose. 'O yes indeed I have', he replies, and, as showing the thoroughness of his mode of working, he adds 'I have spent two whole days in hunting for a suitable text'.[30]

The concordance was utilized to compile lists of excerpts, selections from which could then be introduced if and as suitable into the developing libretto. Elgar's approach was far from rigid, however, and he did not confine himself to material garnered in this fashion. Much was gleaned from other sources, his own reading and correspondence especially, whilst many of the verses on the lists were either never used at all or else surfaced later in the project in surroundings entirely removed from those for which they had originally been intended.[31] The treasury of texts collated from the Bible thus became part of an extensive vocabulary upon which the composer drew in trying to realise on paper his evolving mental conception of *The Apostles*, but it would be a mistake to equate them with the conception itself.

Curiously, the early lists – that is to say, those which were drawn up before the acquisition of a typewriter at the end of October 1902 – are not in Elgar's hand but that of his wife. The waste of time and manpower involved renders it unlikely that he would have sought out the texts only to dictate them to Mrs Elgar; equally improbable is that he would have entrusted the task to her entirely by simply supplying the concordance and a list of ideas for which he required suitable verses – the sheer number of entries under the headings for some words for which lists were prepared would have necessitated her playing a far greater part in the actual selection of texts than Elgar could have allowed. But while he must have chosen the verses from the concordance himself, that source does not give them in full, and he may therefore have written down his references before entrusting his wife with the task of finding and transcribing the texts in their entirety from the Bible. The method would have had the twin advantages of keeping Mrs Elgar busy whilst placing a large number of possible texts at the composer's immediate disposal; as the complete verse is often a considerable expansion from the concordance abbreviation, such a theory might also help to explain the presence in the lists of texts which, it is clear even at this stage, could never have been seriously considered for the scenes in connection with which they were apparently transcribed.

Elgar's approach to the assembly of the text in its early stages is clearly illustrated by his initial draft of the Prologue and Scene I.[32] For the opening, he had his text ready-made, yet he was careful and fastidious in his choice of words from the versions available. Thus he found Luke's rendition of Isaiah a 'better translation' than the original, but had to quote directly from the Old

Testament source when the synoptist's account ended, adding an individual touch by the inclusion of a single word from the Revised Version translation of Isaiah 61,3, 'beauty for ashes' becoming 'a garland for ashes'. He then edited out several words, and removed Isaiah's verse 6:

> Ye shall be named the priests of the Lord; men shall call you the Ministers of our God.

This was later to reappear in a new context in the final chorus of Scene 1, an early example of the careful husbanding of his resources which was to become a characteristic of Elgar's approach to the developing libretto. The musician's train of thought is evident in the consideration of soloists for the passage beginning 'To give unto them a garland for ashes' (an idea which was not taken up) and then a return to a 'Final chorus' at 'For as the earth bringeth forth her bud', the text which was indeed to form the choral climax of the movement, although the demands of small-scale textual and musical unity determined that it was not, in the event, to be final.

Satisfied with this opening, Elgar proceeded to the more arduous task of constructing the first scene. Having not yet decided upon an appropriate title, he headed the draft simply 'no.1'. Subsequently he added the unusual heading 'The Choosing of the Apostles' (queried in the margin by the more conventional term 'calling' which was finally adopted), a phrase borrowed from Henry Latham's study of Christ's education of the Apostles, *Pastor Pastorum*,[33] henceforth a profound influence on the ordering of events in the early part of the work. Although he did not finally adopt the title 'The Choosing of the Apostles' which Latham had given to his Chapter 8, the similarly framed heading with which the author had titled his next chapter, and which was also the subtitle of the book as a whole – 'The Schooling of the Apostles' – became Elgar's own preferred term for describing the educational processes dramatized in the early scenes of *The Apostles*.[34] The clear line of division drawn in the book between the 'Choosing' and 'Schooling' almost certainly influenced his eventual decision to separate his own setting of the Calling from the teaching concentrated in the Beatitudes, whilst Latham's stress on the importance of Christ's itinerant, wayfaring lifestyle to the education and spiritual development of his followers lies behind the 'By the Wayside' scenario finally chosen several months hence as the background for Elgar's pastoral teaching scene.[35]

Deciding to base his account of the Calling on that of Luke, chapter 6, Elgar began by writing out a continuous sketch of the verses which he intended to use. He then contemplated various interpolations into this basic scheme, starting with a prayer for Jesus based on John 17:

> I pray for them: I pray not for the world, but for them wh.[ich] thou has given me: for they are mine [etc.]

which replaced for the time being the idea of an orchestral depiction of Christ at prayer which was to be restored, in modified form, to the final version.[36] Below the sketch, he wrote 'I am not satisfied with this *yet*', perhaps in part because he had already set some of the text towards the end of *The Light of Life* seven years earlier. From here he turned to a chorus to greet the Dawn, the texts for which were drawn from a concordance list compiled for the purpose;[37] again, after this had been discarded one of the excerpts (from Psalm 30) was later recalled for a different purpose (in 'By the Wayside'):

> Weeping may endure for a night
> but joy cometh in the morning.

Three further additions were then considered as means of extending the scene around the narrative of the Calling. The first comprised the text of Mark, 3.14 and the complete list of the apostles according to Luke, the latter idea being almost immediately rejected. Then came a scene of healing, prefaced by a chorus of the sick, to follow Luke's description of 'a great multitude of people' coming to hear Jesus and 'to be healed of their diseases'; ideas for this are scattered throughout the page and also on a separate insert. The most significant interpolation, however, begins with the tentative suggestion, immediately after the Calling, of a 'Chorus (if nec[essarl]y)' to be founded on II Chronicles, 29.11, added to the page as an afterthought. From this small seed was to grow the chorus 'The Lord Hath Chosen Them', which appears in embryonic form on another separate insert and which was eventually to develop to the extent of forcing Elgar to discard the rest of the scene as envisaged in the first draft, and reconsider the position of the Beatitudes, which were intended to form its next and concluding portion.

The various comments scribbled on to the draft at this point show how the growth of the libretto towards its final shape had begun to outstrip the composer's more superficial first thoughts. As the comment 'if necy' shows, when he began the scene, he was clearly searching for ideas by which he might stretch it out to a reasonable size; for the same reason, he considered adding another verse to, or repeating the opening of, the chorus of the sick. As the scene began to evolve along its own lines, however, and the idea of one massive, dramatically static, chorus took hold, he was obliged to reconsider and think in terms of having to 'omit, if too long, the whole incident on this page'.

On the next page of the sketch, Elgar switched from the Gospel of Luke to that of Matthew, thereby (in line with Robinson's *Harmony*) sending Christ back up the mountain from which he had descended to heal the sick, in order to deliver the Sermon on the Mount. It was to be several months before the imaginative device by which the Beatitudes were used as the means of bringing out the individual characters of the chief Apostles was to come to fruition in 'By the Wayside'; here, the blessings are declaimed simply in sequence (Elgar did not even bother to write them out, indicating the sequence merely by a list of numbers and the direction to 'omit 11') and elicit no response. The Apostles as yet do not figure in the action at all, their characterization being delayed in the composer's mind presumably until the incident of the contention planned for the next section. Herein lies a fundamental reason surely for the subsequent abandonment of the scene as it stood and the expansion of the chorus based on the text from II Chronicles. Central to Elgar's idea, as he later told Edward Capel-Cure, was that the Apostles should 'stand out as the living characters', while the character of Christ would remain static, His importance underlined by the simple dignity of His utterances.[38] Yet, in the first draft for Scene I, Christ was the only living character, seen praying to His Father, choosing His followers, healing the sick and preaching the Kingdom of God. Through the continued evolution of the libretto, this flaw was gradually ironed out and the attention of the drama turned increasingly 'to the subjects rather than to the King – to the disciples rather than to the Master'.[39]

After the Beatitudes, Elgar added some further thoughts from the Sermon on the Mount, before attaching to the draft some texts from concordance lists to fashion a short paean of praise; of these, several were later incorporated into the chorus which eventually ended the scene. On such a page as this, and indeed throughout these early stages of work, Elgar resorted without doubt to a patchwork method of construction which has attracted much censure. What is sometimes overlooked, however, is that both here and elsewhere when the text was put together thus, the composer was generally dissatisfied with the results and eventually rejected them as failing to achieve that level of coherence and 'deeper consistency' which his creative mind led him to demand from his own work. Meanwhile, throughout the time spent piecing together these unsatisfactory assemblages, a more unified and integrated pattern of thought was developing in his mind which came gradually to supersede his first efforts. There was never any question, therefore, of these formative attempts passing into the finished work; they were merely a necessary first step, setting the cogs of the creative process into motion. As was often the case with his music, the composer seems to have worked on the theory that with such a huge distance to cover, any progress was to be preferred to none at all, and that it was better, therefore, to work at an unsatisfactory libretto until it was improved out of all recognition or even superseded entirely, than to sit waiting for the perfect inspiration to fall from the sky. In his 'Retrospect' lecture at Birmingham University in 1905, responding to a request that he might shed light on the 'actual labour of composition', he borrowed the following observations from Tchaikovsky:

There is no doubt that even the greatest musical geniuses have sometimes worked without inspiration. This guest does not always respond to the first invitation. We must ALWAYS work, and a self-respecting artist must not fold his hands on the pretext that he is not in the mood. If we wait for the mood, without endeavouring to meet it half-way, we easily become indolent and apathetic. We must be patient, and believe that inspiration will come to those who can master their disinclination.[40]

Elgar was well aware (as was his wife) of his own tendencies towards apathy and indolence, and the great quantity of redundant libretto sketches for *The Apostles*, with their now misleadingly patchwork appearance, testifies to his attempts to overcome them. So while it is possible to conjecture that the various dead ends which his instinct led him to follow in the course of constructing this first draft might have been avoided had he started out with a firm and detailed blueprint for the scene, this was not how his mind operated, and the time and patience required for such methodical preparation might indeed have brought the workings of his imagination to a complete standstill.

Creative considerations apart, there were by this time other reasons also why it was urgently imperative for the composer to get something on to paper. As early as 1 August 1902, just a day after Mrs Elgar first noticed that her husband had begun collecting material, G. H. Johnstone, himself under pressure from Novello, wrote to enquire how the composer was 'getting on with it, & how soon do you think you can finish the Scoring?'[41] Not surprisingly, Elgar stalled for time, promising Johnstone that he would have 'some M.S. ready for you or the publishers to see' 'after the holidays'.[42] This 'M.S.' did not materialize, of course, and, at the end of October, around the time that Elgar finished the first draft of Scene 1, Johnstone re-iterated his request, having since been approached by Novello's great publishing rival, Boosey's:

> Before I reply to them I shall be glad to know when I shall be able to show either them or Novellos some part of the work, the time is quickly coming when it ought to be in the hands of the printers and I should like to get it completed, before the end of this year.[43]

No doubt relieved, then, to have finished a draft of the opening scene even in such an unsatisfactory state, and keen to see the result of his labours in more polished form, Elgar gave the sketch to his wife, who copied it up neatly in her own hand.[44] Meanwhile, he turned his thoughts to the next scene by taking a scrap of paper and scribbling upon it 'pt 1/ Teaching/ Children/ Contention/ Cornfields/ Scene 2'.[45]

It was probably the experience of constructing and then painstakingly transcribing the opening portions of text which provided the Elgars with the impetus to obtain some mechanical assistance in their endeavours. Thus it was that on the last day of October 1902, the composer acquired a typewriter, an 'infernal machine', as he described it to Jaeger the next morning,[46] but one which was to prove indispensable to the development of the libretto in the succeeding months; once established at Craeg Lea, it was pressed immediately into service, and the growth of the text as reflected in the extant sketches assumes a gradually more coherent and legible appearance. From this evidence it is apparent that the first draft of the Prologue and Scene I was not the only extended section of libretto to be prepared before the beginning of November. There is a striking similarity between the method of construction evinced by this draft and that of a large part of the Judas soliloquy which was eventually to conclude the scene of 'The Betrayal'; once again the text is pieced together from various handwritten sources (although, as there are fewer of these, the sketch has far greater continuity than that of 'The Calling of the Apostles') and has then been transcribed, also in hand, by Mrs Elgar. It is therefore not surprising to find both these scenes mentioned in Elgar's letter to Edward Capel-Cure of 3 November already referred to, the chief interest of which lies in its adumbration of the composer's ideas for the pastoral interlude which he wished to set after Scene I. Having just begun to contemplate this in detail, and ever mindful of the pressures upon him, he decided to enlist the help of his erstwhile librettist in its compilation,[47] taking the opportunity also of inviting the vicar's comments on some of his first attempts:

> Will you tell me if any of the enclosed fragments do any *violence* to your feelings – in the selection of words I mean. No one can object to the Angel looking on during our Lord's all night prayer?
> I hope you will like the idea of the Prologue – the Isaiah words read by our Saviour.
> The Judas scene I like but please suggest any words . . .
> Will you sketch out for me a scene in which 'Jesus went about to all the villages *Thro the fields of corn* Contention of the apostles for precedence. Peter, *speaking* dignified, *John* also speaking, softly and graciously, Judas *roughly*, the others as chorus.
> Then with it the lesson of the children. Here the general chorus (S.A.T.B.) can come in – This wd. make my quiet sort of pastoral scene & the chronology of the children episodes in the gospel seems so vague that no violence will be done by putting all these incidents together?[48]

Capel-Cure responded quickly to the request, enclosing 'a sketch of the 'Cornfield' section' and promising to 'try and do better' should Elgar not be satisfied.[49] Unfortunately, no such sketch survives in the vicar's handwriting, and while some of Elgar's own ideas may have been influenced by his suggestions, most of the typed sketches for the Contention and children episodes[50] are so short, fragmentary and inexpertly typed as to point to a very early date for their compilation, and to suggest that they were more likely to have been the catalyst for, than the fruits of, the composer's decision to seek assistance with the scene.

November was a busy month in which engagements in London and Leeds, and work on the *Five Songs from the Greek Anthology* (op.45) effectively put a stop to further intensive work on the libretto of *The Apostles*. Thus very little else of substance may have been achieved by the time that Elgar arrived home from London on the 24th to find a letter from Johnstone informing him that Novello 'would like to see the 'Libretto'' before agreeing to publish the work on Johnstone's terms.[51] Since the beginning of August, he had been able to placate Johnstone by implying in his correspondence that the project – and in particular the libretto – was further advanced than was actually the case. He now deployed similar tactics, outlining in his reply the definitive plan of the work as he then envisaged it (see above, p. 15), but still sending nothing to prove that *The Apostles* was actually underway. Johnstone's reply brought matters to a head with a direct and unambiguous request for the libretto, and it was probably this that finally spurred Elgar, who had no libretto as such and was therefore in no position to send anybody a copy, into action; certainly, just over a week later, he was able to report to Edward Speyer that 'Alice has been busy typing (that's rather a horrible verb) my libretto and has only distributed one '£' amongst all the twelve apostles'.[52] Over the next ten days, for many of which the diary is silent, a makeshift text was typed out and sent to Novello via Johnstone. Jaeger had yet to see it on the 16th, when he wrote optimistically hoping that 'the 'Apostles' are progressing famously',[53] but on the 29th, he was able to report that he had 'read the 'Book' of the Apostles. You have set yourself no small task! Some of the "situations" should give you superb chances for inspired music'.[54]

Exactly how many 'situations' were contained in this draft libretto, given that Elgar had very little available time since the beginning of November for the assembly of new material, must remain partly open to conjecture. Assuming, however, that he wanted to give the publishers the impression that some portions of the work at least were complete, he would certainly have directed his wife to type out the most extensive early drafts, of the Prologue, 'The Calling of the Apostles' (which was in a sense finished, if nothing like finalized) and the Judas soliloquy, all of which had been sketched before the end of October. It would be typical of the composer's stalling tactics to send the unsatisfactory first sketch of Scene 1 as a definitive version at the same time that he was actively contemplating its wholesale revision to incorporate his newly formed ideas of introducing some genuine local colour into the 'Dawn' sequence.[55] What Alfred Littleton at Novello was shown at the end of the year may, therefore, have comprised very little beyond that which Elgar had sent Capel-Cure at the beginning of November; indeed, his reaction to the libretto in this shape echoes Elgar's own description of the excerpts sent to the vicar as 'fragments': 'I could really gather little or nothing from the libretto as it was in such a fragmentary state'.[56]

Thus, at the close of 1902, after some five months of intermittent work, and in spite of G. H. Johnstone's repeated attempts to glean from him a complete text, the sum total of Elgar's achievement probably amounted to little more than a short Prologue, a draft of Scene 1 which was to be entirely recast over the following weeks, and a quantity of mostly undeveloped fragments for various projected sections of the work as far apart as the cornfield and Cornelius episodes. Of the Prologue alone could it be said that the composer was satisfied with his text as the foundation for his most ambitious and far-reaching musical ideas. Yet before the end of December, he had begun work on the vocal score of this one short but definitive portion of the text with such enthusiasm that, by the turn of the year, the Prologue was, in Johnstone's words, 'ready for the printers'.[57] Elgar was truly practising what he was later to preach when he advised Ivor Atkins, who was planning a work for the 1908 Three Choirs Festival but could find no suitable text, to 'Set to work on your new thing at once. Don't wait for words.'[58]

It was adherence to this maxim that was to guide the immediate future evolution of *The Apostles*, with all notion of methodical planning being temporarily laid aside, the casualty of a struggle between creative temperament and sheer pressure of time. The early gestation period of *The Apostles* shows Elgar's to have been an impulsive genius, depending to a great extent on the inspiration of the moment for its best ideas, which would often be pursued to their natural end to the exclusion of his sometimes more calculated, but less inspired schemes. Combined with this was a natural enough tendency to fall back on more amenable work when difficulties arose, and a disinclination therefore to pursue the laborious task of compiling uncongenial stretches of libretto when creative ideas of a more urgent nature – both textual and musical – were crowding in on him. Hence, when the inspiration came, prompted by Longfellow, to begin the work with Christ's speech in the synagogue, he suspended his long-term plans, at a time when they still lacked the thoroughness necessary for so prodigious an undertaking, in order to draft the beginning of the libretto itself, just as, at the end of the year, he was to embark on the music of the Prologue with his ideas for Scene 1 still very much in a state of flux. The first draft of this latter scene clearly caused him much difficulty, and it displays none of the signs of inspiration or enthusiasm which characterize the contemporaneous first sketch of the Judas soliloquy, for example. Judas was the mainspring of the project, as is clear not only from the earliest plans but from as far back as 1899, and Elgar's conception of this antihero and his fate was already well enough formed for him to be able to compile a long stretch of libretto which owed nothing to his sources and antedated by several months his discovery in Archbishop Whateley's *Lectures on the Characters of Our Lord's Apostles*[59] of a reputable authority to back up his individual interpretation of the character. When inspiration did finally descend on Scene I, and Elgar was drawn to incorporate elements of Jewish ritual and to conclude with the massive chorus 'The Lord Hath Chosen Them', the entire unsatisfactory first draft was thrown over. The development of Scene 2 was to follow a similar course, with the linked contention and children ideas pursued for several months before being cast aside in the wake of the composer's sudden decision to set the scene around the declamation of the Beatitudes by the wayside.

Throughout all this work, time was on Elgar's shoulder. There can be little doubt that the obligation to meet the fixed deadline of the Birmingham Festival provided a very necessary inducement to get the project off the ground, yet the pressure of the commission simultaneously rendered its systematic planning a practical impossibility in the time available. From their experience of the many festival works which had passed through their hands, both G. H. Johnstone and Littleton at Novello clearly expected that Elgar would not only have organized his work in advance, but would have substantially completed the libretto before beginning to write the music.[60] Thus he found himself having continually to prevaricate in order to convince these parties that his work was following a predetermined course, when it was in fact evolving slowly, line by line, with long term plans receding into the distance as he grappled with the material of the scene immediately before him.

A significant outcome of these tactics was his decision to set the Prologue, taken partly to persuade Johnstone that the music of the work was well in hand and that, by implication, the libretto was well nigh complete. For the composer, moreover, the move from words to music must have constituted a welcome escape from the difficulties which continued to beset his attempts to assemble the libretto for Scene 1. Although begun out of necessity, however, this change of course – involving as it did the emancipation of his natural creative genius from the restraints under which it had been labouring during his work on the text – proved to be the immediate salvation of the project in creative terms; for as he proceeded with the music of the opening, Elgar's mind began to think in terms of musical structure and development, and this in turn was to contribute enormously to the subsequent development of the text. Clearly, if music and words were to grow successfully in Elgar's particular creative environment, they had to a great extent to evolve together.

Whilst this approach was to prove indispensable to the progress of the project in the short term, it may also have contributed heavily to its eventual abandonment. In earlier choral settings, Elgar had been more or less able to pour his musical ideas into the firm mould provided by a finite, structured, text, while in his later forays into purely orchestral genres he was largely content (*Falstaff* being perhaps the major exception) to stay within the confines of traditional (as he perceived them) forms, adapting these in each case from within as his expressive needs demanded. *The Apostles*, however, presented him with a different challenge, for while his conception of the project was finite in itself, it possessed, in the working out of its textual and musical details, almost unlimited potential for expansion, which could be held in check only if the movement of the libretto was mapped out in advance and the set plan adhered to. The successful completion of the work depended in fact on his devising an entirely new and unique structure into which to channel his inspiration, and this he was never able to do. In the last resort, libretto planning and construction on the scale which the project demanded proved to be an uncongenial, and ultimately self-defeating, discipline for the musical mind of Elgar, despite the enthusiasm with which he had initially taken on the task, and, after the production of *The Kingdom*, he retreated, in later choral works such as *The Music Makers* and *The Spirit of England* into the more familiar and less demanding occupation of setting complete texts gleaned from the works of those whose muses moved more freely in the literary sphere.

Notes

1. Robert Anderson, *Elgar in Manuscript*, London, British Library, 1990, p. 57.
2. On 1 December, Johnstone informed Elgar that the organizers had resolved 'to invite you to write the principal work for the next Festival, and I mentioned that you had a work on 'The Apostles' which was evidently to their satisfaction . . .' (Elgar Birthplace).
3. E. Wulstan Atkins, *The Elgar-Atkins Friendship*, Newton Abbot, David and Charles, 1984, p. 76.
4. Robert Buckley, *Sir Edward Elgar*, London, John Lane, 1904, p. 75.
5. From a proof of an interview given on 14 March 1903 and published in the *Musical Times* in April, p. 228 (BL Egerton MS.3097A, f.26); Elgar removed these words in the proof.
6. As recalled by Arthur Troyte Griffith, and quoted in Geoffrey Hodgkins, *Providence and Art*, Elgar Society, 1979, p. 7.
7. Most of the theological literature surviving from Elgar's library and now kept at the Elgar Birthplace dates from 1903 or later, and hence could not have contributed to any preparatory study. Much, however, is missing; the Severn House inventory (made after a burglary in 1918) mentions a number of volumes which have since disappeared (such as *Cruden's Concordance*, Barry's *Tradition of Scripture* and dictionaries of the Bible by Hastings and Smith), while there seems to be no trace of some books known to have been used by the composer, for example, Hillard's *Life of Christ* and works by Delitzsch and Henry Hart Milman.
8. B. L. Add. MS. 47904B, ff.225–226.
9. Cambridge, Hall, 1894. Elgar Birthplace.
10. ed. B. Davies, London, n.d. Elgar Birthplace.
11. Thus, apart from an early annotation of Luke 7.35–50 in his *Red Letter New Testament*, and the underlining of some scattered verses in a Bible acquired in

Liverpool late in 1902, there are no markings in Elgar's copies of the Gospels to compare with the heavy annotations made in the same volume and others of the Acts of the Apostles, the Epistles of Peter, John and Jude, and Revelation. For *The Kingdom* and the subsequently planned third work, these latter books of the New Testament were the only narrative source, and Elgar had no opportunity for the comparison of different versions of a single event.

12. In this decision, Elgar followed tradition (and Sir John Stainer, whose use of the scene in the oratorio *St Mary Magdalen* he later used as justification), but went decidedly against the scholarship of the time. Alfred Edersheim, in his magisterial survey *The Life and Times of Jesus the Messiah* (London, Longmans, 1887), for example, attributed the legend to the 'cravings of morbid curiosity or saint-worship' and concluded that 'there is not a tittle of evidence for it' (vol. I, pp. 561–3).

13. This was to be a recurrent feature of Elgar's plans; as late as March 1903, he could provide F. G. Edwards with only the vaguest of statements regarding the sequence of events which would follow Pentecost: 'The troubles and trials go on till we reach Antioch' (op. cit.).

14. As Elgar told Canon Gorton in a letter of 7 July 1903. P. M. Young, *Letters of Edward Elgar*, London, Geoffrey Bles, 1956, pp. 120–21.

15. Paragraph 464, p. 254; there are only two subsequent paragraphs – 'Persecution by Herod' and 'Barnabas and Saul separated'.

16. Elgar's underlining of Pinnock's text.

17. Jerrold Northrop Moore, *Edward Elgar: A Creative Life*, Oxford, Oxford University Press, 1984, pp. 378–9. Moore implies that the change of plan occurred after 28 October 1902, as he quotes for that date part of the letter quoted below to Alfred Littleton outlining a 'rough description' of the trilogy; this letter in fact dates from 1903, however, and Moore includes another portion of it under the correct date later in his discussion (p. 419).

18. Letter of 25 November, 1902; Jerrold Northrop Moore (ed.), *Elgar and His Publishers: Letters of a Creative Life*, Oxford, Oxford University Press, 1987, p. 388.

19. ibid, p. 512.

20. loc. cit.

21. Part of an interview published in the *Strand Magazine*, April 1904.

22. By Moore (1984, op. cit., pp. 294–5), who makes the assertion on the basis of Elgar's then conceiving a scrap of music which he linked to the character of Judas (but which was subsequently to be used for the Angel of the Agony section of *The Dream of Gerontius.*)
    In 1894, Mary Frances Baker had prepared for Elgar a libretto drawn from St Augustine's *Civitas Dei*, but this was never part of a larger scheme, and certainly does not fall in with Elgar's description of his 'original lines'.

23. B. L. Add. MS. 47904B, f.233.

24. B. L. Add. MS. 47904B, f.231.

25. *The Divine Tragedy*, 'The First Passover', V: 'Nazareth'.

26. ibid, 'The First Passover', IX: 'The Tower of Magdala'.

27. Moore (1987), op. cit., p. 377.

28. *Strand Magazine*, op. cit.

29. Buckley, op. cit., pp. 84–5.

30. Part of the interview of 14 March 1903 for the *Musical Times*. Elgar removed this exchange when the article was in proof. In fact, in the case of the announcement

of the Dawn from the Temple in Scene I, he was to spend considerably more than two days searching for a text before finding what he wanted outside the Bible, in the Talmud.

31. This is a characteristic of Elgar's musical sketches also, not only in the context of specific works, but across the whole of his composing life.

32. BL Add. MS 47904B, ff.162–9.

33. Cambridge, Deighton Bell, 1890; Elgar possessed the reprint of 1902 (Elgar Birthplace). From the evidence of an isolated sheet of paper upon which he has scribbled the bibliographical details of the book and some page references to Chap. 8 (B. L. Add. MS 47904B, f.239), it seems likely that he first discovered the work through mention of it in another volume.

34. He was in fact so pleased with the term that he was not above pulling the wool over the eyes of his friend Canon Gorton with regard to its true derivation; in his *Interpretation* of Elgar's libretto (written at the composer's request and with his help, and published to coincide with the first performance), Gorton, who clearly did not know Latham's book, wrote:

> It is of the utmost importance that we should note what Dr Elgar himself has termed the schooling of the Apostles. Christ is the Pastor Pastorum – the Shepherd of the Shepherds . . .

'The Apostles': An Interpretation of the Libretto, London, Novello, 1903, p.8.

35. In his preamble to Chap. 9, Latham remarked how Christ's decision to 'change from a stationary life to a wandering one was conducive to the growth of certain qualities valuable for the founders of a Church' (op. cit., p. 270), while Elgar annotated in his own copy the observation that the Apostles probably learnt less from lessons as such than they did from 'words dropt in daily intercourse and from watching their master's doings in the thousand little occurrences of their *wayfaring daily life*' (ibid, p. 231; Elgar's underlining).

36. Here, a short orchestral introduction showing Christ alone and at prayer leads into the prayer and prophecy of the Angel surveying the scene; this again may have been an amalgamation of ideas from *The Divine Tragedy*, which begins with an angel bearing the prophet Habakkuk through the air, and continues by putting into the mouth of John the Baptist some of the words which Elgar later gave to the Angel (beginning 'He shall not strive').

37. BL Add. MS. 47904B, f.176.

38. Letter of 3 November, 1902. Jerrold Northrop Moore (ed.), *Edward Elgar: Letters of a Lifetime*, Oxford, Oxford University Press, 1990, pp. 121–2.

39. As expressed by A. Wheeler in a letter to Elgar of 22 February 1903 in response to the composer's request for Wheeler's opinion as to the relative merits of two texts for use at the end of Scene 1 (Hereford and Worcester Record Office, 705:455:3717). Wheeler's grasp of Elgar's intentions here exceeds that of even some modern commentators, who have persisted in criticizing the composer for underplaying Christ's life and death in order to concentrate on the fate of the Apostles, Judas in particular.

40. 13 December 1905. *'A Future for English Music' and Other Lectures*, ed. P. M. Young, London, Dennis Dobson, 1968, pp. 219–21.

41. Moore (1987) op. cit., p. 368.

42. As quoted by Johnstone in a letter to Littleton of Novello, 6 August 1902. ibid.

43. 29 October, 1902. ibid, p. 385.

44. BL Add. M.S. 47904B, ff.171–3, 31, 174–5.

45. BL Add. M.S. 47904B, f.47.
46. Moore (1987), op. cit., p. 377.
47. Capel-Cure had supplied Elgar with the book of his only previous oratorio, *The Light of Life* (1896).
48. It is interesting to note that Elgar had already by this time elaborated upon the first draft of Scene I to the extent of having introduced the idea of an angel watching over Christ's prayer on the mountain.
49. HWRO 705:445:7897. There seems to be no evidence to support Moore's claim (1984, p. 381) that Capel-Cure responded with a text for what was to become 'By the Wayside'. The sketches make clear that Elgar did not conceive the scene in this shape until after he had discarded the Beatitudes from Scene I in January 1903. Besides, the vicar's letter, which still refers to the 'cornfield' scenario, makes no hint at the great imaginative licence which he would have had to take with Elgar's suggestions in order to produce such a scene.
50. BL Add. MS. 47904B, ff.56, 57v, 58, 64v; a more extended typed sketch on f.57 is the most likely to bear Capel-Cure's influence.
51. Letter of 22 November 1902. Moore (1987), op. cit., p. 387.
52. Letter of 9 December, 1902. Moore (1984), op. cit., 394n.
53. Moore (1987), op. cit., p. 382.
54. HWRO 705:445:8567. Moore (1987), op. cit., 391, dates this letter to the 22nd. Jaeger's writing is ambiguous, but he goes on to recall a promise of the composer's that he would 'play the work to me next time I come to Malvern' and asks, 'Supposing I should be staying in your neighbourhood next week, would you carry out your promise if I came over for a day'. Jaeger came to Craeg Lea on 4 January, which would only fall into his plans for 'next week' had the letter been written on the 29th.
55. These ideas were not to reach fruition until well into January 1903, but Elgar was already thinking along such lines in early December, for on the 8th, he received a reply from Alfred Kalisch to a letter requesting information about the shofar and the Talmud, recommending Elgar to consult Kalisch's Rabbi, F. L. Cohen, which advice Elgar was to take with results which may now be heard in the 'Dawn' and 'Morning Psalm' sections of Scene 1. (HWRO 705:445:3873).
56. Letter of 2 January 1903, from Littleton to Johnston. Moore (1987), op. cit., p. 392. The likelihood of the first typescript of the libretto containing the early drafts of the Prologue, Scene I and Judas's soliloquy is strengthened by the presence amongst the sketches of the remains of typed versions of these drafts. Their survival is due for the most part to their having been cut up and rearranged either during revision of the scenes in question, or else to supply texts for different purposes once the original draft had been discarded. In the case of the Judas scene, there are fragments of two copies of the draft, from which it would seem that when Elgar sent the libretto to Novello, he also kept a copy himself. This, according to a letter from Johnstone to Littleton at the end of the year, was subsequently returned to the composer, who, when he came to work on the revision of the Judas scene, therefore had two copies to work from. Of these, he used the reproduction upon which to write comments and suggestions, before cutting up the original to implement his revisions by rearranging the fragments alongside the new texts which he wished to interpolate.
57. Letter to Littleton, Moore (1984), op. cit., p. 389.
58. Letter of 3 August 1908; Atkins, op. cit., p. 174.
59. London, 1894. Elgar Birthplace.

60. Elgar had only himself to blame for this state of affairs. When he accepted the commission from Birmingham, he clearly gave Johnstone the impression that the work was already underway. Thus when Johnstone first communicated with Littleton about the publishing of *The Apostles*, he reported in good faith that Elgar had 'been at work at it some year or two'. (Letter of 17 June, 1902; Moore (1987), op. cit., p. 361).

3 *The Apostles*: Elgar and Bach as Preachers

Ivor Keys

This essay, an elaboration of an A. T. Shaw Memorial Lecture, has as one of its points of departure the examination of two of Novello's vocal scores side by side: those of *The Apostles* and of the Elgar/Atkins edition of the *St Matthew Passion*. What caught my eye was the division of the music into scenes in each case; for instance 'In the tower of Magdala' and 'In the court of Caiaphas' respectively, and common to both the use of the word 'Prologue'. In their introduction to the Bach edition Atkins and Elgar mention Gevaert and Heuss as their predecessors in dividing the work into scenes, and one is bound to agree with their claim for the English edition: 'There can be no doubt that such divisions are of the greatest help in making Bach's treatment of the Gospel narrative clear to the hearer'. Chronology of course forbids us to link the editorial work on the Bach with the work on *The Apostles*. The Bach edition was published in 1911 for the Worcester Three Choirs Festival, and the Birmingham Festival first performance of *The Apostles* was in 1903. It is also pretty evident that in 1911 other pressures on Elgar, notably work on the Second Symphony, meant that his musical contribution to the Bach (Atkins being in any case responsible for the words) was not large. He acknowledged this in two letters to Atkins[1]: (16 March 1911) 'As to the Passion I don't see how my name is to come in unless I can do some expr.' [Expression marks?], and (3 July 1911 in respect of payment by Novello's for the work) 'I have done so little in the matter (and that little out of friendship for you!) that I cannot say much about figures . . . I think a royalty for you would be best but if my name was or is worth anything (which I gravely doubt) Messrs. N. might be disposed to give me something down, leaving the royalty to you.'

On the other hand it is inconceivable that Elgar would not have known the great choral works of Bach as early as the long gestation of his own libretto and music of *The Apostles*, which Wulstan Atkins reckons at no less than 35 years. What is more, he was intimately acquainted with, and much moved by, the great staple, apart from Handel, of the choral societies' diet,

Mendelssohn's *Elijah*, in which that composer transmitted in nineteenth-century terms what he saw as the ethos of a Bachian oratorio.

A musical genre which has been cultivated for the best part of 300 years is bound in many cases to have spread over ill-defined boundaries, but a definition of 'oratorio' as good as any is that of Howard Smither in the *New Grove*: 'An extended musical setting of a sacred text made up of dramatic, narrative and contemplative elements'. Smither's article makes it clear that by 'dramatic' is meant 'having characters', though in the nature of the case seldom characters acting on a stage. The other two elements – narration and contemplation – are basic to the whole conception. But even so they do not always run in anything like equal harness within the work. As is well known, 'oratorio' originally derives from a building, notably the famous Roman oratory of St Philip Neri in the church of S Maria in Vallicella. 'Oratorio' as a word for the 'music' is first seen in 1640. But from its inception at the beginning of the seventeenth century the musical biblical narrative went hand in hand with spiritual exercises, spoken in sermons or sung in hymns (laude). At the other end of our scale of definitions the English-speaking world stands confused by the overwhelming fame of *Messiah*, which was certainly not introduced by Handel as an oratorio. The wonderfully dexterous biblical libretto by Jennens is virtually entirely contemplation, though often of the most exhilarating kind. There are only six verses of 'actual narration' in the entire work: the passage from St Luke, chapter two, beginning at 'There were shepherds' and ending at 'Good will towards men'. An incomparable example of what Jennens and Handel really meant by an oratorio is *Saul*, in which the chorus not only takes part in the 'action' but, in such a number as the wonderful 'Envy, Eldest-born of Hell', moralizes in the manner of the chorus of a Greek tragedy, with which *Saul* may justly be compared.

Mendelssohn's first oratorio, *St Paul* (1836), makes no bones about interspersing the work with chorales used by Bach, starting with 'Wachet auf' (Sleepers wake) in the opening bars of the overture. In *Christus*, incomplete at his death in 1847, he closes a chorus with 'Wie schön leuchtet der Morgenstern' (How brightly gleams the morning star) on the heels of a journeying trio for the three wise men.[2] In *Elijah* there is no Narrator as such, the action and the *solo* comments upon it being carried almost entirely by named dramatic characters, though sometimes recourse is had to one or more angels. Notable exceptions are the non-ascribed soprano solo 'Hear ye, Israel' which opens part two, and of course the famous alto solo 'O rest in the Lord'. The only chorale-type movement is the quartet 'Cast thy burden upon the Lord'. The chorus, as in Bach's Passions, takes part in the action and also comments in big numbers such as 'Be not afraid'. This logical design is kept up until near the end of the work, when the narrative is at an end and the piece dissolves into miscellaneous pieties. Both the extant Bach

Passions are, in the historical sense I have described, true oratorios but with a specific subject matter. The 'action' is in the hands of a narrator-Evangelist, Christ and other named characters, and of the chorus as 'actors'.

The commentary, born out of the spiritual exercises of the early seventeenth century, is in the hands of the chorus (through whose opening and closing portals we pass) and of soloists over and above, and quite separate from, the soloists who are named. Sometimes the chorus are so moved that they cannot refrain from butting in on the solos with naive cries of 'Come where?' or 'Loose Him! Leave Him! Bind Him not!' in which their passionate interruptions eventually obliterate the commentary/duet. The commentary par excellence, encapsulating the emotions of the audience, and by extension the whole of Christian mankind, was the chorale verse, in which, for all we know, the commenting soloists may have joined.

It is evident from all the Elgar literature that in *The Apostles* and its successor(s) he was equally passionate in seeking to bring home the great story to the emotions of the audience, and by extension to the whole of such mankind as would listen, but he had to eschew the chorale. For one thing it was not part of the Roman Catholic tradition; far from it, it was a Protestant weapon, and a German/Lutheran one at that. Bach's Leipzig audience, as the mighty first chorus of the *St Matthew Passion* unfolded, would only have to hear the tune 'O Lamm Gottes' on ripieno sopranos and organ to know that the subject matter was the spotless Lamb of God, even if, as was very probable, they could not hear all the words. In 1903, three years before The English Hymnal, it may be doubted whether a significant number of English Protestants, though church-going, knew even half a dozen of the chorales familiar to mid-eighteenth-century Leipzig.

At first sight the Birmingham audience had copious means of coming to grips with *The Apostles*. For one shilling they could buy a programme – with eight pages on Brahms's fourth symphony thrown in – which gave them all the words and no fewer than ninety-two music examples, deployed through sixty-one pages of 'Analytical and descriptive notes by A. J. Jaeger'. Following ample precedent from Bayreuth, Jaeger had produced a veritable vade-mecum of leading-motifs, giving to each a pithy, usually one-word title in capital letters. Here is a sample, dealing with the opening of the scene in Gethsemane:

> The RESOLUTION motive (67), with a new, sustained phrase superimposed above it, introduces the scene in Gethsemane; trumpet, side drum, and big drum give it an element of blatancy well in keeping with the situation.

> The gentle WAYSIDE motive (35) – a touching subtlety – accompanies Judas' hypocritical 'Hail'. The PASSION (18), CHRIST (3), APOSTLES (16), CHRIST'S LONELINESS (17), and PETER (57A) motives follow in the order named, as suggested by the text, and the SOLDIERY (23) and CAPTORS (70) themes lead to a fresh and highly original idea when the scene changes to the Palace of the

High Priest. The questionings of the High Priest's servants are always accompanied by passages such as the following, in which idle curiosity seems to be followed by derision and indifference.

Ex. 1

Looked at nearly a century later, such a passage – and there are plenty more of them – seems almost to guarantee that the bemused listener will be shielded from the impact of what Elgar hoped he was doing. Occasionally Jaeger introduces a tentative note into otherwise pat identifications as though they had not secured Elgar's blessing. But the status of the Elgar/ Jaeger friendship has led the majority of historians to follow Ernest Newman's assertion that Jaeger's leading-motive titles 'may be taken to have the composer's sanction'. However, a recent article by Christopher Grogan[3] has relieved us of accepting Newman entirely. What may have given Elgar pause about his dear friend's 'analysis' – and friendship produced in Elgar an almost tongue-tied reticence – may well have been the fear of two aspersions on the work's leading-motive system which arose in newspaper critiques of the first performance[4]. Bennett, for the *Daily Telegraph*, wrote:

> It may be true that the method here so conspicuously exemplified helps the composer in the accomplishment of his work by reducing it to a level of a mere deftness, but it is possible to buy ease as well as gold at too high a price.

Baughan, for the *Daily News*:

> But I must admit that it is apt to be illuminative on paper more than in hearing, unless the invention of themes is distinctive. They must have unmistakable character . . . or else they conjure up no definite ideas, and their constant recurrence either passes unnoticed in the swirl of the orchestral current, or it seems to produce a feeling of irritation; one has a feeling of chasing shadows . . .

One does not have to subscribe to either of these opinions to realize that studying a multiplicity of leading-motives is not likely to lead us to 'Elgar as preacher' since on this showing he (or some of his audience) fell fairly soon after the first hurdle. But we have 'horse's mouth' evidence from Elgar himself about his intentions. They all date from 1903 and in chronological order they are: A short 'pleasant conversation with the editor', mainly on the libretto, published in the *Musical Times* of April (Vol.44, no.722, p.228) containing. . . 'Coming to some of the details of the new oratorio, the composer has not attempted to individualise all the twelve Apostles. Peter, John and Judas only are "speaking" characters. He has had before him (1) the Christ, (2) that the Christian Gospel has to be preached, and (3) that there is need of assistance in proclaiming its message.' The *Musical Times* of July (Vol.44, no.725, pp.449-50) continues briefly from the musical viewpoint, insofar as the musical details even at this late date can be regarded as final. A crucial sentence from our viewpoint is: 'In laying out his oratorio the chorus is an intellectual force, and not a body of people more or less interested in what is going on who are merely called upon to utter reflective commentaries on the action.' This must, one feels, be regarded as an 'if-the-cap-fits' comment on his oratorio-writing contemporaries. Elgar must have known his words to be a false antithesis as far as Bach was concerned.

But the third 1903 quotation makes explicit reference to a Mendelssohnian technique of joining the listener-at-large to the narration. It occurs in a letter of 17th July to his friend and confidant Canon Gorton, rector of Morecambe and founder of the Morecambe Festival, of which Elgar was a distinguished adjudicator and publicist: 'I have as in *Elijah* and *St Paul* etc. *made speeches* [Elgar's underlining] for the characters except the Christ whose words are of course untouched.'[5]

On Elgar's recommendation, an article on the libretto by Canon Gorton was published in the *Musical Times* of October 1903 (Vol.44, no.728, pp.656-7). There are no examples or analysis of the music, and Gorton only gives, as he himself calls it, 'a bald outline of the libretto', making clear that there would be a sequel to the Birmingham oratorio. But one sentence, apropos the Prologue, takes us to the heart of the Bach/Elgar connection: 'Jesus, *marked out as the Son of God*, is endowed by the Holy Spirit for the ministrations among men' [my underlining].

After clefs, the first thing that almost every composer of Elgar's day would write – probably in sketches, and certainly in the next stage – was a key-signature. Elgar chose A flat, with the melody starting on the third. I quote him from the July *Musical Times* article:

Ex. 2

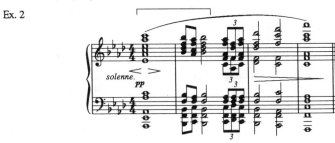

In the *St Matthew Passion* A flat occurs thrice: as the key of a chorale (No.16), as the starting and ending point of the tonally wayward Recitativo

'Ah, Golgotha!' (No.69), but climactically and unforgettably in No.73, allotted by Bach to both choirs together:

Ex. 3

The auxiliary-note figures marked in both examples are not a piece of resemblance-fancying. Bach's two-bar phrase and the words there enshrined are seminal to Elgar. The words are obviously seminal, in the sense that if millions more people – not simply 'the centurion and they that were with him' – had not acknowledged that 'this was the Son of God' there would have been no *St Matthew Passion,* nor any Gospel to teach. We can hardly assert that Elgar did not go along with his opening theme (Ex.2), being called by Jaeger THE SPIRIT OF THE LORD. Elgar quotes it in his *Musical Times* article but it is introduced thus:

> The Prologue – beginning with the words 'The Spirit of the Lord is upon me' – opens with a short orchestral introduction, in which the following theme, inseparably connected throughout the work with the foregoing idea, is prominent.

Although this theme obviously has pride of place as being the first music heard, and although the previous paragraph in the article speaks of 'the theme representative of the Apostles themselves', the reference seems to be not to the A flat opening theme but to the two preceding musical examples in the article establishing the connection between the Gregorian Gradual 'Constitues eos' (promising power to the Apostles) and the Grandioso E flat theme at figure 49 (vocal score page 39), to the words 'The Lord hath chosen them, They shall be named the Priests of the Lord.' The most striking (and therefore the most 'public') of the uses to which the A flat theme is subsequently put are not so much references to the Apostles (or to the Spirit of the Lord) as to the kernel of what they have to preach – the Salvation through the acknowledgment of Christ as God. See the following in particular, the references being to the current Novello vocal score:

(Page 51) The choral response, *ppp tranquillo,* to Jesus's words 'He that receiveth Me, receiveth Him that sent Me'.

(Page 92) The stilling of the storm and the saving of the impetuous Peter from his abortive walk on the sea wrings from the awe-struck Apostles

'Thou are the Son of God', and the auxiliary notes become a mysterious enharmonic sequence.

(Page 99) Peter's declaration 'Thou art the Christ, the Son of the living God' is endorsed by Jesus singing 'Blessed are thou' whilst the theme is spectacularly driven home, even to an untutored audience, by a pause on the first chord rising from *pp* to *ff* and down again, and using the same key (A flat) to achieve a subconscious reference back to Bach.

(Page 143) At Peter's denial the theme is denied thus:

Ex. 4

(Page 166) The colossal shade of Bach forbids Elgar any approximation at the actual words 'Truly this was the Son of God' unless it be that the final *pppp* A flat carries the merest hint of the tonality. Paradoxically, the word 'Truly' takes up the orchestral rendering of 'Eli, Eli . . .' (My God, my God why hast thou forsaken me?) to link Jesus's tragic cry of bereftness with the barely audible assertion of the witnesses on Golgotha.

Where possible Elgar like Mendelssohn has carried on the narration through a dialogue of the characters, but in the early stages at any rate he uses an Evangelist and a tenor at that. With a full symphony orchestra constantly to hand, Bach's use of the entirely conventional 'full-stop' punctuation – a perfect cadence on continuo – would be a distancing touch of antiquarianism, and instead Elgar, at any rate initially, uses an introductory phrase. What happens to it, to the untutored ear rather than the analytical eye, is an interesting example of the fluidity with which Elgar carries the ear along. Directly after the opening 'portal' chorus (Jesus's reading of Isaiah 61 universalised into many voices) we hear this (page 12):

Ex. 5

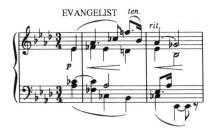

Syncopated and slowed, this 'signs off' the Evangelist and leads to the orchestral depiction of the night. The next voice to be heard is Gabriel (soprano) singing in the distance to

Ex. 6

The tutored, especially with Jaeger's help, will recognise the 'Angel' figure from *Gerontius*; the untutored, without a nice regard for intervals, will feel Ex.6 as an enhanced, literally heightened, version of Ex.5, which has grown a tail, and this tail will be in evidence when the tenor resumes. The next piece of narration (page 68) now begins and ends with the 'tail', but preceded by the falling fifth from Ex.5, the rhythmical shape, as so often in aural perception, being more telling than the intervallic one. This may begin to sound like an analyst's playground, but the psychological effect of these evolutions is greatly to reinforce the sense of a continuing narrative, not one where we interrupt the proceedings by going back to an identical position at a lectern. Indeed after the long 'Mary Magdalene' episode the next narrative recitative is preluded by 'Jesus' music, with vestiges of the tail (page 97), and at the next (page 104) we have fifths up *and* down, and we might as well acknowledge that we are now in the presence, not for the first time, of a Magdalen motif.

After an interval, of three-quarters of an hour according to the programme-book, we need to get our bearings again; accordingly after the orchestral prelude the Evangelist has his original introduction. Thereafter there is no more tenor-Evangelist, but the comparatively few pieces of straight narration are given to male chorus, then contralto solo, and most beautifully to four-part women's chorus for Peter's weeping, where Elgar would not have proposed to meet Bach on his own solo ground.

After 'Golgotha' we part company with Bach. The *St Matthew Passion* ends very much on earth, possibly *in* earth, with, in the final sarabande, the organ contributing its lowest possible note, the 32-foot C. In his final chorus Elgar unites heaven and earth, with indeed an outright quotation from *Gerontius.*

But the final parallel with Bach and enhancement of his notions is to be found in the magnificent Judas scene in and outside the Temple. Number 25 in the *St Matthew Passion* (page 43 in the Elgar-Atkins vocal score) is a commentary on the Agony in the Garden on three planes, subjective-solo, objective-chorus, and orchestra. Jesus has just uttered the words to slow orchestral heart-beats: 'My soul is exceeding sorrowful, even unto death;

tarry ye here and watch with Me'. We are at once involved. The solo (non-Evangelist) tenor is heard for the first time, without any preamble, as though his reaction 'O Grief!' cannot wait for an introduction, and he sings an arioso in a spectacular foreground, representing each individual amongst us. The chorus represent our communal reaction in the background *piano sempre* during the intervals of the tenor solo, by singing line by line a verse of the Chorale 'Herzliebster Jesu'. The foreground orchestra adds a new colour with the oboes *da caccia* entering for the first time to spread a purple tint over the scene, and the repeated semiquavers in the bass represent, as so often in Bach, the quickly trembling heart.

At the Temple (page 146) Elgar also employs three planes, the soloist being Judas, who not only sings his 'own' words, e.g. 'I have sinned in that I have betrayed the innocent blood' but adds Biblical comment that we take to ourselves, e.g. 'Whither shall I go from Thy Spirit?' (The few sentences of narrative are given to the contralto.) The background equivalent to Bach's quiet chorale is given to the chorus representing the singers in the Temple, using as a communal expression psalm 94, 'O Lord God, to whom vengeance belongeth, Lift up Thyself, Thou Judge of the earth'.[6] The orchestral bass accompanies the psalm-singing with a menacing ostinato rhythm (crotchet rest on the beat, followed by three crotchets) and later also uses slow repeated-note crotchets suggestive not so much of the heart-beats as of the imminent funeral march of the anguished Judas, and at the same time preparing a funeral march for Jesus, and by a triple symbolism evoking the ineluctable approach of our own death and of God's judgement. The role of the chorus is amplified also. At Judas's confession they reply (as indeed does Bach's chorus) 'What is that to us? See thou to that,' and they interrupt his second attempt at confession with 'Selah!' at the tops of their voices. Now 'Selah' occurs in the psalms as an occasional directive as to singing or ceremonial; its meaning is uncertain. Elgar seems to have used it as a rough and rude equivalent of *tant pis*. In a letter of June 29th 1910 to Frank Schuster he writes: 'There are fine rows going on over the first performance [of the Violin Concerto] and I am desperately annoyed at several things: selah!'.[7] Another letter, to Troyte (Nov.12, 1913) allots a whole paragraph to the single exclamation.[8] The shattering effect of Selah! is immediately topped by the horrific transformation from background to all-enveloping foreground of the psalm-verse 'Lord, how long shall the wicked triumph?'

After another meditation the chorus is used again to relay, from outside the Temple, the dreaded 'Crucify Him' to the desperate ears of Judas (and ourselves). After Judas has hanged himself we can hear from inside the Temple a verse of the psalm proceeding as though nothing else had happened: 'He shall bring upon them their own iniquity', a terrible reminder that one of God's worst punishments is to allow man to have his own way. It is hard to imagine a more telling and searing sermon than this scene of Elgar's.

By way of coda we may note how *The Apostles* struck home to the young composer John Ireland. He wrote in 1912 an anthem, still a favourite: *Greater love hath no man*. In it we are summoned by Peter's Second Epistle, chapter 2, to be 'a holy priesthood', like the Apostles. At bar 74 there occurs what is impossible to believe is an unconscious reminiscence, the restatement of the theme from *The Apostles* (page 5, figure 5) now to the words 'That we, being dead to sin . . .' Yet more Elgarian is the fervour of this theme sung in unison, complete with the inner chromatic counterpoint in octaves on the organ, to the words, from Peter II chapter 2 again: 'That ye should show forth the praises of *Him who hath called you* out of darkness into His glorious light' [my underlining].

Notes

1.   Atkins, E. Wulstan, *The Elgar-Atkins Friendship*. Newton Abbot, 1984, pp.215 and 220.
2.   Mendelssohn, ed. Keys, *Three excerpts from Christus*, Addington Press, Royal School of Church Music, 1979.
3.   'My dear Analyst'. *Music and Letters* 72 (1): pp.48-60, based in part on Moore, Jerrold Northrop, *Elgar and his Publishers: Letters of a Creative Life*, Oxford, 1987.
4.   They are both to be found in Moore, Jerrold Northrop, *Edward Elgar: a Creative Life*, OUP, 1984, p.417.
5.   Young, Percy, *Letters of Edward Elgar*, London, 1956, p.121.
6.   Known to organists as the far-from-background basis of the Reubke sonata.
7.   Young, Percy. op. cit., p.197.
8.   Young, Percy, ibid., p.214. See also Atkins, E. Wulstan, op. cit., p.97.

4 'The True Foundation': The Symphonies

Robert Meikle

No composer seems to have been so preoccupied throughout his life with the symphony as was Elgar, and at the same time to have produced so few works in the genre. One of his earliest attempts at composition concerns the famous occasion when he wrote a symphony based on Mozart's 40th,[1] and his last years were largely taken up with work on the BBC's commission for a Third Symphony. As early as 1898 he was suggesting to Ivor Atkins that he might write a symphony for the 1899 Three Choirs Festival based on the life of General Gordon of Khartoum;[2] the proposal was accepted, and on 1 March 1899 the *Musical Times* confidently reported that 'Chief among [compositions 'on the stocks'] is the new symphony for the Worcester Festival, which is to bear the title "Gordon".'[3] But the project fell through, perhaps because he had been too busy with the *Enigma Variations*, whose première took place on 19 June 1899, or perhaps because, as he indicated in a letter to Ivor Atkins, he could not afford it.[4] At the beginning of the new century there was further talk of a symphony: in November 1900 Alfred Rodewald offered financial assistance during its composition, and on 20 January 1901 a letter from Alice Elgar to Jaeger seemed to assume that it was on the way: 'I think there cd. be no *nobler* music than the Symphony. I *long* for it to be finished & have to exist on scraps.'[5] But for a while he was busy with the *Cockaigne* Overture – which Elgar himself conducted at its first performance on 20 June 1901; then in October he was writing to Richter about '. . . the symphony I am trying to write . . .: but I have much to do to it yet.'[6] Nothing more was said of the project that year; then, in 1902, a proposed commission for the 1904 Leeds Festival elicited the possibility of a symphony.[7] An indication that something was definitely under way came in a letter of October 1903: '. . . All the incidents [of a car journey] are being worked into the Symphony in E flat dedicated to Hans Richter by his friend Edward Elgar.'[8] But just as *Cockaigne* had interfered in 1901, now another overture, also symphonic in conception but also smaller than a full-scale

45

symphony, *In the South*, intervened, monopolised the first two months of 1904 and took the place of what might have been a symphony at the Covent Garden Elgar Festival in March of that year. By 1905 his thoughts were back at a symphony, but '. . . the Symphony does not come . . .'⁹ Finally, by the spring of 1907, it was impossible to put off the project – either consciously or unconsciously – any longer. On 27 June 1907 Alice Elgar noted in her diary that Elgar was 'Playing great beautiful tune,'¹⁰ and almost exactly fifteen months later, on 25 September 1908, the full score was completed. The first performance was given in Manchester on 3 December of the same year by the Hallé Orchestra, conducted by the dedicatee, 'Hans Richter, Mus. Doc., true artist and true friend.' Both in the Free Trade Hall and at the London première in the Queen's Hall on December 7, the Symphony in A flat (probably the only symphony in the entire repertoire in that key) was rapturously received by audiences and critics alike. Comparisons with Beethoven and Brahms were on everyone's lips, and within a year it had been performed no less than 82 times.¹¹

Although at least one of the sketches which eventually were to form part of the Second Symphony dates back to 1903, the actual process of composition took far less time than the First: after Op. 55 came the Violin Concerto (1909–10), and the Second Symphony followed close behind. Work began in earnest in November, 1910, and was to run concurrently with the new edition of Bach's *St Matthew Passion* that Elgar was preparing with Ivor Atkins. By 28 February 1911 the Symphony was finished. It was dedicated to – though not necessarily inspired by – 'the Memory of His late Majesty King Edward VII', and carried an inscription from Shelley, 'Rarely, rarely comest thou, Spirit of Delight!' However, its reception at its first performance three months later on Thursday 24 May did not match that accorded the First Symphony. For one thing the hall was by no means full – perhaps after the *Dream of Gerontius* and the Violin Concerto earlier in the week audiences had had a surfeit of Elgar – and he himself sensed that there was something less than fulsome in the applause: 'What's the matter with them, Billy?' he complained to W. H. Reed; 'They sit there like a lot of stuffed pigs.'¹²

There was little talk of a further symphony during the war years, but by 1920 Shaw was beginning to sow the seeds: 'If I were king, or a Minister of Fine Arts, I would give Elgar an annuity of a thousand a year on condition that he produced a symphony every eighteen months.'¹³ Presumably he pestered Elgar during the ensuing years, but in 1932 his enthusiasm took the tangible form of suggesting that the BBC commission it. By the end of the year his persistence was rewarded, and the formal commission was announced on 14 December.¹⁴ In some ways the gestation of the Third Symphony parallels that of the First: the same gathering together of sketches from years before, the same confident rumours circulating (even prior to the formal announcement of the commission) that the work was well under way, and the same encouraging assurances from the composer himself that all was going well: 'I am as forward with the work as I hoped to be . . .' (24 April 1933), then three days later, 'I like your idea to announce the Symphony for the May Festival of 1934 . . .' and, on the same date, to Sir John Reith at the BBC, 'I presume it will be correct for me to send my MS . . . *direct* to the publishers . . .'[15] The saddening difference was of course that he died before the work could be finished, and with instructions to W. H. Reed that no-one should attempt to complete it from the remaining sketches,[16] though it is clear that in any case not enough survives for that to be possible.

Consequently, the outcome of a commitment to the symphony that spanned nearly all of his working life, from the apprenticeship with Mozart's 40th to the unfinished Third Symphony nearly sixty years later, is two works in the genre, with barely two-and-a-half years between them. Perhaps Elgar sensed that he was writing almost at the end of an era, stretching back a century and a half, when it could be taken for granted that any composer worthy the name would produce a respectable collection of symphonies, whereas now the changes taking place in musical styles were as radical as any that the evolution of music had ever witnessed. But whatever the reason, Op.55 and Op.63 manifest a number of intriguing and unique paradoxes, among them their structure and content, their relationship to each other and to their composer, and their composer's attitude towards them.

'No survey of [Elgar's] orchestral output can deal exclusively with the notes and harmonies as written in the scores. Although by technical analysis one can isolate the virus [*sic*] in any particular passage, and although the music itself is strong enough to be self-sufficient examined and heard purely as a musical structure, yet by excluding extra-musical clues and associations, whether personal or literary, a dimension is eradicated.'[17] With these words Michael Kennedy advocates an approach to Elgar's symphonies that is guided primarily by non-musical issues, that is, by 'meanings', by any clues that biographical information might hold for them, and by, one assumes, what the critic himself might make of the works when heard in the light of such information. And to be sure, some of Kennedy's own interpretative responses to the works ring as true as any. Yet I question whether any composer can be so secure in the embrace of his devotees that his works become somehow exempt from an investigation that might wish to seek out and assess their qualities simply as music. Such an investigation would look not for a 'virus', not for a pervasive, infectious strain running through the music, but rather for the component which is still as crucial in the twentieth century as it was when Leopold Mozart coined his term for it in the eighteenth: 'il filo';[18] In other words, it would ask whether the symphonies are indeed 'strong enough to be self-sufficient examined and heard purely as [musical structures]'. Nor need it be simply an arid, clinical dissection, but rather an enquiry to discover if there is musical as well as biographical evidence for both the affection in which the symphonies are held by some and the scepticism with which they are regarded by others.[19] There are few enough such investigations in existence: descriptive résumés abound, all the way from the introductory articles in the *Musical Times* immediately prior to the two premières, to the most recent biographies published in the last decade or so. Yet, with Diana McVeagh's admirable study as a rare exception, there are few insights into, and even fewer detailed scrutinies of, Elgar's actual method of constructing a symphony movement. I propose to try to open a few doors onto this aspect of his compositional processes. How does he build a movement? What is his attitude to tonality? To form? To motivic relationships? Nor do I find such an enquiry into his technique a negation of the man's presence in the Symphonies, but rather an alternative means to reveal it. 'Adequate performances of the two Symphonies never fail to convince the writer that for each there is a programme of some kind . . .,' wrote Basil Maine in 1933, but he immediately went on to acknowledge that familiarity with the programmes is not sufficient to reveal what he called the 'inner life' of the works.[20] And we have Elgar's own authority for such a line of enquiry: in his Birmingham University lecture of 13 December 1905 appears the remark from which this essay takes its title:

> Turning to the question of absolute music: I still *look upon music* which exists without any poetic or literary basis as the true foundation of our art . . . . I hold that the Symphony without a programme is the highest development of art. *Views to the contrary are, we shall often find*, held by those . . . who would deny to musicians that peculiar gift, which is their own, a musical ear, or an *ear for music.*[21]

I shall return later to evidence which suggests that this was not Elgar's last word on the subject, but there can be little doubt of the value that he places on what Maine was to call the 'inner life' of a symphony, and it is to that dimension that we now turn.

The first basic but significant observation to make about Elgar's op.55 is that few symphonies in the entire repertoire, nominally assigned a key, spend so little time in their tonic as this First Symphony spends in A flat major. Just under half of the first movement (about 300 bars out of some 630) is in A flat, and the second and third movements completely ignore it. The finale begins in D minor, touches briefly on A flat at 110 and 111, and there are four bars of A flat at 141₅; only on the return of the so-called motto theme, at 146, is the tonic key of the Symphony finally confirmed, with the result that, of more than 400 bars in the movement, only a mere 80 or so have any allegiance to A flat, a situation that must be unprecedented in the history of the symphony.[22] But there are two principal reasons why A flat imposes itself as the tonic: first, it frames the entire work – it is the first and the last key we hear; and secondly, both melody and accompaniment in these two passages are almost completely diatonic in A flat. Both at the beginning of the work, and, even more strikingly, in the huge *tutti* from 146 to 148 which marks the climax of the finale, there is scarcely an accidental to be heard.[23] These two solid anchorage points in A flat at beginning and end seem to have allowed Elgar to work at times in an idiom so chromatic that it has either caused confusion over the definition of keys, or it has even become atonal.

To begin with, almost every commentator on this Symphony has declared the first subject (at the *Allegro*) to be in D minor, a key both convenient, since the key signature is reduced to one flat, and beguiling, since D minor is a tritone away from the tonic, and moreover the finale begins in D minor. Yet every other piece of evidence we can adduce, beginning with our ears, tells us that the key is in fact A minor, that the first two melody notes could not possibly be leading-note-to-tonic, that the chord in the second bar is a dominant 7th, not a secondary 7th, and that the chord in bar 8 is V of V, not V of V of V (See Ex.1). Our ears will also recall that bars 7-8 of the introduction come to rest on the supertonic: Ex.3(a) below demonstrates that these two bars anticipate bars 7–8 of the first subject almost note for note, with the result that the B natural at ₁6 (i.e. the last note of Ex. 1) can hardly be any other than a supertonic, as was the B flat in bar 8.

Ex. 1

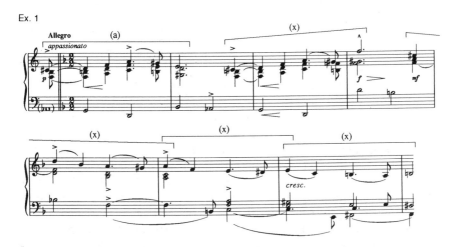

Further evidence confirms the suspicion that the one-flat signature has little to do with the key: the Preface to the Elgar Complete Edition of the work reproduces a sketch of the beginning of the *Allegro:* it is at the same pitch, but has a key-signature of one sharp.[24] Clearly Elgar was experimenting with key-signatures, looking for the most helpful one, and that of one sharp was discarded after a couple of bars. Then we have Elgar's own word on two separate occasions: almost a year after it was completed, he writes to Jaeger, 'As to the symphony – the general key is A flat – the signature of one flat means nothing. It [*sic*] is convenient for the players.'[25] Finally, writing to Ernest Newman about the recapitulation (at 32, where the melody is at the same pitch as in the exposition), Elgar commented that the treble '. . . gives a feeling of A minor . . .'[26] But although the A flat-D tritone link and the neat but illusory notion of placing both the first movement and finale *Allegros* in D minor must now therefore be discarded, there are nevertheless different relationships – now of semitones – elsewhere in the work which emerge to recall this first movement (the recapitulation of the main theme of the finale in E flat minor at 134, for example, after its first appearance at 111_6 in D minor).

Probably the A minor of the first movement's first subject was self-evident to Elgar, but he knew full well that some tonal aspects of the work as a whole might appear odd. In the letter to Jaeger quoted above, he demonstrates in manuscript the relationship between the A flat of the first movement and the F sharp minor of the second: A flat can function as the dominant of D flat, which in turn can enharmonically become the dominant of F sharp. So F sharp in its relation to A flat is, as it were, IV of IV.

> 'This is a sort of *plagal* (?) relationship,' he went on, 'of which I appear to be fond (although I didn't know it) – most folks run through *dominant* modulations – if that expression is allowable & I think some of my twists are defensible on *sub*-dominant grounds. [And he might have gone on to point out that the D major of the third movement is IV of the relative major of F sharp.] All this is beside the point because I *feel* & don't invent . . .'[27]

Subdominant inflections are even more striking in the Second Symphony: not only is the climactic chord in bar 3 the subdominant, but in the D flat chord of bar 6 we have already reached IV of IV, and Elgar contrives, by an ingenious accumulation of harmonic devices, actually to launch into the recapitulation on a chord of A flat rather than the tonic E flat (at 42_1). In the second movement, which is in C minor, one of the principal subsidiary themes (at 76) is in F, while the wistful fragment in parallel thirds (which had first appeared at $_370$) leans towards the subdominant. One of the first important tonal digressions in the finale (at 137) leads to D flat, and the second subject (the 'Hans himself' theme, as Elgar called it – at 139)[28] is in A flat, not the B flat that 'most folks' would have selected). But a generalized preference for the subdominant over the dominant is not Elgar's sole preoccupation in arranging the tonal structure of his symphonies, and there are in addition wider matters to be considered.

Ever since the evolution of the symphony in the mid-eighteenth century as an independent genre, tonality had been one of the most crucial of its components. The establishment of a tonic, departure from it, rapid and closely-packed digressions to other, temporary, tonics, the re-presentation – quite literally, the recapitulation – of material in the tonic that had initially been encountered in an alien key, leading to the final reconciliation of these successive tonics through a return to the home key: such issues were the very stuff from which the symphony was built. As the eighteenth century gave way to the nineteenth, concepts of tonality and of potential key-relationships widened, but the dynamic tension between tonic and non-tonic keys endured. No aspiring symphonist, even in the highly-chromatic days of the early twentieth century, could possibly ignore the issues raised by tonality. It had evolved through and along with the symphony; indeed, it was one of the things that the symphony had always been 'about.' Consequently, an investigation of Elgar's treatment of tonality will tell us something about Elgar the symphonist. Let us consider parts of two movements regarded respectively to be among his weakest and his best – the finale of the First Symphony and the first movement of the Second.

The *Lento* introduction to the last movement of the First Symphony is much more restless than that to the first movement: it fluctuates tonally far more (beginning in D minor, it passes through D major, B flat major, F minor and A flat major – there is even a hint of F flat/E major – before it returns to D minor), and it also contains more thematic material, both as reminiscence and anticipation. At the double bar (*Allegro*) a turbulent, D-minor theme appears, which we take to be the first subject, and which is followed in due course by the theme that was originally to have been the second subject (at 113 – and redolent of César Franck) and then by the second subject proper (at 114 – often, and with good reason, likened by critics to Brahms; I shall return to these two themes later, when we come to Elgar's treatment of melody). They lead in turn to a three-fold statement (each progressively louder and higher: in D minor, F major and A flat minor) of what we might nominate as the movement's motto – the *quasi*-march theme that had been quietly adumbrated in bars 6–9 of the introduction. A fourth, climactic outburst of this theme in D minor prepares the way for a restatement, still in D minor, of the theme from the beginning of the *Allegro*, and it soon appears that we are possibly into a development section, though if that is the case, it is an odd exposition to have ended, just before 120, in the tonic.[29] All three principal themes of the movement (that is, the first and second subjects and the *quasi*-march) are developed, and evaporate (at 129) into a shadow of the motto that had begun the work,[30] proceeding in turn to the most radiant passage in the whole movement. We hear now an extended statement, in augmentation and in canon, of the *quasi*-march theme, which sets out in E flat minor, digresses briefly, and returns to it at 134. Now begins the recapitulation, and here we can examine Elgar's tonal procedures with more detailed reference to the score.

The passage from 134 to 143 (that is, the recapitulation) retraces exactly the route that the exposition had taken from 111_6 to 120, except that the recapitulation is one bar longer. But if we compare the pitches of the two sections, we find variants between them that can only be called haphazard. They are set out in Table 1.

Table 1
Exposition and Recapitulation in the finale of Symphony 1

Exposition	Recapitulation	Distance of Recap. from Exp.	Adjustment: compare
111_6–112_3	134 – 135_3	semitone up	
$112_{5\text{-}6}$	$135_{5\text{-}6}$	tritone	112_4 & 135_4
$112_{7\text{-}8}$	$135_{7\text{-}8}$	maj. 3rd down	$112_{6\text{-}7}$ & $135_{6\text{-}7}$

Bars $135_{7\text{-}8}$ are repeated at $135_{9\text{-}10}$

$_4113$–$_1114$	$_4136$–$_1137$	tone down	$_{5\text{-}4}113$ & $_{5\text{-}4}136$
114 – 116*	137 – 139*	maj. 3rd down	$_1114$ & $_1137$
*: Second subject.			
116 – 116_5	139 – 139_4	semitone up	$_1116$ & $_1139$

The above passage is one bar shorter in the recapitulation: bar 116_5 does not reappear at 140.

116_6–$_1120$	140–143	min. 3rd up.	The altered link at $_1140$.

It is the same in the recapitulation of the first movement in the Second Symphony. Table 2 summarizes the differences in much the same way as Table 1, though rather more concisely.

This continual side-slipping in these two recapitulations, with a dextrous alteration here and a new juxtaposition of sequences there, creates in each situation a reprise whose tonal relationship to its exposition is constantly changing. The effect is that we lose all sense of the tonal pressure, of the exploitation of tension between the tonic and other keys – whether the traditional 'related' keys or not – that had hitherto been fundamental to the symphony as manifested through sonata-form structures. Moreover, it is difficult to escape a sense that these long, repeated paragraphs, deprived as they are of coherent and, because their relationship to the exposition is constantly changing, of logical tonal relationships with the exposition, acquire an almost frantic quality in what becomes discernible as a search to

Table 2
Exposition and recapitulation in the first movement of Symphony 2

Recap.	Compared with Exposition.	
$42\text{-}_3 43$:	second bar-1:	same pitch
$_{2\text{-}1}43$:		new
$43\text{-}44_2$:	1-2:	4th up
$44_{3\text{-}4}$:	$2\text{-}2_2$:	tone down
45:		23 bars cut, from 2_3-7
45-52	7-13:	tone down; $_2 52$ is new
52:		10 bars cut, from 13-15
52-54	$5\text{-}6_4$	tone down; taken from part of the cut passage between 2_3 and 7
$54\text{-}_1 63$	15-24:	4th up; some bars omitted
$63\text{-}63_4$	$31\text{-}31_2$:	min 3rd up & augmented
$63_{5\text{-}6}$	$_2 2$ & 2:	same pitch
$_4 64\text{-}64_4$	repeats previous 6 bars, and the last two a second time	

The movement ends with further brief references to earlier material, some contracted (just before 65) and some expanded (the two bars before 66).

avoid too slavish a résumé of the exposition.[31] To be sure, these paragraphs are disguised with consummate skill, and in a field in which Elgar's mastery is beyond dispute: his scoring – or rather, in this context, his re-scoring. Time and again a passage which appears on an early hearing to be 'new' turns out to be a restatement of something heard earlier, transposed and re-scored but otherwise unchanged, unless by the addition of a counter-melody (as for example the fanfare-like figure which appears at 121 in the finale of the First Symphony, and which is incorporated into the recapitulation at 134). One of the most striking instances of this re-scoring practice can be seen in a comparison of figures 6 and 53 in the first movement of the Second Symphony: the material is basically the same in each case, with 53 being a tone below 6, but the later passage having been radically re-scored.

Let us now turn to the third movement of the Second Symphony, the movement marked 'Rondo' by Elgar, but which can quite readily – perhaps more readily – be regarded as a scherzo, and which has elements of sonata form as well.[32] In fact, its dimensions as a rondo are far from clear, as Table 3 shows.

The alternative set out in Table 3(a) seems to be a straightforward rondo structure, though inevitably some paragraphs become unwieldy in their dimensions: both appearances of B are huge, and it contains two themes – the first no further away from home than the tonic minor – together with a return of material from A in a form that recalls Loge's Magic Fire, from

Table 3
Possible rondo and scherzo dimensions in the third movement of Symphony 2

3(a) *Rondo I*

A	B	A	C	A*	B	A (& coda)
Beginning	93	103_7	107	116	122_3	132
Bars in length:						
73	140	54	108	66	147	53

3(b) *Scherzo and Trio*

Scherzo				*Trio* (with traditional repeats)				
A (with repeat);	B	A^2	a	a;	b	a^2;	b†	a^2
Beginning	92	103_7	109	110	111_3	112	$_8113$	114

†: This longer b repeats the lead-in to the trio from 107.
Scherzo Da Capo (no repeats)

A*;	B	A^2
116	122_3	132

3(c) *Rondo II*

A	B	A	C	A	D	A*	B	A	C	A (& coda)
Beginning	93	98	100	103_7	107	116	122_3	126	129	132
Bars in length:										
73	69	24	47	54	108	66	68	31	48	53

*: This section includes, from $117-122_2$, the 'ghost' music from the first movement.

98–100 and from 126–129. B is therefore about double the length of A, and becomes uncomfortably top-heavy. After the 'hammering' music derived from the first movement, at 122_3, the momentum of B returns, and the movement '. . . picks up simply its former mood . . . ,'[33] and inexplicably carries on as if nothing had happened, as if the intervening tumult had changed nothing. There are recapitulatory side-slips (at 123_8 and 125) and the Loge music is extended.

However, a scheme along these lines has two drawbacks. First, it makes the form not all that different from that with which Elgar quite deliberately chose not to label the movement – scherzo and trio. Table 3(b) shows how the movement could be regarded in that light, and a comparison with Table 3(a) shows that the two schemes are identical, except that the scherzo plan fills out C in more detail as a trio. Secondly, when listened to as a rondo, the movement lacks the feature which had characterized that particular form for over 100 years, and which would impart to it the spirit of its rondo-forerunners, irrespective of any qualms about the actual labelling of sections: it wants that sense of building up the listener's expectations at the end of subsidiary sections, sure in the knowledge that the refrain is just around the corner, and the consequent satisfaction when it duly reappears. The problem is once again tonal, for at 93, supposedly the beginning of the first episode, no amount of bounding energy can disguise the fact that we have moved no further away from the key of the refrain than to its minor, where we will remain for close on 60 bars. And if we do not move away from the tonic, there is little that can be done to create a sense of returning to it.

Table 3(c) proposes a rondo with a greater number of sections, and thus of episodes and refrains. It has the advantage that no section becomes impossibly top-heavy, but the appearance of B twice in the tonic minor still upsets the tonal balance, and the reliance on rhapsodic returns of the A refrain (the 'Loge' sections) at 98 and 126 is not entirely satisfactory. Still, we are closer, in this version, with its kaleidoscopic shifts to and from the refrain, to the essence of the rondo.

One further, large-scale sonata-form movement must be briefly examined – the finale of the Second Symphony. Its main theme dates back to Elgar's Italian trip to Alassio in 1903–4,[34] though it could hardly be more English in spirit. There is something about its placid, unruffled, even slightly self-satisfied air, that imparts the unmistakeable atmosphere of a Sunday bandstand in the park. The band is out of sight – probably just beyond the rhododendrons – and so we cannot hear all the instruments; but the lower ones come over quite well, and the occasional chirp from flutes, clarinets and oboes is carried by the afternoon breeze. The second subject ('Hans himself') appears first in A flat and is stated three times before it turns quickly to B flat minor at $_4$142 – its own subdominant side – and thence to a B flat major which sounds slightly odd after so much A flat, as if it were somehow not the dominant key at all. The development uses 'Hans', but is so angular and contrapuntal, with wild, almost Mahlerian eruptions in the strings, that it scarcely seems to belong to the same work. A climax in B minor gives way to the quieter section (reminiscent of the second movement of the Brahms *Deutsches Requiem*) that Elgar labelled, 'Braut's bit'.[35] The recapitulation virtually retraces the steps of the exposition, with barely an alteration to be heard, except for the amendments necessary to bring the second subject, and hence the whole movement, round to the tonic. But since the second subject had been in A flat, with a modulation to its dominant (i.e., the tonic), so now the second subject, in E flat, modulates to *its* dominant (that is, B flat), and the presence of the dominant key so close to the end of a sonata-form movement creates a sense of unease, despite its outward confidence. The final close in E flat wistfully recalls the beginning of the work, and perhaps symbolises the weakness of the movement as a whole: for all the spirit of the first three movements seems to have been drained away, and we are left with only shadows – grandiose, but shadows all the same – of their former spontaneous vigour, fitted into that structure somewhat disparagingly known as 'text-book sonata form'.

From the anxious side-stepping of recapitulations in the First Symphony to the uneasy subdominant excursions in the finale of the Second, we find what Michael Kennedy has rightly discerned as a restlessness in the 'curious tonality' of the Symphonies, 'which is constantly and violently switched about'.[36] But on the evidence of these movements, it is a restlessness which urgently seeks to find a path forward, not a controlled turbulence articulated by the confident grasp of a sure tonal framework.

There is one particular passage in the First Symphony, however, in which a theme is recapitulated in the 'wrong' key, obviously quite deliberately, and to magical effect. The return of the principal theme of the slow movement (at 100) takes its normal course for five bars, and then side-steps (at 100_6), to continue a fifth higher than in the opening statement. That first statement had led to a cadence in F sharp minor, so this return now correspondingly aims a fifth higher, that is towards C sharp minor, only to turn (at 102) to C sharp major. It is in that key rather than the tonic D that the second main theme of the movement now appears; but the reason soon becomes clear. Elgar is saving the final return of the tonic for one of the most touching moments in all his music: the *Molto espressivo e sostenuto* theme at 104. (And this semitone relationship between the C sharp major of the second theme and the D major of the *Molto espressivo* is a distant echo of the semitone between A flat of the introduction to the first movement and the A minor of the first subject.)

Much has been written about Elgar's use of the sequence and of repetition as a means of generating momentum, and I do not intend to dwell on them at length here. But it is interesting to make two comments. The first is that, in the Symphonies, these devices appear most frequently in the movements that present the most marked problems in sustaining a musical argument across a large, spacious span of time – first movements and finales. In fact, if one were to cut from the first movement of the Second Symphony every phrase that either repeats or is in sequence with its immediate predecessor, it would not be surprising to find the movement reduced to about half its present length. Sequences help to keep a musical idea moving, they are an aid to development, and in subsequent appearances after the first they can be strung together in a new order.[37] And a study of this first movement shows that each of these needs is met by the use of sequences. Speculation rather than comment might be a more fitting word for the second observation provoked by Elgar's devotion to the sequence: for they are so insistent, so pervasive, so relentless, almost, that one wonders to what extent the forthcoming edition of the *St Matthew Passion* was in Elgar's mind while he was writing the Symphony. Certainly it cannot have been far away, and an examination of the recapitulation in the first movement will demonstrate that Elgar has learnt much from Bach's ability to reshape sequential passages. Although the prevailing moods of the two works could hardly be more different, two movements of the *Passion* provoke particular conjecture as possible influences. One of the potential models is the opening movement, with its powerfully-flowing 12/8 metre, and especially the sequences on, for example, pp.3–4,[38] ' "See Him," "Whom?" "the Bridegroom Christ." ' The other, No. 75 (p. 176, 'Make thee clean, my heart, from sin') is again in 12/8, this time in a major key, and in addition with leanings towards the subdominant – a feature which would undoubtedly have attracted Elgar's attention.

If, then, a suitable image for Elgar's treatment of large-scale forms might be that of a surging energy as a mask for caution, even uncertainty at times, it would be a mistake to assume that his harmony and chromaticism were either uncertain or prudently conservative. The indebtedness of various aspects of his writing, especially phrase-structure, to predecessors such as Brahms and César Franck, has been pointed out on innumerable occasions. The characteristic repetitive rhythms of many of his melodies also trace their ancestry to, among others, Brahms. But harmonically Elgar is firmly in the first eventful decade of the twentieth century. When we listen to the almost completely diatonic introduction to the First Symphony, we may well need to remind ourselves that it was being composed at exactly the same time as the work which was to lead twentieth-century music into atonality – Schoenberg's Second String Quartet; but no reminder of the imminent disintegration of tonality is necessary when we hear the first subject – not only at the beginning of the exposition, but even more markedly in the recapitulation, where Elgar himself was pleased to draw attention to its mild bitonality.[39] At times it is possible to suggest that such-and-such a tonally indeterminate passage is in the process of moving from one key to another (there are many such moments in the third movement of the Second Symphony);[40] there are other progressions which are suspended in no key at all, as are the four chords which drift lazily through the slow movement of the First Symphony (See Ex. 2); and the first five bars in the melody of the 'ghost' episode, as Elgar called the famous passage which first appears at 28 in the Second Symphony,[41] contain eleven of the twelve notes of the chromatic scale. The whole-tone scale makes a brief appearance between 127 and 128 in the third movement of the Second Symphony as an extension of the 'Loge' music referred to above, and the first cadence chord at the end of the same work (at 171_4) is a version of the *Tristan* chord,[42] but transformed in almost exactly the same way that Debussy had devised in 1894 to bring to a close his *Prélude à l'après-midi d'un faune*. With hindsight, of course, we know that Elgar was to venture no further toward the dissolution of tonality; but there are moments in these two Symphonies when he sails close to the edge.[43]

Ex. 2

Tonality and harmony both look in two directions: tonality sometimes shaped with great skill and sometimes quite unsure of its direction, harmony looking both backwards to a more diatonic age and forwards towards the disappearance of traditional hierarchical chord relationships presupposed by and reinforcing the existence of a tonic. And if we turn to Elgar's treatment of melody we can see a further paradox, demonstrating an analogous split between on the one hand great skill in devising a coherent thematic framework, and on the other an uncertainty which could find itself inserting themes at the last minute.

In the First Symphony, the motto theme needs to strike a fine balance: it must preserve sufficient individuality to enable it initially to persist in the listener's memory as a point of stability, and finally to return as a consummation of the whole work. At the same time, if it does not generate other themes, it will be left in noble isolation at the beginning and the end, with a few passing reminders *en route* from the one to the other. Elgar fulfils both requirements, through just such explicit reminders on the one hand, and ingenious metamorphoses on the other. The quotations are self-evidently clear enough (48, for example); Ex.3 shows some of the less obvious thematic derivations.

Even more striking than the melodic affinities are some of the rhythmic echoes from bars 7–8 of the introduction: see the segments marked (x) in Ex.3, either with or without the first tied note and the last dotted note. Perhaps the most surprising, and also the most satisfying, of these relationships is that with the *Molto espressivo* theme at 104, as demonstrated in Ex.3(d). Its 'descending steps [with some octave displacements] could be heard as emergent from the Symphony's motto,' writes Moore.[44] So too could the prominent dominant and subdominant notes in its second and fourth bars, and in addition the rhythm of these first four bars twice sets out the rhythm

Ex. 3

of figure (x). The first sketch for this *Molto espressivo* theme dates from August 1904, a full three years before composition began in earnest, and it is almost as if the work somehow germinated from it, rather than from the opening motto which nominally sets the Symphony in motion. We should note, too, that, in addition to the close kinship of their main themes, further links exist between the second and third movements. For instance, the D-major *Adagio* does not completely abandon the second movement's F sharp minor: it reappears at bars 5–6 and again on the approach to the return at 100, where D major emerges from an interrupted cadence in F sharp minor. Nor should we overlook the fact that both themes are rounded off by a triad of F sharp minor – at $_2$56 and $_2$94.

Elgar's treatment of thematic relationships in the First Symphony demonstrates as subtle an integration of many principal themes as one would encounter in a work by a classical master. Yet such skill co-exists side by side with a manipulation of other themes that at times appears almost gauche. There is for instance a fleeting but curious moment in the first movement of the First Symphony, when in the recapitulation (at 35) we hear only the second phrase of the first subject (in F minor). Had the first phrase (marked [*a*] in Ex.1) been included, the result could have been long-winded; but it is missing, and as a result the second phrase, played alone, sounds lopsided. But it is in the finale of the same work that the most serious structural issues emerge for, as Robert Anderson has shown,[45] some important insertions were made at the manuscript stage of the full score. The least complex involved the addition of the motto in the introduction (which sounds entirely convincing); much more curious was the last-minute inclusion of the 'Brahmsian' second subject. We must imagine the movement planned, complete with climaxes,[46] the sketches fleshed out, the whole in the process of being written out in full score, when suddenly the composer decides that his existing second subject (at 113) is inadequate, whereupon he *inserts*[!] the melody from 114–116. Expository material must needs be developed, so Elgar now adds a passage of exactly the same length between 127 and 129, and after this 'token' development, only the recapitulation and the *stringendo* in the coda provide further references to this newly-implanted melody. Anderson offers possible, and non-musical, reasons for the addition of the theme (Elgar's recent involvement with Brahms's Third Symphony, or perhaps some kind of homage to Richter, the dedicatee of the Symphony, and soon to be the conductor of the first performance), but given the fundamental issues of the relationship between form and content raised by the composition of a symphony, we can legitimately wonder what kind of symphonic mind inserts a second subject as an afterthought, at the stage of preparing the manuscript full score.

The similarity between this 'new' second subject in Elgar's finale and that in the finale of Brahms's Third Symphony, and the fact that the end of Elgar's Second quietly recalls the beginning, just as the close of Brahms's Third had done the same, together with Elgar's own documented admiration for Brahms's Third, all dispose us – if we wish to investigate possible further parallels – to concentrate on this particular Brahms Symphony. It is however in a comparison of the finales of the two composers' First Symphonies that a number of intriguing correspondences emerge. Not all can be adequately demonstrated here, and close reference to the scores is indispensable: in the following summary, numbers in parentheses refer respectively to bar numbers in Brahms and to rehearsal numbers in Elgar.

The two movements each open with a slow, brooding introduction, presenting both a fragment which might turn into an important theme (the Brahms does; the Elgar does not), and a short, chordal theme which will reappear later, scored at one point for prominent trombones (47; 109₄). The Elgar bears a more-than-passing relationship with the initial counter-melody in Brahms's woodwind: see Ex.4(a). There are marked accelerations in the two introductions, either by tempo indication or by diminution of note-values (8 and 18; 110); in the *Allegros* a dotted crotchet-quaver figure appears prominently (far more so in the Elgar), as Ex.4(b) demonstrates (148; 111₆).

Ex. 4(a)

Ex. 4(b)

there is no explicit thematic connection between these two quotations, but their combination of steps and angular leaps does give them a marked resemblance to each other. Elgar's two second subjects (in addition to the harmonic affinity of the first with César Franck) resemble the continuation of Brahms's second subject in their use of crotchets in pairs and triplets (132; 113 & 114). Both expositions reach climactic phrases in their initial keys (we recall that the Elgar is in D minor, not the tonic A flat), and repeat them a third higher: Brahms moves from C major to E minor, Elgar moves from D minor to F major, and extends the process to A flat minor and eventually back to D minor (168; 118-120). After their expositions, the two works immediately present quite lengthy statements of their first subjects in their original keys (185; 120), and the development processes which follow (Brahms is of course amalgamating development and recapitulation; Elgar gives us the two sections) treat an introduction figure contrapuntally

(234; 122); these two 'developments' lead to further restatements of introductory material, the one powerful and the other serene, but both imitative (285; 130), whereupon the two works pick up their previous momentum (302; 134). Finally, both move to massive climaxes in which earlier themes – subdued at their first presentations – now appear in a glorious *tutti* (407; 146). Elgar's climax is a *Grandioso* presentation of the Symphony's motto, Brahms's of the trombone chords from bar 47: and if ever Brahms might have felt the need for the direction, *nobilmente*, it would have been over this chorale theme in his First Symphony.

Some of the themes in this comparison between Brahms and Elgar resemble each other quite closely, while others could not be more different; the prevailing moods of the two works are markedly contrasted, and the proportions of their various sections are also different (though the two *Allegros* are almost exactly the same length – 395 and 393 bars respectively). Any one or two sporadic similarities could be put down to coincidence or to some unconscious assimilation process; but we cannot ignore such an accumulation of correspondences, and if we leave on one side the actual content of the events in these finales, concentrating instead on the frequent parallel occurrences of the events themselves, we find in Elgar an indebtedness that cannot but question again his ability, on the evidence of his First Symphony, to create a large-scale symphonic *Allegro*.

If a degree of scepticism qualifies admiration for the First Symphony, however, barely a single caveat need be entered for the Second. We have already noted the propensity for harmonic and tonal relationships in this work to incline towards the subdominant by the frequent introduction of a flattened seventh, a tone below the tonic; now we can observe in thematic construction the equally subtle phenomenon of the step of a semitone, at times merely oscillating between major and minor third, but at others shifting between dominant and raised fourth, and thereby counterbalancing the harmonic lean towards the subdominant by implying a melodic shift in the direction of the dominant. Ex.5 shows the most striking, but not all, of such instances; Ex.5(a) indicates chromatic moves to a raised fourth, that is, the leading-note of the dominant, while Ex.5(b) shows those themes which incorporate a semitone shift, but have no implications for the dominant.

The connection between the 'ghost' theme of the first movement (at 24) and the main theme of the third movement could not have a more brilliant demonstration than at 118, where the 'ghost' takes over from the scherzo with barely a hint of the eruption that is almost upon us. Finally, the version of the *Tristan* chord already referred to, which forms the final cadence at the end of the work, contains A natural, the sharpened fourth of E flat; the chord's final resolution onto E flat unobtrusively but effectively reconciles the Symphony's A natural with its tonic.

Ex. 5(a)

Ex. 5(b)

There are other clear and significant melodic instances of semitone relationships, usually appearing as an appoggiatura, and beginning as early as bar 2 of the first movement. From there, it reappears on innumerable occasions, some of the most prominent of which are indicated in Ex.6.[47]

Ex. 6

There are still further, fleeting thematic relationships: that between $_2$2 and 93 will be immediately apparent. Less obvious, perhaps, is the affinity in melodic outline between $_2$2 and 73, or the fact that the brief, linking figure at $_3$8 returns to fulfil the same function in the third movement, at 115. And all these interconnections are to do with the manner in which themes are constructed, with their recurrent figurations and devices. They take no account of the more notorious reminiscences – virtually quotations – principally of bars 2 and 3 of the first subject,[48] and the re-emergence at 118 in the scherzo-rondo of the theme from the first movement: 'Now, gentlemen,' remarked Elgar in rehearsal of this passage, 'at this point . . . I want you to imagine that my music represents a man in a high fever. Some of you may know that dreadful beating that goes on in the brain – it seems to drive out every coherent thought. This hammering must gradually overwhelm everything.'[49]

Evocation of the Sunday afternoon bandstand in the Second Symphony cannot but bring us to the issue of Elgar's so-called Englishness. The delight taken in this 'English' quality by almost every writer on Elgar's music is matched only by their perplexed inability to put their finger on its source. 'Englishness in music cannot be defined . . .,' writes Diana McVeagh; Vaughan Williams, in an obituary tribute of 1935, observed that '. . . he has that peculiar kind of beauty which gives us, his fellow countrymen, a sense of something familiar – the intimate and personal beauty of our own fields and lanes..,' while Neville Cardus gave up on definition and instead enlisted the pen of W. S. Gilbert: 'Yet in spite of all temptations to belong to other nations, he remained an Englishman.'[50] But if Englishness there be in his music, then the qualities that proclaim it must be embedded in it: they can be nowhere else.

A detailed exploration of this phenomenon is outside the scope of this essay, but when so many commentators place such emphasis upon it, a possible explanation, and a pointer for further study, might be indicated here. In a little-noticed article almost forty years ago in *The Gramophone*, an American linguist and musician, Robert A. Hall, Jr., proposed a possible link between 'Elgar and the Intonation of British English.'[51] He observed that, 'Two of the most striking features of British English intonation . . . are a wide range of variation in pitch and a predominance of falling patterns', and went on to identify exactly the same characteristics in Elgar's melodies. These are, '. . . a tendency to large leaps, often of a seventh . . . [combined with] . . . a predominantly falling trend . . . ', an observation which we could confirm by opening at random the slow movement of the First Symphony, to look no further. 'No wonder, then,' Hall continued, 'that the English feel there is something peculiarly "all their own" about Elgar . . . According to our hypothesis, this phenomenon is due, at least in part, to his reflecting in his music the two most characteristic features of British English intonation, its wide pitch-range and its predominantly falling patterns. Since, however, we normally have a very hard time sorting out or even identifying features of intonation, the Englishman simply feels an "instinctive" affinity to English music . . . without knowing why. Our hypothesis, moreover, would give much fuller content to Elgar's somewhat mystifying remark that "music was in the air all around you and you merely had to grab what you wanted and as much as you wanted."' The authors of the obituary in the April 1934 *Musical Times* almost stumbled on the same explanation: '. . . what. . . brings us back to Elgar again and again is a property that exists for us alone, a *speaking* quality to which our ears are attuned and the ears of foreigners are not.'[52]

It was with some reluctance (he declined the offer at least once) and after considerable persuasion that Elgar agreed on 25 November 1904 to accept an appointment to the new Chair of Music at the University of Birmingham. His formal training, such as it was, had not been academic, he had no experience of academic teaching, and he was sceptical of and ill at ease with the English academic musical establishment.[53] It is clear that in an academic milieu he felt insecure and on unfamiliar ground: the very conditions he attached to his acceptance reveal both his misgivings about the responsibilities of academic life, and an underlying fear that he was perhaps not the best man for the job.[54] However, within a year of his appointment he duly delivered the six lectures to which he had committed himself, and which included the famous Inaugural Lecture, 'A Future for English Music'. Yet they make odd reading: not only do they contain some of the most controversial views he had ever expressed – on critics, English musicians, absolute music, and so on – not only does their style, although literate and clear, seem stilted and uncomfortably 'correct' beside the easy fluency of his letters, but also one of the principal ideas which he propounded is more than once clearly contradicted by his own music, that is, the concept of absolute music as the 'true foundation'. It is as if he felt it incumbent on him to utter opinions that would command respect in academic circles.[55] Yet nearly every remark that has come down to us from Elgar concerning the two Symphonies is descriptive, or programmatic, in some extra-musical way or other. His first thoughts on the composition of a symphony were that it might commemorate General Gordon, while in the Symphonies themselves, the briefest survey of his comments would include, in op.55 for example, 'There is no programme beyond a wide experience of human life with a great charity (love) and a *massive* hope in the future;' at rehearsals he would suggest to orchestras that they play the trio in the second movement (at 66) 'like something you hear down by the river'; 'The rest is silence' in a 1904 sketch of the end of the third movement.[56] Descriptions of the Second Symphony are even more explicit: 'The spirit of the whole work is intended to be high & pure joy . . .'[57] On the *Più lento* at 28 in the first movement: it

'. . . might be a love scene in a garden at night when the ghost of some memories *comes through it*, – it makes me shiver.'[58] On the second movement: '. . . the feminine voice [at 78] *laments* over the broad manly 1st theme – and may not [87] be like a woman dropping a flower on the man's grave?' And of course three themes were identified with specific individuals: 'Windflower' (Mrs Alice Stuart Wortley) at 106 in the third movement, 'Hans [Richter] himself' at 139 in the finale, and Lady Elgar, or perhaps Mrs Stuart Wortley again, at 152 in the same movement, which he labelled, 'Braut's bit'.[59] Two years later, the whole tenor of his *Musical Times* article introducing the 'Symphonic Study,' *Falstaff*,[60] takes it for granted that there is nothing at all untoward in musical motifs representing people and events. And all this from the man who had extolled absolute music as the 'true foundation', and who had been reported in the *Birmingham Post* as saying, in connection with the Third Symphony of Brahms, that '. . . music, as a simple art, was at its best when it was simple, without description'.[61]

As I have suggested earlier, this programmatic approach to Elgar's Symphonies has become the norm, and a recent article in *19th Century Music* proposes interpretations relating the Second Symphony to his personal life that are even more radical still than any yet aired.[62] Intriguing though these readings are, however, we must not forget that there is also a place for investigations of a different kind. 'The symphony is the work of a musical brain, and what it has to convey is the music of which it consists. Beside this, all other meanings . . . exist and revolve round each other in a smaller dimension.'[63] These words advocate an attitude to the symphony which is the very antithesis of most of the writing to date on Elgar's Symphonies, although they were written in an article on Elgar's Second, in an attempt to restore what its author called 'our sense of proportion'. Yet there is no mutual incompatibility here, for an exploration of these two works as 'the work of a musical brain', reveals their creator just as surely as do the interpretations of moods and programmes both putative and documented. Michael Kennedy finds in both Symphonies '. . . the musical expression of the contrasts and conflicts in his make-up . . .: exuberance followed by depression; restless gregariousness followed by loneliness and withdrawal; optimism giving way to a resigned fatalism and distrust of "providence"; a deep nostalgia for the vanished days.'[64] So too, in his handling of the raw materials of symphonic structure, do we find this unique co-existence of opposites: the massive confidence of flawlessly-placed climaxes (always worked out first, we remember) and the desperate attempts to create a form that will convey them to us; harmony as nostalgic for a diatonic past as Mahler, and almost as aware as he of the approaching chromatic void;[65] adventurous formal structures side by side with almost prosaic sonata forms; bold juxtapositions of key-centres and tame expositions that bring us back to the tonic; immense self-assurance across the whole spectrum of individual symphonic techniques, and a self-doubt that can only weld them together as mosaics.

'I have written out my soul in the Concerto, Sym II & the Ode & you know it,' Elgar wrote to Alice Stuart Wortley on 29 August 1912, '& my vitality seems in them now. . . in these three works I have *shewn* myself.'[66] In that confession – to which I think we could with justification add the First Symphony – he almost seems to be recognizing what we can now confirm eighty years later, that the years from 1908 to 1912 mark the summit of his output. The outbreak of war, the death of his wife and advancing age meant that – with the possible exception of the Cello Concerto – he was not to attain to such heights again. And in the two Symphonies it remains above all the quality he singled out in that letter – the sheer vitality,[67] and a vitality which can be calm as well as animated, both placid and exuberant, vitality almost as the life-force – that, as surely as he depicted Hans, portrays Edward himself.

Notes

1. Moore (1984), pp. 80–1. Just how many attempts Elgar made at a G minor symphony is unclear: in the *Strand* article of 1904 quoted in Moore, he states that he 'wrote a symphony' thirty years earlier (so presumably in or around 1874) not only of the same length but also with the same instrumentation as Mozart's 40th. But Moore appears to identify this exercise with fragments of a symphonic Allegro and Minuet dating from 1878, and scored for an orchestra that includes four horns, not two, as in Mozart.
2. Moore, op. cit., p.246.
3. *Musical Times*, 1899, Vol.40, 161.
4. Moore, op. cit., p.270. '. . . I have had to write to Canon Claughton . . . & withdraw my new work from the scheme – the reason is merely the pecuniary one & this is insurmountable.'
5. ibid., pp.338, 340.
6. ibid., p.358.
7. ibid., p.376.
8. ibid., p.420.
9. Letter to Richter of 19 February 1905, quoted in Moore (1984), p.455.
10. ibid., p.514.
11. ibid., p.557.
12. Reed (1946), p.105.
13. Shaw, (1920), p.9.
14. Anderson (1990), p.177.
15. Letters quoted in Moore, op. cit., pp.810–11.
16. Quoted in Kennedy (1982), p.129. For details of the plans for the Third Symphony and the surviving sketches, see particularly Anderson (1990), pp.175–83; Kent (1978), pp.196–216; Moore (1984), pp.803–21; and Reed (1936), pp.169–223, including facsimiles of the sketches.

17. Kennedy (1970), p.7.
18. 'Good composition, sound construction, il filo – these distinguish the master from the bungler - even in trifles.' Leopold Mozart to his son, 13 August 1778, in Anderson (1966), p.599.
19. For affection, see, for example, Moore (1984), pp.599–611, and *passim*; for a degree of scepticism, see Carner (1980).
20. Maine (1933), Vol.2, pp.306–7.
21. Young (1968), pp.206, 207. Elgar's italics.
22. References to the scores are by rehearsal numbers in the Novello edition; subscript numbers on either side indicate numbers of bars before or after the rehearsal numbers.
23. Two rhythmic characteristics which lend further strength to this immensely broad melody (and hence stability to A flat major) are first, the steady crotchets in the bass, which cannot but be a distant echo of the persistent quaver accompaniment in the second movement of Beethoven's *Eroica* Symphony, and secondly, the tendency of the melody to become even broader still by constantly leaning towards 3/2 time.
24. Elgar (1981); reproduced from British Library Add. Ms. 47907A, f.31.
25. Young (1965), p.276. This point is confirmed by various passages in the Symphonies, such as, for example, the 140 or so bars from 22 to 32 in this first movement: about 120 bars have a key signature of two sharps, yet D major and B minor are only two of the many keys through which the music passes.
26. Letter of 23 November 1908. See Moore (1984), p.531. (Yet no more than eleven pages earlier, on p.520, Moore himself writes of the key changing from A flat major to D minor at the double bar – that is, at 5_3). See also Maine (1933), pp.126 and 129, and Kennedy (1982), p.244, for assumptions that the first subject is in D minor.
27. Young (1965), p.277.
28. It seems pretty clear that Elgar is referring to Hans Richter, although the spirit of another Hans whom Elgar held in high regard – Hans Sachs – is frequently to be heard in this movement. See 143, for example.
29. The first movement had gone through much the same procedure: a restatement of the first subject (though in augmentation) at the original pitch (14_8), followed by a further fragment (at 16_6), leading to a threefold drive of Wagnerian intensity towards A minor, the key of the first subject. Only at the last moment does the cadence (at 18) turn to C major.
30. Elgar creates this sense of the distant image not only by the dynamics, but also by requiring just the last desks of violins and violas to play – and in addition, his own 1930 recording has a marked *meno mosso* at this point, although it is not indicated in the score.
31. '. . . the music [of the A flat Symphony] turns upon itself down many a labyrinthine way . . . ,' writes Neville Cardus (1958), p.210.
32. Mitchell (1957), p.121. and Parrott (1971), p.72, are two of the very few commentators who have recognized that this movement is also a Scherzo.
33. McVeagh, op. cit., p.166.
34. Kent (1976–7), p.57.
35. Kent (1976–7), p.25.
36. Kennedy (1982), p.248.
37. Elgar referred to sequences as '. . . waterwheels, the devices that enable composers to carry on by repetition,' and observed that, 'The masters, from Bach to Wagner, are all deeply indebted to [musical waterwheels].' See Moore,

pp.684–5. However, it is difficult to contradict the notion that at times Elgar can become too indebted.

38. Page references are to the vocal score of the Elgar/Atkins edition, and the text is as revised by Atkins (see Moore, 1984, p.595).

39. See the letter already quoted in Moore (1984), p.531. 'As [the treble] gives a feeling of A minor & [the bass] of G maj: – I have a *nice sub-acid feeling* when they come together at 32.'

40. See also McVeagh (1955): 'Elgar is a tonal composer, for although he writes long stretches where it is impossible to pin down the key, so that apparently tonality is weakened and obscured, yet it is precisely this that opens up a harmonic hinterland beyond the immediate foreground.' (p.196).

41. Kent (1976–1977), p.42.

42. See Dennison (1985), p.107. Although the influence of Wagner is more widespread in his music than that of probably any other composer, Elgar belongs to that select group of composers who were able thoroughly to absorb and exploit Wagner's idioms while still retaining an unmistakable individual voice.

43. Indeed, it is probably just as well – though a melancholy reflection – that he did not live to complete the Third Symphony. Fred Gaisberg of the Gramophone Company noted in his diary (27 August, 1933: quoted in Moore [1984], p.816) that, 'The whole work strikes me as youthful and fresh – 100% Elgar without a trace of decay. He makes not the smallest attempt to bring in any modernity. It is built on true classic lines and in a purely Elgar mould . . .' Nearly sixty years later that is not quite the compliment that Gaisberg no doubt intended. See also Kent (1978) p.216: 'Had the *Third Symphony* been completed with such stylistically unvaried material, it would probably have been a disappointing successor to Elgar's two previous symphonies.'

44. Moore (1984), p.537.

45. Anderson (1990) pp.101–3.

46. See C. S. Terry's note in the Athenaeum Club (quoted in the Elgar Complete Edition Preface to the full score, p.vi): 'In every movement its form, and above all its climax, were very clearly in his mind – indeed, as he often told me, it is the climax which invariably he settles first.'

47. Perhaps the most complete lack of appoggiaturas in the finale contributes in some way to an inescapable sense of its detachment from the rest of the Symphony.

48. The quotation of this fragment of the first movement at the end of the second (between 87 and 88) is the one reference which seems like an interposed reminiscence and not a fully-integrated moment in the musical argument of the *Larghetto*. It is framed by a 6/4 chord of C major, and the resulting parenthetical feel is not counteracted by the pedal G that supports its four bars.

49. From Shore (1938), p.135. Quoted in the Preface to the Elgar Complete Edition of the Second Symphony, p.viii.

50. McVeagh (1955), p.214, Vaughan Williams (1935), p.16, and Cardus (1958), p.211.

51. Hall (1953), 6–7.

52. H. G., W. McN., (1934), p.307. My italics.

53. See Young (1968), for the details of the appointment and the texts of the lectures given at Birmingham. Some of Elgar's views are summarized in Kennedy (1982), pp.174–6.

54. Moore, op. cit., p.447. See especially the first two conditions and the last: '1. That I should not be expected to reside in Birmingham. 2. That I do not deliver

more than six lectures or addresses in the first year . . . 5. That the post be not advertised, even pro forma.'

55. See Young (1955), p.328: 'This utterance, given once and in an academic society where he was notably ill at ease, was made because he felt it the correct statement in regard to time and place.'
56. Kennedy (1970), pp.53, 55; Anderson (1990), p.97.
57. Kennedy (1982), p.237.
58. Moore (1984), p.603.
59. Kent (1976–7), p. 58.
60. Elgar (1913).
61. As reported by Ernest Newman; see Young (1968), p.105.
62. See Gimbel (1989), especially p.239: 'Thus [in the Second Symphony] Elgar resigns himself to his art. The result of his Judgement [that is, in the derivations from the motive of that name in *The Dream of Gerontius*] . . . is to deflect his forbidden obsession [with Alice Stuart Wortley] and return to his true Spirit of Delight, his music, with the spirits of Richter and Rodewald to assist him.'
63. McNaught (1951), p.61.
64. Kennedy (1982), p.243.
65. He voiced his awareness in a lecture at Birmingham University on 5 May 1914, in which he recalled an earlier address: 'I suggested to you that . . . the main development [of music] would be chromatic harmony and strange blending of keys . . . that it was vulgar to twist our scale, which was good enough for Beethoven and Brahms and Bach, and make it do the monkey tricks I foretold would be forthcoming.' Moore (1984), p.663. (He appears, however, to be recalling his 'Retrospect' lecture and not, as Moore suggests, the inaugural 'Future for English Music' lecture. See, for example Young (1968), pp.203ff.)
66. Moore (1984), p.639. The other works he refers to are of course the Violin Concerto and *The Music Makers*.
67. It is fascinating to observe his use of the same word, 'vitality,' seven years before to identify exactly the quality lacking in the music of his English predecessors. See Young (1968), p.37.

References

Anderson, Robert (1990). *Elgar in Manuscript*. The British Library: London.

Atkins, E. Wulstan (1984). *The Elgar-Atkins Friendship*. David and Charles: Newton Abbot.

Cardus, Neville (1958). *A Composers Eleven*. London.

Carner, Mosco (1980). *Major and Minor*. Duckworth: London.

Colls, Robert, and Philip Dodd, eds. (1986). *Englishness: Politics and Culture 1880-1920*. London.

Dann, Mary G. (1938). 'Elgar's Use of the Sequence'. *Music and Letters* 19: 255-64.

Dennison, Peter (1985). 'Elgar and Wagner'. *Music and Letters* 66: 93-109.

Elgar, Edward (1905). *'A Future for English Music' and other Lectures*. Ed. Percy M. Young (1968). Dobson: London.

Elgar, Edward (1908). *Symphony No. 1*, Op. 55. Elgar Complete Edition; Novello: London (1981).

Elgar, Edward (1911). *Symphony No. 2*, Op. 63. Elgar Complete Edition; Novello: London (1984).

Elgar, Edward (1913). 'Falstaff'. Musical Times 54: 575-9.
Gimbel, Allen (1989). 'Elgar's Prize Song: Quotation and Allusion in the Second Symphony'. 19th Century Music 12(3): 231-40.
G[race], H[arvey] and W[illiam] McN[aught] (1934). 'Edward Elgar June 2, 1857 – February 23, 1934'. Musical Times 75: 305-13.
Gray, Cecil (1924). A Survey of Contemporary Music. London.
Hall, Robert A., Jr. (1953). 'Elgar and the Intonation of British English.' The Gramophone 31: 6-7.
Howes, Frank (1966). The English Musical Renaissance. London.
Kennedy, Michael (1970). Elgar Orchestral Music. BBC: London.
Kennedy, Michael (1982). Portrait of Elgar. (Rev. & enlarged ed.): Oxford University Press: London.
Kent, Christopher (1976-1977). 'A View of Elgar's Methods of Composition through the Sketches of the Symphony no. 2 in E flat (op. 63)'. Proceedings of the Royal Musical Association 103: 41-60.
Kent, Christopher (1978). Edward Elgar: A Composer at Work. A Study of his creative processes as seen through his sketches and proof corrections. Ph.D. Dissertation, King's College, London.
Maine, Basil (1933). Elgar, his Life and Works. 2 vols. Bell: London.
McNaught, William (1951). 'A Note on Elgar's Second Symphony'. Musical Times 91: 57-61.
McVeagh, Diana (1955). Edward Elgar, his Life and Music. Dent: London.
Mitchell, Donald (1957). 'Some Thoughts on Elgar (1857-1934)'. Music And Letters 38(2): 113-23.
Monk, Raymond, ed. (1990). Elgar Studies. Scolar: Aldershot.
Moore, Jerrold Northrop (1984). Edward Elgar: A Creative Life. Oxford University Press: Oxford.
Moore, Jerrold Northrop, ed. (1987). Elgar and his Publishers: Letters of a Creative Life. 2 vols. Oxford University Press: Oxford.
Mozart, W. A. (1966). The Letters of Mozart and his Family. Ed. Emily Anderson. 2nd ed., 2 vols. Macmillan: London.
Musical Times (1899). Announcement of the anticipated 'Gordon' Symphony: 40: 161.
Musical Times (1908). 'Sir Edward Elgar's Symphony'. Unsigned article, 49: 778-80.
Newman, Ernest (1911). 'Elgar's Second Symphony'. Musical Times 52: 295-300.
Parrott, Ian (1971). Elgar. Dent: London.
Reed, W. H (1936). Elgar as I knew him. Gollancz: London.
Shaw, G. Bernard (1920). 'Sir Edward Elgar'. Music and Letters 1: 7-11.
Shore, Bernard (1937). The Orchestra Speaks. Longmans Green: London.
Shore, Bernard (1950). Sixteen Symphonies. Longmans, Green: London.
Tovey, Donald Francis (1935). Essays in Musical Analysis, Vol. II. Oxford University Press: London.
Vaughan Williams, Ralph (1935). 'What have we learnt from Elgar?' Music and Letters 16(1): 13-19.
Young, Percy M. (1955). Elgar O.M. Collins: London.
Young, Percy M. (1965). Letters to Nimrod. Edward Elgar to August Jaeger 1897-1908. Dennis Dobson: London.

5   The Soul Enshrined: Elgar and his Violin Concerto

Michael Kennedy

'Aquí está encerrada el alma de . . . . .' 'Here is enshrined the soul of . . . . .'
This quotation from Lesage's *Gil Blas* which Elgar inscribed at the head of the score of his Violin Concerto, ranks in evocativeness with *Von Herzen – möge es wieder – zu Herzen gehn!* ('From the heart – may it again – go to the heart') on Beethoven's *Missa Solemnis*. It also provides us with an Elgarian enigma equally as intriguing as the 'unheard' theme of the *Variations*, but more susceptible to solution. Whose soul? And why? As far as the music is concerned, there can be little doubt in the listener's mind that it enshrines the soul of Edward Elgar himself. He poured all his most characteristic ideas and stylistic features into a work for which he had a deep and abiding affection. It is, perhaps, not surprising, for the violin was his instrument and although 'Dorabella' (Dora Penny, later Mrs Richard Powell) was told[1] that his tone was 'cold', in this Concerto he filled the solo part with all the poetic and expressive warmth he must have craved as an executant.

Charles Sanford Terry, the Bach scholar who, as will be seen, was close to Elgar during the final stages of work on the Concerto, was given a first proof of the full score by Elgar in October 1910. To it he attached a note[2] he typed on 12 November 1910, two days after the first performance: 'I have never heard Elgar *speak* of the *personal* note in his music except in regard to the Concerto, and of it I heard him say more than once when he was playing it over as it was produced: I *love* it'. With the exception of *The Dream of Gerontius*, and more than in the case of the symphonies and *The Music Makers*, Elgar certainly confided to paper more of his feelings about the Violin Concerto than about any of his works.

But Elgar himself hinted that the 'soul' of the Concerto was feminine. He said as much to one of his biographers, Basil Maine, according to Ernest Newman, writing in the *Sunday Times* on 21 May 1939; and since Maine was alive at the time and did not deny Newman's assertion, it is presumably true. Writing to his close friend Nicholas Kilburn on 5 November 1910, Elgar translated the quotation – which, in the original, reads 'Aquí está encerrada el alma del licenciado Pedro Garcias' – as 'Here, or more emphatically *in here*, is enshrined or simply enclosed – buried is perhaps too definite – *the soul of* . . . . . ?? The final "de" leaves it indefinite as to sex or rather gender. Now guess'. Terry, in the note already quoted, remarked: 'While I was looking over his shoulder, he wrote "de la" in red ink under the "del", but thereafter he took the trouble to consult a Spanish friend . . . whether the word "del" would leave the sex of the soul's possessor undetermined. Eventually, he made it "de"'. Already, in the letter to Kilburn, there are five dots after "de". Elgar knew that, in printing, the customary indication of an omitted passage is three dots, so his use of five was obviously deliberate.

Where did Elgar find this quotation, which is so peculiarly apt for his purpose and has an authentic Elgarian ring? It is quoted in Oliver Wendell Holmes's *The Autocrat of the Breakfast Table*, which was published in the Everyman Library in 1906, when Elgar may well have read it. In Lesage's book, the inscription is on a roadside gravestone which is found by two students. One of them scoffs at it as ridiculous – a soul cannot be enclosed in a grave. But the other looks closer and finds beneath the stone a purse containing money and a note saying: 'Be my legatee, you who have been wise enough to unravel the meaning of the inscription and make better use of my money than I did'. There is no evidence that Elgar knew the original story and it obviously has no connection with the Concerto.

So whom did Elgar have in mind as the feminine soul of his Violin Concerto? There are four possible candidates – all, curiously or conveniently, with names or nicknames containing five letters – of whom Mrs Alice Stuart Wortley – later Lady Stuart of Wortley – seems to me to have the strongest and most convincing claim. But before examining her connection with the work in some detail, a brief history of how the work came to be written is necessary. It is known that Elgar was composing a violin concerto in November 1890, after the first performance of his concert-overture *Froissart*. Alice Elgar's diary twice refers to it. Against the second reference, Elgar at some time later scribbled: 'Since destroyed'. Sketches for violin concertos in A minor and E flat are to be found in sketchbooks, now in the British Library, covering the years 1902–3 and 1905–6.

The impetus to compose the work we know as Op.61 came from the Austrian virtuoso Fritz Kreisler (1875–1962). Elgar first met him, so far as is known, at the Leeds Festival in October 1904 when Kreisler was soloist in the Brahms Concerto in a concert in which Elgar conducted *In the South*. A year later they coincided again at the Norwich Festival. It was at this time that Kreisler said in a newspaper interview that he considered Elgar to be the greatest living composer. 'I place him on an equal footing with my idols, Beethoven and Brahms. He is of the same aristocratic family. . . I wish Elgar would write something for the violin. . .' A few days later, on 21 October 1905, Elgar's sketchbook contains music headed 'First sketch of Violin

Concerto 1905'. Twelve bars of slow introduction in B minor precede the first seven bars of the Concerto as we know it followed by a different continuation[3]. On another page, marked '2nd theme', are bars 131–145 of the first movement.

Elgar told Kreisler of the existence of the sketches, but nothing further happened for three and a half years. In the meantime he completed the oratorio *The Kingdom* and composed the *Wand of Youth* suites and the First Symphony. In April 1909 Elgar and his wife stayed for a month at Careggi, near Florence, in a villa rented by a wealthy American friend, Mrs Julia Worthington, known to her intimates by the Browningesque nickname 'Pippa'. There Elgar composed his greatest part-song, *Go, Song of Mine*, and another entitled *The Angelus* which he dedicated to Alice Stuart Wortley, whom he had known since 1902. She was the daughter of the artist Sir John Millais and the wife of Charles Stuart Wortley, M.P. for Sheffield 1880–5 and for its Hallam division 1885–1916. Her friendship with Elgar had been formal for seven years, but in March 1909 it grew closer and this dedication was a sign of increasing intimacy. During his stay in Careggi, Elgar also reverted to the Concerto sketches, adding some more of the first movement and mapping out most of the slow movement.

Back at home in Hereford Elgar continued to work on the Concerto. Alice Elgar's diary entry for 19 August states: 'E. possessed with his music for the Vl. Concerto'. He played some of the themes to Dora Penny, who stayed at Plas Gwyn that month and recorded the occasion in her book[4]. They sat outside until dark, after watering the garden with the hose, and Elgar went to the piano 'when the windows were wide open and curtains drawn back, and lovely scents came in from the garden'. He seems then to have laid the work aside, for in October he looked at some sketches that he had composed in 1903 and became, to quote Alice Elgar again, 'quite inspired with Symphony No.2'. The next mention of work on the Concerto in her diary is not until 10 January 1910. On two days of that month, the 20th and 24th, Elgar asked Lady Speyer, wife of the financier Sir Edgar Speyer, to play through the slow movement (*Andante*) for him and a group of friends. As Leonora von Stosch, she had been a pupil of the Belgian violinist Eugene Ysaÿe. 'All loved it much', Alice faithfully notes, 'it was repeated'. Among the listeners were Charles and Alice Stuart Wortley. The former was so moved that he asked to borrow the music; Elgar later gave him some of the sketches. But Elgar himself had doubts and on 7 February wrote to Alice Stuart Wortley: 'I am not sure about that Andante & shall put it away for a long time before I decide its fate. I am glad you liked it. I hope your husband will not think I imagine the sketches to be worth having – but people ask me for them sometimes & *don't* get them'. However, on that same day, as we know from his dated sketchbook, he worked 'in dejection' on bars 23 to 26 of the first movement and on bars 131 to 139, part of the '2nd theme' he had composed in 1905. These two themes came to be of the utmost significance to him. He called them his 'windflower' themes after the little white *anemone nemorosa* about which he wrote[5] that it was happily named because 'when the east wind rasps over the ground in March and April', it merely turned its back and bowed before the squall. 'They are buffeted and blown, as one may think almost to destruction, but their anchors hold, and the slender-looking stems bend but do not break. And when the rain clouds drive up, the petals shut tight into a tiny tent, as country folk tell one, to shelter the little person inside'.

These themes were associated with Alice Stuart Wortley, probably because she particularly admired them. She responded to his doubts about the *Andante* by passionately urging him to continue with the Concerto. It is apparent that the intensification of their relationship occurred between January and May of 1910 and was based on her love of the Concerto and of his music generally. This does not imply that it became a physical and adulterous relationship. Neither would have embarked on such a risky and disloyal course, whatever their personal inclinations might have been. But Elgar's letters to her at this time reveal that he was at any rate spiritually 'in love' with her and that he felt a powerful bond between them forged by what he recognized as her instinctive understanding of his personality as expressed through his music. Perhaps, too, there was an element of flattery that he, the Worcester shopkeeper's son, should be so close to one who moved in aristocratic circles, though he had plenty of other women friends who did and were of noble birth, which Alice Millais was not. From February 1910 onwards he always called her 'Windflower', after the themes which for him enshrined her soul. Every year he sent her the first windflowers he found growing in Herefordshire or Worcestershire. Henceforward, there were always 'Windflower' themes in his music, particularly in the Second Symphony, the O'Shaughnessy ode *The Music Makers* and the Cello Concerto. The Violin Concerto, the symphony and the ode constitute a trilogy in which Elgar composed an autobiographical testament of his feelings for Alice Stuart Wortley. As he wrote to her in 1912: 'I have written out my soul' – significant word – 'in the concerto, Sym.II & the Ode & you know it . . . in these three works I have *shewn* myself'.

Her encouragement lifted the cloud which had settled over composition of the Violin Concerto. A note on one of his sketches says: 'This is going to be good! "Where Love and Faith meet, there will be Light". February 7, 1910, 6.30 pm, Queen Ann's [*sic*] Mansions'. (Elgar had a service flat at this time in Queen Anne's Mansions, St James's Park and was there from 16 January to 9 February 1910.) His love, her faith. For the rest of their lives, they kept 7 February as a personal anniversary. On 1 May 1910, Elgar gave her nearly forty pages of his composition draft of the first movement (now in the Birthplace Museum) with a note: 'Burn these sketches if you do not keep them – I am not vain enough to think you want them!! E.E.' These sketches contain evidence of their working together on the Concerto, for beneath two deleted bars Mrs Stuart Wortley has written: 'This is to remain. W.' and '& this also. W.' In fact, the bars were not restored to the finished work.

Originally pinned to sketches of the two 'windflower' themes which Elgar gave her was a cutting which tells us more about the relationship between Elgar and his Windflower even than his letters. It shows, as I interpret it, that he had confided to her the history of his broken engagement, in 1883, to the Worcester violinist Helen Weaver. She was the daughter of another shopkeeper in Worcester High Street and had been a student at Leipzig Conservatory, where Elgar had visited her. Their engagement ended when she contracted tuberculosis and emigrated to New Zealand, where she recovered, married, and died in 1927. This rupture deeply affected Elgar, although whether, as has been claimed, he 'never got over it', nobody can know with certainty. It is feasible that the thirteenth of the *Enigma Variations (Romanza, ***)*, although overtly connected – as all documentary evidence proves – with Lady Mary Lygon's voyage to Australia, is also a memory of Helen's (Nelly's) departure for New Zealand. The elegiac tone of the clarinet's quotation of a lively phrase from Mendelssohn's overture *Calm Sea and Prosperous Voyage* – which, notwithstanding that its title was apt for Elgar's purpose, they may well have heard together in Leipzig – suggests a dark and secret memory. There is a theory, favoured by Ernest Newman, Leopold Stokowski and Elgar's godson E. Wulstan Atkins[6], that the asterisks of the Variation XIII and the dots of the Violin Concerto inscription conceal the same person, Helen Weaver.

When Ernest Newman wrote his *Sunday Times* articles about Elgar's enigmas in the spring of 1939, he received a letter (hitherto unpublished) from Clare Stuart Wortley, Windflower's daughter. 'I venture to say', she wrote,

> that I do not think Elgar can have attached any significance to the number of dots following the Spanish phrase which he placed before the Violin Concerto, because I possess that phrase written out by his own hand, followed by only four dots! He came to tea with my mother on Sept.22 1910. . . He wrote the phrase out for her on a piece of our own notepaper and dated it. Probably he simply wrote it down to make it clear to her. . . A proof, which he also gave her, shows five dots; but although he had corrected the printers' "del" to "de", he did not make any correction to the five dots. This seems to show that he was indifferent in the matter – don't you agree?

Newman did not agree, sensibly. He replied to her on 18 May:

> I take it that Elgar wanted to do two things, (a) to dedicate the concerto to someone, or the memory of someone, who had five letters in his (or her) name; (b) to hide the identity of this someone from the world. Now isn't it

probable that, being the expert mystifier he was, he deliberately put people off the scent here and there by making it look as if there was no particular meaning to be attached to the *five* dots?. . . Five is a very curious and unusual number of dots to get into print all by mere accident.

He followed this up five days later:

> I am pretty sure I know the name: the whole facts of the case were given me by a correspondent (unknown to me personally) who was an intimate, long ago, of both Elgar and . . . . . I myself had for many years been sceptical about the 'Lady Mary Lygon' as the subject of the 13th Variation . . . but I hadn't any information that could give point and body to my suspicions. After receiving the information about the '. . . . .' I asked my correspondent whether the person 'enshrined' here was the same as the one covered by the three asterisks [*Romanza* ***] and I was told that they were one and the same. . . The details are very curious and sad.

It is in the nature of music that it can say two things at the same time, and if both Helen and Lady Mary are commemorated in the *Romanza*, why should not Helen and somebody else be the 'soul' of the Concerto? The emotional burden of the Concerto is 'what might have been', and this would have applied equally to Elgar's thoughts of Helen and 'Windflower'.

The cutting Elgar pinned to the sketches he gave to Mrs Stuart Wortley was an extract from an article which appeared in the *Daily Telegraph* of 30 April, 1910, written by its art critic Claude Phillips, who was a friend of Elgar. Phillips mentioned Titian's 'Nymph and Piping Shepherd', which he described as 'the most wonderful love-poem of Venetian 16th century art'. He then described the painting and it was this passage which Elgar appended to the sketches:

> It is twilight, and soon will be night, with the lovers, who dally still in the sombre air shot with silver. The poetry of the early years has come back, intensified by something of added poignancy, and of foreboding that is tinged, it may be, with remorse. This last passion has something that the earlier passion has not; in one sense it is nearer to earth and earthiness; in another it is infinitely higher and more far-reaching, more typical of the love that in its heights and depths, in its tender light and sombre, fitfully illumined shadow is truly that which to the end of all things must hold and possess man.

If the quotation of those words was not a declaration of love, then what was the point of sending them to her? It was part of the process of '*shewing myself*'.

Elgar took a rest from composition from 1 to 10 April 1910 when he accompanied his friend Frank Schuster on a motoring tour of Devon, Cornwall and Wiltshire. On 3 and 4 April they visited Tintagel where the Stuart Wortleys frequently stayed. From the London flat (No.7) at 58, New

Cavendish Street, which he and Lady Elgar had rented for three months, Elgar wrote on 20 April to Alice Stuart Wortley: 'I am now ablaze with work & *writing hard*; you *should* come & see (& hear it!)'. He continued to send her progress reports: 27 April: 'I have been working hard at the Windflower themes but all stands still until you come & approve'. 28 April: 'It is so dreary today & the tunes stick & are not Windflowerish – at present'. On 7 May, the day after King Edward VII died, he wrote to Schuster: 'I have the Concerto well in hand & have played (?) it thro' on the P.F. & it's *good*! awfully emotional! too emotional but I love it: Ist movement finished & the IIIrd well on – these *are* times for composition'. On 12 May Lady Speyer played Elgar the completed first movement.

Next day Elgar went to Bray, near Maidenhead, to stay at Schuster's Thames-side home The Hut and to work on the Concerto. After a break to fulfil conducting engagements, he returned there, writing to Schuster beforehand (27 May): 'I want to *end* that Concerto but do not see my way very clearly to the end – so you had best invite its stepmother [Alice Stuart Wortley] to The Hut too. Do'. Meanwhile, another musician had joined the team of advisers and helpers on the Concerto. This was W. H. Reed, a violinist in the London Symphony Orchestra (and later its leader), whom Elgar knew well and liked. Elgar met him in Regent Street and sought his aid on 'some questions of bowing and certain intricacies of violin technique'.[7] Reed called at New Cavendish Street on 28 May. He found Elgar 'striding about with a number of loose pieces of MSS. . . Some were already pinned on the backs of chairs, or fixed up on the mantelpiece . . .' From this unconventional session came the harmonics in the slow movement at bars 20–21 before cue 47 and, in the same movement, the leap of a 12th up the G string in the *ad lib* passages of bars 38–39, four before cue 51. Over this last example, Reed recorded, 'we had great fun . . . The first time we tried it in this way instead of going to a more reasonable position on the D string, the effect so electrified him that he called out "good for you" when I landed safely on the E with a real explosive sforzando'. In the afternoon, Alice Stuart Wortley formed the audience. Four days later, Elgar delivered the first movement to Novello.

The next two months were devoted to completion of the Concerto, at Hereford and The Hut. He was now at work on the long accompanied cadenza in the *finale* which is the glory of the Concerto. He wrote to Alice Stuart Wortley on 16 June: 'Here is one of your own flowers. I have just been walking round between work: it goes well & I have made the end serious & grand I hope & have brought in the real inspired theme from the 1st movement – Frank approves. I did it this morning . . . the music sings of memories & hope'. Three days later, again to her: 'The work goes on and the pathetic portion is really fixed'. Four days later: 'I am appalled at the last movement & cannot get on – it is growing so large – too large I fear & I have headaches. . . I go on working & working & making it all as good as I can for the owner'. He wanted her to be present when Reed was to play through the first movement and *finale* in Plâs Gwyn on 30 June. To Schuster, on the eve of this play-through, he wrote: 'This Concerto is *full* of romantic feeling – I should have been a philanthropist if I had been a rich man – I *know* the feeling is human & right – Vain glory!. . . You will like the cadenza which is on a novel plan I think – accompanied softly by a few insts. & – it comes at the end of the last movement – it sadly thinks over the 1st movement'.

Reed again found scraps of music-paper pinned all round the room, 'many different versions of the same thing with different bowings to be tried for each. . . The Cadenza was in pieces; but soon the parts took shape and were knit together to become an integral part of the concerto'.[8] On this occasion, Ivor Atkins, organist of Worcester Cathedral, accompanied Reed at the piano while Elgar 'strode about the room, listening and rubbing his hands excitedly. He would dash up to us with a pencil and scratch something out, writing an alternative in the margin, or add an *allargando* or *tenuto* over a certain note to make it stand out: always trying every possible effect in tone gradation, slurred or detached bowing, harmonics or natural notes'. In the cadenza, 'the *lento* between 105 and 106 nearly moved him to tears as he repeated it again and yet again, dwelling on certain notes and marking them *tenuto, espress, animato* or *molto accel*, as he realized step by step exactly what he sought to express'.

One of the most poetic features of the Concerto is the *pizzicato tremolando* for the strings of the orchestra with which Elgar accompanies the soloist in the cadenza. The effect he wanted he called 'thrumming'. He wrote to Nicholas Kilburn on 15 March 1911: 'Let the good men lay by their bows. . .& *rustle* 3 or even 4 fingers *flatly* (not hooked) over the strings'. Writing to Ernest Newman, who was writing the programme-note for the first performance, in September 1910, he said: 'The sound of distant Aeolian harp flutters under and over the solo'. Elgar had an Aeolian harp in the crack of a partly opened window at Plâs Gwyn and loved to listen to 'its fairylike improvisations' (Reed's phrase) as the breeze set its strings vibrating to produce 'a shimmering musical sound of elfin quality'.

The day after the Hereford play-through, Elgar travelled to London to give Fritz Kreisler his first glimpse of the Concerto. The violinist was 'much impressed' (Alice Elgar's diary). 'He said at one passage "I will shake Queen's Hall"!' After 9 July, Elgar was engaged on the orchestration. Reed played it through several times on 26 July – 'Cadenza *wonderful*' Alice Elgar shrilled in her diary, and on 5 August she could record 'E. finished his orchestration of his most booful Concerto – Very happy over it. D.G.' Elgar wrote to Terry: 'I have put the last note to the last movement in the full score and have lit a pipe!'

Kreisler played the complete work to Elgar in the Novello board room on 2 September. 'You must not expect a finished performance, because I must always leave the technical study of the violin part of a new work to the end, in order to command it musically the better', he had warned the composer beforehand. Next day, the Elgars went to Gloucester for the Three Choirs Festival. With them were Julia Worthington, at whose Italian villa the work had been started, Alice Stuart Wortley, and Dora Penny. Both Kreisler and Reed were performing in the Festival and both played through the Concerto to this admiring private audience, Reed on 4 September, Kreisler on the 8th. Among the listeners was Robin Legge, music critic of the *Daily Telegraph*, who wrote later that he had 'never seen a keener enthusiasm in one musician for the work of another than Kreisler showed for Elgar's Concerto'.[9] Kreisler and Elgar worked on it again on the 9th, when Kreisler said: 'You have written an immortal work'.

Throughout October Elgar worked on correcting proofs of the score, assisted by C. S. Terry. Kreisler again played through the work in London on 15 and 17 October, when Alice Stuart Wortley turned pages for Elgar and Alice Elgar for Kreisler. The piano arrangement was published on 4 November. Elgar wrote to Windflower: 'How I detest its being made public'. The first performance, conducted by Elgar, was given in Queen's Hall at a Philharmonic Society concert on 10 November. The First Symphony was also in the programme. It was an evening of pouring rain but, as Lady Elgar recorded, 'Crowd *enormous*. Excitement intense – Performance wonderful. Enthusiasm unbounded – *Shouts*'. After the concert Schuster gave a dinner-party in his London home in Old Queen Street. Among the guests was the 21-year old Adrian Boult, who recalled Elgar's saying to Claude Phillips: 'Well, Claude, did you think that was a work of art?'

It was the last time – with the exception of the wartime pieces – that an Elgar composition received anything but a muted welcome. The Second Symphony, *The Music Makers, Falstaff,* the chamber music and the Cello Concerto were all to be accorded half-hearted applause at their first performances. 'The radiance in a poor, little private man's soul has been wonderful and new and the concerto has come', he had written to Alice Stuart Wortley on 25 October. Its coming marked the end of the Elgar era.

A few days before the first performance, for which Mrs Stuart Wortley had a spare ticket of which to dispose, Elgar wrote to her: 'I wish I could use it & you might conduct – but you will be conducting the concerto wherever you are'. After rehearsing for the second London performance on 30 November, he wrote to her: 'The concerto at 9am in the dark was divine – all seats empty, but a spirit hovering in Block A [where the Stuart Wortleys always sat in Queen's Hall].' In letters to her for the rest of his life he referred to the Concerto as 'your' or 'our own' Concerto and to the Second

Symphony as 'your symphony'. From this evidence, it is difficult to deduce any conclusion except that hers was the 'soul' of the work.

Yet according to her book,[10] Dora Powell was told by Lady Elgar that the subject of the inscription was Julia Worthington (Julia or 'Pippa', another five-letter candidate). There is no evidence to support this assertion – no letters of any significance between Elgar and his American patron have ever come to light. Assuming Mrs Powell's statement to be correct, one wonders if Alice Elgar herself knew or was being deliberately misleading. Elgar also gave some sketches headed 'The Soul' to Adela (five letters again) Schuster, sister of Frank, but not too much importance need be attached to this gesture.

The success of the Concerto was not confined to the first performance, for which Kreisler received a fee of £200 and Elgar of £100. Kreisler played it three more times in London by 16 January 1911, once with Sir Henry J. Wood conducting. He also played it, conducted by Wood, in all the major provincial cities. In 1913 he introduced it to Russia in St Petersburg, with Serge Koussevitzky conducting. Generously, he said the finest performance he ever heard was given by Ysaÿe in Berlin in 1912. Ysaÿe never played it in Britain because of a dispute with Novello about what he regarded as the excessive performing fee they were charging.[11] After the First World War, Kreisler seemed less interested in the Concerto. When he played it in the United States, he cut it (as did Yehudi Menuhin) and he evaded several efforts to persuade him to record it. Jascha Heifetz took it up (and recorded it) and nearly all other international virtuosi of the instrument have taken it into their repertory. The first violinist to record it, with Elgar conducting, was his former pupil Marie Hall in December 1916. The Concerto was savagely abridged and, for accompaniment of the cadenza, Elgar wrote a special harp part (there is no part for harp in the full score). Curiously, in his analysis of the Concerto included in his book *Violin Master Works and their Interpretation* (New York, 1925), the great Russian violinist and teacher Leopold Auer wrote: 'The cadenza has been shaped by a master hand; and the fact that the harp is the outstanding instrumental support of the solo violin gives the cadenza an especially rhapsodic quality'. One can only surmise that Auer was writing without reference to the score or he would surely not have committed such a blunder. But a 'rhapsodic quality' is what the music of the Concerto has throughout its course. The violin is poet, orator, muse, singer and shooting-star in this Concerto. One may hear it, without knowledge of any of its history as recorded in the preceding pages, as 'pure music' and be entranced, dazzled and moved. Yet it would still be impossible to miss the deeply personal nature of the music. Charles Sanford Terry heard Elgar say to Ivor Atkins that he would like the *nobilmente* theme of the slow movement [five bars after cue 53] to be inscribed on his tombstone. In that theme, beyond any doubt, the soul of Edward Elgar is enshrined; in the

Concerto as a whole he enshrined the soul of Alice Stuart Wortley. Once, when she missed a musical evening at his London home, he told her that someone had asked him: Where on earth is Mrs W. in all this music? 'I said *to myself* "Everywhere – and alas! nowhere". But you see they all thought it was nothing without you & so did I.'

Notes

1. Dora Powell, in a letter to Clare Stuart Wortley, 15 May 1939: 'My stepmother used to say that his playing was very hard and cold, which always made me wonder. I can easily imagine that he had a fine technique'.
2. Quoted in *Elgar Complete Edition*, Vol.32: *The Concertos* (Novello, 1988), p.xxxi.
3. These sketches are in the Library of Congress, Washington D.C.
4. Powell, Dora M. (1937). *Edward Elgar: Memories of a Variation*. London, rev. 3/ 1949.
5. *The Times*, 28 April, 1923.
6. See his *The Elgar-Atkins Friendship* (Newton Abbot, 1984), pp.477–80.
7. Reed, W. H. 'The Violin Concerto', *Music and Letters*, Vol.xvi, January 1935, pp.31-2, 34.
8. Reed, W. H. (1936). *Elgar As I Knew Him*. London.
9. *The Daily Telegraph*, 26 September 1910.
10. Powell, op. cit., p.86.
11. For a full account of this episode, see Moore, J. N. (1987). *Elgar and his Publishers*, Vol.II. Oxford, pp.747-60.

6 *Falstaff*: Elgar's Symphonic Study

Christopher Kent

The composition of the symphonic study *Falstaff* occupied Elgar between April and September of 1913[1] and in common with several other of his major works it had an earlier genesis. This is suggested by sketches made during the Worcester Festival of September 1902[2]; although these are headed 'Falstaff', only one of the themes of this sketch occurs in the eventual work.

In the introduction to his analytical essay on the work[3] Elgar shows an impressive knowledge of Shakespearean critical writings. He stressed that his work was 'based solely on the Falstaff of the historical plays (1 and 2 Henry IV and Henry V.)' rather than 'the caricature in The Merry Wives of Windsor . . .' Elgar then described his composition as follows: 'The musical interpretation, or, as it is preferably called study of the character of Falstaff, is practically in one movement, with two interludes, to be noted later, and falls naturally into four principal divisions which run on without break. These divisions are not shown in the score, but it is convenient to cite them as follows:

> I. Falstaff and Prince Henry;
> II. Eastcheap,- Gadshill, – The Boar's Head, revelry and sleep;
> III. Falstaff's March, – The return through Gloucestershire,
> – The new King, – The hurried ride to London;
> IV. King Henry V.'s progress, – The repudiation of Falstaff,
> and his death.'

The sketches show this four-fold division to have been clear in Elgar's mind throughout the composition of the work. Within this framework, however, there were significant changes to both the detail and to the title of the work. In the copy of the miniature score of *Falstaff* that Elgar gave to Alice Stuart Wortley (E.B. ref: 1456) is a fragment of MS paper which contains what is likely to have been the first sketch for the opening theme of the work. This is headed simply: 'Falstaff (tragedy)'. Then, in the first section of the main volume of working sketches (B.L. Add. MS. 47907B ff.1–5) other designations appear: 'Symphonic poem' (f.5), and 'Character study' (f.2), but the latter was deleted in favour of 'Symphonic Study (in C minor), with two Interludes in A minor . . .' Full transcriptions of these plans appear in Appendix One.

Although they show the four-fold scheme of the work to have been consistent in Elgar's mind there were uncertainties over the inclusion and placing of the two Interludes. The first of these: "Jack Falstaff, now Sir John, a boy, and page to Thomas Mowbray, Duke of Norfolk" (76^1-80^7) is not mentioned in the plans and there is sufficient evidence in the sketches to support the conclusion that it was not part of the original scheme of the work. Two sketches of the end of Section II are transcribed in Ex.1.

Ex. 1(a)   B.L. Add. MS. 47907B f.75

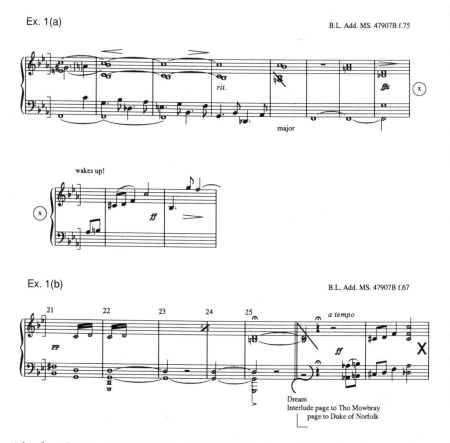

Ex. 1(b)   B.L. Add. MS. 47907B f.67

The first (Ex.1a: B.L. Add. MS. 47907B f.75), shows Falstaff settling to sleep on an F major chord (with a 4–3 suspension), followed by an *ffz* and a direct '⊠' to what is now 81^1 with the note: 'Wake up!' The second sketch (Ex.1b: B.L. Add. MS. 47907B f.67) contains the end of the same passage now transposed up a tone to end on the dominant of C minor. This chord of G major is shown tied across the double bar to what is now figure 87[1]. Beneath this, at a later stage, Elgar has added a pencil note with an arrow indicating the insertion of 'Dream Interlude page to Tho[s] Mowbray/ page to Duke of Norfolk'. Some indecision also existed over the second Interlude since this is not mentioned in what would seem to be the first plan, and in the second plan, a reference to Shallow is deleted.

Even if the overall plan for *Falstaff* were clear in Elgar's mind the same cannot be said of some of the musical material. In common with many of Elgar's works the sketches for *Falstaff* reveal that many themes and motifs pre-date the main period of composition, and furthermore, they are often part of complex chains of migrations and relocations.

The disarming innocence and tranquillity of the violin solo in the first Dream Interlude is such that it is difficult to accept that it had a previous location; yet this was the case. It first appears in the short score sketch for the *Coronation March* of 1911,[4] in which it was intended as the second theme, before being replaced by the Trio. However, the initial material of the *March* can itself be related back to the thwarted *Rabelais* ballet project of 1902. This can also be seen from the sketch of the Trio of the *Coronation March* (B.L. Add. MS. 63161 f.8) where, at the foot of the page, Elgar has encircled a syncopated fanfare figure with the note: 'Falstaff'. Sure enough, this figure re-emerges with apparent spontaneity to arouse Falstaff from the slumbers of the first Dream Interlude and to herald the march of his scarecrow army at the beginning of section III (83[1-5]).

This deft manipulation of short cellular ideas that figures prominently in Elgar's mature compositional technique was first compared to a mosaic by Frank Howes.[5] It is arguable that *Falstaff* sees the culmination of this practice, which was tending to lead him towards ever leaner textures and a predominance of concise motifs. Though Elgar would have most probably resented this comparison, it suggests that he was moving in a similar direction to Debussy. Few of Elgar's more extended melodies in *Falstaff* can be related to conventional phrase structures or seen to conclude with the cadences that their openings might lead us to expect. For example, the main theme of Prince Hal, apparently secure in E flat major at its outset, is answered in its minor mode. It is only in the two Interludes of *Falstaff* that Elgar permits any relief from the continuous assemblage and evolution of motifs.

The sketches of *Falstaff* reveal one of the most extensive examples of Elgar's manipulation of a single motif that can be traced through the sketches of several works. This motif is the descending chromatic flourish in the horn parts of the 'mock battle' episode in Section III (88[1]–96[7]). In Ex. 2 the various sketches are collated in a temporal sequence.

Ex.2a (p.3 of Sketch Book II. B.L. Add. MS. 63154 f.10) relates to the Judas scene of *The Apostles* and dates from April or May 1903. The deleted word

'Judas' is followed by words which indicate the three other placings: '[Simon] Magus Crowd Falstaff'.

Ex. 2(a)

B.L. Add. MS. 63154 f.10 Sketch Book II p.3

It duly appears in the working sketches of *The Apostles* (B.L. Add. MS. 47904A f.169) with the note: '? Christ being mocked' (Ex.2b). Note that Elgar has cross-referenced this to his Sketch Book using his customary abbreviation system: '3/II', indicating page three of Sketch Book II. Ex.2a also contains the note: 'to 48 VIII'.

Ex. 2(b)

B.L. Add. MS. 47904A f. 169

This relates to a sketch for the setting of the words 'We do hear them speak' from the 'Crowd' scene, 'In Solomon's Porch' in the Pentecost section of *The Kingdom*. Although Elgar also rejected this location, it is significant that he considered it as part of a fugal texture, dramatically appropriate to project the amazement and confusion of the crowd at the diverse spiritual utterances of the Apostles.

Ex. 2(c)

B.L. Add. MS. 63160 Sketch Book VIII p.48

In *Falstaff* Elgar drew this distinctive idea into the mayhem of the 'mock battle'. First, he placed it between a repetition of a four-bar phrase of vigorous invertible counterpoint (Ex.2d. B.L. Add. MS. 47907B f.95). Only the final four quavers at the end of the preceding phrase required adjustment to accommodate the inserted flourish which is complete with scoring details. (A similar procedure can be seen in the sketches of the development section of the first movement of Elgar's Second Symphony.)[6]

Ex. 2(d)

B.L. Add. MS. 47907B f.95

This location was also abandoned in favour of the second episode of the Shrewsbury Fight, where, in its final setting, the motif becomes a plosive focal point, heralded by trumpet calls (Ex.2e).

Ex. 2(e)

B.L. Add. MS. 479678 f.90

This fluent relocation of themes is also evident within the working sketches of *Falstaff*. Elgar's decision to remove the reference to 'Sneat's noise' led to the displacement of a distinctive theme in oscillating thirds with characteristic touches of diatonic dissonance. This was eventually to find a place in the second Dream Interlude (Ex.20 in Elgar's Analytical Essay) but two of its original placings can be seen from the sketches. The first (B.L. Add. MS. 47907B f.53), shows how this idea might have followed the 'cheerful, out-of-door ambling' theme that precedes the midnight caper at Gadshill (Ex.3). In this sketch, the music of figure 99^5 continues as at 51^{1-6} which in turn leads to the material now at 103^1. The second location (f.56) was to have been at figure 34^1, where it appeared instead of the 'mysterious semiquaver passages'.

Ex. 3   B.L. Add. MS. 47907B f.53

An equally intriguing reflection of Elgar's creative thinking to be revealed in the sketches for *Falstaff* concerns the theme of section II of the work which symbolized his hero's 'boastfulness and colossal mendacity.' The earliest sketch (B.L. Add. MS. 47907B f.129), written in semiquavers, is marked 'Fuga'. What would appear to be the next sketch in the temporal sequence of events (f.66) shows a working as a three-part fugato which has the deleted title: '(Bardolph drunk) <u>fatuous sound</u>'. The intended scoring was for bassoons doubled by bass clarinet, and later with trombones and tuba. Note the flatulant exclamations at each leap in the line! (Ex.4)

There is also a non-fugal metamorphosis of the theme as a march (B.L. Add. MS. 47907B f.58), but ultimately, it was in the flight from Gadshill (fig.44^1) that Elgar gave full rein to its fugal character. The essence of Elgar's mature polyphonic technique can also be seen in the fluent melodic counterpoint at fig.27^1. Here this same theme combines with the rising cycle of fifths of the 'substantial material' associated with Falstaff's vision of himself as 'a goodly portly man . . .'[7]

A further example of Elgar's process of seeking out the full symphonic

Ex. 4

B.L. Add. MS. 47907B f.66

potential of these two themes can be seen in an unfulfilled planning sketch on f.60v. of B.L. Add. MS. 47907B (Ex.5). This shows a motif extracted from Ex.4 extended sequentially over a pedal-point between statements of *Falstaff's* 'portly' theme.

Ex. 5

B.L. Add. MS. 47907B f.60v.

Throughout the MSS of Elgar's mature works there are frequent revisions of conclusions. His dislike of commonplace melodic endings and cadences was expressed in the well-known letter to Jaeger of 26 March 1906:

> It is easy (!) enough to write a melody – except the last two bars:
> I am sure that it is the difficulty of avoiding a 'barn door' ending
> that has kept the modern school from symmetrical melody.[8]

Though it may be difficult to find 'barn door' endings in the completed scores of Elgar's works of international stature, their sketches often reveal the suppression of commonplace gestures. (Some particularly notorious examples can be found in the sketches of the first, second and fourth movements of the second symphony.)[6]

The conclusion of *Falstaff* is no exception, with its two extensions to the coda which were made at the orchestration stage. These are contained on two additional pages bound into the front of the MS full score (see Appendix 1). It may have been Elgar's first intention to conclude the work at bar 17 of fig. 136 with a perfunctory unison C. This is suggested by a double bar, pauses and an emphatic *forte* on p.215 of the manuscript full score. The effect of such a conclusion would have been for Falstaff's death to have occurred almost immediately after his repudiation. There would have been no portrayal of Falstaff's decline with its important implications for dramatic as well as musical balance. Elgar achieved this with his next extension of the score to bar 8 of fig.146. Ghosts of the orchard, Honest Gentlewoman and Prince Hal themes flit across the score as Falstaff, 'so shaked that it is most lamentable to behold', sinks towards death. This first extension ended with a rather unsubtle *forte* chord of C for full orchestra which punctuated the end of the clarinet solo. This is present on f.41v. of B.L. Add. MS. 47907B and on p.229 of the MS. full score which also has the note: 'fine/Edward Elgar: /Hampstead.'

From the next page of the MS. full score (p.230) it appears that Elgar reduced the level of this chord from *forte* to *mezzo forte*, and then to have extended it for three additional bars rising to *fortissimo*. A further 'Fine' indication follows. The final revisions can be found on the two additional pages bound into the front of the MS full score. The first of these contains 146[8-13], and beneath bars 11 to 13 is the following instruction in Elgar's hand: 'Instead of the last bar in MS / score [referring to p.230] substitute this.' It is preceded by a note to the engraver: 'N.B. the orchestration of / these bars remains / as written except tam picc'. Thus the famous side drum solo came as a later idea. It first appears in a short score sketch on f.35v. of B.L. Add. MS. 47907B as an insertion between two *pizzicato* Cs which follow the A minor 6/3 chord at 146[16].

It remained for further refinements to be added to the side drum solo, possibly at the proof correction stage. These are the *fermata* at 146[11], which is not present in the MS, and the G.P. in 146[18], which may also have been an afterthought arising from a *fermata* originally placed above the flute stave.

The above revisions to the conclusion of *Falstaff* confirm Elgar's unease over commonplace endings. Only in the approach to the first intended close at 136[17] is there any sign of V–I cadences in C minor, but these (in the strings), are deflected by the E minor interjections of the clarinets and bassoons. The second intended close at 146[8] approaches I via IV with an added sixth (after the dominant seventh at 145[6] had remained unresolved)

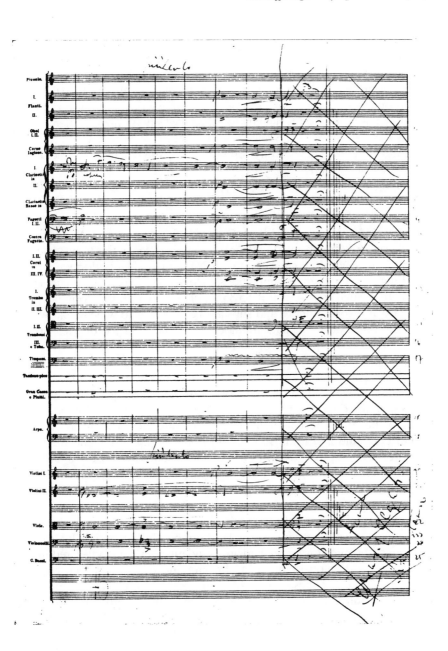

Figure 1   Elgar's first conclusion of *Falstaff*

but in the last eight bars the final C major chord is again set beside its
E minor mediant.

Looking at the overall tonal structure of *Falstaff* it is only in the March of
the King's Progress in section III (114^1) that Elgar's declared tonal centre of C
minor is presented in a conventional manner. Falstaff's principal theme
which opens section I revolves about the dominant of C, but it is denied a
tonic resolution and leads directly to Prince Hal's two principal themes in E
flat (4^1) and E minor (7^1). Similarly at the end of section I (16^{11}) any tonic
resolution of this theme is firmly contradicted by the B flat minor opening of
the Eastcheap section.

Among Elgar's mature orchestral works, *Falstaff* is the only case where
significant revisions were made to the printed score after the first performance.
Some copies of the miniature score were printed before the first performance
and were received by Novello & Co. from the engravers, F.M. Geidel of
Leipzig on 26 September 1913. Elgar presented copies of this to his wife and
to Alice Stuart Wortley (see Appendix 5). During the first performance Alice
Elgar made a number of annotations in her copy. Apart from customary
superlatives such as 'wonderful' (p.35), 'delightful (p.37) or 'glorious' (p.65)
there are also some queries and substantive criticisms to which Elgar was to
respond. She noted the page numbers of some of these queries on the
flyleaf of her score: pp. 97, 101 and 120.

An 'x' placed above 71^6 might have arisen from some ragged ensemble at
the pause. For this, or for some other reason, in the revised edition of the
score Elgar moved the pause to the previous bar. Possibly it was to give the
conductor an opportunity to consolidate the new tempo by beating it
through the rest. The comment on p.97 is indistinct; it might be read as
'rough here' and if read thus in conjunction with the comment 'shade/too
fast' on p.100 and the querying of the *poco sostenuto* on p.101 it could be
that the first performance had become in this vicinity. Conversely, the 'no' at
the *animato* on p.120 might suggest that the tempo had sagged or that the
ensemble may have become insecure.

Notwithstanding his wife's remarks there were other passages that Elgar
decided to alter of his own volition. Furthermore this apparently limited first
printing of the miniature score had an abundance of wrong notes, redundant
accidentals and inconsistencies in phrasing and dynamics which required
correction. Many of these corrections are evident from Elgar's conducting
copy of the full score which is in the collection at the Birthplace Museum.

The most significant alteration concerned pp.129–130 (128^{1-9}) which were
queried by Alice Elgar in her score during the première with the note:
'melody more/marc.[ato]'. Elgar duly strengthened the scoring of the melodic
line at this point by adding the second and fourth horns and third trumpet in
128^{1-4}, and from 128^{5-12} he added the brass to the original strings and
woodwinds. The two versions are compared in Figures 2 and 3.

There were a considerable number of adjustments to dynamic and expressive details with many added 'hairpins' and changes to aspects of phrasing and articulation. Other alterations are of a more substantial nature and this suggests the correction of some initial miscalculations in balance. Falstaff's growing somnolence prior to the first Dream Interlude (p.73, fig. 73^{1}f.) provides an interesting example. In the revised edition a *molto tranquillo* is added, the divided cellos and muted horns are reduced from *p* to *pp* to give the incipient snores of the tuba more prominence, and 'hairpins' are added to the fragments of Falstaff's main theme in the bassoon and clarinet parts.

Adjustment of dynamic markings also took place in the vigorous two-part counterpoint of the Shrewsbury fight episode (91^1–92^1, pp.92–93) where the marking for the bassoons and string basses was increased from *p* to *f*. In two instances (4^4 and 125^{10}) between the editions Elgar transposed a low written B flat (concert E flat) for cor anglais up an octave. Presumably it had transpired that many of the instruments in normal use in 1913 extended only to E natural. Conversely, at 130$^{14–15}$ (p.33) the first trumpet part is extended to low E flat (concert F) after stopping at B flat in the first edition.

Removals of or adjustments to slurs can often be explained in terms of the technical idiosyncracies of the instruments concerned. In the first edition where several instruments doubled a line, Elgar often phrased them identically. The revisions in the second edition are often more idiomatic. For example in 24$^{1–5}$ (pp.28–29) the lower strings were originally phrased in the same way as the woodwind. In order to facilitate more intense tonal projection the bowing was altered from one to two strokes per bar. Similarly in 26$^{1–8}$ (pp.30–32) the bass trombone and tuba parts were at first slurred but then altered to tonguing.

More subtle emendations included the removal of the bassoon doubling from the first two notes of the 'cello line at 8^1 (p.8) so that the *tenuto* and *glissez* could emerge more clearly. Further refinements were also made to the scoring of Falstaff's death scene. In the revised edition a *con sord.* direction is inserted at the C major chord for brass (146$^{6–10}$), and to the hushed tamburo piccolo solo the term 'muffled' is added to the existing *con sord.*

We might conclude from the above that in the redeployment of material from other projects, completed or abandoned, *Falstaff* is not dissimilar to several of Elgar's major works. In the localized alterations to the structure and ordering of detail, *Falstaff* is again no exception and reflects working habits that are evident in *The Dream of Gerontius* as well as in the oratorios and symphonies. As an example of Elgar's uncertainty over conclusions *Falstaff* stands second only to the extension of the *Enigma Variations* finale. In the alterations to the orchestration and details of dynamics *Falstaff* is perhaps more of an exception. Moore[9] has suggested that the reason for this

Figure 2   Fig. 128f. as in the first edition

Figure 3   Fig. 128f. as revised after the first performance

may have lain in Elgar's 'uncertainty'. Psychologically this may be arguable, but from a purely musical viewpoint the agile and economical textures of the work were a new departure requiring even greater deftness in their scoring. Elgar's awareness of this is amply evident in the revisions made before and after the first performance.

Notes

1.   See Appendix 2
2.   See Appendix 1
3.   Elgar, Edward. *Falstaff by Edward Elgar. Analytical Essay by the Composer.* Reprinted from the *Musical Times* of September 1913. Novello, London, 1913, p.5.
4.   BL Add. MS. 63161 ff.3v., 5–6 and 8.
5.   Howes, Frank, 'Elgar (1857–1934)', *The Heritage of Music,* vol.III, ed. H. Foss, Oxford, 1951, 138–152.
6.   Kent, Christopher, 'A View of Elgar's Methods of Composition through the sketches of the Symphony no.2 in E flat (op.63), *Proceedings of the Royal Musical Association,* vol.103 (1976–7), p.41.
7.   Elgar, op.cit, ex.8, p.9.
8.   Hereford and Worcester Record Office, ref: 705:445:8757.
9.   Moore, Jerrold Northrop, *Edward Elgar, A Creative Life,* O.U.P., 1984, p.655.

Appendix 1

The manuscript material relating to Elgar's work on his Symphonic Study *Falstaff* is extensive. While the bulk of it stems from the main period of composition (April to September 1913), there are, in common with many other of Elgar's works, a number of themes which originated in earlier works but were discarded and recycled into a later project. Conversely, there are ideas which Elgar earmarked for *Falstaff* but never used for the work. The material in these categories is as follows:

B.L. Add. MS. 63154 ff.12,18 & 10v. (Sketch Book II pp.13,18 & 10)

The contents of p.13 of this MS. which is headed: 'Falstaff Castle House/ Worcester Festival/Sep 1902', were not used in the actual work nor have any concordances in other sketches given indications as to whether Elgar made use of it elsewhere. Above the first bar Elgar deleted the title 'Hudibras'. It is a detailed working sketch beginning in C minor stemming from a horn fanfare which is repeated in E flat with the note 'add' and then tried contrapuntally. There is also a theme in F marked 'dolce' of which the last two bars were moved 'from on page 26' (f.28) where they are headed 'Turn ye', a reference to *The Apostles*. The two bars at the very end of the page are encircled and marked 'laughs!/good'; the second of these is the only part of this material that was eventually to be used in the work. It can be seen in the Gadshill escapade between figs.43 and 44, albeit with harmonic alterations.

Page 18, which contains sketches for the setting of The Lord's Prayer in *The Kingdom* concludes with an incipit marked 'falstaff' but this does not appear in the eventual work. Folio 10v. is stamped 'COLISEUM MASQUE' and entitled 'Falstaff' above and contains a theme in G minor, which appears in *The Crown of India*.

Although not directly related to any material of the work it bears comparison with figs. 63–4, where a texture founded upon a quaver perpertuum mobile is also joined by a descending chromatic countermelody. This folio also contains the motif that appears at fig.152 in *The Kingdom* .

B.L. Add. MS. 63154 f.4 (Sketch Book II p.3)

This sketch shows the theme familiar in *Falstaff* at fig. 90^{7-10} etc. at the beginning of a remarkable chain of relocations. These are collated in Ex.2 of the main text. It was first considered for the 'Judas' section of *The Apostles* (a) specifically for a reference to '?Christ being mocked' (b) (B.L. Add. MS. 47904A f.169), then , the references '[Simon] Magus & Crowd' and '48 VIII' lead to a draft for the scene 'In Solomon's Porch' in the Pentecost section of *The Kingdom* (B.L. Add. MS.63160 f.32, Sketch Book VIII p.48). Its final incorporation into the 'Shrewsbury Fight' episode of *Falstaff* (d & e) is also discussed in the main text.

B.L. Add. MS. 63161 ff.5-6,8, & 3v. (Sketch Book IX pp.8-10,13,& 6)

In this short score sketch for the *Coronation March of 1911* (itself discarded from the thwarted Rabelais ballet of 1902) the thematic material of the first Dream Interlude of *Falstaff* appears as the second theme. This is shown to have been discarded in favour of the Trio on f.8 (p.13) of the MS; but this sketch is not irrelevant to *Falstaff* either, since at the foot of the page is the syncopated fanfare which heralds the march of the hero's Scarecrow Army (figs. 83 and 85 ff.), but with a number of differences in both pitches and rhythms.

B.L. Add. MS. 63161 ff.29 v-33 (Sketch Book IX pp.56-63

Elgar also sketched the following materials in this MS., apparently during the main period of composition. There is nothing to suggest that they were not originally intended for the work.

pp.56–7: 55^1–57^8
p.58: three unused incipits: the first is entitled: 'pistol & C'.
pp.60–61: 17^1–25^2
p.62: 24^1–25^3 passim.
p.63: 20^9–21^1

B.L. Add. MS. 47907B

This source contains the main body of working sketches. There are 130 folios whose contents vary from short incipits, through evolutionary drafts to fair copies in short score complete with scoring indications. Most of the latter are in ink, but the former are a mixture of ink, pencil and crayon. Several different kinds of MS paper are used but the most widely found is of fourteen staves by Boosey and Co., London.

The contents fall into three categories:

A ff.1–5: these contain verbal plans of the title and sections of the work as follows:
f.1 'Symphonic Study in C minor, with two/Interludes in A minor "Falstaff"..
E. Elgar' op.<Character Study> [the latter deleted before the main title is written out again]
f.2 'Falstaff i. At Court. {Falstaff/pr.Hy/ij. At Gadshill/ and the Boar's Head {Robbery in dark/Boar's Head/Doll &/Sneat's noise [*q.v.* Henry IV Part II, Act

II, Scene 4]/& sleep./?iij. To Shrewsbury –/ and back./{realmarch/&/ mock march/& real march [deleted]/fighting/iiij. King Henry V^th^ progress/ and the End {as sketch/ repudiation/ & death.'

f.4 (attached to f.5) is an illustration of a 16th century Italian fool's mask (Narrenmaske) from the Kaiser Friedrich Museum, Berlin.

f.5 'Falstaff./ Symphonic poem/ Edward Elgar./ op.

perhaps cut out of an article or catalogue.

f.5v. Main features/i. At court/<Courtly conversation/with p. Hy. > / ij. At Gadshill & <Highway robbery> /the Boar's Head/Revels/Sneats' noise/ sleep/iij. <At> To Shrewsbury/<Marching - (Shallow.)> /Scarecrow army../ and back./iiij End. Kg Hy V.'^s^approach /march. &^c.^ see sketch /End. progress &/the End.

B ff.6–49: these contain some of the fair copy sketches from which the full score was made with references to the page numbers of the latter. They are arranged in order of appearance in the completed work with paginations 1–20 by Elgar. Some of these leaves are headed: I, II or IV to identify the section of the work that they belong to, viz:

'Falstaff I' ff.6–23 [000^1^–16^11^]

'Falstaff II' ff.23v.–36 (or 24-39) [17^1^–75^8^]

[III is identified later (f.83 ff.) but occupies 81^1^–101^8^]

'IV' ff.37v–43 [107^1^–146^19^]

Interlude No.1. (originally 'Intermezzo I') ff.46–7 [76^1^–80^7^]

Interlude No.2 (originally 'Intermezzo II') ff.48–9 [102^1^–106^6^The above versions of the Interludes are both fair copies of the arrangements for pianoforte.

C ff.50–130: these extensive working sketches relate to all four sections of the work and to the Interludes.

Elgar Birthplace MS.66

On various dates during 1913 Elgar gave or sent to Alice Stuart Wortley (Windflower) fair copies in short score of several portions of the work. It is clear from Alice Elgar's diary (see Appendix 2: *Chronology of Composition*) that Mrs. Stuart Wortley was not less a close companion and confidante during Elgar's composition of *Falstaff* than she had been in the cases of the Violin Concerto and the Second Symphony. The details of this material are as follows:

1. 'Ap[ril] 17:1913' 103^1-8^ written in halved note lengths (cf. B.L. Add MS. 47907B f.128)

2. 'May. 26. 1913' 4^1^–5^2^ headed: 'a scrap of Falstaff for the Windflower's/ return.' It is marked 'Allegro/nobilmente. (Very full & rich)' and has differences in dynamics.

3. 'May 27: 1913' On verso 'Farewell to the Hut) July 1913'.118^6–119^8 marked 'p espress^0, and in the last bar 'dolce'. At the end the composer noted: 'written on Tuesday night after you left/ & now Good night – /EE' (29 July)

4. 'July 8: 1913' 63^3–64^9 followed by a two bar coda so as to cadence in G minor and form a self-contained piece. On the last system is 140^{1-4} a tone higher and marked 'slow'.

5. 'Sunday <u>Aug 3 1913</u>' 19^1–20^{15}, this paste-over was not copied out expressly for Alice Stuart Wortley but was taken from the existing working sketches and given to her with an apologetic heading: 'I have no minute to copy all this/ out – I hope you can make out/ this sketch which I have inked over'. In the course of this sketch pp.8–10 are referred to as if the material had been orchestrated on the corresponding pages of the full score, but the latter do not contain it. (It does not occur until pp.30–33.) This might be interpreted as a sign that Elgar intended to place this material sooner, or that these numbers relate to further short score sketches, but there are no suitable parallels among these either.

6. No date. 102^1–106^6: a complete short score working sketch of the 'pastorale' with details of instrumentation. This too was drawn from the material now in B.L. Add. MS. 47907B since the latter only contains a plan and a few fragments (ff.99v.–101 and 128) and the fair copy of the pianoforte arrangement (ff.48–9) to which there are page references.

Alice Stuart Wortley's copy of the Miniature Score ref: E.B. 1456

Bound between the title page and the first page of music is what may have been the original sketch of the opening theme of the work. It is in pencil and is headed 'Falstaff (tragedy)'. The incipit which follows it would appear to be unrelated to the final work. It is undated, and since it has been trimmed it is not possible to determine which of Elgar's sketch books it might have come from.

Fitzwilliam Museum MU. MS. 733 (23.H.21).

This, the MS full score of *Falstaff* was presented to the Fitzwilliam Museum by Carice Elgar-Blake in 1968. There were six leaves missing (pp.1, 24, 39, 99, 100 and 202) but with the exception of p.39* these were acquired at a Sotheby's sale on 23 November 1977 and reconstituted. The MS comprises 230 pages of single sided score paper of 28 staves with four percussion lines

---

* Page 39 appeared as lot 528 in Sotheby's sale of 29 May 1992 and was acquired by a private individual.

measuring approximately 337 x 454 mm. A further double-sided sheet of 26 staves is bound into the front of the MS (295mm. x 430mm.) numbered '1' and '2' with instrument names in Elgar's hand. This contains 146^8 to the end. As a whole the MS is essentially an ink fair copy, with minor alterations in pencil or red ink, which Elgar prepared with some haste in view of the many crooked and roughly drawn bar-lines. The rehearsal numbers have been inserted with a rubber stamp and there is no foliation.

In private possession

An eight page MS of the first 'Dream Interlude' (76^1–80^7) given to Edward Speyer. It is a tone lower (ie. in G minor), a fact that the composer related to Speyer in an accompanying letter written from Hampstead on 17 July 1913:

'My dear Edward:
Enclosed I venture to send – with much shyness – a separate little movement (Interlude) from Falstaff; – this is the original score. I have had to copy it (transpose it) into the score which goes to the printer so that this little book of eight pages is more original than the original score which is printing.

We enjoyed our time with dear Tonia & you extremely. I am sorry my indigestion has returned & I am looking for an almshouse.

My love to you both. Your ever affecti[onate]' [E.E.]

Appendix 2

A Chronology for the Composition of Falstaff from Alice Elgar's Diary

(HWRO ref: 705:445, Accession no. 7416, parcel 3)

1913

17 April: 'E. vesy porsley . . . C. to Lecture – Alice S[tuart] W[ortley] to tea – A. to see Mrs Laffery'. On this visit Elgar gave Mrs Stuart Wortley a copy of 103^{1-8}

25 May: '. . . E. beginning to turn to Falstaff'

26 May: 'E going on with Music Gott sei Dank'

27 May: 'E going on with Falstaff, & trust he is better. A.& C. to Oriana Concert E's Evening Scene, <u>most</u> beautiful & well sung. Then to Brickdale party frightful jammed crowd. Dr. Blair in evening with E.'

28 May: 'Very hot – Alice S.W. drove E. into town to try new coes after hearing some Falstaff music to her joy.'

15 June: 'E. at The Hut' [Frank Schuster's home at Bray, near Maidenhead]

16 June: 'E. at The Hut. Alone all day & worked hard at Falstaff . . .'

18 June: 'E. busy . . .'

19 June: '. . . E. immersed in his music–'

20 June: '. . . E. busy with his great musics.'

22 June: '. . . Ranee & Lady Colvin came. E. played to them & they were radiantly happy over Falstaff . . .'

26 June: 'E. vesy hard at work . . . E. to French play with Alice S.W. – she came back & had tea & heard Falstaff.'

27 June: '. . . E. very absorbed in Falstaff, orchestrating all the morning. Beautiful things he was writing.'

4 July: '. . . E. going on with his Falstaff.'

7 July: '. . . Whittemore to lunch. E. played him some Falstaff . . .'

8 July: '. . . E. writing hard not so vesy hapsy.'

10 July: 'A. to Novello for E. to see Mr. Littleton about Falstaff – Were they going to have it ? A. Littleton wanted it. So it was arranged . . .'

11 July: 'E. happy with his work. A. to Novello with 1st portion . . .'

16 July: 'E. hard at work . . .'

17 July: 'E. much absorbed . . . A.S.W. drove E. to Barnet & Hadley. Gerald Cumberland called in the morning & had a talk with E. & wrote in the 'Daily Citizen' next day.' [See Appendix Three below]

18 July: '. . . E. very absorbed in Falstaff - Very happy over it, D.G . . . E. & A.S.W. for drive . . .'

19 July: 'E. very absorbed & happy in his music . . . D.G. for days seeing E. better & happy with his work'.

20 July: 'A.S.W. took E. for drive. E. working all the morning . . .'

21 July: 'E. working . . .'

26 July: 'A.& E. motored to The Hut . . . Lionel Holland there and Alice S.W.'

28 July: '. . . E. working in Garden room [at The Hut]. Decided to go to Tan-yr-Allt [Penmaenmawr]'

29 July: '....E. busy in garden room - Alice S.W.left...'

30 July: 'Frank [Schuster] motored E.& A. to station. Home all well . . .'

31 July: '. . . E. working at high pressure . . .'

2 August: 'E. working very hard. Alice S.W. to tea.'

3 August: A.S.W. to tea & drive E. out –

4 August: '. . . A. & C. to see Ramsdens. Alice S.W. came in aftn..E.working at very high pressure – <u>nearly</u> finished his work'

5 August: '. . . Left Severn House about 10.30 [for Penmaenmawr] E. down at 4 a.m. A. made him tea &c &c & finished his great work Falstaff – D.G.'

8 August: 'E. vesy busy with his notes on Falstaff . . .'

9 August: '. . . E. vesy busy with his Falstaff notes'

18 August: 'E. busy . . . Mr. Devenport came & brought metronome . . .'

19 August: 'E. very busy'

20 August: 'E. very busy'.

21 August: 'E. busy writing & correcting . . .'

22 August: 'Much excitement about Dr. McNaught who was to be at Wardour St at 8.30 to correct proof & return immediately but E. had registered letter so it was too late. E. finishing & correcting & c –'

23 August: 'E busy with proofs & notes . . .'

26 August: '. . . Proofs coming constantly . . .'

27 August: '. . . E. recd. proof copies of his notes on Falstaff. It looks splendid fine literary work.'

1 September: Left Tan-yr-Alt - Good journey home found all safe & well - D.G. Very glad to leave the house wh. we disliked very much - cold & ugly & uncared for. Sorry to leave the Sea delighted to leave the disagreeable Welsh – '

21 September: [E. at The Hut] '...E. expected parts to correct & Mr. Reed at Hut to help him but only very few came – '

22 September: Orchestral parts only arrived this very morning from Germany – Orchestra played straight from them – Very few mistakes & they really read wonderfully – Falstaff sounded magnificent & wonderful – audience greatly impressed – '

2 October: [First performance at Leeds] '. . . E. rather hurried it & some of the lovely melodies were a little smothered but it made its mark & place. E. changed very depressed after – . . .'

18 October: '. . . Harold Brooke to lunch & finish correcting Falstaff score . . .'

Appendix 3

The Daily Citizen, 18 July 1913

'I have, I think, enjoyed writing it more than any other music I have ever composed, and perhaps, for that reason, it may prove to be among my best efforts. Certainly, the character of Falstaff, with its variety, richness, and fecundity of feeling and thought, provides ample material for a creative musical work. But it must not be imagined that my orchestral poem is programme music – that it provides a series of incidents with connecting links such as we have, for example, in Richard Strauss's "Ein Heldenleben" or in the same composer's "Domestic Symphony". Nothing has been farther from my intention. All I have striven to do is to paint a musical portrait – or, rather, a sketch portrait. . . . I have finished all the preliminary sketch-work, and of the actual scoring, only a little remains to be done. I shall say 'good-bye' to it with regret, for the hours I have spent on it have brought me a great deal of happiness.'

Appendix 4

Alice Stuart Wortley's copy of the Miniature Score (E.B. ref: 1456)

This is bound into a volume of beautifully tooled green leather which contains in addition to the score, Elgar's article on *Falstaff* from the September 1913 edition of the *Musical Times*, a guide book to Studley Royal and Fountains Abbey, a short press profile of Elgar: 'The Man as he is', written during the Leeds Festival by G.C. and the programme of Landon Ronald's first performance of *Falstaff* in London on 3 November 1913 in an all Elgar programme which also included the Variations and Second Symphony. This performance of *Falstaff* was the first to include the revisions. Pasted to the verso of the flyleaf of the score is a ticket admitting Mrs C. Stuart Wortley to the first performance of the work in Leeds Town Hall on 2 October, and between the title page and the first page of music is the initial sketch of the opening theme referred to above. Elgar's formal inscription is at the head of the first page of music: 'To Alice Stuart Wortley/ from Edward Elgar/ Leeds/ Sep 29 1913 p124.' The significance of 'p124' is not clear, on the page in question, which also contains rehearsal number 124, Elgar has written:'124 x 2 ='. Were this page to have been the only one in the score on which the page and rehearsal numbers were in tandem it might have served as a possible explanation, but that is not the case. There are no other markings in the score.

The guide book is initialled 'A C SW by Elgar and inscribed: A memento of a/ lovely day./ October 2. 1913/ to the W[indflower]./ from Edw.'

Appendix 5

Alice Elgar's copy of the Miniature Score (in private possession)

This is inscribed on the title page: 'To C Alice Elgar/ from her loving Edward/ Oct 1: 1913'. On the flyleaf are references to pages 97,101 & 120 which relate to three of the following comments which were written into the score in feint pencil during the first performance.

p.5 'not/ legato / enough.'

pp. 16,18 & 22 'fine'

p. 35 'wonderful'

p. 37 'delightful' bottom margin.

p. 46 'melody / not heard' bottom margin

p. 55 'beautiful' r.h. margin.

p. 65 'glorious' r.h. margin.

p. 71 the 'X' above 71^6 in Elgar's hand could relate to the moving of the fermata to the previous bar in the revised edition.

p. 72 'wonderful' l.h. margin.

p. 84 'splendid' l.h. margin.

p. 90 'fine' r.h. margin.

p. 94 'fine' l.h. margin.

p. 97 'rall. here' in Elgar's hand, top margin.

p. 100 'shade/ too fast' l.h. margin.

p. 101 the *poco sostenuto* at 99^{10} is encircled with a '?' above.

pp. 103 (102^1) & 106 'beautiful' l.h. margin.

p. 114 'Carac' l.h. margin. The phrase beginning at 114^1 had reminded Alice of the opening theme of *Caractacus*

p. 120 the *animato* at 121^1 is encircled with the remark 'no' possibly in Elgar's hand.

p. 127 'fine' at 126^6 r.h. margin.

p. 128 'glorious' top margin. At 127^1 Elgar has inserted a missing F clef into the Fagotto part.

p. 129 at 128^1 there is the remark 'melody more/ marc.'

p. 136 'lively' l.h. margin.

p. 145 in 143^{12} '? 2 Vio' in the top margin in Elgar's hand.

p. 146 'wonderful' l.h. margin.

7 'Ghostly Stuff': The Brinkwells Music

Ivor Keys

The 'ghostly stuff' of my title was Elgar's own phrase, referring to the first movement of the Piano Quintet in a letter to the dedicatee, Ernest Newman.[1] Taking the word in its straightforward sense as 'spooky' (Elgar perhaps meant no more in the context of the letter) it is easy to see its relevance to that particularly haunting movement. But the question of what the music is haunted *by* is an altogether broader one which will be examined later, though not by pursuing the search for what Newman called the 'quasi-programme that lies at the heart of the work', a quest in which there is little mileage at this time of day.

In the three 'Brinkwells' chamber works and the Cello Concerto we are dealing with a huge ghost: the resurrected, post-mortem composer himself. In *The Music Makers* (1912) Elgar set, with overwhelming pathos and finality, the closing words of the contralto soloist; 'a singer who sings no more' and signed as a composer his own death certificate, his own 'Novissima hora est' from *Gerontius*. Literally, *Falstaff* is a year later in final form, but both works date in sketch from 1902 and the latter is probably only edged out by Birmingham Festival rehearsal deadlines. The musical language of leave-taking is a slow triple time with a searing or yearning first-beat dissonance, prepared as a suspension or unprepared, but in any case persisted in to the point of obsession. It can by now do the quintessential Elgar no harm to suggest a comparison to the choral echoes of 'No more' to that other master of nostalgic loss, Delius. Witness this from the antecedent masterpiece, *Sea Drift* (1904):

Ex. 1

108

The first performance of *Sospiri*, which Kennedy justly describes as 'a wounded heart-cry', came just within World War I. Otherwise the war-time evoked nothing (as far as the public was concerned) except pieces allied to words or stage action, or a patriotic concoction such as *Polonia*. It is significant that the *pièces d'occasion* of World War I seemed not to serve any significant purpose in the second. Elgar in 1915 seemed to be conniving in his own death as a large-scale composer in writing to Alice Stuart Wortley: 'After all, nobody *wants* any real music'.[2] All the more surprising is the resurrection brought about, apparently, by the delightful discovery in 1917 of the cottage at Brinkwells in Sussex, north of Fittleworth, west of Pulborough. To most non-natives Sussex means seaside and Downs, and even in these well-populated days there is a wooded remoteness, bordering on the mysterious, about this patch of no-man's-land near Surrey, nestling behind the tiny barriers of the Arun to the east and the yet smaller Rother to the south. Roman antiquity is near at hand: the villa at Bignor and the venerable Stane Street. Elgar's happiness at Brinkwells is well documented, and to it we may mainly ascribe the bringing into shape (one must be a little vague in these mysterious matters) of the astonishing series of four big works, in every sense. Their final allocation was: the Violin Sonata, op.82, the String Quartet, op.83, the Piano Quintet, op.84 and the Cello Concerto, op.85. But this is only an ultimate chronology. A theme from op.85 was written down well before the rest of it, and not at the time of sketching ascribed to any particular work, and apparently op.83 was begun before op.82. It is not perhaps too fanciful to think of this gigantic ghost coming back to life to write not four works, but one thirteen-movement work in E minor or thereabouts. (The Piano Quintet is the one not 'in' E, but has a big, fairly firm central movement in E major.) One is justified in using the inverted commas, because all four pieces show a marked unorthodoxy in the use of tonality, whether looked at on the small or large scale. Of course systematized atonality has nothing to do with Elgar's style, but we are more than justified in using the phrase 'calculated unorthodoxy' since calculation comprises so great a proportion of the process of composition, especially in 'absolute' music. There are of course earlier examples of this penchant for surprise. On a large scale in the First Symphony we have the stately introductory motto in A flat giving way to an allegro which is suddenly, and at length, in D minor, in a sense the furthest away from A flat, being exactly halfway up the chromatic scale, but not having any immediate harmonies in common. On the smaller scale we can see Elgar's evident delight in beginning the first Pomp and Circumstance March, a D major piece if ever there was one, on a trumpet E flat. Let us now examine, mainly from this point of view, the four works in their ultimate order, hoping that the subheadings will not detract from what they have in common.

Sonata for Violin and Piano, op.82

This was published in 1919, and first performed in March 1919. For what it is worth, no key is mentioned on the title-page. The work begins with one bar in A minor, but at this stage one cannot depute more than a tinge of the subdominant to the music, since the two F sharps in the second bar, within two seconds of the start, make sure that the listener is at home in E minor (whether he consciously knows it or not). What the A-to-E progression does do is to sow the seed for the emphatic plagal cadence at the end of the movement, and, with decorations, at the end of the work. The conservatism of the instrumental writing – as though Debussy and Ravel had never existed, let alone Schoenberg – might lead us to expect orthodox destinations in the form, making for a 'second subject' paragraph in G major. The music takes care almost entirely to defeat this expectation. One place, though rather early, where this might occur is at the 'big-tune sign-post' at Fig. 3. (The rehearsal marks are included for optional verification, not essential for the gist.) But here we have instead another E minor theme, slightly allied to the first, making as though for G major, but sliding away through sequences which momentarily (Figure 4) bring us within reach of B minor, another possible 'second subject' key. But this in turn is undermined by sequences based on the first subject, more directly alluded to. The purpose of this apparent pettifogging is to point to Elgar's enigmatics. Have we already stumbled, without proper clues, into the 'development'? Are we supposed to know, or care? Then at Figure 5 we arrive at a theme analogous in its 'still centre' effect to the quietly obsessive chorale passage in the Piano Quintet. Here is the violin part at this point (it is punctuated by periodical chimes on the piano):

Ex. 2

This outline is reminiscent of the second main theme in Vaughan Williams's antecedent song Silent Noon (1903). If the reminiscence is conscious we could remark that there must have been silent noons aplenty in and around the composing studio at Brinkwells. The use of the bottom G in the violin's arpeggiation in Ex.2 gives a decidedly E minor tinge to what might otherwise be a C major tune. Feelings of orthodox G major do not obtrude at this stage, not even when the pedal G gets transferred to the piano. Not until thirty-two meditative bars later do we get a *fortissimo* G chord, but even then in second inversion, and if because of this we incline to consider that the exposition ends here or hereabouts we have to contend with an almost immediate lapse into F sharp minor, gently crowned on the piano by a prefiguring of the first phrase of the Piano Quintet.

Unorthodoxies continue in the ensuing development based not on the beginning of any subject, but on the movement's fifth bar, spun out into no fewer than six limbs of a sequence, cocking a snook at the rule-of-thumb 'three are enough', a received wisdom of the Stanford school. But the moment of recapitulation is obvious enough even if Elgar had not – with a touch of irony? – marked it *Come prima.* Our bearings thus found, it seems clear that the 'silent noon' stillness stands for the 'second subject', though it does not show any signs of wanting to be recognized in a home tonality; indeed it is momentarily lodged in G, as though to confuse the issue. A notable absentee now is the quotation from the Quintet, if that is what it was. The pre-ordained plagal cadence is marked by a crescendo on top of *fff.*

If the Quintet is ghostly stuff then so is the capricious opening and close of this sonata's second movement. Its heading – Romance – promises a strangeness and yet, following Mozart's and Brahms's usage, a trace of surface charm. Elgar does not encourage us to look for a *frisson*, describing it to Alice Stuart of Wortley as 'a fantastic, curious movement with a very expressive middle section'. It has a slightly Spanish air, with its guitar-like off-beat *pizzicati* and the castanet-like triplets of a slowish bolero. There is as yet no key-signature; the caprices of the music would make one an encumbrance. C sharp minor might have the most votes, except that the frequent catch-phrase ending on C sharp attracts an A beneath it each time. Paradoxically it is the middle of the movement which settles to a key signature, of B flat. The light relief disappears with magical abruptness, giving way to what Elgar describes, with an evasion of direct personal pride, as 'a melody for the violin – they say it is as good or better than anything I have done in the expressive way'. The following example shows the step into the distance, distance not only in its key but in its trance-like floating. Yet the continuity is there in the transfiguration of the 'catch-phrase' fourths and fifths on the other side of the whole bar's stillness. Elgar is the master of modulatory transitions, but here 'transition' is not the word:

Ex. 3

The rapt distance of Elgar's B flat – a straight enough key to most composers – has notable other examples in both concertos: in the Violin Concerto it directly follows, *semplice*, on the B minor of the first movement, and in the Cello Concerto, as here, it is the central crux of an E minor work. Nor is this the only likeness: the passionate outpouring is almost continuous – four beats rest in the sonata, six in the Cello Concerto; both inherit the slow triple time from *The Music Makers*, and both end on their dominants as though their singer has not the strength to sing further in that strain.

The whimsical phantom's return, muted, decides to end in A, so that the plagal cadence feeling is renewed with the onset of the third movement in an E major, which seems unequivocal, except that its counter-statement after twelve bars is in A, another turn to this particular screw. The tone of the subjects is on the whole more extravert, with some expected keys in expected places. But this sets in relief a remarkable series (Fig. 43) of enharmonic pp gropings, produced by what one might call 'come-what-may' short sequences in which the experimental master can make an artistic effect by seeming to lose his way. Another *Come prima* seems to put us on the homeward way, especially as some of the music is gone through again, rather than really recomposed. But this is to prepare another step into the distance, the resumption of the *dolcissimo* middle of the second movement. But in a sense this 'cyclic' idea is neither distant nor an excursion at all, for it is mainly in the home E major that we have avoided so long, and its psychological effect is to bring us to the haven where we would be, in a way which the Cello Concerto does not, cannot, seek to attain.

String Quartet, op.83

As with the Sonata, this work was published in 1919 and first performed in public in 1919, and the title-page does not mention a key. The gravitation towards plagal cadences in the Sonata has already been noticed. The essence of this cadence is that it avoids using the leading note, in E minor the progression D sharp to E. Elgar was not immune to contemporary reaction against dominant-bound harmonic progressions and definitions, fuelled in England by renewed interest in church modes and in the activities, with Vaughan Williams a powerful adherent, of the English Folk Song and Folk Dance societies. Elgar would never have been pedantic enough to insist on flattening the leading note in a *cadence*, a tiresome mannerism in some of his feebler 'muscular-Christian' contemporaries. There are plenty of D sharps in his E minor. But the first two bars of this work, with harmonies using D rather than D sharp, take the melody up from E to the syncopated and accented D above, then let it fall to B. One is reminded of the opening melody of the Serenade for Strings of many years before. The introduction of a flat seventh falling to a fifth in a basic minor scale leads naturally, for modern ears, to a slight but interesting ambiguity in the combination of minor key and relative major. In these cases, and more specifically in the Cello Concerto, the combination is E minor and G major, and in the Serenade the music does indeed immediately proceed to a counter-theme in the key of G much sooner than any second subject in the relative major would naturally come. But in the Quartet Elgar maturely plays on these ambiguities – perhaps 'relativities' is the more appropriate word. At Fig. 3 the opening theme is begun again. At this place, where the tonality might be expected to move further afield, the opposite occurs. The syncopated top note is enhanced upwards and the bass altered to make a quite unambiguous dominant harmony leading naturally to a full-close in the tonic key instead of a transition. This cocking of a snook at Stanfordian rules of composition is slyly compounded by a *poco rit*! But within two bars the music does slide away simply and quickly to G major harmony, but what does the first violin play above it? A tune beginning on E, D sharp, E, thus putting E minor on G, whereas the opening, as we have seen, put G on E minor. The E start to this new-old subject makes an 'added-sixth' effect (not a common tonic harmony in Elgar), whereas the climactic re-statement at Fig. 6, *fortissimo*, is certainly in E minor notwithstanding the G in the bass. Assuredly the two keys are 'relative' to each other, not to say inextricable, in Elgar's paradoxical way. The recapitulation is straight and punctual to balance the turbulent come-what-may sequential passages which with their twelve-eight time and wide-leaping range recall and build upon the Second Symphony. The freedom and daring of the part-writing are a proper tribute to the shade of Beethoven. So is the very touching way, at Fig. 14, in which the first violin 'sighs' with a gulp in the throat, in the reprise of the second subject. The technique of silences on the principal beats of what would otherwise be continuous melody is a momentary recreation of Beethoven's sobs in op.130, or in the *Klagender Gesang* of the piano sonata op.110. There *is* some straight dominant in the lead-in to the last cadence, but the last chords of the movement run, most beautifully, direct from C major to E, thereby relating the music in advance to the key of the slow movement. But perhaps this process has begun slightly before the end, when in the coda Elgar twice conspicuously flattens the second note of his scale to F natural, a touch of the 'Phrygian' from church days?

The overall marking of the middle movement as 'agreeable' – *piacevole* – is certainly true enough, but perhaps does not prepare us for its surprisingly large scale. It is in no hurry to cease being a trio, the first violin not entering till the twenty-third bar, and even here for twelve bars at any rate it simply doubles the tune's restatement at the octave above. Nor is the opening the only three-part writing, for there are leisurely sequences employing the four instruments but only three at a time, and at the recapitulation there is the very Elgarian texture of a top, bottom, and middle part (here the tune, not a counterpoint) in octaves. As a single-line melody the main subject would clearly be in C, for a longer period, at that, than late Elgar usually offers. But in the opening six-bar phrase, with not an accidental in sight, there are four root-position chords of A minor, an immediate resurfacing of our relatives. The quotation of bars 15 and 16 enshrines the mixture in harmony which often beautifully suffuses the movement – top and bottom in C, middle (viola) in A minor. Note the sign-posting *espress.*

Ex. 4

It perhaps goes without saying that we look in vain for anything approaching a 'subject' in G, or any modulation into that key. The only partly contrasting melody is marked, as much as anything, by the texture spreading to four real parts (momentarily five because of double-stopping). As though obsessionally echoing the procedure of the first movement this second subject complements the first using now A minor with a strong tinge of C, and throwing new light on Ex.4.

It is in this movement that there comes into its own the long-breathed capacity for still rumination which is one of the striking features of the Piano Quintet. There are 72 bars at *piano* or less, excluding a few accents, and the last 32 are muted.

To print *Finale* over a last movement seems to promise something ebullient, if not brash. The music reverts without preliminaries to E minor, perhaps connecting itself to the middle movement by its first two notes being C, E. As in the corresponding part of the Cello Concerto there is a rhythmical swagger here, helped on by the punctuation of a quasi-orchestral rat-a-tat figure. Wide and quick modulations do not prevent the first part coming to a full-stop on the tonic E, fifty-two bars into the piece. Elgar's new key-signature here permits us to know, though our ears do not immediately tell us, that the secondary subject paragraph begins at any rate in A major, standing in the unorthodox relationship of sub-dominant major to the erstwhile tonic minor. Not only that, but the almost immediate introduction of G naturals into the tune puts us into the sub-dominant region of the *new* subdominant. The process of extrication is the function of the rest of the movement. The viola makes the rat-a-tat figure into a pattering rain of semiquavers, taken up as it were on the brass which uses them in the Cello Concerto, and eventually becoming a torrent through the whole texture. As for the recapitulation, it is perhaps best seen in a moment of near-stillness (Fig. 49) rendered the more significant by its proximity to a gentle re-use of the harmony of Ex. 4. But this stillness serves to enhance the sustained burst of energy which carries the music home, a far cry from the shrug of the shoulders which dismisses the Cello Concerto.

Quintet in A minor for Pianoforte, 2 Violins, Viola and Violoncello, op.84

The priority of the piano is emphasized by its separate line and larger type on the title-page. It was published, and first performed in public, in 1919. On the autograph score the first and last movements both have the same inscription: Brinkwells/1918. At the proof stage Elgar had that of the first movement changed to 'Bedham'. The Ordnance Survey shows the hamlet of Bedham as scarcely a mile, as the crow flies, from Brinkwells, so one is bound to attribute Elgar's odd insistence to some seminal, visionary experience there which he wished to acknowledge to a public which would mostly be totally ignorant of this semi-private geography. These country impulses are a well-known fact of his life, and particularly his penchant for trees, whether as ghostly or as potential firewood. One of his most mysterious utterances featuring trees is the music set to his own words in the technically difficult and partly almost atonal part-song *Owls*, subtitled 'an epitaph', op.53, no.4. Its refrain is a hurriedly muttered 'What is that?' followed by the soft hoot of 'nothing'. We have Elgar's warrant for connecting this with owls. We note on the map the secretive-looking woods above Flexham Park near Bedham and note that the legends of accursed Spanish monks therein may spring from Algernon Blackwood's imagination[3] and proceed to the music, which is enigmatic enough.

If one performs or hears the first four notes – A G A D – with the D four times as long as each of the others, there is no doubt that D, not A, will establish itself as the key-note even with no harmony. The muttered comments of the unison strings, *pp* and *serioso*, confirm this, as does the fact of the four-bar answering phrase ending on A, making the effect of a I–V half-close – an odd start for a work announcing itself as being in A minor. This key is not firmly established till just before the plangent wail of the strings (Fig. 1), eighteen bars into the piece, and even here the prominent B flats, 'Phrygianising' the scale by lowering its second note, leave more than a vestige of D minor in the air. One is chary of guessing how much plainsong Elgar would have encountered in liturgical use at St George's Worcester – probably, given the date, rather little – but the A G A D phrase is by far the best-known setting of the Compline Antiphon *Salve Regina* with the fourth note as the 'final' of its undoubted Dorian mode. (The antiphon can be found on p.276 of the current *Liber Usualis*, if indeed anything can now be described as 'current'.)

At the ensuing *Allegro* Elgar goes to the other extreme. The B flats disappear, and A minor is confirmed by two thunderous full-closes. At this point the performers, and perhaps some of the audience, have to ask themselves whether the previous music has been merely introductory. Elgar's deliberate baffling-tactics are continued by a reversion to the strings' wail (Fig. 4) followed by a duet on the violins, first *p*, plaintive and hesitant, then *ppp* (*sic*) and truly ghostly. If there are any 'Spanish' features here they could be the persistent lowering (again) of the second note of the scale, though it is here mainly a major scale, making a Moorish augmented second with the C sharp; the piano accompaniment, and later the *pizz* of the lower strings, makes a guitar-like effect, at a tango speed but without the characteristic dotted rhythms. But there is a compensation for the 'stop-go' effect of these changes which is vital for the integrity of the music: the 'Salve Regina' opening, the accompanimental figure of the allegro, the 'Spanish' violin duet and its climax in the orthodox key (at last) of a second subject all have at their onset the shape of a written-out 'lower mordent', the second (auxiliary) note being either a tone or a semitone before the first and third. Ex.5 shows the violin duet. Note Elgar's very precise bowing:

Ex. 5

The next example shows the 'real' second subject, also heard an octave below on the lower strings but, characteristically, with the cello above the viola. Note also how the second bar of Ex.5 is greatly enhanced by the accented, wider interval up and down:

Ex. 6

It is time to economize, but readers with a score could add to these examples the hauntingly repeated chorale-like eight-bar phrases beginning at Fig. 9. We must certainly note a semiquaver figure of the same 'mordent' kind which becomes the tail that wags the dog in the ensuing *fugato* whose slightly scholastic beginning worried Bernard Shaw. It is to make a final drastic appearance in the Cello Concerto.

Such very strong motivic links are clearly meant to be recognized, since they occur at the head of all the relevant themes. It is not a case of semi-hidden correspondences, perfectly legitimate though such a composing technique could be, as indeed in late Brahms. Brahms also of course uses 'migrating mordents' in his Second Symphony though with less wan material. But this very cohesion gives Elgar warrant for the very unorthodox treatment of the sonata form in the waywardness of most of the tonality. The orthodox key of Ex.6 does not last long; at its restatement it is allowed to wander sequentially towards the one key not to be expected at this stage: A minor.

The central part of the movement (Figs.8 to 14) hovers largely round E minor when that key might ordinarily have been enshrined earlier in the scheme. A symptom of this stay in the dominant minor is the use throughout this section of the one-sharp key signature. Such development which Elgar uses here is of the six-eight theme which does in fact mark the recapitulation, and which is extended till the triumphant return of Ex.5 *con fuoco* and *ff* (Fig.18). But in what key? E major again, *not* A, and for long enough to warrant a four-sharp key signature. By this time it need hardly be said that the recapitulation of Ex.6 is also in an unorthodox key – B major – and is mainly a ghost of itself at that. Indeed when the music at last returns, by way of the opening motifs, to its shadowy tonic, anchored by the piano's *pp* drum-roll on A, we could even now not feel truly at home. But Elgar of course has the answer to this: we have been experiencing only the first movement of three.

Compensating for these vagaries is the mainly serene *Adagio* in E, which has something of the romantic stillness of the slow movement of Brahms's A major Piano Quartet. A characteristic of this 'late' style is the standing quietly transfixed on a chord four bars at a time, which is pretty lengthy at crotchet = 54. As though obsessed, the movement uses E minor, not major, for its climax.

Intent on dispelling the long certainty of the Adagio's close the 'wail' from the first movement returns. At last it *does* sound introductory, rather than posing a question as to where the last movement proper begins. At the allegro there is at last an unambiguous A major announced, as though to answer previous questions, by a unison theme *con dignità*. Not only is this main theme deliberately square (as in the last movement of the Second Symphony) but its four-bar periods are so persistent that we are no fewer than 72 bars into the music before the rhythmic pattern is broken, by a second subject paragraph. This is led off by a galumphing syncopated theme – the kind of thing which Clara Schumann found distressing in Brahms's second version of his op.8 Trio. But its determined ordinariness offsets some precipitous modulations. We are not yet out of the haunted woods; from afar we hear in succession the Salve Regina, the 'chorale' and the violin duet (Ex.5) now become a ghostly waltz, and the cello even plays the sadly falling chromaticism of Ex.10.

Cello Concerto, op.85

First public performance 1919. Published in piano score 1919, in orchestral score 1921. Both sketches of the 9/8 opening, the one in the British Library and the one sent to Windflower, now in the Birthplace, had the word *serioso* added by Elgar, interestingly enough since this was the printed designation of the opening of the Quintet. If it seems certain that the 9/8 theme was the starting germ it is not too fanciful to see the falling declamation of the cello's eventual opening as growing out of the germ's shape, to the extent of identical notes at important places. Tovey[4] calls it 'recitative-like', importing the term from Elgar's own use at the opening of the fourth movement (which is not quite the same melody, but near enough). When the 9/8 theme begins on F sharp it is wan and quiet; when it starts on the tonic E it is ff. The contrasting themes are still in E minor or major. In this respect there is no symphonic propulsion or any avoidance of tonic full-stops. The E major is enhanced by the semi-modalism of the E minor, even – most unusually for Elgar – by giving the first subsidiary theme (Fig. 7) to the woodwind with consecutive octaves top and bottom.

The purpose of the short re-introduction of the 'recitative' to start the second movement (*not* entitled a scherzo) is not just a cyclical binding. The short length of the first movement does not in itself necessitate this. The purpose is rather to establish E as the 'key note' or 'final' of the very Dorian shape of the cello's *Allegro molto* figure, which might well otherwise be heard in G.

Ex. 7

Transposed and transcribed for comparison, here is by far the most common Gloria Tone used in the Introit of a Mass (*Liber Usualis*, p.14):

Ex. 8

Glo–ri – a ..... et Spi–ri – tu– i Sanc – to .... A – men.

Here yet again is the amalgam of minor and relative major, so determinedly played upon by Elgar as to deny the relative major its orthodox function as a 'second subject' destination. Indeed this moment is marked by a playfully abrupt lurch into E flat major (Figure 22). Short and quick though it is, it is this movement and not the first which uses symphonic deployment, and it is the erstwhile E flat theme which is recapitulated in G, allowing the movement, whatever it started in, to end unequivocally in that key despite a last-minute attempt by muted horns to cloud the issue.

The effect of the slow movement is of a ceaseless outpouring, or a seamless garment. There are only six beats when the solo is not playing, at one juncture when another theme might conceivably have been introduced. But this would be quite contrary to the miraculous flood of the whole, 'ending' on the dominant; the inverted commas point the paradox: the threnody comes to an end, but the enduring sorrows cannot be assuaged by a tonic conclusion.

The last movement permits itself a second subject (Fig. 47) in G, the first having been more wholly in E minor than most. This other subject Tovey calls 'dignity at the mercy of a banana-skin'. But it doesn't quite come out of the blue, as its rhythmical affinity with the second movement demonstrates. It is a rhythm which is also Schumannesque, and marked by typical and fantastical alterations of speed.

Ex. 9

From the second movement

From the last movement

The recapitulation is suddenly enlivened by the *ff* semiquaver figure which spurted out of the *fugato* of the Quintet, now with the heavy brass lending an air of irascible impatience to a Cockaigne-like bombast. But now other music is coming home to roost. As the funereal shades gather in slower four-four time we hear, with the harmony on *ppp* strings and the top line reinforced by the solo *ff*:

Ex. 10

This dying fall and the characteristic rhythm of the previous example are intertwined as relief from ebullience in the last movement of the Quartet (see bars 4 and 5 after Fig. 44 which show the same key and the same falling bass as well).

So to the desperate paroxysm of farewell with its obsessive rhythm of two whole beats followed by two halves. The lonely alto voice at the end of *The Music Makers* had introduced the obsession in words whose pallid optimism did not ring true: 'You shall teach us . . . things that we dreamed not before'. In the final triple time of the Concerto the rhythm expresses a dying cry. The extraordinary ghost of Elgar Redivivus at Brinkwells becomes, as far as big music goes, 'a singer who sings no more'.

This essay is in part an elaboration of a lecture I gave to the Elgar Society in 1985. This included so many live illustrations, short and longer, as to make it impossibly expensive and laborious to reproduce for reading. I am the more deeply indebted to Diana McVeagh for the pains she took to send me a detailed résumé based on a tape of the lecture, without which this essay would have been a harder task, to say the least.

Notes

1. Kennedy, Michael (1968, 1982). *Portrait of Elgar.* London, O.U.P., p.276 in the second edition.
2. Kennedy, ibid., p.269.
3. See Atkins, Wulstan (1984). *The Elgar-Atkins Friendship.* Newton Abbot, David and Charles, p.295.
4. Tovey, D. F. (1936). *Essays in Musical Analysis*, vol.3: *Concertos.* London, O.U.P., p.201.

8 Elgar and the Irish Dramatists

Percy M. Young

I

As the twentieth century opened a new phase of political development commenced, with the ambitions of small European nations increasingly disturbing the assumed authority of greater powers. These greater powers themselves were by no means immune from the contagion of nationalism, and in 1901 Elgar's own sense of patriotism was stimulated by the accession of Edward VII. But as he prepared the *Pomp and Circumstance* Marches and the *Coronation Ode* – which together may seem to have represented the *ne plus ultra* of English self-satisfaction – he was innocently drawn into the affairs of Ireland, with his acceptance of an invitation from George Moore, Irish novelist and playwright, to contribute incidental music to a play.

This was the time of revival of the Gaelic language, which – under pressure from a politically motivated Gaelic League – had begun to make its way into the Irish school curriculum (in Gaelic-speaking districts), even if as a foreign language. The revival of the language was accompanied by rediscovery of Irish myth and legend and the establishment of Irish Literary Societies – in London as well as in Dublin. In 1897, when he was living in London, Moore was visited by Edward Martyn – wealthy landowner from Galway, barrister, man of letters, and neighbour of Moore in the Temple – and W. B. Yeats. Yeats, conspicuous for his vigorous efforts on behalf of Irish nationalism – both political and literary – at the time was also living in London.

> I waited for the servant to leave the room, and as soon as the door was closed they both broke forth, telling together that they had decided to found a Literary Theatre in Dublin . . . A forlorn thing it was surely to bring literary plays to Dublin! . . . Dublin of all cities in the world![1]

Martyn and Yeats were able to assure Moore of the support of Lady Isabella Augusta Gregory, a wealthy young widow with a keen interest in Irish folk

121

poetry and legend, whose home at Coole Castle, in Galway, was to become famous for its literary associations. In 1899 the existence of the Literary Theatre was marked by the production of two plays: Martyn's *The Heather Field* and Yeats's *The Countess Cathleen* – subtitled as 'A Miracle Play'. There being no professional company in Ireland their performance, in the Antient Concert Room in Dublin, was by a group of actors recruited in London. A second season followed with a programme comprising *The Bending of the Bough*, by Martyn, revised by Moore, Martyn's *Maeve*, and Alice M. Milligan's *The Last Feast of the Fianni*. At this point Yeats and Moore were persuaded into collaboration, jointly to provide a dramatized version of the legend of *Diarmuid and Grania*, which would be the principal event in a third season of Irish plays.

In a colourful passage in *Ave* Moore describes his journey from London to Coole, where he and Yeats would work together during the autumn of 1900. When coming through Galway Moore wondered how it must have been in the fourth century,

> when Grania fled from Tara with Diarmuid; that was her adventure; and mine was to write Ireland's greatest love-story in conjunction with Yeats . . . a wonderful act the third would be, the pursuit of the boar through the forest, the baying of Finn's great hounds – their names would appear beautiful in the text – Barn, Skealon, Lomaire . . .[2]

From the nearest station to Coole – at Gort – Moore arrived by bicycle at the lodge gates of the Castle. Here, he significantly ruminated,

> A horn[3] should hang on the gatepost, and the gate should not open till the visitor have blown forth a motif; but were this so Yeats would be kept a long time waiting, for he is not musical. It was pleasant to follow the long, blue drive for nearly a mile, through coarse fields, remembering the various hollows as they came into view, and the hillocks crowned by the hawthorns that AE [George Russell] painted last year.

Yeats and Moore 'spent many pleasant hours, quarrelling as to how the play should be written', until, her patience beginning to pale, their hostess disposed that Moore – better versed in the practicalities of theatre – should assume ultimate control.

For performance of the play recourse had again to be made to the English theatre, so that the first performance of *Diarmuid and Grania* was to be by Frank Benson's Shakespeare Company, based at Stratford-on-Avon. That music – of as Celtic character as could be supposed – should be a necessary ingredient of Irish drama was generally, enthusiastically and uncritically, accepted. The actress Florence Farr (friend of Bernard Shaw) had been inspired to compose gloomy, vaguely modal, quasi-recitative settings for Yeats's *The Countess Cathleen* (1892) and *The Land of Heart's desire* (1894).[4]

In the matter of music in the theatre Moore was less concerned with authenticity than with effectiveness. Having a strong recollection of Elgar's *Caractacus*, which he had heard at the Leeds Festival in 1898, he took advantage of being at Bayreuth in the company of Henry J. Wood, to ask Wood, whether he thought that Elgar would be interested in contributing some music to *Diarmuid and Grania*. He read some of the text to Wood, who promptly wrote to Elgar on 20 August,[5] suggesting that he, if interested, wrote directly to Moore. Two days later Moore, in acknowledging a letter from Elgar, indicated the kind of music he would need:

> ... I received your letter last night and was glad to hear from you. Henry Wood told me he had written to you about the drama I read to him at Bayreuth. I regret to say I know very little of your music – only a few pages but these are full of beauty and I should be pleased if my drama inspires you to write an opera ...

That Elgar should write an opera – preferably on an Irish subject – now began to show itself as an obsession.

> The best way perhaps would be for you to indicate to me the treatment you wished, for the merit of a libretto is measured by the music it inspires. These are however matters for later consideration. For the moment my concern is to get you to write me a few pages of music for the death of Diarmuid.

Continuing his letter, Moore became practical:

> I feel that I must have music for the end of the play and I cannot entertain the thought of casual music – a funeral march taken out of an opera and arranged to suit the occasion or a couple of Irish melodies arranged with harp accompaniment. My last act passes into a forest and horns are heard from time to time (hunting horns) and if I have the casual horns blowing whatever notes the local horn player thinks will do I shall lose all interest in the play ... A moment comes when words can go no further and then I should like music to take up the emotion and carry it on.[6]

Moore went on to propose that, as he was going to be in London in the near future and Elgar would also be there – for rehearsals for the Gloucester Festival – they should meet. Arrived in London he wrote from the Hotel Belgravia on 4 September:

> I shall come to your rehearsal tomorrow and when it is over I shall go to Brighton probably by the 4 or 4.40 train and I will ask Benson about the orchestra, the number of first violins etc., and will let you know on Friday. There is one horn call at the end of the second act, but I think you will agree with me that it should be the simplest, three or four notes. When you have read the third act you will be able to tell me about the music though not about the play for it really is necessary to read the first two acts of a three act play,

but if you are not too disappointed with the third act I feel sure you will like the other and if you do, it will give me much pleasure to do the versification for you. I think I can say that I like music sufficiently to know how to subordinate it to the music.[7]

The note in Alice Elgar's Diary about the rehearsal, on 5 September, of the newly written *Cockaigne* (a work as far away as imaginable from the prospective music for *Diarmuid and Grania*) was brief – and to the point – 'very splendid'.

Writing from his house in Dublin – 4 Upper Ely Place – on September 7, recalling the rehearsal, Moore suggests the difficulty – whether for performer or listener – of realizing the character of the new music of the new century:

> You stopped the orchestra so often that I did not receive an impression of the music as a whole, but I think I was able to appreciate the beauty of the writing and many passages seemed to me extremely novel and rich.[8]

An enclosed memorandum[9] reveals that the constitution of the Gaiety Theatre band could hardly have suggested contemplation of a major work. There being two first violins, one each of other strings, two horns, two percussionists (one drum, two Tympanum, and simbals [sic]), with oboe, bassoon, trombone, and celeste, its resources were fully stretched for the ordinary business of interval music.

However, if Elgar should require more resources (within reason) it would, no doubt, be possible to oblige him. Moore then goes off into a private investigation of the properties of the cornet – in the process getting confused as to the different significations of cornet in various parts of Europe:

> Until today I believed the cornet to be a non musical instrument that did not enter into a musicians' [sic] score unless the subject were a village dance in which case I can imagine Berlioz introducing the cornet for local colour, but today the manager of the Gaiety tells me that the cornet exists in Wagner, and in Gounod's scores. Is this so?

Anticipating that in the course of the next week Elgar should receive the text of the first two Acts, Moore hoped, 'you will want to use them as the basis of an opera text'. Benson would begin rehearsing the play in a few days' time, first in Liverpool and then in Birmingham, to one of which rehearsals Elgar might like to come if he could not be in Dublin for the first performance. Moore breaks the news that the Irish Literary Theatre would not be able to pay any fee for the use of the music. If, however, Benson's hope of a performance in Belfast were realized Benson might then be able to find some money for the composer. Beyond this was a possibility that Mrs Pat Campbell, now in management and on the lookout for new material, might take the play. Further testing his fund of optimism, Moore considered that there could be a good chance of acceptance of the play for a German production in an unspecified theatre. This, however, would be conditional on success in Dublin . . .

Sending the first two acts on 10 September, Moore suggested,

> if you decide to write the opera I think the best plan will be for you to reduce the text yourself in the f[ir]st instance for by so doing you will be in the position of one who had written his own libretto or nearly . . . I must see you soon about the opera. There is another legend I need to see you about. A furious correspondence has been going on in the press as to how the music should be written. Some of the letters are very funny. I'll show you a couple next week.[10]

The inspiration provided by Florence Farr in respect of the kind of music to be held evocatively appropriate in the context of Irish drama (as yet presented to the public through the medium of English) led the promoters of the Irish Literary Theatre to issue a prospectus, informing all and sundry that

> Mr. Edward Elgar. . .has arranged to write some incidental music for the third act [of *Diarmuid and Grania*], consisting mainly of horn-calls, and music of the immortals, to be introduced at the death of Diarmuid, and some symphonic music for the burial. Certainly the Wagnerian 'horn-calls' and 'music of the immortals' – because Dr. Elgar is a close follower of the Bayreuth Master – will sound strangely amid the primitive scenes of bygone centuries, and at once will conjure up the well-known painting, wherein King David is represented as playing before Saul on an iron grand piano.

It was what he considered the provinciality of Irish artistic and dramatic concepts (liable to be drawn, for political reasons, into a tightening Gaelic discipline) that caused Moore in due course to concern himself with Irish affairs from a distance. It was the fact that in his experience of Elgar's music he discerned in it – as well as an English sensibility – a realization of broader areas of European culture, which could enrich a national culture. So he was interested not only in what Elgar could do for *Diarmuid and Grania*, but what he might be encouraged to do one stage later. His determination that Elgar should compose an opera became the leitmotif of the whole sequence of his letters to Elgar over a decade.

Opera was produced on shoestring finances in Dublin in 1901, so that Elgar's orchestral requirements led to discussion between Elgar, Moore, and the Manager of the Gaiety Theatre. He, hearing that Elgar spoke of requiring more players than were immediately available, pointed out that as the Theatre was a small house, two first violins would be perfectly adequate. Elgar, he reminded Moore, did not know the acoustics of the house. In a postscript to his letter of 17 September, Moore commented:

Here Lohengrin is played with orchestra of 27. Perhaps the best way would be to write for the number of instruments mentioned in your letter, and I will do the best I can to get the extra instruments.

It seems that one 'extra' player was a horn player, for whom Moore was willing to pay himself. After all, he claimed, 'these performances will be a turning point in the artistic life in Dublin'. His enthusiasm, clearly stirred by Elgar, ran into his next busy letter, of 2 October:

Dear Dr. Elgar:

You seem to have been having a good time. I think I can see you with your head full of ideas and the pen running swiftly. I shall not be surprized to find that the music you have written is among your best music. It will be to your advantage to come to Dublin to see the play – I am thinking now of the opera which you are contemplating writing. The Benson Company are at present in Birmingham and they will be there till the 20th. May be I shall slip over next week to see a few rehearsals, and I might, if [there] is time, take you in on the way, either at Leeds or at Liverpool. Cross country journeys are difficult. The truth is I have an immense number of things to attend to just at present. Besides my own play I have to rehearse a play in Irish that Dr. Douglas Hyde has written. I do not know Irish and will have to rehearse it through the medium of translation. This is only one item. There is a great deal of organising to be done and I do not like to be away from Dublin longer than I can help. Moreover there is my own writing and I have promised some things which must be done within a certain time. It will be safer if you will send me the small score at your convenience, and if you will at the same time let me know if you will come to Dublin. Your presence will be of the greatest assistance and I beg of you to come *if you possibly can*. I can put you up here and Mr Hyland would be likely to get you the musicians you want. But if you cannot come to Dublin I will try to take you in on my way either to or coming from Birmingham. It will be a great treat to hear you play the music, but do let me know if you can come to Dublin as soon as you can find time to scribble a note; and do send me the small score for I shall not feel safe until I have the music.

Forgive my importunity, but my anxieties are many; there is an accumulation just at present and I am anxious to strike one off the list.

Very truly Yours,

George Moore

PS Your writing is very difficult to read and the postscript – something about it being easy to read I cannot make out.[11]

Moore was neither the first nor the last to complain of Elgar's writing. Moore's own, with all the signs of haste and many imperfections of punctuation is hardly better.

Dr Douglas Hyde (1860–1949), founder of the Gaelic League and author of a recently published *Literary History of Ireland,* intended his play, *Casadh an tSugain (The Twisting of the Rope)* – the forerunner of many Irish peasant plays – to be performed by members of the Gaelic League on the same bill as *Diarmuid and Grania.* This was a political gesture, bringing into the open an apparent difference between the ideas of Hyde, on the one hand, and of Yeats, Martyn, and Lady Gregory, on the other. For Hyde, the Gaelic – 'Irish' he called it – language was the foundation on which a mass movement urging national independence, should be established. For the others, while sympathetic to the cultural value of a language that had only barely survived in spoken form, the exposition of essentially Irish ideas and ideals to the wider world could only be expressed by means of English.[12]

With a performance of the *Enigma* coming up at Leeds and the first performance of the first two *Pomp and Circumstance* Marches, at Liverpool, to be followed within the month by further performances of the Marches in London and *Gerontius* in Manchester, Elgar also was well occupied. He gave no sign that he felt obliged to take note of Irish cultural-political matters.[13] The repeated note in Alice's Diary that he was 'very busy' with '*Diarmuid*' was an understatement. This work was occupying him on 28 and 30 September. On October 2 and 3 he was 'finishing' the score, which was sent to Dublin on 4 October.

Two days later Moore wrote that he had

> received the score but I cannot find words to thank you sufficiently. I have sent for a copyist – he is coming to see [us on Monday] and will [do] his work here. I never give out a [MS] for the parts to be copied until it has been copied here. I know my fear is groundless but the annoyance of having a Ms lost would be too great to be borne. I shall send the copy to Kinsore on Tuesday – I doubt if it can be copied in a single day; then the parts will be copied and I will send them to you for correction. I forgot to call your attention to the blare of trumpets that announces the arrival of Finn and feared you would overlook it[.] It was a pleasant surprise to find you had not. I am rehearsing the Gaelic play next day – five amateurs and the Irish language make an anxious time. The little play is very pretty; it will act about 25 minutes and will be a great success for – including the Chief Secretary [of Ireland] we are all interested in the language movement. My plans are to go to Birmingham next Thursday or Friday. Mrs. Elgar writes that you will be in Leeds till the 10th[,] then go to Liverpool – if you could come over here for the 21 – if you come over on Sunday you could rehearse the music on Monday. It would be better still if you come over on the Friday – you could rehearse the music on Saturday. (interlined addition) On second thoughts I see that that will not do – There <are> is a morning performance[s] on Saturday and you could not get the band[.] Again thanking you for the music and hoping you will be able to come to Dublin (Benson will not arrive till the 20th).[14]

On 10 October Moore while asking for a setting of a charming lyric by Yeats – prescribing the Florence Farr treatment – reported progress:

I enclose a letter from Benson and words for the song [words by Yeats, 'There are seven that pull the thread']. I feel it is a great shame to trouble you with them, my hope is that the trouble will be a slight one. The little song would probably be sung without an accompaniment, a mere little folk chant, and this you could probably arrange in an hour or so, at least I hope so. The copyist is still at work, he is very slow, but he will finish the score today. I fancy he is a fairly good musician, I know he sings at sight very well, and I know he has a good appreciation for your music for he has pointed out and sang several passages to me. He called my attention to a beautiful phrase written for the clarionet and he said quite simply: 'It is a most beautiful phrase, and I am sure upon the instrument will effect [sic] the hearer deliciously. I long to hear the music, and I am going over next week to see a rehearsal and shall try to meet you at Liverpool and you will play it for me. Moreover I want to persuade you to write the opera. My copyist is a genial dull little man, but he seems quite overcome by the beauty of the music. He sings in the Palestrina choir and composes a little himself, and I have no doubt has got a very excellent idea of your music from the manuscript.[15]

Although that letter was mistakenly sent to Elgar at the Grand Hotel in Leeds instead of to the Queens, it did, as Moore surmised, eventually catch up with him. In the meantime Elgar had received another letter supplementing its predecessor:

Benson wrote to say that he thought Laban (old woman of the play) shall sing a crooning song while Grania filled out the ale. The woman who plays Laban [Lucy Franklein] used to sing in opera so there will be no difficulty – the music will be a mere nothing. . . . In a letter I wrote yesterday . . . I told you how beautiful I thought the music. There is nothing more beautiful in Wagner; the frase [sic] on the clarionette brings tears to the eyes and the wailing march is overpoweringly beautiful. I enclose the words of Laban's song. Can you scribble some notes underneath the words, just a little chant, hardly above a monotone. But the way you will do this will be different from any one else's way and will give me such pleasure.[16]

The score and parts duly arrived at the Gaiety and the conductor invited Moore to the band room one day to hear a run-through of the Funeral March. Moore later recalled his first impressions:

When it was over, the conductor turned to me saying:

There's your march. What do you think of it?

It will have to be played better than that before I can tell, a remark the orchestra did not like, and for which I felt sorry but it is difficult to have the courage of one's convictions on the spot, and, while walking home, I thought of the many fine things that I might have said; that Elgar had drawn all the wail of the *caoine* into the languorous rhythm of his march, and that he had been able to do this because he had not thought for a single instant of the external forms of native music, but had allowed the sentiment of the scene to inspire him. Out of the harmony a little melody floats, pathetic as an autumn leaf, and it seemed to me that Elgar must have seen the primeval forest as he wrote, and the tribe moving among the falling leaves – oak-leaves, hazel-leaves, for the world began with oak and hazel.[17]

Overhanging that description is a sense of the woodland music in *Caractacus*, which Moore had remembered from Sheffield.

In response to a request from Jaeger that he should send a score of his 'Irish Play music' to Novellos, Elgar significantly responded, 'The irish play music I am having *copied* out for Wood as I may (silentium) utilise it for an opera later'.[18]

At the end of the first night of *Diarmuid and Grania*, according to the *Irish Times*, the audience, having called for the author was rewarded with an injunction by Yeats: they should join with him and Mr. Moore, he said, in supporting a movement to provide a true national theatre, instead of spending large sums in importing 'very vulgar plays' from England. This comment, in view of the performances of *King Lear* to take place later in the week when Elgar's Funeral March would be used as interval music, was somewhat surprising.

The play came in for severe criticism. James Joyce, a nineteen-year old student at University College wrote a savage essay, rejected by his College magazine, but published independently as 'The Day of the Rabblement',[19] of which the value was somewhat impaired by his unsuccessful submission of a play of his own to the Irish Literary Theatre. Some critics found *Diarmuid and Grania* too 'modern' in atmosphere, some ridiculed Benson's appearing in tartan trews to play the hero, others disapproved of the introduction of a live goat into the cast, while the public at large disliked discovering that Grania 'was not as perfectly virtuous as an Irishwoman should be'.[20]

On 23 October Moore expressed his feelings about the performance to Elgar:

> I did not write to you at once because I wished to tell you something a little less casual than the impression after a first performance. The piece went very well last night and I am quite satisfied how it has come out on the stage. I am therefore more anxious than ever before that you should write an opera on the subject. Whatever the merits of the piece may be one merit it certainly has it has inspired some of the loveliest music. Every time I hear the Dead March I hear something new in it. It is at once beautiful and cultured. It seems to me more like Schopenhauer than anything else. I am always comparing one thing with another, for without comparison I do not become clear to myself. If you can write the whole opera in the same inspiration I cannot but think that you will write an opera that will live. There are 10 operas by Wagner, one by Beethoven, one by Mozart, and one by Gluck, and I shall not be surprised if you were the fourteenth. The little song will probably be very popular, and you will make a good deal of money by it when you publish it, but it is the number that I care for least. Of course I knew it was written between posts and

it is a beautiful bit of writing, but I do not think it is a number you will leave if you write the opera.

Moore was obsessed with the *Diarmuid and Grania* music to the point of repetitiveness.

> I think you did me a great service by writing it, but I think you did yourself a service too, for I am sure that all your admirers will say that his [Diarmuid's] death march is among the most beautiful music that you have composed. I do not want to be effusive but I do not think anybody has composed more beautiful music! . . .[21]

A hostile review of the play in *The Fortnightly*, together with its rejection by the German friends whose opinions he had sought, shook Moore's faith in the subject. Moore indicated something of Elgar's feelings in his letter of 15 January 1902:

> There is something in what you say, about the death march – but the prehistoric air does not matter. You must be historic or prehistoric and I don't suppose you want to write historic drama. Wagner has not a monopoly of the prehistoric any more than the French Jews have of the historic.[22]

Elgar, writing to Alfred Littleton, began to take leave of Diarmuid and Grania, although, perhaps, a little reluctantly: 'I don't think the play will ever be heard again although it may be resuscitated as Moore talks of rewriting some of it'.[23]

In 1905 Moore published a highly original, Tourgeniev-inspired,[24] novel – *The Lake.* Distinguished by its psychological insights, and by the poetic quality of the writing, with reflections of Moore's early life in county Mayo and vivid memories of educational experiences in a Catholic seminary in England, this concerns the vocation of priesthood. Set within an Irish village community, *The Lake* centres on the conflicting urges and intentions in the mind of the priest – Father Oliver Gogarty, his love for the young schoolmistress – Nora Glynn, whom he had sent into exile, and the teeming life of a secret countryside. With its symbolism, the prose, from time to time, captures phrases that might well seem to have escaped from familiar Elgarian territory:

Father Gogarty, in one of his letters, writes to Nora Glynn:

> . . . You have been to Derrinrush: you know how mystic and melancholy the wood is, full of hazels and Druid stones. After wandering a long while I turned into a path. It led me to a rough western shore, and in front of me stood a great Scotch fir. The trunk has divided, and the two crowns showed against the leaden sky. It has two birch-trees on either side, and their graceful stems and faint foliage, pale like gold, made me think of dancers with sequins in their

hair and sleeves. There seemed to be nothing but silence in the wood, silence, and leaves ready to fall.[25]

Moore discovered patterns of music in *The Lake* for Lady Cunard, when he wrote to her from Fontainbleau in August 1905:

> There is some pretty landscape music in the book – it is my landscape book – and some of the landscape is a memory of the forest. 'The forest is like a harp', the breeze lifts the branches and a bird sings: a touch of art was added to the vague murmur I hear and the Siegfried music . . .[26]

By 1908 Moore felt a sense of exasperation as he saw Elgar's fame soaring far beyond the limits normally set for British composers. On 9 July he wondered whether Elgar had read *The Lake*, a copy of which he had sent to him with one of Lord Howard de Walden's *Lanval*.

On 14 July Moore, having received an apparently unenthusiastic letter from Elgar, took up the objections given and somewhat abruptly suggested that Elgar, in respect of the desired opera, should pull himself together – or 'you will go on to the end of your days without ever discovering a libretto . . . and English music will be the poorer'.[27] Two days later an apologetic letter followed, with a revised project, suggestive of ideas harboured at one time by Alice Elgar:

> What I really would like would be for you to write an opera on a noble subject, nobly developed, and not write one on a subject – let us say like 'Carmen' in which there are smugglers and soldiers, toreadors & card players & I do not know how many other things, all in scraps . . .[28]

A note of hope lingers in Moore's reply to an invitation to dine with the Elgars:

121 Ebury Street,
Thursday Dec 4 [1913]

Dear Elgar:

I got a letter this morning from Lady Elgar asking me to dinner tomorrow night. If we are alone it might be well for me not to dress. It seems that libretto can be talked about in a jacket, will you let me know.

Truly yours

George Moore[29]

By this time whatever thoughts Elgar might have had on a 'noble subject, nobly developed' had been subsumed into *Falstaff*, a work of which the first signs are in the Sketches which came into being during the initial phase of exhortation from Moore in 1902.

On 11 May 1914 the subject of *Diarmuid and Grania* was regretfully closed by Moore – going back once again to square one:

121 Ebury Street,
SW
May 11th 1914

Dear Elgar:

I am very much obliged to you for writing that the Grania music was going to be done at the Queen's Hall. I went to it, and my feeling during the whole time was that I had never heard more beautiful music – and you know that I have heard some very beautiful music. My feelings of pleasure, however, were dashed by ones of disappointment. After hearing the music last Sunday, I can no longer believe, if I ever believed it, that you were wise in refraining from writing an opera. I am sure you would have done better with Grania than you did with 'The Crown of India', and I believe you would have made more money. When I dined at your house you spoke to me about a world-wide subject. Well, if you do write an opera, I believe it will not be on a world-wide subject: in my opinion, a writer should begin with an obscure subject and make it world-wide. It is true that I am doing just the very contrary myself. I have returned from Palestine and I am writing the Fifth Gospel: but I am not responsible for the vagaries of human nature. Wagner, who was the least commonplace of men in his writing as well as in his music, could not have avoided commonplace if he had chosen Charles and Cromwell: it seems to me a subject as disastrous to the musician as to the writer. But Grania inspired you to write some of your very best pieces of music, and as I have said, one of the most beautiful that I ever heard: so it really seems unaccountable wilfulness on your part not to go on with it, unless indeed you feel that you are not an opera composer. Of course one cannot go into another man's soul. I am busy, as I say, at present, writing the Fifth Gospel but if you were going to write this opera, I would rewrite some parts of it, and you could get someone to versify it. I suppose Yeats would raise no objection, though he may be annoyed of my picture of him in 'Vale'.

Sincerely yours,

George Moore[30]

In 1901, while Elgar was constructing a Gaelic persona, his friend Ivor Atkins was exerting his own influence in Dublin, as one of the adjudicators for the Feis Ceoil – a large-scale competitive festival, patronized by the Dublin establishment. It was after the performance of the 'New World' Symphony in Dublin in 1901 that a decision was taken, by offering a Prize for an 'Irish Symphony' (such works by Stanford and Sullivan already existed!), to provide a Hibernian challenge to Dvořák. At the Feis Ceoil of 1902 – Atkins was again adjudicating – the prize-winning work was declared to be Signor Michele Esposito's 'Irish' Symphony,

1   *Top*: Elgar at Fair View, 1898; *bottom*: George Moore by Henry Tonks, 1901

Gaiety Theatre, Dublin.

Lessees
Manager
Telegrams—"GAIETY, DUBLIN."
Telephone, 592.

MICHAEL GUNN, Ltd
Mr. C. HYLAND

PROGRAMME .... ONE PENNY

FOR FIVE NIGHTS AND
MATINEES—

WEDNESDAY, AT 2.30 P.M. - - DIARMID AND GRANIA
SATURDAY, AT 2.30 P.M. - - - KING LEAR

THIS (TUESDAY), and WEDNESDAY EVENINGS, OCTOBER 22nd
and 23rd, 1901, at 8,
BY REQUEST OF THE IRISH LITERARY THEATRE,

MR. F. R. BENSON

WILL PRODUCE

A New and Romantic Play in Three Acts, entitled :

DIARMID AND GRANIA.

By GEORGE MOORE AND W. B. YEATS.

King Cormac	the High King		Mr. ALFRED BRYDONE
Finn MacCoole, the Chief of the Fianna			Mr. FRANK RODNEY
Diarmid			Mr. F. R. BENSON
Goll	his Chief		Mr. CHARLES BIBBY
Usheen	Men		Mr. HENRY AINLEY
Caoelte			Mr. E. HARCOURT WILLIAMS
Fergus			Mr. G. WALLACE JOHNSTONE
Fathna	Spearmen		Mr. WALTER HAMPDEN
Griffan			Mr. STUART EDGAR
Niall	a Head Servant		Mr. MATHESON LANG
Conan the Bald	one of the Fianna		Mr. ARTHUR WHITBY
An Old Man			Mr. H. O. NICHOLSON
A Shepherd			Mr. OWEN
A Boy			Miss ELLA TARRANT
A Young Man			Miss JEAN MACKINLAY
Grania	the King's Daughter		Mrs. F. R. BENSON
Laban	an old Druidess		Miss LUCY FRANKLEIN
	Serving Men, Troops of the Fianna, &c.		

Act 1		THE BANQUETING HALL IN TARA
Act 2		DIARMID'S HOUSE
Act 3		THE WOODED SLOPES OF BEN BULBEN

Special Music Written by Dr. EDWARD ELGAR.

Acting Manager			Mr. A. SMYTH-PIGOTT
Stage Manager	For		Mr. LEONARD BUTTRESS
Assistant Stage Manager	Mr. F. R. BENSON.		Mr. EDWARD BROADLEY
Advance Representative			Mr. JAMES FOX

To be Followed on Monday, Tuesday, and Wednesday Evenings by

'THE TWISTING OF THE ROPE.'

By DOUGLAS HYDE, LL.D.
Cast filled by Members of the Gaelic Amateur Dramatic Society.

Thursday, Friday, and Saturday, and Saturday Matinee - **KING LEAR.**

ORCHESTRA.

Overture ...			Shakesperian		*Jules Guilton*
Selection ...			The Lily of Killarney		*Arr. by G. R. Chapman*
Excerpt ...			Songs without Words		*Mendelssohn*
Funeral March			Diarmid and Grania		*Dr. E. Elgar*

BOX OFFICES at Messrs. Cramer, Wood & Co., 4 & 5 Westmoreland-street, open from 10 a.m. to 5.30 p.m. Saturdays, from 10 a.m. to 2 p.m. Also at Shelbourne Hotel, and in the evenings at Theatre, from 5.45 p.m. to 9 p.m. Saturdays, from 2.15 p.m. to 9 p.m. All Letters and Telegrams to Box Office, Cramer's, 4 and 5 Westmoreland-street.

PRICES—Balcony Stalls (Dress), **5s.** Balcony (bonnets allowed), **4s.** Pit Stalls **3s** Upper Circle, **2s.** ; Pit, **1s.**; Gallery, **6d.** Private Boxes, **20s., 30s.,** and **40s.** Children under twelve years of age half-price to Balcony Stalls, Balcony and Upper Circle. **Early Doors** to Upper Circle, Pit and Gallery, **6d.** Extra—Open at 7 o'clock. Matinee at 1.30 o'clock. **ORDINARY DOORS**—Evening at 7.30. Commence at **8.** Matinee at **2.** Commence at 2.30.

MONDAY NEXT—
THE LATEST LONDON SUCCESS,

THE WEDDING GUEST

By J. M. BARRIE, Author of "The Little Minister," &c.
From the GARRICK THEATRE, LONDON.

This Theatre is Disinfected with "Jeye's" Sanitary Compounds.

QUIRK, PRINTER, WICKLOW STREET, DUBLIN

2 Playbill for *Diarmid and Grania*, 1901

3   Elgar by William Strang, 1911

4   Alice Stuart Wortley by her father, Sir John Millais, 1887

5   R. A. Streatfeild in 1913

6   Photograph of Elgar by E. O. Hoppé, c. 1915

7 Two studies of Elgar at Severn House, Hampstead, 1919

8 *Top*: Elgar as seen by Hugh Deane, c. 1927; *bottom*: Laurence Binyon by William Strang, 1901

a masterly work of very great power and beauty. Of the four movements the Scherzo, a most inspiring jig, is, at first hearing, the most attractive. The Symphony was received with great enthusiasm by a large audience.[31]

Elgar's 'Irish' music had been addressed to the wrong audience.

II

It was under the management of Harley Granville Barker and J. E. Verdrenne in the early years of the century that Bernard Shaw became a household name. On 16 September 1907 a season of Shaw plays under this management opened at the Savoy Theatre with a new production of *You never can tell*. For this production the sets were designed by Arthur Troyte Griffith, whose diversity of artistic talent has generally remained hidden behind his transmutation into a Variation. Concerning Troyte's association with this Shaw production his sister wrote:

Yes – I remember when 'The Devil's Disciple' was produced in London he told us to go & see it, & to notice the hero, whose part was taken by a rather short man, when he had to get a match-box off the mantelpiece, as he (Troyte) had made it much too high! being himself over 6 ft. He did know Shaw & used to go long walks with him arguing on all kinds of subjects.[32]

Barker commended Troyte in this manner:

Words fail me to express my admiration of you. I have never had so much trouble taken off my hands before. I'll write to you on Monday or Tuesday about Act III Scene 3.

Elgar, having been advised by Troyte to see the play duly did so on 19 September, with Julia Worthington as his companion. Meanwhile Barker was dealing with Troyte's detailed drawings for the next production, of Shaw's 'Diabolonian' play, *The Devil's Disciple*. This opened on 14 October and on 2 November Elgar went to see it with Alice, who reported in her diary: 'To B. Shaw's play with Troyte's scenery. Very nice. Play unconvincing'. Nor did Elgar think much of the play. His conversion to Shaw, the dramatist, was yet to come.

In the following month, in a letter to Colonel Mapleson, Shaw replied to a suggestion that he should write a libretto for an opera for Saint-Saëns:

10 Adelphi-terrace,
London W.C.
December 4,1907

My dear Colonel Mapleson:

Unfortunately I have a prior engagement with Richard Strauss, which is at present rather hung up by the fact that I want to write the music and he wants to write the libretto, and we both get on very slowly for want of practice.

I wonder whether Elgar would turn his hand to opera?

I have always played a little with the idea of writing a libretto, but though I have had several offers nothing has come of it.

When one is past fifty and is several years in arrear with one's own natural work, the chance of beginning a new job are rather slender.

Yours faithfully,

G. Bernard Shaw[33]

It was some years before Shaw thought again of the possibility that Elgar might write an opera. Before that happened Elgar's interest in the theatre was stimulated by a significant development in the career of Granville Barker. It was his production of *The Winter's Tale* at the Savoy Theatre, in 1912, that was appreciated by those weary of the false heroics of conventional Shakespeare production as the real beginning of modern theatre. Inevitably there were those who considered Barker's interpretation as heretical, but – amid the discord of opposing criticism – Elgar came down firmly on Barker's side in a letter both perceptive and generous:

Severn House
42 Netherhall Gardens,
Hampstead N.W.

Oct. 22 1912

My dear Barker:

We went to 'A Winter's Tale' with great hopes & remained to obtain great joy – I congratulate you most sincerely on a *splendid* production. I will not write at length as I hope I may see you soon I should dearly like to talk of it to you. I hope you are happy over it *yourself* – a lot of preposterous nonsense has been written but that won't affect you I trust. I always have in mind the sentence of Coleridge 'The true *stage-illusion* (in this & in all other things) consists – that in the mind judging it to be a forest, but, in its remission of   the judgment that it is not a forest'. All the modern writers get no farther than this & do not understand how to express it: you have in 'A Winter's Tale'   got just the right amount of 'illusion' & barring a few such things, the whole 'play' – acting, scenery & (on this occasion) music were to me *one* & near perfection.

> All good wishes &
>   kindest regards
>
>   Very sincerely
>
>   Edward Elgar[34]

It is not beyond possibility that this event affected the direction of Elgar's reading, for during the next year he gave much thought to Shakespeare. From spring to autumn in 1913 he was, on and off, dedicated to his interpretation of Falstaff, which came out as near an opera as a symphonic poem could be. On 7 April Alice's diary carries a sad and revealing note. A Mrs. Crawshay had 'talked of Nobel prize', to which was added, 'Pray it may be given to E.'

At that time the Elgars were much given to theatre-going. On several occasions they went together to see the current box-office winner, G. C. Hazelton's *The Yellow Jacket*. On 21 June Alice and Carice went to see an 'Irish play'. Remarkably it was John Millington Synge's *Riders to the Sea*. It is a pity, perhaps, that Elgar did not see this play, and that George Moore did not draw attention to its music-dramatic possibilities. The career of the opera composer was much in Elgar's mind at the time, for on 14 June he went to see a film. The subject was the life of Richard Wagner, which, according to the Diary, he found 'very harrowing, creditors interrupting composition etc. Splendid how possessed he was with his work & no opposition stopped him'. (How different it was for an English composer.) Later in the year Elgar went to performances of *Boris Godunov* and Pélléas and Mélisande, and on Boxing Day the whole family returned to Bernard Shaw, to a performance of *The Doctor's Dilemma*.

Towards the end of his life Elgar's interest in drama was stimulated by Barry Jackson, one of the most innovative of theatre directors of his time. It was through Jackson's enterprise in making Shaw the centre of the first Malvern Festival – with a place of honour reserved for Elgar – that Elgar's relationship with Shaw came to a climax of mutual understanding. Each, it seems, came to see in the other an image of what he himself might wish to have been.

On the Saturday before the English premiere of *The Apple Cart*, on 19 September, at Shaw's request, Elgar was asked to open an Exhibition devoted to Shaw's career in the Malvern Public Library. Elgar's speech was faithfully recorded in *Berrow's Journal*. Well-prepared for the occasion – perhaps, too well-prepared – this speech carried behind its fluent phrases ideas and quotations that had been aired before. Here and there, echoes of ancient misgivings and prejudices could be heard.

Sir Edward said that he had been asked to declare the exhibition open. Having said that much, it was absolutely unnecessary for him to say anything more [Laughter]. He was glad they approved – [Laughter] – but he felt constrained rather to embroider that, because although it was one of the greatest honours he ever had, to introduce anything of his friend Shaw, he had some doubt – as people always had, he believed – as to his fitness for the post, and he was very well assured that he was not better fitted than any other. It was usual to ask a lot of silly rhetorical questions, such as 'Why am I here?'

He recognized in the invitation an example of the boldness of Sir Barry Jackson, for on an occasion like that they ought to have asked a practised speaker, some one who could really bring before them the glorious career of Bernard Shaw. That he could not do. As he had said, it was a bold thing, but the man that found that Shakespeare flagged a little in their minds and put him in modern dress, could do anything [Laughter]. If, after the next fortnight, they flagged ever so little, Sir Barry might give them one of Shaw's plays, 'Heartbreak House', in classical costume. He thought their author, judging from some photographs which escaped the censor last summer, when he was in an extremely abbreviated costume, might be able to take a part himself and give another performance of 'Arms and the Man' [Laughter].

Sir Edward went on to say that in opening the exhibition, he could claim one qualification. He was a great theatre-goer, and he knew the works of their friend, Bernard Shaw, from beginning to end. He held what he believed was a sort of record. It was the fashion nowaday, in the lesser Press, to go in for records. He thought he was the only person who had been to twenty-nine theatrical entertainments in one month, and he would add for the benefit of actors, actor managers, and producers, that he had paid for his seats [Laughter]. He might also say that the adventure owed him something, because some of the performances were so bad that he did not sit out the second act [Laughter]. He would not specify which these plays were.

Malvern people were fortunate in having Sir Barry Jackson among them [applause] – and in having the new Theatre which stood on ground where, in ancient times, he [Sir Edward] piloted many a fair musical performance to rocky disaster [Renewed laughter]. Malvern ought to be proud of the new Theatre as it was of having Mr. Shaw – the two went together. They could not have had Mr. Shaw without the Theatre and the Theatre brought Mr. Shaw to them. He left them to decide who was to be congratulated most. 'At any rate we congratulate ourselves', continued Sir Edward, 'I am speaking as though I lived here still. We congratulate ourselves on having a Temple of Art which really is a credit to any town. [Hear, hear] As our Chairman has said, the Theatre has justified itself by your being able to have a Festival here – a unique Festival in the annals of the Theatre, which pays tribute to a unique person.

Sir Edward said that was not the time or place for him to give a history of Shaw plays. He believed that many interesting mementoes of early days were in that room, memories stretching back to the first plays, through some trials and some troubles, to those triumphs which led them to the recognition Mr. Shaw deservedly had today. The wonder of the series of plays he would not dilate on. One masterpiece after another had been rather shattering to the nerves of some of them. He had sometimes thought that Shaw had thrown a play at them, the British public, in the spirit in which Sterne gave the ass a macaroon. They would remember that Sterne questioned himself afterwards whether he gave the macaroon to the ass from any good motive, whether it was intended as food, or whether he wanted to know from curiosity how the British public, he meant the ass [Laughter], would eat a macaroon. Sometimes he [Sir Edward] had a suspicion that Shaw was giving the public a macaroon, and wondering what the dickens it was going to do with it [Laughter]. This was a thorny – it might be a thistley – subject.

The British public was now entirely alive to what it owed to Shaw, and they were looking forward with an interest, not to be measured by newspaper paragraphs, to the productions of this latest play, 'The Apple Cart'. Many hypotheses had been ventured as to what it was all about; at present it was a mystery. Some local agriculturalists found satisfaction in the choice of the title [Laughter]. For a play produced in a cider country nothing could be better [Renewed laughter]. They were anticipating a very cheap and good advertisement from the production. He feared, however, that the acid in the play was more Shavian than salic [Laughter]. So much would be said and written on the dramatic side of Bernard Shaw in the next week that he would not trouble them with his feelings and criticisms, but there was one side of the great man on which he could speak with some certainty. English literary men had rarely been musical. When they had been, they had been treated with a little contempt by men who were not musical. Gray, the poet, was one of the greatest musical amateurs of his time, but was never treated seriously, and kept his music out of sight as much as possible.

Having referred to De Quincey and Disraeli as literary men who knew a great deal about music, Sir Edward said, 'Bernard Shaw knows a lot more about music than I do [Laughter]. We won't grumble at that [Laughter]. He was a musical [*sic*] critic, and a good one, in those dull days when the two universities and the Colleges of Music used to do nothing but sit around and accuse one another of the cardinal virtues [Laughter]. I am going to quote Swift. Shaw "drenched a desperate quill". That's good! [Laughter] He wrote for our enlightenment much in favour of what I call elastic and natural music, to the destruction of the pedant, and his knowledge and feeling for music is beyond that of most professional musicians. Among the records shown here I hope there is a manuscript of one of his early criticisms'.

Sir Edward went on to say that that exhibition resulted from a suggestion by Mr. Lucas, the Librarian, and he congratulated him. [Applause] It was a very happy idea, but many of the things, the choice, and, he believed, were due to that gracious and lovable personality, Mrs. Shaw. [Applause] What they owed to that lady in artistic things and help, he would not go into now, but he thanked her, and was sure they did, for all she had done to make that exhibition what it was. [Applause] Its effect and influence should be stimulating and uplifting, and he once more congratulated Malvern on having been chosen as the place for the festival, and if the example was followed by other towns in England, so much the better. He had left to the last Shaw as his friend. Of course, in public life, and having decided opinions one way and another, some people thought his friend a little angular at times, and a little fierce. Nothing could be further from the truth. Shaw was the most amiable of men. He was the best friend a man could have, the best friend to young artists, the kindest and possibly the dearest fellow on earth. [Applause] Sir Edward then declared the exhibition open.

From Shaw there was this tribute to Elgar:

. . . as a matter of fact Sir Edward is one of the greatest composers of the world. If you make the utmost allowance for the very greatest of his contemporaries you must say that he is one of the four best composers in the world. If you asked me to name the other three I could name one or two pretty quickly, but when I came to the third I should be very much puzzled.

That is something for England to be proud of. But I do not think England is proud; that is the disgraceful thing about it . . . I am seriously and genuinely humble in his presence. I recognise a greater art than mine and a greater man than I can ever hope to be.

Seconding this vote of thanks the senior member of the Library Committee maintained the elevated character of the occasion by observing of the two previous speakers that 'it was quite certain that one would go down to posterity as the Shakespeare and the other as the Handel of our generation'.

The September issue of *The Musical Times* somewhat tartly observed of Shaw's comments:

. . . It deserves to be placed on record also as being apparently the only public utterance in which Mr. Shaw has acknowledged himself to be second to any creative artist, living or dead.

Notes

Letters in the Hereford and Worcester Record Office = HWRO
1. George Moore (1911). *Ave*, p.44
2. ibid., pp.342–3, and Moore (1957). *Letters to Lady Cunard, 1895–1933*, ed. Rupert Hart-Davis. London, p.31 ff.
3. As will be apparent from his correspondence with Elgar, Moore had an obsession with horns; cf. *Ave*, p.197, concerning performances of *The Ring* in the early 1890s he noted, 'It was the horns announcing the Rhine that reawakened my musical conscience'.
4. See Liam Miller (1977). *The Noble Drama of W. B. Yeats*. Dublin, p.37, and for 'The Fool's Song', p.118; Florence Farr's *The Music of Speech* was published in 1909.
5. HWRO 705:445:2263.
6. HWRO 705:445:2266. Elgar's early experience in respect of Irish folk music consisted of nine bars (in his Sketch Book 5) of a 'Fantasia on Irish Airs', for Violin and Piano, based on T. Moore's version of 'The pretty girl milking her cow'. (*Irish Melodies*, ed. M. W. Balfe (1859), p.127)
7. HWRO 705:445:2322; see *Salve*, p.101 – 'Elgar sent six horn-calls to choose from, and, in my letter thanking him for his courtesy, I told him of the scene in the third act, when Diarmuid, mortally wounded by the boar, asks Finn to fetch water from the spring. Finn brings it in his helmet, but, seeing that Grania and

Finn stand looking at each other, Diarmuid refuses to drink. This, and the scene which follows, the making of the litter on which the body of Diarmuid is borne away to the funeral pyre, seem to me to crave a musical setting. It is a pity to leave such a scene unrealized; and how impressive a death-march would come after Grania's description of the burning of Diarmuid.

8. HWRO:445:2259

9. HWRO:445:2325

10. HWRO:445:2260

11. HWRO:445:2329. Moore may have in the first place have expected a piano score; however, a full score came almost immediately.

12. A useful discussion of Douglas Hyde's activities and intentions is given in Conor Cruise O'Brien's review of J. E. and G. W. Dunleavy's 'Douglas Hyde; A maker of modern Ireland', *Times Literary Supplement*, 21 June 1991, p.9.

13. Elgar was persuaded to take a position on an Irish political situation in 1914, when he became a signatory of the 'solemn Declaration' against Home Rule.

14. HWRO:445:2261, the last part of this letter was confusingly modified.

15. HWRO:445:2265, see *Salve*, p.77, the copyist, 'a tenor from a cathedral choir', is unflatteringly described: 'H smelt like a corpse, but no matter, a score is a score, and Benson had to receive a copy of it within the next fortnight. The conductor at the Gaiety wanted to copy the parts, so that he could learn the music'.

16. HWRO:445:2328

17. see *Salve*, pp.77-78.

18. The Funeral March was played at a Queen's Hall concert on 18 January 1902. Appropriately it was conducted by Henry Wood.

19. Published in *Two Essays*, with F. J. C. Skeffington's 'A Forgotten Aspect of the University Question', by Gerrard Brothers.

20. See Joseph Hone (1936), *The Life of George Moore*. London, p.239.

21. HWRO:445:2331

22. HWRO:445:2258

23. *Elgar and his Publishers*, ed. J.N. Moore (1987). Oxford, p.342

24. *The Lake* was conceived as one of a series of stories – inspired by Tourgeniev's example – to be published together as *The Untilled Field*. It was finally published separately.

25. *The Lake*, 1921 ed., p.154.

26. *Letters to Lady Cunard*, p.45.

27. HWRO:445:2272

28. HWRO:445:2271

29. HWRO:445:2338

30. Broadheath, Birthplace, item 737.

31. *The Musical Times*, Vol.43, 1902, p.405.

32. Letter from Miss Lillian Griffith, 15 February 1955.

33. *St James's Gazette*, cutting in Broadheath Birthplace file.

34. B. L. Add. MS. 47897, f.90, an isolated letter in a collection.

9 Elgar, Streatfeild and *The Pilgrim's Progress*

Christopher Grogan

The idea of composing an opera recurs throughout Elgar's career from about 1897. His own enthusiasm for such a project was genuine enough, if sporadic; in 1909, whilst on holiday at Careggi, he went so far as to commence a new sketchbook with the title 'Book of Opera in 3 Acts',[1] but of this, and several similar schemes, nothing became until, in his last years, the composer embarked earnestly upon an adaptation of Jonson's *The Devil is an Ass*, to be called *The Spanish Lady*. Prior to this, he professed himself unable to discover a plot of sufficient interest and originality to fire him, but he remained always open to suggestions, and these were forthcoming both from such eminent sources as George Moore, W. S. Gilbert, Laurence Housman and Laurence Binyon, and from a host of less gifted opportunists who sent him scripts through the post and even, on one occasion, journeyed from America to Italy to hunt him down. 'E. dragged out to see him', wrote Lady Elgar of this encounter with one Mr Welch,[2] and one can imagine with what reluctance he went. Most of these literary offerings have since disappeared – many, indeed, perhaps never progressed beyond the planning stage – but one at least survives complete and this, while having been considered only briefly by Elgar, retains some significance both in its unconventional purpose and design, and in its subject, *The Pilgrim's Progress*, anticipating by nearly forty years the production of an equally unconventional, but thoroughly characteristic, stage work by that pioneer of modern English opera, Ralph Vaughan Williams.

The adaptation of Bunyan's allegory was the work of R. A. Streatfeild, from 1898 until his death in 1919 an Assistant Keeper in the Department of Printed Books of the British Museum. The friend and literary executor of Samuel Butler, whose *The Way of All Flesh* and other posthumous works he prepared for publication, he edited works by Darley and Smart and translated Ibsen's lyrical poems. His interests extended also to music, in which capacity he served as critic for *The Daily Graphic* from 1898 until 1902, and wrote enduring studies of Handel and of opera.[3] In order therefore to gain some insight into *The Pilgrim's Progress* and the impetus behind its creation, it may be helpful first to say something about his thoughts on the latter subject, and on English opera in particular.

I

At the heart of Streatfeild's writings lies his strong advocacy of modern English music, and especially of the need of the national art to free itself from foreign influence and establish its own identity. His fervour derived in part from bitter experience; in the introduction to a collection of his articles published in Paris in 1913[4] (itself a testament to his crusading zeal), he remembered how in 1889, when Hans Richter included in a concert otherwise devoted to Wagner a symphony by Parry, 'l'auditoire', at the beginning of the English work, 'se leva avec affectation et quitta la salle du concert', leaving only 'un petit nombre de vaillants partisans de la musique nationale' to represent the national interest. After this experience, Streatfeild laboured to achieve for indigenous music the same respect that English audiences seemed happy to accord to its European counterparts.

He longed also for a truly national school of operatic composition and performance, frequently discussing ideas and movements from the past history of the genre in other countries in terms of their potential suitability for emulation by his own. Undoubtedly, he found his ideals most perfectly realised in the work of Weber, and he took the opportunity to compare the situation inherited by that composer in the Italian-dominated operatic scene of early nineteenth-century Germany with that of English opera in his own time:

> those who at this moment are struggling to place the latter upon a footing worthy of the greatest nation in the world may read with interest and profit the address to the amateurs of Dresden which Weber published in one of the most widely-read newspapers . . . 'The Italians and French have made respectively for themselves a distinct class of opera, in the form that gives the genius of each nation free play. The Germans, however, strenuous in the pursuit of knowledge, and ever ardent in progress, try to appropriate for themselves whatever they admire in others' . . . Had Weber never written *Der Freischütz* he would still have done more than any man of his time to establish German opera upon an abiding basis. But it was in *Der Freischütz* that his fight for recognition of home-grown opera found its crowning triumph.[5]

The appeal to Weber's achievement was apt, for as Streatfeild pointed out, without his lead there might have been no Wagner, the acclaim accorded to *Der Freischütz* in London in the 1830s having helped to initiate the popular growth of German opera in England which culminated in the capital's great Wagner productions of the 1880s.[6]

In Streatfeild's view, Weber had founded German opera by 'turning to the melodies of his native land', and he argued that if England was to emulate his success, it had to 'begin by building upon a similar foundation'.[7] A whole generation of young musicians who would wholeheartedly have endorsed this prescription was coming to prominence even as he wrote; but at the turn of the century, the English music he heard remained so intent on 'appropriating for itself what it found admirable in others' that it could make no original contribution of its own. Streatfeild's survey of British composition immediately prior to the rise of Elgar constitutes a true catalogue of faint praise:

> We had, it is true, composers whom we ourselves honoured, whose music we loved and admired: Parry, whose great choral works are animated by the mighty breath of Handel and Mendelssohn; Stanford, who gave us symphonies, quartets and cantatas uniting the gentle melancholy of his native Ireland to the form bequeathed by Schumann and Brahms: Sullivan, whose operettas had been the delight of London for more than twenty years. But it was no longer possible to conceal from ourselves the fact that our music had not a cosmopolitan character. We might amuse ourselves as we chose among our insular fogs, but we could not pretend to form a part of the great international confraternity of art.[8]

If he thus diagnosed a chief obstacle to the resurgence of British music, however, he also discerned a slight clearing of the 'insular fogs' in some of its operatic productions. It was ambition to succeed in terms of contemporary German music-drama that was stifling native talent, and Streatfeild reserved his admiration on the whole for less ambitious efforts such as Stanford's *Shamus O'Brien*, which he commended both for its 'typically Irish subject' and for its status as a 'genuine comic opera, the dialogue being interspersed with music'.[9] In Stanford's apparent retreat from the challenge of modern music-drama to a *Singspiel* of the *Der Freischütz* type, he perceived a genuine advance for a country still in its operatic infancy. After all, did not Wagner himself 'recommend a budding bard to start his musical career with a *Singspiel?'.*[10] The way forward – at least in the short term – lay with the lighter forms of opera, and it was in the works of Gilbert and Sullivan that Streatfeild discovered, not surprisingly, the most promising foundation for his 'ardently desired' national opera. Unlike most of his compatriots, Sullivan

> owed very little to anyone. His genius was thoroughly his own and thoroughly English, and in that lies his real value to posterity. For if we are ever to have a national English opera, we shall get it by writing English music, not by producing elaborate exercises in the manner of Wagner, Verdi, Massenet, Strauss or anybody else. Most great artistic enterprises spring from humble sources, and our young lions need not be ashamed of producing a mere comic opera or two before attacking a full-fledged music-drama.[11]

Streatfeild had little doubt that, should a greater man than Sullivan – but one equally untrammelled by foreign influence – emerge from this company of young lions, English opera might indeed rise again from the ashes.

He saw more behind the malaise of the genre in England than the pursuit of continental modes of expression, however. As a literary scholar, he took a keen interest in libretti [12] (his textual observations, indeed, being frequently more astute and rewarding than his musical criticism), and it was to the poor quality of these that he attributed in great part the low achievement of English opera in the late nineteenth century. Frequently he bewailed the failure of a promising work through a text which was 'thoroughly dull', weighed down with 'unmitigated gloom', or simply 'balderdash'. Neither were these criticisms unreasoningly negative; his own views regarding the role of the libretto and the relationship between music and drama were clear and considered, but to get some idea of these, it is necessary to step beyond his discussion of the parlous state of native opera to consider his thoughts on the greater productions of the continent.

Streatfeild's basic thesis was that pure drama and opera were incompatible, because the essence of opera was lyrical and hence undramatic. Closely interlinked was a critical standard setting inspiration above technique, probably derived from his mentor Samuel Butler's notions of 'gnosis' and 'agape'.[13] With Butler he shared also his love of Handel, and using that composer as his model, he argued:

> Handel's view of opera differed completely from that of our times. He treated it lyrically, not dramatically, and who shall say that he was wrong? In our time opera has tended more and more to approach the confines of drama. Disregarding the one immutable convention by which opera exists as an art form – the substitution of song for speech – we aim at a bastard realism, striving to bring the song of opera as near as possible to the spoken accents of drama. Nothing can make opera realistic, it is conventional in essence; the less lyrical and the more dramatic it is, the less has it a reason for a separate existence.[14]

The whole history of the genre he viewed as a conflict between the opposing forces of the lyrical and the dramatic, and in the lives of Gluck and Wagner he saw the struggle personified; each had pursued the cause of dramatic truth in his theoretical writings, but had produced his greatest music when he abandoned, or at least compromised, these theories to the demands of lyrical expression. Wagner's attempts to weld 'drama and opera into one harmonious whole' were 'doomed from the outset by the simple fact that the two are perfectly distinct art-forms, each with its own peculiar set of conventions';[15] for this reason his most enduring achievement was *Tristan and Isolde*, which Streatfeild considered one of the most perfect conceivable examples of what an opera should be, since it is almost devoid of incident and deals entirely with emotion. This is the true province of music, which strictly speaking has nothing to do with incident. It cannot heighten the dramatic effect of a 'situation'; it is merely a drag upon action, whereas its power of expressing emotion is unlimited.[16]

But even *Tristan* suffered from Wagner's pursuit of realism, through his 'wilful avoidance of the possibilities of choral effect',[17] the chorus being for Streatfeild one of the conventions upon which the validity of opera as a distinct art-form was founded.

It was in the late works of Verdi that Streatfeild found the closest approximation in late nineteenth-century opera to his ideal balance between the dramatic and the lyrical. Although he considered the subject of *Otello* not entirely suitable, having 'too much action and not enough pure emotion', he relished the manner by which this obstacle had been overcome, with musician and librettist combining to 'hasten over the merely dramatic passages and linger upon scenes in which speech under stress of feeling rises naturally into song . . . Thus the purely lyrical passages and the scenes of emotion which lend themselves to legitimate development are given their proper value in the general scheme, instead of being drowned . . . in one vast ocean of symphonic harmony.'[18]

II

Considering such views alongside his trenchant criticisms of English opera plots and his own literary aspirations, it is scarcely surprising that Streatfeild should eventually have been drawn into attempting some practical expression of his ideas. In this, as in all his musical activities, he would have been encouraged by William Barclay Squire, then in charge of the printed music collections of the British Museum. Whilst still a Cambridge undergraduate, Squire had provided Stanford with his first libretto, an 'admirable condensation', as Streatfeild was later to describe it, of Moore's *The Veiled Prophet*.[19] For his own subject Streatfeild turned to a very different source, but his choice of *The Pilgrim's Progress* accorded well with his stated priorities for the revival of national opera. In both its derivation from the popular tradition and its established status as a folk-epic, the allegory is English to the core; yet it has also exerted a more general influence by virtue of its universally applicable spiritual message.[20] Moreover, in its incorporation of supernatural folklore and elements of nature, it has much in common with such manifestations of German Romanticism as Streatfeild found most appealing in *Der Freischütz*. He dubbed Weber the 'inventor of local colour in music',[21] and would have been equally quick to appreciate what has been termed the 'mixture of realism and romance'[22] in Bunyan's scenic descriptions which, while symbolic, are also localized and referential.[23] It is perhaps significant that the Romantic age was the first to afford 'special consideration to Bunyan as an imaginative writer, and to *The Pilgrim's Progress* as a work of art'.[24]

Where Bunyan's work differed from the text of *Der Freischütz*, and most other operas of Streatfeild's acquaintance, was in the straightforwardness and absence of dramatic conflict of its plot, a great attraction for one who believed that music could add nothing to a dramatic situation and would only have its expressive powers attenuated by vainly attempting to elucidate the details of a typical opera text. Although a great deal happens in the course of Christian's journey to the Celestial City, there are no sub-plots, no intrigues, no earthly love-entanglements, and hence no complicated knots to be unravelled. In Streatfeild's view, opera had ideally to concern itself less with drama and more with character, as this relied for its depiction on the expression of emotional states which he considered music's true province. Mozart, he believed, excelled all other operatic composers because of his unique powers of 'limning a character in a few dexterous touches and sustaining it tirelessly through every changing stroke of fortune';[25] for this reason also, *The Pilgrim's Progress* might prove eminently suitable for Streatfeild's purposes, Bunyan's faculty for succinct characterisation being quite as renowned as Mozart's in his different sphere.[26]

In Streatfeild's lifetime, indeed, it was upon such purely artistic facets of his genius that Bunyan's stature largely rested. As one contemporary put it, 'Modern readers . . . approach *The Pilgrim's Progress* not so much for edification, for the sake of the religious and ethical doctrine set forth in it, as for its narrative and dramatic excellence'.[27] For many, the work had outlived its original didactic intent, T. R. Glover's assertion that it was 'one of those permanent books which survive their own theories' epitomizing a corpus of critical reaction that stretched back to Coleridge,[28] as well as providing an interesting parallel to Streatfeild's view of the music of Gluck and Wagner. But in Bunyan's case, Streatfeild, however unfashionably, undoubtedly perceived the theory – the specifically Christian, if not narrowly Puritanical, message – as being of the utmost importance. Not only was it the basis of the allegory's universal appeal but, perhaps more significantly, it would furnish him with the high and noble sentiment which he required for his own work. The simple progress from darkness to light, from despair to salvation, of the allegory could provide the perfect antidote to the predominating gloom of most English operas, as it might also counter the trend towards decadence of such works as Richard Strauss's *Salome*, of which Streatfeild observed: 'Many critics quite the reverse of prudish have found its ethics somewhat difficult of digestion . . . [although] more advanced spirits . . . contend with some justice that a work of art must be judged as such, not as an essay in didactic morality'.[29] It is perhaps not fanciful to see here a reflection of Streatfeild's own equivocation in the face of the Straussian challenge, as both a committed Christian and a critic of the musical arts. Clearly he had misgivings, and it can scarcely be doubted that there was something of a missionary purpose behind his own choice of subject.

III

Exactly when Streatfeild embarked upon his task is not known; the earliest evidence of his seeking any advice about the project dates from September 1914, and was addressed not to a composer but to the stage designer Norman Wilkinson. Six weeks after the outbreak of World War I, to which he here alludes, Wilkinson returned to its author a copy of the manuscript which he had 'enjoyed reading', promising to 'bear it in mind. When this upheaval subsides lets hope we shall be able to patch ourselfs up & do things again!'[30] Wilkinson was in fact something of a musical dilettante, keeping a harpsichord in his Chiswick home and having to his credit some settings of the early poetry of Yeats. But he had made his reputation during the immediate pre-war period by designing sets and costumes for Harley Granville Barker's Shakespeare productions at the Savoy Theatre, and it is as a response to his contribution in this field, rather than to his modest musical gifts, that Streatfeild's interest in him may be attributed.

Barker's achievement in these productions had been revolutionary, a complete reappraisal of Shakespearean staging for the new century. In an attempt to revive the spirit of the earliest performances, he overturned the illusionist, 'fully upholstered'[31] settings of Irving and Tree, along with their edited texts and spotlights on the main characters, and replaced them, in *A Winter's Tale* of September 1912, with non-realistic backgrounds on painted silk curtains, a complete text, stylized movement and all-encompassing white lighting. It was Wilkinson who was largely responsible for the distinctive look of the production, which the critics found disconcerting but which was central to Barker's idea.[32] In December of the same year, they collaborated on a less contentious *Twelfth Night*, before proceeding, in *A Midsummer Night's Dream* in January 1914, to attack late nineteenth-century conventions with renewed vigour. The enduring symbol of the approach was Wilkinson's design for the fairies, whom he dressed and painted entirely in gold, the intention being to 'unblinker the spectators' eyes'[33] to Shakespeare's substantial immortals. Harold Child, drama critic of *The Times*, was one of the many who came away from the theatre with his mind going 'back to the golden fairies . . . one's memories of this production must always be golden memories'.[34] Child was then becoming involved in the revival of English opera, working with Vaughan Williams on the text of

Hugh the Drover, and it is likely that another critic much preoccupied with that revival, Streatfeild, would also have attended the production and been impressed by the fairies, such was his love of the supernatural as represented upon the stage.

This, moreover, was only one feature of a production which he would have found much in sympathy with his own ideals. Barker and Wilkinson had succeeded in creating a new tradition of Shakespearean staging much as Streatfeild wished to see new blood pumped into national opera, and he would have been keen to discern aspects of their achievement which could usefully be translated on to the musical stage. One important device developed by Wilkinson had in fact already appeared in an operatic context in England; a coloured curtain and non-illusionist decoration had been a feature of Gordon Craig's production of *Dido and Aeneas* at the Hampstead Conservatoire in 1900.[35] The rejection of realism would have appealed to Streatfeild not only as echoing his own dissatisfaction with 'bastard realism' in opera, but more specifically, in that the approach would adapt well to the dream sequences of *The Pilgrim's Progress*, as also would Barker's emphasis on stylized movement enhance the presentation of the work's allegorical figures.

Streatfeild may further have been encouraged by Barker's advocacy of traditional music of a recognizably English provenance. For *A Winter's Tale*, as Arnold Bennett noted disapprovingly, there was 'no music',[36] by which he meant that there was not the orchestra which the audience expected; instead, 'actors disported over the whole stage, romping in vigorous rustic dances . . . accompanied by pipe and tabor'.[37] In common with such contemporary musicians and folk-song collectors as Vaughan Williams and Cecil Sharp, Barker's intentions were entirely serious; there was no laughing at rustic folly, but a genuine desire to catch something of the spirit of a more rural age and culture, as is apparent from a tirade delivered by him to W. Bridges-Adams regarding the latter's production of *A Midsummer Night's Dream* at Stratford in 1919:

> I don't care whether the audience laugh or not at seeing Starveling and Bottom and the rest go on like fifth-rate unskilled music-hall knockabouts. What you do by allowing it is to move them (the audience) suddenly out of the Shakespeare Theatre into the fifth-rate music hall . . .
> Besides – consider this. Here is Cecil Sharp teaching on one side of the town the beauties of folk-dancing. Here are you contradicting everything he says by making your rustics fall in a heap when they attempt a bergomask. No, no, no.[38]

It was to Sharp that Barker himself had turned for the music to accompany his 1914 production. Clearly, Mendelssohn's famous score could have no place in such a consciously innovative context, and Sharp assembled instead a score consisting for the most part of folk tunes, with a few stylistically similar inspirations of his own thrown in;[39] he also choreographed the dancing. He justified the rejection of Mendelssohn's score not on any grounds of quality, but because 'we of the present generation are no longer under the influence of the wave of German Romanticism which swept over this country sixty or seventy years ago, and, therefore, his music comes to us as an echo of a past age, the expression of an ideal which is not ours'.[40] Streatfeild too was conscious of the importance of establishing a new sense of identity in English music, following the example of his admired Weber in pursuit of a similar result. But whereas Weber had developed his national idiom in the context of the Romantic movement of which he was in many ways a product, Streatfeild and Sharp, and the larger movement to which they belonged, were convinced that, a hundred years later, their hopes for a genuinely English school of composition could not be fulfilled until the last vestiges of German Romanticism had been purged from the musical language.

In seeking the assistance of Norman Wilkinson, then, Streatfeild was acknowledging an achievement in English drama which he hoped to see emulated by the nation's opera. The two would have been acquainted through a range of mutual friends both in the artistic and theatrical world and at the British Museum. Laurence Binyon, for example, who worked alongside Streatfeild, was himself a poet and playwright and a friend of Barker, and was also associated with such men as the artist Charles Ricketts, who, like Wilkinson, had worked on designs for Barker's productions.[41] Another frequenter of the British Museum and the London theatres, especially since his acquisition of a large house in Hampstead in 1912, was Edward Elgar. He first attended Barker's *A Winter's Tale* on 18 October that year, with his wife and Alice Stuart Wortley; according to Lady Elgar's diary, the party was 'much delighted & thoroughly admired & enjoyed it', so much so that the composer returned just over a week later. He also wrote a revealing letter to the producer:

> We went to 'A Winter's Tale' with great hopes & remained to obtain great joy – I congratulate you most sincerely on a *splendid* production . . .
> I hope you are happy over it *yourself* – a lot of preposterous nonsense has been written but that won't affect you I trust. I always have in mind the sentence of Coleridge "The true *stage-illusion* (in this & in all other things) consists – not in the mind judging it to be a forest, but, in its remission of the judgment that it is not a forest." All the modern writers get no farther that this & do not understand how to express it: you have in 'A Winter's Tale' got just the right amount of "illusion" & . . . acting, scenery & (on this occasion) music were to me *one* & near perfection.[42]

The following year he saw Barker's staging of Arnold Bennett's *The Great Adventure*, the success of which, as producer told author, made possible the 1914 *A Midsummer Night's Dream*. Of this latter, Elgar was perhaps a little less enamoured, although we have only his wife's report that the evening had been 'very interesting but not satisfying';[43] she too retained a vivid memory of Wilkinson's fairies, 'rather good', she thought, 'as it saved them from being like pantomime fairies'.

IV

Streatfeild probably met Elgar for the first time in 1912, for at the beginning of December that year, he was invited to tea at Severn House, a 'nice interesting man', Lady Elgar noted approvingly, and 'quite devoted to E.'[44] The friendship deepened steadily over the following months, and in 1915 occurred two events which strengthened it further. In February, Elgar was obliged on health grounds to resign from the Hampstead Special Constabulary. But his desire to play an active part in the domestic war effort remained and, on 5 April, Streatfeild persuaded him to enlist in the Hampstead Volunteer Reserve. The two sometimes went to drill together, Streatfeild bringing Elgar home and occasionally staying for dinner. Also on 5 April, Elgar revealed that he had abandoned a setting of Binyon's poem 'For the Fallen', so as not to steal the thunder of Cyril Rootham, whose version (already accepted for publication by Novello) would be completely eclipsed by the appearance of an Elgar setting. Lady Elgar reported Streatfeild's reaction as '*distressed . . .* because he [Elgar] had so generously retired in favour of Wrootham – but quite *angry* too (quite right)'. When on 25 April, he visited again, in company with the Binyons, and heard some of the proposed music, he knelt beside the composer, 'enraptured'; his enthusiasm then took a practical turn as he approached Augustus Littleton at Novello and persuaded him 'with no very great difficulty'[45] to publish both settings. Furthermore, when Rootham took exception to what he regarded as Elgar's breach of faith in issuing his work, Streatfeild, 'so kind and like a champion',[46] took up the cudgels and wrote to the aggrieved composer, justifying Elgar's behaviour and his own, having first established from Binyon that Rootham had in any case never been given the exclusive right of setting the poem.

After such gallant behaviour, Streatfeild became a firm favourite with Lady Elgar,[47] and his visits to Severn House continued regularly until suddenly, on 22 July 1917, she was 'grieved to hear sad accounts of our dear friend Streatfeild'. Whatever calamity had befallen, it was sufficient to send him out of the Elgars' lives, and he is not mentioned again in the diary until 8 February 1919, when Lady Elgar was 'shocked to hear' that he had 'died a few days since – The Keeper Brit. Museum rang up & told us in answer to my note asking him to lunch on Sunday – a real loss of a devoted friend'.[48]

Streatfeild's very real devotion arose not only from his love of the Elgars' hospitality, but from a keen appreciation of Elgar's achievement in English music. In his most extended article on the composer,[49] he hailed him as the saviour of national musical pride, appearing when 'the hopes of even the most patriotic music-lover in England had sunk almost to zero', and attaining a status from where he was 'destined to carry the fame of England far afield'. His earliest encounter with Elgar's music occurred in 1896, when he was present at the first performance of the oratorio *The Light of Life* and recognized at once that 'a new voice had arisen in England'; he subsequently followed the composer's career with close, and not uncritical, interest. As with others whom he held in particular esteem, he came to regard Elgar's essential genius as residing primarily in his lyrical gifts. Thus he preferred the 'freshness of inspiration' of the cantata *King Olaf* to its successor *Caractacus*, which he considered 'a success of technique rather than inspiration', the musical fabric based too studiously on the Wagnerian principle of leitmotif. Such sentiments are entirely consistent with his views on music generally. Wagner he saw standing 'like a mighty monument at the end of a blind avenue, magnificent in solitary splendour but leading nowhere',[50] and he felt that many of the composer's theories had no validity outside his own work; the leitmotif especially had 'degenerated into being merely a clever arrangement of labels' in the hands of musicians 'untouched by the fire' of Wagner's genius.[51] In Elgar he perceived an artist whose lyrical gifts should not be allowed to drown in the Wagnerian sea. Furthermore, he found in him a rare mastery of musical characterization, manifested in the 'frenzied terror of the dying man' in *The Dream of Gerontius*, for example, and in the 'interpretation of individual emotion' in parts of *The Apostles*, although here too (unlike *Gerontius*) he found the composer's genius hampered by his reliance on leitmotif techniques.

Clearly then, there were features of Elgar's style which might have prompted Streatfeild to believe that here was the composer in whose gifts rested the potential to produce an opera which could revitalise the genre in England. Moreover, he perceived in this music an involvement with spiritual matters comparable to those charted by Bunyan in *The Pilgrim's Progress*. Whilst appreciating the 'vivid picturesqueness' and 'dramatic power' of the soul's journey in *The Dream of Gerontius*, he believed that it was in the two Symphonies and the Violin Concerto that Elgar had 'written the story of his own soul';[52] his lengthy discussion of the First Symphony in these terms reflects strongly his own preoccupation with Bunyan's allegory:

> With this summons to a higher life [the opening motto theme] are contrasted the wiles of the world, the flesh and the devil. Bewildering siren calls seem to summon the hero to destruction. Pleasure spreads her net around his feet, the call of the ideal sounds brokenly and fitfully and through the maze of changing harmonies winds ever the dark and sinister theme of sin . . .
> The Scherzo seems to carry us into the world of sheer hard work . . . We seem to be plunged into the midst of the human struggle for existence, and a

curiously abrupt and square-cut melody shows us the hero bracing himself for his life's task . . .

[The *Adagio* is] a movement of extraordinary beauty, in which the deepest and purest aspirations of the soul of man are clothed in sound . . . He seems to be moving in a world of spiritual ecstasy, through an air growing ever more rarefied . . .

[In the finale] the hero seems to be sunk in the lethargy of despair. Memories of his old life, of his early struggles and ambitions, flit idly across his mind, but they cannot rouse him to action. At last with a supreme effort he shakes off his torpor, and throws himself once more into the fray. From this point onwards all is feverish energy and exaltation. The horizon seems to widen, the air to grow purer. The magnificent theme of the ideal, transfigured and glorified, seems, like a vast tree, to spread its branches over all, and the work ends in a blaze of triumph and splendour.

The correspondence between this hero's journey, and that charted in *The Pilgrim's Progress* is pronounced, not only in the general theme of spiritual growth, but in many specific details. The account of the symphony's opening, for example, parallels Christian's call, his setting out towards the wicket-gate and the 'higher life' beyond, also his temptation by Obstinate and Pliable, representing the 'wiles of the world'. Similarly, the 'sheer hard work' of the scherzo recalls the Hill Difficulty, and cleaner air of the slow movement that of the Delectable Mountains. Most noticeably, the hero's plight at the start of the finale and his conquest over his own torpor owe not a little to Christian's imprisonment in the dungeon of Giant Despair and his sudden release upon remembering that he possesses the Key of Promise.

Whether or not Streatfeild originally adapted *The Pilgrim's Progress* with Elgar's music in mind, the two men certainly discussed the project, for when the composer acquired the libretto after his friend's death, he noted that it remained the 'property of the executors, lent to me in case I should carry out the plan of R. Streatfeild that I should write music to it'.[53] But the continuation and intensification of the war after 1914 put any immediate practical realization of the plan out of reach. Norman Wilkinson, after contributing to a highly successful production of Hardy's *The Dynasts* at the Kingsway Theatre in December 1914, followed Granville Barker to America. The conflict effectively signalled the end of Barker's directing career in England, and also cut short Wilkinson's artistic development; essentially a pacifist, he was unable to reconcile himself to the brutalities of war. Subsequently he returned to England, working for Nigel Playfair and then the Stratford Festival, but he never regained the heights of his work for Barker and died in February 1934, a few days before Elgar, another artist whose creativity may be viewed as having been profoundly affected by the four years of upheaval. When Streatfeild himself died in February 1919, it might well have been expected that his ideas for *The Pilgrim's Progress* would expire with him.

Several incidents, however, may have combined to recall his work to Elgar's memory. In October 1919, Walford Davies wrote to enquire why the composer had never attempted an opera, to which he replied, 'I have never found a subject I cared about – I wanted something heroic and noble, but I am only offered blood and lust . . . '.[54] But there could be no subject more heroic and noble than that chosen by Streatfeild. Then early in 1920, with his wife seriously ill, Elgar took over the writing of her diary, and noted, on 10 February, that he had recently been reading the works of Samuel Butler; very soon afterwards, he began to make enquiries of Barclay Squire as to the possible whereabouts of Streatfeild's text. On 7 April, Lady Elgar died. The composer was prostrated, but not apparently to the point of his interest in *The Pilgrim's Progress* being snuffed out altogether; perhaps he sought some creative work to take his mind off the grief to which Squire referred in his letter of 25 May:

> I have written to Wilkinson to ask if he has a copy of Streatfeild's libretto, &, if so, to send it to me. I will then write to Mrs Streatfeild to ask what she wishes done with it. In any case I should propose to endorse the copies with a statement that the copyright belongs to her, as Dick's executrix & residuary legatee. Perhaps she may wish to leave them in your hands: I don't see that in hers there will be any chance of their ever being made use of.
> Indeed you didn't make an exhibition of yourself. I feel deeply what a mark of friendship it was on your part to come and see me & I quite understand what an effort it must have been.[55]

Both the answering tone of this letter and its allusion to Elgar's visit suggest that it was he who continued to take the initiative in the matter of the libretto. The discussion of copyright also reflects a typical concern of the composer who was always keen in the pursuit of his own rights and those of others, musicians especially.

Wilkinson replied, enclosing a copy of the script and asking Squire to 'let me know if any scheme does materialize or is at least contemplated as regards a theatre version of the book with music as I have always felt something could come of it, especially with Elgar's hand in it'.[56] Having also acquired a second copy, Squire next obtained Mrs Streatfeild's permission to send them on to Elgar, which he did, 'endorsed as I suggested', on 7 June.[57] Upon receiving them, Elgar made some notes on the envelope and then opened it to peruse the contents; it remains to be discussed exactly what he found when he did so, and why no work on *The Pilgrim's Progress* was subsequently forthcoming from his pen.

V

Of the two typescript copies which Elgar acquired from Barclay Squire[58] one retains the greater interest for being accompanied by a 'suggested' prologue[59] and some notes on how the libretto should be set. These may have been added when the script was sent to Wilkinson; at all events, they post-date the text itself by some considerable time. The notes are undeveloped and fragmentary, and were intended only to adumbrate ideas which might be utilized or discarded in the course of active collaboration with a musician. Nevertheless, they are sufficiently coherent to demonstrate that Streatfeild's deliberations regarding opera had led him to devise a rather different synthesis of words and music; this he described as 'symphonic drama'. Although the term might seem to contradict his ideas about the basic incompatibility of drama and music, the inconsistency is somewhat mitigated by the nature of the union which he had in mind:

> during the two sections of the drama the music should be continuous, giving the impression of a continuous march or progress, illustrated by occasional vocal scenes at moments of intense lyrical or dramatic feeling, the form thus corresponding somewhat vaguely to that of opera, with its recitative rising at certain intenser moments to lyrical song.[60]

The intention that the text should be spoken over a continuous thread of music whilst the plot advanced, rising to song only at climactic moments, was a logical enough development of the methods of Verdi in *Otello* which he so much admired. But the scheme also owed something to Wagner, whose 'use of the orchestra as a means of lyrical expression' was in Streatfeild's view, 'the one really important legacy'[61] which he had left to the world.

Yet in one respect, Streatfeild was to demand from his orchestra even more perhaps than Wagner had done. The sequence of events in his libretto may be summarized thus:[62]

> *Scene 1: The Calling of Christian:* May procession introducing Christian and Christiana; Christian, dejected, reads from his book; Evangelist appears and shows him the way to eternal life; he rushes away from the crowd, who pronounce him mad.
> *Scene 2: The Wayside Cross:* Christian arrives at the cross, weeps with remorse, but is cheered and sent on his way by the Three Shining Ones.
> *Scene 3: The Palace Beautiful:* Faithful, reclining on a couch, is tended by Piety, Prudence and Charity; Christian enters, the two are armed and go forth together.
> *Scene 4: Valley of the Shadow of Death:* Christian, alone, is called back by unseen voices and the image of his wife; he fights with Apollyon; Faithful appears in time to tend his wounds.
> *Scene 5: Vanity Fair:* Chorus of pedlars and salesmen; Christian and Faithful arrive, cause a riot, are tried and found guilty; Faithful is martyred at the stake.
> *Scene 6: Bypath Meadow:* Christian meets a shepherd-boy; is joined by Hopeful in company with Messrs. By-ends and Facing-both-ways; these two are disillusioned and turn back; Christian persuades Hopeful to leave the path and enter the meadow.

Scene 7: Doubting Castle: In the dungeon, Christian despairs, but is comforted by Hopeful; the voice of Giant Despair exhorts them to suicide; Christian remembers the Key of Promise, and the prisoners escape.

Scene 8: The Delectable Mountains: Christian and Hopeful encounter the four shepherds, who answer their questions and send them on their way with a blessing.

Scene 9: The River of Death: Christian and Hopeful come to the river; Christian vacillates but is encouraged by his friend; they enter and re-emerge wearing white robes; concluding chorus of praise as they enter the Celestial City.

There was to be no continuous plot, therefore, but rather a series of tableaux either taken from the allegory or (as the May procession, concocted to make a suitably bustling opening)[63] devised by Streatfeild himself. The connection of these tableaux into a coherent narrative was to be the primary role of the orchestra in the scheme:

> the symphonic interludes between the various scenes are not mere interludes, but integral parts of the drama, describing those portions of Christian's progress, which are not represented upon the stage. For example after Scene 1 (Christian's departure from the City of Destruction[)], the music should first show the enthusiasm of Christian for his pilgrimage, his pride in his superiority of his fellow-Townsmen, abruptly ending with his fall into the Slough of Despond – with how much definite realism this should be treated is left to the wise discretion of the musician – his humiliation & despair after this episode, his resumption of his pilgrimage, & his passing weariness & languor lead naturally on to the second scene . . .
>
> It is unnecessary to describe these symphonic interludes in detail. I merely suggest the general scheme of their treatment. A particularly important one, however, may be mentioned, that which follows 'Bypath Meadow' . . . The musician has here to represent first the wandering of the pilgrims through fair meadows & by rippling brooks, next their straying from the path & increasing difficulties as darkness falls upon them, & finally their apprehension by Giant Despair and their imprisonment in his dungeon.
>
> Scarcely less important is the symphonic movement following the next scene, the escape of the prisoners from the dungeon, their rapture at finding themselves once more in freedom, their eager resumption of their journey, and the gradual melting of noontide rapture into the serene tranquillity of evening.

While Streatfeild clearly believed music to be capable of rendering this detailed series of events with some precision (the language here recalls his impressions of Elgar's symphony), he was asking much of any potential collaborator to provide a score sufficiently vivid to do so effectively without visual assistance of any kind. The scheme also compromises his own thesis that music could not deal with incident, and would no doubt have been adapted and developed to great advantage in the course of being worked upon by a musical mind. No such union was forthcoming in Streatfeild's lifetime, however, and to Elgar, seeking a viable libretto for a first opera, it must very soon have become apparent that this disjointed text, with its half-baked notions of a new fusion between music and speech, was *sui generis* and, separated from its author, artistically redundant. His annotations of the text are cursory, amounting to no more than a questioning of Streatfeild's use of the word 'moody' to describe Christian's mental state at the beginning of Scene 1, and a suggestion that the protagonist's speech ending 'What shall I do to be saved?' might be 'shorter'. After correcting a typing error at the start of Scene 2, he appears to have lost interest altogether.

This was no doubt partly due to his state of mind following the death of Lady Elgar; *The Pilgrim's Progress* was perhaps the first victim of a creative lethargy which was to afflict the composer for the next decade. Nevertheless, there are further, artistic, reasons, why he may have felt disinclined to pursue the scheme. A clue to these may be found in Streatfeild's treatment of Christian's encounter with Mr By-ends. In the original, Bunyan's powers of characterization are at their height here, vivid,[64] precise and witty, in their observation of a hypocrite looking for the easy way to salvation. Streatfeild, while retaining the character, discards the humour and puts in its place an entirely straight-faced sermon delivered by Christian to his wayward acquaintance outlining the perils to be faced on the road to the Celestial City:

> The journey must be made afoot, by paths
> O'er grown with thorn and bramble and beset
>   With foul morasses; mountains must be climbed
> And valleys traversed; and on every side
>   Are hidden dangers, giants in the path
> And devils that withstand us on our journey.

So although Bunyan's message remains, the subtle art by which it is so effectively put across is entirely absent.

The rejection of the lighter aspects of Bunyan's genius is consistent throughout Streatfeild's text and is a reflection not so much of a humourless mind,[65] as of the author's missionary intent leading him to jettison many of the aesthetic properties of *The Pilgrim's Progress* in order to underline its didactic purpose. Such an approach, if faithful enough to Bunyan's own aims, was out of tune with the artistic climate of the early twentieth century when Streatfeild conceived the project, and even more so by 1920, when Elgar came to peruse his friend's text. In a famous article of 1921,[66] Ernest Walker dismissed the Victorian oratorio idiom as a spiritual compromise, 'full of powerful, non-artistic associations . . . always edifying but . . . free from any pressingly personal appeal to spiritual emotions'. Streatfeild's libretto, for all his forward-looking ideas on the development of opera, belongs to this reactionary class, and would have repulsed Elgar, who had laboured as hard as anybody to rid the oratorio of its complacency.[67]

Perhaps Streatfeild's worst mistake was to substitute his own verse for the original text, thereby rejecting what was for many the foundation of Bunyan's art as an allegorist and writer of stature. Commenting on the 'low' style of *The Pilgrim's Progress*, Coleridge had cautioned that 'if you were to polish it, you would at once destroy the reality of the vision'.[68] His words were echoed nearly a century later by Robert Bridges, who added: 'this some of his warmest friends do not perceive, when they Victorianise his spelling'.[69] Streatfeild transformed more than just the spelling, recasting the whole narrative into sickly and often feeble verse designed to appeal to middle-class Anglican sentiment of the late nineteenth-century:

> O weary way, O tired feet!
> O grievous burdon of my sin,
> That weighs upon my spirit so
> I can no further go.
>
> . . .
>
> Had I but known the weariness and pain
> I must endure,
> I ne'er had ta'en the strait and narrow way,
> That leads thro' briar and thorn unto the eternal day![70]

This is very close in tone to Longfellow's versification of the Gospels in *The Divine Tragedy*, and it would certainly have attracted an earlier generation, possibly even at one time Elgar, whose youthful enthusiasm for Longfellow – inherited from his mother – bore fruit in *The Black Knight* and *King Olaf.* But the mature composer was not attracted to Longfellow's religious outpourings; although he developed some scenes in *The Apostles* from ideas in *The Divine Tragedy*, he left the poetry strictly alone, going to the Bible (mostly the Authorized Version) in search of a more robust and enduring diction. Perusing Streatfeild's text less than two years after the end of the Great War, he would have found its language as anachronistic as its idiom.

When Elgar consigned the scripts to his desk, the history of Streatfeild's plans for *The Pilgrim's Progress* came effectively to an end. The idea of composing a musical stage work on the subject reminded very much alive, however – as it had been for more than a decade – in the mind of a composer more active than Elgar. Ralph Vaughan Williams's preoccupation with the allegory was to culminate in the production of his 'morality' *The Pilgrim's Progress* at Covent Garden in 1951,[71] but he had first been involved with the work as early as 1906, when he provided the music for a theatrical adaptation staged at Reigate Priory.[72] Following its provincial success, this was expanded and transferred to the Imperial Theatre, London, in 1908, where it is highly probable that Streatfeild would have seen it. As in his own libretto, a 'dramatised version' of the text replaced Bunyan's original diction, and the action was divided into a number of tableaux. For the music, Vaughan Williams drew heavily on his recent researches into folksong, an emphasis which would have pleased Streatfeild;[73] the composer's use of 'Sellenger's Round' to accompany an opening dance of Puritan girls anticipates Sharp's incorporation of the same tune at the beginning of his music for Barker's *A Midsummer Night's Dream*. Five years later, Vaughan Williams was himself to collaborate with Barker and Norman Wilkinson on a production of Maeterlinck's *Death of Tintagiles*, whilst in the same year, 1913, he also embarked upon an operatic project, *Hugh the Drover*, 'English to the roots in . . . dramatic atmosphere and melodic background'[74] and a positive and individual response to Streatfeild's challenge to English composers to emulate Weber and found a national opera upon national themes. It is perhaps a just cause for speculation, therefore, how Streatfeild might have been received had he approached Vaughan Williams at this stage of his career, rather than Elgar, with his ideas for *The Pilgrim's Progress* and the revival of English opera.[75]

Notes

1. BL, Add. MS. 63161.
2. Quoted by P.M. Young, *Elgar O.M.* (London 1955), 148.
3. *Handel* (London 1909); *The Opera* (London 1897). All subsequent references to this book are to the 3rd edition, revised and enlarged (London 1907). The volume eventually ran to a 5th edition (1925), revised by E. J. Dent.
4. *Musiciens Anglais Contemporains*, trans. Louis Pennequin (Paris 1913). The chapter on Elgar was also published separately, both in the Netherlands (see n.8 below) and Italy (as 'Un Musicista Inglese' in *Rivista d'Italia*, October 1912).
5. Streatfeild, *Modern Music and Musicians* (London 1906), 184.
6. For a full account of this phenomenon, see E. W. White, *A History of English Opera* (London 1983), 243–59 etc.
7. *The Opera*, 349.
8. 'An English Musician: Edward Elgar', *De Nieuwe Gids*, Aflevering IV (The Hague 1912).
9. *The Opera*, 335.
10. ibid, 344-345.
11. loc. cit.
12. In the autumn of 1912, Streatfeild visited Modena in order to transcribe and translate the letters of Handel's librettist Paolo Rolli. See his 'Handel, Rolli and the Italian Opera in London in the Eighteenth Century', *Musical Quarterly*, 3 (1917), 428–55.
13. Defining 'gnosis' loosely as 'technique', and 'agape' as 'charm', Butler found only the former in most serious music, which he disliked, and the latter in the work of the very few composers whom he admired. For him as later for Streatfeild, Handel represented the height of musical achievement, to whom all previous music had led, and since whose death the art had entered into terminal decline. Whereas Handel appealed to the musical 'man in the street', Bach, because of his preoccupation with contrapuntal techniques, 'goes over

the head of the general public and appeals mainly to musicians'; Handel was the greater, for 'the greatest men do not go over the masses, they take them rather by the hand'. Of Beethoven also he complained, 'I do not greatly care about gnosis, I want agape', while *Parsifal* he found 'compact of gnosis as much as any one pleases but without one spark of either true pathos or true humour'. Opera in general he disliked (preferring even Handel in his oratorios), the more so as it became more dramatic; 'music', he said, 'should never be combined with acting to a greater extent than is done, we will say, in the "Mikado"'. All these views may have had their influence on Streatfeild's more reasoned and sophisticated musical thought, as also Butler's patriotic love of the Savoy operas; 'Englishmen', he proclaimed, 'should stick chiefly to Purcell, Handel and Sir Arthur Sullivan'. See 'Handel and Music', in *The Notebooks of Samuel Butler* (London 1919), 110–34.

14. *Modern Music and Musicians*, 66.
15. ibid, 276. These arguments were not new; as early as 1876 at Bayreuth, Hanslick had argued that 'continuous dialogue belongs to the drama, and sung melody to the opera', describing Wagner's 'method of uniting them' as 'unnatural'. Henry Pleasants, ed., *Eduard Hanslick Music Criticisms 1846–99* (Harmondsworth 1963), 141.
16. *Modern Music and Musicians*, 272.
17. *The Opera*, 202.
18. *Modern Music and Musicians*, 292.
19. *The Opera*, 335. *The Veiled Prophet*, completed in 1878, was first performed at Hanover (in a German translation) in 1881; its first English performance was at Covent Garden in 1894 (in Italian). Early in 1905, Barclay Squire (then only briefly acquainted with the composer) tried to interest Elgar in another libretto of his own, set in Sweden and 'essentially romantic with a supernatural element' (Hereford and Worcester County Record Office, 705:445:2299). He had already offered it to Stanford, who apparently completed the first act before putting it aside because of the hopelessness of getting the opera produced.
20. See Roger Sharrock, introduction to the Penguin edition of *The Pilgrim's Progress* (Harmondsworth 1965), 26.
21. *Modern Music and Musicians*, 191.
22. Sir Charles Firth, introduction to the Methuen edition of *The Pilgrim's Progress* (London 1898); reprinted in Roger Sharrock ed, *'The Pilgrim's Progress': A Casebook* (London 1976), 91.
23. The flashflood in By-path meadow, for example, is clearly taken from life in the flat counties of eastern England with which Bunyan was familiar.
24. J. W.Mackail, *'The Pilgrim's Progress': A Lecture Delivered at the Royal Institution of Great Britain March 14, 1924* (London 1924), 21.
25. *Modern Music and Musicians*, 137.
26. Mackail (op. cit.) is typical in emphasizing Bunyan's 'extraordinary power of characterization' in *The Pilgrim's Progress*. 'This applies not only to the main figures, but to all those incidentally introduced. Each one of them has only to be mentioned in order to become fully alive'.
27. ibid, 10.
28. T. R. Glover, 'On the Permanence of *The Pilgrim's Progress*' (1915), repr. in Sharrock (op. cit.) 126. Coleridge, writing in 1830, noted that 'the interest' of the book was 'so great that in spite of all the writer's attempts to force the allegoric purpose on the Reader's mind ... his piety was baffled by his genius, and the Bunyan of Parnassus had the better of the Bunyan of the Conventicle'. ibid, 53–4.

29. *The Opera*, 316.
30. BL Add. MS. 47895, f.44. Wilkinson here echoes the more or less general assumption of the time that the war would be short-lived.
31. Dennis Kennedy, *Granville Barker and the Dream of Theatre* (Cambridge 1985) 123.
32. Barker referred to this aspect as 'decoration', eschewing the term 'scenery', with its suggestions of realism.
33. Kennedy (op. cit.), 161.
34. Quoted by J. C.Trewin, *Shakespeare on the English Stage 1900–1964* (London 1964), 57.
35. Craig described the setting thus: 'a plain blue background . . . lights from above placed on a proscenium . . . a colour scheme – very little movement'. E. W.White, *The Rise of English Opera* (London 1951), 145–6. Four years prior to this, Frederick Delius had written: 'I don't believe in realism in opera', and his later expansion of his ideas to Philip Heseltine reveals much in common with Craig and Barker, although a more direct influence on his thought was Strindberg: 'realism on the stage is nonsense, and all the scenery necessary is an impressionistic painted curtain at the back, with the fewest accessories possible'. Quoted by Christopher Redwood, 'Delius as a Composer of Opera', in *A Delius Companion* (London 1976), 233.
36. 3 October 1912. *Arnold Bennett: The Journals* (Harmondsworth 1965), 354.
37. Kennedy (op. cit.), 129.
38. Letter of 20 August, 1919, Eric Salmon, ed., *Granville Barker and His Correspondents* (Detroit 1986), 437–8.
39. Opening with Sellenger's round, the music also made use of 'The Sprig of Thyme', 'Greensleeves' (for the bergomask of Act V, Scene 1, anticipating its adaptation for Shakespearean operatic use by Vaughan Williams in *Sir John in Love*) and 'Lord Willoughby' (which usurped the position of Mendelssohn's wedding march in the same scene). Although Sharp in his introduction to the published music emphasised his use of 'timeless' folk-music, belonging to 'no period', rather than potentially limiting and 'precious' Elizabethan music, several of the tunes are in fact specifically Elizabethan provenance. *The Songs & Incidental Music Arranged and Composed by Cecil J.Sharp for Granville Barker's production of 'A Midsummer Night's Dream' at the Savoy Theatre in January 1914*, London and Taunton 1914, pp.10–12.
40. ibid, 12.
41. Ricketts' acquaintance with both Streatfeild and Wilkinson is apparent from his journals. Cecil Lewis, ed., *Self-Portrait: Taken from the Letters and Journals of Charles Ricketts, R.A.*, collected and compiled by T. Sturge Moore (London, 1939). Wilkinson developed the colonnade of curtains in the forest scenes of *A Midsummer Night's Dream* from an idea of Ricketts'.
42. BL Add. MS. 47897, ff.90–91. Barker and Elgar were already acquainted, the producer having attempted to involve the composer in a number of theatrical schemes involving J. M. Barrie (in 1910) and Laurence Housman (in 1914). The Elgars were among the 150 guests invited to Barker's and Barrie's cinematographed supper party on 3 July 1914. In 1925, on being unable to attend a performance of Barker's *The Madras House* with Alice Stuart of Wortley, he wrote to her: 'If you *do* see Barker please be an angel & give him warm messages from me – tell him I was at the *1st* of this play (& all the others) & know every syllable of it'. Jerrold Northrop Moore ed., *Edward Elgar: The Windflower Letters* (Oxford 1989), 304.

43. Diary, 13 February 1914.

44. ibid, 1 December 1912. Streatfeild became one of Elgar's theatre companions, accompanying him on 20 May 1913, for example, to *The Yellow Jacket*, a 'Chinese play done in a Chinese manner', by Hazelton and Benrimo. At the end of October 1913, Streatfeild was in Leeds with the Elgars for the premiere of *Falstaff*.

45. Letter from Streatfeild to Rootham, 28 March 1916. The letter is quoted in full in J.N. Moore ed., *Elgar and His Publishers*, (Oxford 1987), 788.

46. Diary, 27 March 1916.

47. He became the more so when he recommended one of her sonnets to the editor of *The Bookman*, who published it in August 1915; Streatfeild's own contribution to the issue was the loan of three postcards he had received from Samuel Butler, used to illustrate an article on the author by George Sampson. Lady Elgar's sonnet, entitled 'ENGLAND, AUGUST 4th, 1914, A RETROSPECT' may be found in P.M. Young, *Alice Elgar: Enigma of a Victorian Lady* (London 1978), 177; Streatfeild appears to have been instrumental in persuading Lady Elgar to tone down to 'savage' her original denunciation of the Germans in the poem as 'devilish'. (Letter to Lady Elgar of 9 July 1915, HWRO 705:445:6362.)

48. The 'sad accounts' of July 1917 probably refer to the onset of the progressive insanity which was to result in Streatfeild's early retirement, his committal to Camberwell House and eventual early death at the age of 52. How little of the detail of this sad demise was known to the Elgars may perhaps be guessed from Lady Elgar's belated luncheon invitation.

49. See n.8 above. All Streatfeild's impressions of Elgar's music quoted here are from this source.

50. *Modern Music and Musicians*, 275.

51. loc. cit. The accusation, deriving originally from Ernest Newman, was by this time already a commonplace of Elgar criticism, especially of *The Apostles* and *The Kingdom*.

52. This impression corresponds very closely to Elgar's own comment to Alice Stuart Wortley (embracing also *The Music Makers*, but not the First Symphony) that he had 'written out my soul in the Concerto, Sym II & the Ode . . . in these three works I have *shewn* myself'. Letter of 29 August 1912, in J.N. Moore ed., *Edward Elgar: The Windflower Letters* (op. cit.) 107.

53. BL Add. MS. 47895, f.50. Elgar was as receptive to operatic suggestions at this period as at any other of his career. In July 1913, at Frank Schuster's house in Bray there was 'much talk of opera for E.' during a visit by Sidney Colvin of the British Museum, although it is not known if Streatfeild's name was mentioned (Diary, 28 July 1913). In the following years, Elgar went on to compose two of his most extended stage works, the incidental music to Algernon Blackwood's *The Starlight Express*, and the ballet *The Sanguine Fan*.

54. Letter of 8 October 1919. P. M. Young ed., *Letters of Edward Elgar* (London 1956), 259.

55. BL Add. MS. 47895, f.45. Streatfeild was unmarried; the reference here is to his mother.

56. 28 May 1920. ibid, f.47.

57. ibid, f.49.

58. After Elgar's death, the parcel containing the two copies was found by his daughter, who sent it to W. A. Marsden at the British Museum. The museum received it initially for a period of ten years, pending a claimant, but, as none was forthcoming, the libretti were eventually incorporated into the collection in

March 1953, one copy to the Department of Printed Books, the other (containing Streatfeild's notes and Elgar's few annotations) to the Department of Manuscripts (Add. MS. 47895).

59. This prologue has been formerly attributed to Elgar himself (see for example P. Willetts, *Handbook of Music Manuscripts Acquired 1908-67* (London, British Museum, 1970), 29), but it is clearly in Streatfeild's hand.

The prologue, of which there is a summary only, no text, was to be of two scenes, describing Bunyan's own conversion. The first scene shows him playing games with friends in the market-square at Bedford. Deriding the parson who reproves them, they continue their sport until Bunyan hears a voice from heaven, is suddenly converted, begins preaching, causes a riot and is arrested. In the second scene, in prison, Bunyan is seen falling asleep and beginning his dream. How effective this would have been on stage is debatable; Bunyan's crimes were hardly such as would have provided great dramatic contrast with his conversion; even those to which he confessed in *Grace Abounding* amounted only to bell-ringing and playing hockey on Sundays, such things as 'would have passed for virtues with Archbishop Laud', as Macaulay once observed. In any case, Bunyan's own conversion was not instant, and much of the power of his allegory in such scenes as the dungeon of Giant Despair springs from its autobiographical basis.

60. Unfortunately it is nowhere specified in the libretto at which points speech was to rise into song, a circumstance which suggests a gap in time, encompassing also a change of intention, between the composition of the libretto and the addition of the notes. The libretto itself contains few musical directions, but implies that the entire text was to be sung. The opening chorus was to begin with 'a lively rhythm', Christian and Hopeful were to 'exeunt singing' into Bypath meadow, while the verdict of 'Guilty' to be pronounced in turn by each of the jury at the Vanity Fair trial is particularly directed to be 'spoken'. A pencilled addition to the beginning of Scene 8 (The Delectable Mountains) asks that the shepherd's pipe tune be 'solemn & quiet – an evening counterpart to the morning pipe of the boy in Scene 6'.

61. *Modern Music and Musicians*, 277.

62. There was to be no subdivision by acts, the curtain coming down after each scene. Streatfeild suggested an interval after Scene 5 (Vanity Fair).

63. It is in this opening chorus that the style comes nearest to that of the English light opera which Streatfeild saw as the basis of a future national opera:

> Mayday! Mayday!
> Lads and lasses, haste away!
> Hither comes the Queen of May,
> Clad in all her fine array.
> Scatter flowers before her feet,
> Primrose pale and violet sweet,
> Let us all make holiday,
> Cheer the Queen upon her way!

Here the influence of German's *Merrie England* (first performed in April 1902) is clear, with Streatfeild's text closely echoing Basil Hood's opening May chorus:

> The May Queen comes,
> let her path be spread with roses white
> and with roses red, etc.

64. So vivid, indeed, that 'Mrs By-ends . . . though she does not appear in person, we know as well as if we had been familiar with her all our lives from her husband's incidental words'. Mackail, (op. cit.), 21. Vaughan Williams went along with this assessment to the extent of personifying Mrs By-ends in his adaption of the book.

65. Streatfeild's abundant charm and sense of humour are attested by his double-edged comment regarding Lady Elgar's hospitality (Diary, 27 July 1916), that 'this is the most difficult house to leave . . . like the garden of Armida, when you are in you cannot get out'; also by a story related by him to Ricketts (op. cit.), 'about Madam Calvé the singer and her morals. Her manager said once, "I don't care who she makes love to, but I do wish she would leave the scene-shifters alone whilst they are at work".'

66. 'Free Thought and the Musician', *Music and Letters*, 2 (1921), 55.

67. Walker singled out *The Apostles* and *The Kingdom* for their contribution to the renaissance of oratorio, in the libretti of which, although they 'resemble those of the older type . . . there is not a trace of the old lethargic taking things for granted, it is all a ringing sacramental challenge to the individual soul'. 'A Generation of Music', in *'Free Thought and the Musician' and Other Essays* (Oxford 1946), 73.

68. Quoted by Sharrock (op. cit.), 53.

69. From *The Speaker*, April 1905. Ibid, 115.

70. This is part of a 36-line soliloquy, comprising most of Scene 2, during which an effusive Christian first bewails his lot, then acknowledges his sins, and finally turns to the Cross for forgiveness. Bunyan has merely: 'He ran thus till he came at a place somewhat ascending; and upon that place stood a Cross, and a little below in the bottom, a Sepulchre.

71. It is curious how often Vaughan Williams's career shadows that of his older contemporary in its completion of his unrealised plans. In addition to *The Pilgrim's Progress*, one thinks of *Sancta Civitas* (which Elgar acknowledged made it unnecessary for him to complete his oratorio cycle), the *Five Tudor Portraits* (on poems of Skelton suggested by Elgar), and the use in *Sir John in Love* of a lyric – 'Do but look on her eyes' – from Jonson's *The Devil is an Ass*, which Elgar considered for *The Spanish Lady*. See Barry Jackson, 'Elgar's "Spanish Lady"', *Music and Letters*, 24 (1943), 5.

72. This was devised and produced by Mrs W. Hadley, the idea having come originally from George Macdonald, a Victorian minister and author of children's books. See Daphne M. Foraud, 'Vaughan Williams at Reigate Priory', *Composer*, 54 (1975), 15–18.

73. Streatfeild had been acquainted with Vaughan Williams's music since 1902 when, as a member of the Magpie Madrigal Society, he had been involved in an early performance of the part-song 'Rest' at St.James's Hall. In his French introduction (see n.4), he placed Vaughan Williams alongside Grainger and Balfour Gardiner as the most eminent of the composers of the folksong school, although he remained cautious as to whether 'ce mouvement artistique est destiné à produire un résultat durable'.

74. A. E. F. Dickinson, *Vaughan Williams* (London 1963), 248.

75. An exhaustive comparison between Streatfeild's and Vaughan Williams's libretti is beyond the scope of the present article, but a few salient points should be mentioned. There exist a few interesting similarities (beyond the inevitable ones determined by the common source). Both composers eschew the title of 'opera'; Streatfeild's original title (before he coined the term 'symphonic drama')

was 'A Mystery founded upon Bunyan's allegory', closely anticipating Vaughan Williams's 'A Morality founded upon John Bunyan's allegory . . . ' Like his predecessor, Vaughan Williams was conscious that the subject did not invite conventional operatic treatment, and he too arranged his libretto into a series of tableaux, with the important difference that he retained a coherent thread of plot throughout (whilst omitting far more of the original than Streatfeild). The two conceptions also share their use of a Prologue, Vaughan Williams (who also characteristically provides an Epilogue) taking his from Bunyan's own preamble, with the author as character standing front of stage and introducing his dream. But behind these common traits lies a fundamental difference in approach. Vaughan Williams's text reflects a more secular, humanistic treatment. Where Streatfeild jettisons the art of the original as superfluous to its message, Vaughan Williams sees it as essential, keeping (for the most part) Bunyan's diction and emulating his gift of characterization (the By-ends scene is truly comic in his hands). Bunyan's message is conveyed in such a way as to appeal, the composer said, to 'anyone who aims at the spiritual life', an approach which Elgar, in 1920, would have found perhaps more conducive to his own inspiration than Streatfeild's more limited vision.

10 'fyrst the noble Arthur'

Robert Anderson

Arthur was not the first play by Laurence Binyon (1869–1943). He had a *Paris and Oenone* produced at the Savoy Theatre, London, in 1906. Nor was it Binyon's first play with incidental music by a distinguished composer; that had been *Attila* at His Majesty's in 1907, for which Sir Charles Stanford wrote his op.102. *Arthur* was not the first collaboration between Binyon and Elgar; that was *The Spirit of England*, a setting (1915–17) of three Binyon poems published in *The Times* soon after the outbreak of World War I. Yet for Elgar his *Arthur* music, undertaken with much hesitation early in 1923, became the first link in a creative chain that was snapped only at his death more than ten years later. Binyon based his play on Malory's *Le Morte D Arthur*. When Caxton printed Malory's work in 1485, he mentioned in his preface the 'three noble Crysten men' most worthy to join the heroes of antiquity. They were 'fyrst the noble Arthur', then Charlemagne, and finally Godfrey of Bouillon, a leader in the first crusade. In Elgar's case the sequence was Arthur, *The Spanish Lady*, and Symphony No.3.

Elgar and Binyon first met at Ridgehurst, the home of Edward Speyer, German banker and enthusiastic patron of the arts. Alice Elgar recorded the date in her diary as 1 December 1901. Speyer used to note in his visitors' book the weight and height of Ridgehurst guests. In 1901 Binyon was about half a pound heavier than Elgar's 10 stone 6 pounds; he was $1^1/4$ inches shorter than Elgar's 5 foot $9^1/2$ inches. In boyhood Binyon had been uncertain whether to be poet or painter. He was now an assistant in the Department of Prints and Drawings at the British Museum, an expert on Blake and English watercolourists, with a developing interest in the art of the East.

The impetus for the writing of a play about King Arthur came first from Sir John Martin Harvey, actor and theatre manager who had begun his career with Henry Irving when only 15, and had managed the Lyceum Theatre since 1899. Binyon dedicated the play to the Martin Harveys: 'Memory goes back to the June day, now long ago, when first I undertook to write for you a play out of Malory's pages on a theme long pondered by you both . . . How much the play owes to you, both in framework and in detail, none knows so well as I'.[1]

Malory's source was the French cycle of Arthur stories. 'For, as the Freynshhe book seyth' is a recurring refrain. Just as Malory made gripping narrative from the complex web of his original, so Binyon was equally involved in 'rejecting and recasting; in the search for essential structure'. Often Binyon echoed Malory as, for instance, when the young Elaine is wasting for love of Launcelot. 'Am I nat an erthely woman?' writes Malory, 'And all the whyle the brethe is in my body I may complayne me, for my belyve ys that I do none offence, thou I love an erthely man'. Binyon changes little: 'I am an earthly woman, and love an earthly man. Is it so great an offence to love?' Binyon has a less easy time over Launcelot's and Queen Guenevere's betrayal of the king. When the friend and knight without equal is finally banished to Brittany, Binyon's Arthur shifts emotionally from one foot to the other: 'He did to me the wrong that least is pardoned, / Yet almost I forget my manhood now'. By contrast Malory has a ready escape route: 'for love that tyme was nat as love ys nowadays'.

Binyon approached Elgar about *Arthur* in late 1922. He had previously been assiduous with libretto suggestions for an opera, made usually through Alice Elgar. None had been accepted; he was no more successful with the 'Peace' Ode he offered in the autumn of 1918.[2] After Lady Elgar's death in April 1920 and Elgar's sinking into virtual musical silence, it can have been with little hope that Binyon put his request to Elgar for incidental music to the tragedy. The play was to be produced in three months' time, on 12 March, at the Old Vic Theatre, which had established a reputation under its manager, Lilian Baylis, for fidelity in Shakespeare and an adventurous operatic policy.

On this occasion, however, his wife's death acted as a spur to Elgar. She had enjoyed Binyon's company and admired his work. She had tried to further his operatic ideas, and had striven hard for Binyon when Elgar gave up the war poems on the grounds that Cyril Rootham had a prior claim to 'For the Fallen'.[3] By 24 January Binyon had so far broken down Elgar's reserve that he put Lilian Baylis in touch with him:

> I have seen Miss Baylis to-night. I told her you wanted to know what resources she could provide, & she offered to write direct to you . . . I think she would do all she could to meet your wishes, as she realizes what a distinction it would be for the Old Vic. No other music would be played. They don't want much in the way of quantity.[4]

Lilian Baylis was herself no mean musician. She had been a child prodigy on the violin; she later taught music in South Africa and ran a ladies' orchestra. She became manager of the Old Vic in 1898, and a nine-season plan had seen the production of all thirty-seven Shakespeare plays. She now wrote to Elgar:

> Laurence Binyon has just been in and has told us the wonderful news that you are willing 'to write a little music' for 'Arthur' which we are producing here on

March 12th. We are all so thrilled by your kindness that I cannot attempt to thank you adequately.

I enclose a list of the instruments which compose our regular orchestra, and my conductor, Charles Corri, would be happy to call on you at any time to discuss further details, should you wish it.

Robert Atkins, who will produce the play, has promised to let me know the scenes for which he would suggest music, in addition to the overture and the entr'acte for the long interval, and I will forward this to you as soon as I can. I do not quite understand from Mr. Binyon whether you are willing to write all the music that is to be used, or not?[5]

Charles Montague Corri (1861–1941) conducted the Old Vic operas and was the gifted scion of a long-established musical family. Robert Atkins (b. 1886) had toured as an actor with John Martin Harvey, and joined the Old Vic in 1915. His Shakespeare repertoire included Caliban, Prospero, Sir Toby Belch, Richard III, Macbeth, King Lear, and Iago; from 1920 he was responsible for productions, including the three parts of *Henry VI* and the first English performances of Ibsen's *Peer Gynt*. Lilian Baylis wrote again on 27 January that Atkins 'respectfully wondered whether it would be possible to mark the pauses, of a minute or two, only, which will occur after each scene, by playing the motif which represents the character who dominates the following scene'.[6]

Elgar was now virtually committed and was anxious to secure the right setting for composition. His daughter Carice had been married just over a year, and he put a proposal to her on 28 January:

I have half-promised (you will understand) to write some incidental music for Binyon's play to be produced in *March*: I see the stage manager tomorrow (Monday) and shall decide for or against – I've seen Binyon dear little man, to-day but the theatre (Old Vic) may make difficulties etc.

NOW

this is the point: *IF* I do it can I come to you for (say) a week & work at the *piano* score in your drawing room: every morning – I *cant* do it at the flat. – I should not be much trouble & shd be (D.V.) writing sketches which I can complete here or anywhere. It might be a bore to Henry (& dogs) & you may be having people, etc.etc. but, again, it might not 'urt you.?? If you wd. rather not have me (& I shall quite understand if you do not) I shall go to Perryfield if they can have me.

Will you send me a wire as soon as you can on receipt of this just saying 'Yes dearest father' – or 'No, you drivelling old blighter' – which is more of this age & what I expect.

I shd. bring a mike [microscope] . . . [7]

Carice agreed, and on 31 January Elgar summed up the position for Binyon:

I have seen Mr.Atkins & compared notes – there is not much difference betn. your views & his – the scenes (save perhaps in *one* case) *must* be 'linked' with music – two minutes sort of thing but no 'formal' break.

Now: the position, or rather *my* position is this: I *want* to do it but since my dear wife's death I have *done nothing* & fear my music has vanished. I am going to my daughter's tomorrow & shall be quiet & things arranged for me as of old: my wife loved your things & it may be that I can furnish (quite inadequate) music for 'Arthur' – Can you give me three more days to 'try'?

I have not written to Miss Baylis or Mr. Atkins because I want you to know how the matter stands in my mind.

Anyhow I am delighted with your work & wish to do my small elucidating part.[8]

Binyon was overjoyed, as he wrote on 2 February: 'I simply can't thank you enough. Even should you find that the spirit does not move you, I shall always prize the recollection of your wish to do this music for my play. But I can't help hoping'.[9]

Elgar went to his daughter's at Chilworth near Guildford on 1 February; he stayed until 10 February. Carice's diary[10] gives some idea of the effort it was for him to resume composition. The day after his arrival he was 'not very well, tried writing but did not "go"'; he answered a letter from his 'Windflower', Lady Stuart of Wortley, and expressed pleasure in reunion with the terrier he had given Carice on leaving Severn House:

Your letter reached me here (Carice's) this morning – I am so sorry; I am to be away for a little time & am *thinking* of the music: I will let you know what happens about it.

Meg is a darling & quite one of the prettiest Aberdeens – such a love.[11]

The next day Elgar and Carice were 'out in morning & got some pond weed', presumably for the microscope. *Arthur* made no progress, and there was no improvement in Elgar's health, which required 'Epsom salts'. On 4 February he was 'better – trying to work in morning'; the next day there was renewed gloom: 'Father not well & disinclined for work'. There was improvement for the next four days, and Carice could twice write, 'Father busy all morning'. Recourse was had to Father Cyril, a local priest, on the afternoon of 7 February, about setting the 'Ecce sacerdos', needed for the climax of the battle scene in *Arthur*. As with Alice in earlier days, there was often cribbage in the evenings, and Carice thought her father finally 'seemed sorry to go'. During the latter part of his stay Elgar wrote again to Binyon, who replied on 9 February: 'Thanks so much – Your note was good to get. I am very glad you like the play, & I am sure your "touches" will give it just the atmosphere needed'.[12]

Work on *Arthur* continued at Perryfield[13] and Brighton, from where he wrote to the Windflower on 19 February: 'I have been away a long time – a very long time & had "nothing to report" as the old war telegrams used to say. I have worked at the Binyon music & have nearly finished it – one or two Windflowerish bits – but it is short'.[14] That same day Lilian Baylis answered an Elgar letter of 16 February:

> ... I hear from Mr.Corri that you mentioned the inclusion of a harp to Mr.Atkins. I fear that the least this instrument would cost for rehearsals and the 9 performances would be £20; we did make it clear to you in our letter of January 24th. ... which instruments were in our orchestra, so that I hope that you will not feel that this additional expense is essential. We sincerely trust that Laurence Binyon's play, with the great attraction of your music, will attract a large enough audience to cover the expenses.[15]

The Old Vic orchestra consisted of two first violins, one second, a viola, double bass, flute, clarionet, one cornet (or trumpet), piano. To the list he had been sent Elgar added '? Harp ? Cello ? Trombone 2 Cornets ?'. In the end he included also timpani and a bell in F. Elgar was now at work on the full score[16] and noted in a memorandum: 'pp.1–30 sent to Mr.Corri Feb 22 1923'. This took the music to the end of Scene III. Lilian Baylis acknowledged its receipt the same day:

> Mr.Corri is already at work on the music you sent over this morning; thank you so much for being so prompt.

> We are all looking forward with the keenest pleasure to the 12th. March. I am hoping that the unique combination of your music and Mr.Binyon's verse will result in the play appealing to both our Shakespeare and Opera audiences, and that we shall have a repetition of the success of Peer Gynt, which was solely owing to this double attraction ...

> I hardly dare to suggest that we increase our debt of gratitude to music by saying that if our little orchestra gives you the satisfaction you hope for, it would be a fitting climax to your kindness if you could conduct at the opening performance? ... [17]

By 23 February Elgar was within sight of the end, as he wrote to his niece, Madge Grafton:

> I have been overwhelmed with this *Arthur* music – I am writing entr'actes etc but have now done the heavy work & take the first lucid moment to write to my niece. How are yer? How are yer? I am very well, but tired. The poor mike has been deserted during this wave of music ...

> Now I have just eaten a scrap of fish & must go back to my writing.

> Monday should see the end of the M.S.[18]

It did, and Lilian Baylis acknowledged its receipt on 26 February.[19]

Elgar's full score now numbered 120 pages, a few of which were used for scene titles and cue lines without music. He had jotted ideas for *Arthur* in a pre-war sketchbook originally designated 'Arden / Opera in three acts'.[20] On the opera's title page (the work appears to have made little progress) Elgar noted in pencil a brief 'contents' list of *Arthur* motifs. On page 5 was music for the 'Banquet?'; page 8 has the 'gregorian' introduction to the final scenes in the Amesbury convent; and page 9 contains the 'Elaine?' theme. These ideas and others were adumbrated in the 'Arden' book; but the bulk of the sketching was done on sheets now bound together and held at the British Library.[21] Through these sketches, often not in sequence, and sometimes much jumbled, Elgar threaded his way to the making of his full score. The score contains a typed list of music required, with pencil annotations by Elgar. Against the page numbers of Binyon's printed play are brief indications of the type and length of music needed:

7.	Intro: (short) to Sc.I.
22.	2 min. Intro. to Sc.II
36.	2 or 3 min. Intro. to Sc.III. / (Music begins before end of Sc.III. / and carry on into
42.	5 min. Intro to Sc IV / (p.44, Banquet music. / p.63. Barge (pp) / p.66 Barge < > to end of scene.

INTERVAL.

67.	2 min. Short intro to Sc.V. / no wait between Sc.V. and Sc.VI.
76.	? Sc.VI.
92.	2 min Stormy intro. to Sc.VII / Chant (Monks). / – – end in silence
115.	Intro: (Gregorian) to Sc.VIII.
123.	do. Repeat as link with Sc IX. / near end repeat < > / slow curtain.

FINIS.

In the event this skeleton brief was much exceeded, and Elgar added notable music to the battle of Scene VII when the play was already in performance.

Binyon's Scene I is set in Sir Bernard of Astolat's castle. Lavaine, the younger son, surmises that the noble guest his sister Elaine has nursed back to health is the Launcelot sorely missed from Arthur's northern wars. The older son, Torre, knows the court gossip, and roundly pronounces Launcelot 'the Queen's paramour', foretelling disaster for the lovelorn Elaine. When Launcelot confesses his identity, Lavaine insists on following so glorious a knight to court; Elaine is left to pine away. Elgar introduces Scene I with the doom-laden sequence of chords that will eventually bring down the final curtain on the tragedy. There follows the Elaine motif (Ex.1), music which Elgar could well describe as 'Windflowerish', and a 'Chivalry' theme of knightly pride (Ex.2), developed at considerable length till it dies away to curtain-up. The 'Elaine' music recurs twice during the scene, once when she realizes Launcelot loves another, and then to accompany the sad dialogue between father and brother as Launcelot leaves.

Ex. 1

Ex. 2

Elgar now changes the mood abruptly, with 'attacca' for the Introduction to Scene II. There is more of the 'Chivalry' theme, courteous at the outset, but wrenched to a powerful climax before returning in initial simplicity, now 'Nobilmente', and leading to its own augmentation as an impressive 'Arthur' theme (Ex.3) in G minor. The curtain reveals 'A room in the Palace at London. At the back a colonnade, through which is seen a rose hedge'. In colloquy with Bedivere, King Arthur hints that his recent victory was tainted by treason. Bedivere points the finger at the king's nephew, Mordred. Arthur's concern is such that he fails to notice the quiet entry of Queen Guenevere, who gently hints at loneliness. Launcelot, now healed, tells what he owes to Elaine, but is still torn between loyalty to Arthur and love for Guenevere. The queen misunderstands his aloofness, which she jealously attributes to feeling for Elaine.

Ex. 3

Scene III returns to Astolat, where Elaine rouses herself sufficiently to dictate a final letter to Launcelot. She then requests her father that her dead body be fitly arrayed and placed in a barge: 'Let old Simon, dumb Simon, take me, and steer downstream to Thames. So I shall come to him'. Elgar's Introduction begins slowly in a drooping sequence. The 'Elaine' music runs its course once more, and at the end of the scene four last bars accompany Torre's forlorn question, 'Oh, father, will she really die?' There follows the 'Link to Sc IV'.

Scene IV is at Westminster: 'A vast circular banqueting hall with steps to the river in front. The hall is hidden at first so that only the stairs are seen'. Elgar's Introduction is grandly processional, beginning with the joyous theme of 'King Arthur's Fellowship' (Ex.4) in the brightness of D major. It is succeeded by the broad treatment of a theme for Guenevere as 'The radiant Rose of Britain and the world' (Ex.5). The music changes to the nervous A minor semiquavers of the 'Banquet' motif (Ex.6), music that pursued Elgar to

Ex. 4

Allegro maestoso

Ex. 5

Ex. 6

The Spanish Lady and the Third Symphony. Recapitulation brings back the 'Fellowship' and 'Rose of Britain' themes, and this most extended of the Introductions ends with a final flourish of 'Fellowship'. When the curtain rises, the 'Banquet' rhythm continues *ppp* as the brothers Gareth and Gaheris discuss the 'red sleeve' Launcelot wore at the joust. Lavaine explains it was the gift of his sister, Elaine. This red sleeve is at the core of Mordred's plot to make the queen betray herself and thus split the realm to his advantage. Inner curtains are drawn back to 'disclose the Round Table spread for a banquet'. There is much music during the scene. The 'Banquet' semiquavers often accompany dialogue, taking on a sinister aspect as Mordred draws the threads of his plot tighter. The 'Rose of Britain' signals the queen's entry and toasts to her, the motif subtly varied as discord threatens. In the absence of the king on state business, a health to the 'Fellowship' is drunk; but this theme too takes uneasy turns. Mordred, pretending that Launcelot's red sleeve must be a favour of the queen's, proposes 'Red wine to the red sleeve'. There is much embarrassment, and the semiquavers return as Lavaine tells once more that the sleeve is Elaine's. Mordred presses his advantage and now assumes Launcelot will be bringing a bride to court. Guenevere manages to drink 'to Launcelot's fair bride', but immediately makes to leave the feast, which breaks up in confusion. Launcelot comes from the king's council, and Guenevere at once confronts him. At the height of their altercation, Guenevere hurls a final taunt: 'Ah, false and faithless, you will go to her'. This is the cue for Elgar's 'Elaine' motif in response to the stage directions: 'a barge appears with the body of Elaine upon it. It is steered by a very old dumb servant. It glides very slowly to the steps which lead down to the river. Launcelot alone sees it first'. The music continues wistfully till Guenevere tries to question the steersman. It resumes while Launcelot reads the letter in Elaine's hand. Arthur enters, and Guenevere, begging forgiveness of both men, departs silently. 'Is love so terrible?' asks the king, thinking not only of Elaine, but of the 'world of fire in Guenevere'. Launcelot, charged with the burial of Elaine, steps into the barge and knows 'There's no end now but exile'. The 'Elaine' music sounds once more, and Elgar noted on his score: 'This number finishes act'. The interval followed.

Binyon's Scene V is set in the queen's tower at night. Elgar's Introduction has sombre muted strings, while a solo violin muses sorrowfully across the crotchet pulse. Uneasy triplets enshrine Guenevere's anxiety in a 'Fear' motif that twice recurs as she imagines watching shapes in the darkness. Launcelot enters by a secret passage and tells of his decision for exile. A moment of passionate talk is interrupted by Mordred and four accomplices, bent on avenging the king's honour. In what ensues Binyon follows Malory exactly, so that Launcelot succeeds in slaying all but Mordred. Guenevere knows that 'from this hour all's war and ruin', since Mordred will be first to the king.

The king's tower is the setting for Scene VI. When planning the *Arthur* music, Elgar was uncertain whether anything would be needed at this point. He made contingency plans: 'N.B. If Intro: is required play from 114–116 (*better alter to 10–20*)'. Both sets of cue numbers enshrine the augmented 'Arthur' theme (Ex.3); the latter pair has it in context of the whole Introduction to Scene II. Neither plan was needed, and Elgar noted Binyon's decision: 'Author's direction No Intro to Sc VI'. Arthur questions Gawaine about the break-up of the banquet. He suspects there was insult to Guenevere and that it may not have been baseless. Gawaine champions Launcelot, contrasting him with Mordred's aptness for 'dissension, rancour, envy, strife'. As Gawaine makes to depart, Mordred enters with his tale of murdered friends and Launcelot's guilt. Gawaine refuses to arrest the queen, so Arthur summons his young brothers, Gareth and Gaheris, for the task. They go unarmed, and Gawaine is full of foreboding. Arthur understands the significance of the moment:

> I feel the creeping of the rust that dims
> Excalibur, and those lamenting Queens
> That come to take me draw like shadows near.

A messenger tells that Launcelot has rescued the queen; Arthur now has no alternative to war. This was Elgar's cue for a 'Drum Roll $ff > pp$', to continue as background to further tidings that Gareth and Gaheris have been killed by Launcelot, and Mordred is 'leagued with rebels in the West'.

Elgar's 'Stormy intro. to Sc.VII' depicts not only the hostility between Launcelot at his castle of Joyous Gard and the royal camp, but also the fierce warring of the elements. Four hammered minims, balefully chromatic, launch a powerful movement that starkly recalls the 'Chivalry' motif and expands it into a fanfare call for Arthur. This is combined with Guenevere's 'Fear', and later with the climax of the 'Elaine' music, so that the various strands of the tragedy are tautly knotted. 'Arthur' appears in augmentation, and the 'Fear' triplets drive the piece to its dramatic end. Arthur is weary of the conflict, but Gawaine is implacable over his brothers' death so that noise of the quarrel 'goes over the seas even to Rome'. There are trumpet calls for a parley, Launcelot's based on a minor 6th (Ex.7), Arthur's echoing the 'Chivalry' motif (Ex.8). The exchange of views merely hardens attitudes on both sides. Binyon directs that 'The storm breaks with blinding violence as the battle begins'; and Elgar resumes the musical warfare of his Introduction. At the height of the battle a distant trumpet, muted, spans the notes of a diminished 5th. Elgar notes a cue for '*distant* chanting "Ecce sacerdos"', the words of solemn welcome to a bishop that he had first set in 1888. Elgar now used the traditional music from the *Antiphonale Romanum*, and specified further: 'chant (in full) *pp* approaching'. The bishop states his errand: 'Our Holy Father on the seat of St. Peter hath sent me hither with his commands'. Launcelot is to surrender Guenevere to Arthur. She is to be unharmed, and the combatants are to be at peace. The bishop's work is done, and Elgar had the 'chant resumed *mf* marching off'. Guenevere is brought from Joyous Gard, and Launcelot accepts the doom of exile. He and his knights depart to music Elgar wrote after the play had opened. On 15 March 1923 Carice 'Went to Father's Flat found him writing extra piece of music for Arthur'. It was based on Launcelot's trumpet call, the minor 6th leading to slow, heartsearching chromatics. Guenevere's only wish was for the 'nunnery at Amesbury'; Arthur was left to utter the names of those he loved most, Launcelot and Guenevere. Originally the scene was to 'end in silence'; but from 18 March Elgar's 'Repeat as curtain begins to fall' meant a further playing of the new Launcelot music.

Ex. 7

(afar)

Ex. 8

Allegro

f   *ff*

The Introduction to Scene VIII, the nunnery at Amesbury, is Elgar's 'gregorian' from the 'Arden' Sketchbook, a slow, obsessive tune moving always within the compass of a 4th (Ex.9). The convent bell tolls three times during the music. The nun Lynned tells Guenevere the king has come. The queen recoils from an interview but asks, 'How looked he?' While Lynned describes him 'in the ghostly morning mist', 'Almost like a spirit', the augmented 'Arthur' theme is quietly played till he addresses the queen. He must now fight his last battle, against Mordred. His motif sounds again '*pp* a *few bars*' at the words,

> I feel the wizard sword Excalibur
> Like an impatient spirit within my hand,

> As if he heard voices recalling me
> Out of this ended world.

The 'Arthur' theme is heard for the last time as the king utters the queen's name and disappears into the shadows.

Ex. 9

Elgar's brief for the end of the play was a repetition of the 'gregorian' music, once as Introduction to Scene IX, and again during the slow final curtain. This scheme was modified. The programme announced only eight scenes, and it seems the action in the convent was to run on without a break. Binyon had Lynned tell the queen about Bedivere's arrival with tidings of Mordred's and the king's end, and how Arthur's body had mysteriously disappeared:

> . . . in the place was sound
> He knew not whether of water or in the air,
> A music new to mortals, and the smell
> As of flowers floating through the dark, as if
> The passing of that spirit sweetened earth.

The final stage direction indicated 'a wide distance of moonlit water, over which glides a barge, bearing King Arthur, and the three Queens sorrowing over him, to the island of Avalon'. This presented a problem in production, and it is uncertain how Robert Atkins solved it. It may even have been omitted. Elgar's last instruction about the 'gregorian' music to close the play was 'repeat till ready'. But ready for what? His own answer was the sequence of doom-laden modal chords that started the evening. Yet he was not altogether happy with the end, as he wrote to Binyon on 18 March: 'The end of a play which depends upon two persons or one only is always risky: for *theatrical* purposes I shd have liked Arthur & *all* his train to march mistily past, seen through a window on the stage R. – however you know best'.[22]

Binyon expressed pleasure to Elgar in the way rehearsals were going: 'Everybody is working hard. We did the banquetting scene this afternoon... The Elaine is charming'.[23] Elaine found favour with Elgar too. The part of Arthur was taken by Wilfrid Walter, originally a designer and painter, who had planned the sets for Pavlova's London seasons; at the Old Vic he had been responsible for stage sets from 1919 and had also played Bottom, Falstaff, Othello and Antony. Douglas Burbidge was Launcelot; at the Old Vic since 1922, he had been Hotspur, Brutus, and the Caesar of *Antony and Cleopatra*. The Mordred, Rupert Harvey, also arranged the fights in *Arthur*, he had toured as Shaw's Professor Higgins after the war, and at the Old Vic had been Bassanio, Mercutio, Hamlet, Pericles and the Button Moulder in *Peer Gynt.* Florence Buckton, the Guenevere, had an early acting career in New York; she became the Old Vic's leading lady in 1921 on the strength of her Andromache in *The Trojan Women* of Euripides.

Elgar began rehearsing at the Old Vic on Friday 2 March. *The Sunday Times* expressed surprise at Elgar's latest venture: 'Fancy the greatest composer in England conducting ten musicians in the Waterloo Road!'.[24] Elgar was sufficiently encouraged on the Sunday to wonder whether the Windflower might not come to the next rehearsal:

> There is a rehearsal (orch.) at the Old Vic at *one* o'clock on Tuesday; – if you could possibly come at such an odd hour I shd. be only too delighted but I foresee that it is an impossible time
>
> We tried the entr'actes on Friday eveng – a curious sound I think from such a small but very good-hearted seven!
>
> I shall have to decide on Tuesday whether or no I conduct on the first night – a weighty judgment
>
> I am not at all well & am depressed [25]

The Windflower was able to come, and so was Carice, as noted in her diary for 6 March: 'Went to London to hear father's music of Arthur rehearsed at Old Vic lovely – Lady Stuart there – Lunch with Father at Waterloo & back to Flat for tea'.

Elgar at rehearsal was graphically described in *The Sunday Times* of 11 March:

> Sir Edward Elgar's patience all through the long and trying rehearsals of 'Arthur', the poetic drama by Laurence Binyon, was monumental. He composed the music to please his friend the author, and he sat about for hours at the Old Vic, last Friday, smoking his pipe, just as Barrie does during rehearsals. Degas missed a wonderful picture as England's greatest composer, his face half-lit by the light in his pipe, waited at the conductor's desk while the stage hands struggled with the scanty properties, and Lilian Baylis sat in the box admiring him.
>
> Elgar passed a minute of the time by paying a compliment to Jane Bacon, who will play Elaine. 'Had I seen you in that dress before', he said, looking at the white robe she wears in her death scene, 'I should have written more beautiful music. I think I'll take it away and re-write it'.[26]

Elgar did conduct the première on the evening of 12 March; but he insisted on the five extra players his scoring required, paying for them himself. Some of his closest friends were there, as is clear from Lord Stuart of Wortley's diary for that day: 'Early dinner & went with A.S.W. to Old Vic to see Ist production of 'Arthur' (Binyon & Elgar). Sir G. Arthur & Lady Arthur joined us in a box. Supper aftds at Savoy. Selves, G.Arthurs, L.Binyon, E.Elgar, F.Schuster'.[27]

Lilian Baylis expressed her gratitude the next day:

> It would be impossible to thank you adequately for your kindness to us with regard to the 'Arthur' music. I can only hope that you will realise that it is the amount of my gratitude which makes me dumb.
>
> It was very kind of you to provide the extra musicians yourself, and had you spoken to me about it before-hand I would gladly have arranged for them to be there myself, as the booking for last night was good.
>
> If, as Mr.Corri has told me, you really would be good enough to conduct at another performance, and could manage to arrange to take either, or both, of the performances on Saturday, March 31st. when the booking is good, I will arrange for the extra musicians to be here at my own expense.[28]

On 18 March Corri requested the five guineas owing for the extra players, and Elgar sent a cheque the next day. Corri also touched on the question of extras for further performances: 'you must *quite understand* I cannot promise to have the *same* gentlemen – but would do my best. The others are quite conversant with the music & you should have an easy time'.[29]

The Windflower went twice more to *Arthur*. Carice saw her there on the afternoon of 15 March and noted that the performance, starting at 2 p.m., had been lengthy: 'Had lunch at Simpson's & to Old Vic   Lady Stuart there – Very beautiful play. & Music sounded lovely – not over till 5.30'. On that occasion Elgar was not conducting and was glad of the opportunity to see the play with the Windflower. In a letter the next day he was gloomy that so few had rallied round him for *Arthur*: 'I forgot, – Blackwood sent a telegram – that's all'.[30]

He wrote again to Lady Stuart on 27 March: 'I am not sure about conducting at the Old Vic: on Saty but I *may* do both performances if they can get the extra instrumentalists. Carice is coming'.[31] The extras were found, and Elgar conducted the two performances. Carice went first to his flat: 'on to Pall Mall Restaurant to lunch   Lady Stuart & Mr.Reed there – & on to Arthur'. Socially the afternoon had been hectic, as he implied in a letter to the Windflower of 6 April: 'I could not get away down to you at the interval as I was held up: after the performance I had to rush off with C. – Mr.Reed had to leave early and all was confusion'.[32] How much of the music did Reed hear on this occasion? And how much did he remember?

Critical reaction to the play was lukewarm. *The Times* of 14 March sensed little vitality in the characterization. Binyon had not

> taken the opportunity which the theme presents of making Arthur alive in the council chamber, so that he may, by contrast, appear the more vividly in his personal life. Launcelot is flat virtue, Elaine flat pathos, and Guenevere crude in her contrasts. It is, perhaps, a literal fulfilment of the legend, but has all its

crises and swift movement; it yet lacks interest because the thought with which it is woven is spun so thin.

The acting is good, though nowhere of particular distinction. Mr.Douglas Burbidge, Mr.Walter and Miss Florence Buckton were handicapped by having been given so few of the mind's subtleties to interpret, and Miss Jane Bacon is a beautiful, though sometimes too tremulous, Elaine.

There was no mention of Elgar's music, which had to wait till the April *Musical Times* for due appreciation. Ferruccio Bonavia wrote: 'In the tender phrases which characterise the unfortunate Elaine, and in the musing phrases which prepare us for the clash of arms, the Elgarian idiom is evident even though there is not the faintest likeness between this and any other music of his'.

On the day of the first performance Binyon inscribed a copy of the play to Elgar: 'in affectionate admiration and regard from his grateful L.B.'[33] Characteristically Elgar noted on the fly-leaf an 'Erratum p.93', where 'beseiged' is wrongly spelt. Elgar acknowledged the gift on 18 March and summed up his view of the critics:

Very many thanks for the copy of *'Arthur'* & your inscription which includes more than I deserve. It was the greatest pleasure to be associated with you in the matter of production & I hope you are pleased with the reception of your work. This is not the day I fear for big things but there are some still left amongst theatre people who can see & feel great stuff.[34]

For Binyon the *Arthur* experience had been stimulating. He was ready for another play, and hoped Elgar was ready for more music, as he wrote on 11 April: 'I am so very glad you enjoyed the play & inspiriting it with music, which I hope will herald more – I enjoyed it all enormously, & not least your coöperation. I hope to write a better – a really good play – some day'.[35] Binyon's next play might have been a 'St.Joan'. Sybil Thorndike commissioned him for such a play that year. Shaw's *St.Joan* was completed on 24 August, a fact unknown to Sybil Thorndike for some months. Shaw was insistent that Sybil Thorndike must be *his* Joan, and Binyon gave up the project.[36] Whether he also deprived the world of some 'St.Joan' music by Elgar we cannot know.

Was there any future for the *Arthur* score? It hardly seemed so as the 1920s moved on. Ivor Atkins was anxious that Elgar should produce a suite from the music for the 1926 Three Choirs Festival at Worcester. He planned a Friday evening concert in the College Hall on 10 September. The *Siegfried Idyll* was to precede the interval, the first performance of the *King Arthur* suite (conducted by the composer) was to follow. Atkins had the programme printed and sent a proof to Elgar. By the side of the proposed new work Elgar wrote, 'alas! no.', and firmly crossed out the entry.[37] He explained to Atkins on 8 June: 'I am just off to town & must return you your pretty proofling with dismal marks & remarks. The day (week, month, year, era, age, eon) is past for ever'. This was not quite true, as appeared two years later. Elgar wrote to the music publisher William Elkin on 26 June 1928 and added a postscript: 'When I come up I shd like to talk to you about the "Fan Ballet", Starlight Express, the music I wrote for Binyon's "Arthur" & anr. trifle; wd a sort of short "Suite" (Arthur) be worth considering?'[38] The 'Arthur' idea was not pursued, but it may have been at this time that Elgar added a memorandum to his *Arthur* sketches. It referred to the moment in Scene IV when the curtains are drawn aside on the Round Table and the banquet. The D major introductory music had now settled in A minor, and Elgar wrote: '[Mem. for concert version *coda* in D]'.

Basil Maine first approached Elgar about a possible study of his life and works in May 1931.[39] The book was published in 1933, with the story continued past Elgar's 75th birthday to the end of 1932. In neither text nor index is there mention of *Arthur*, alone among Elgar's completed stage works. The reason is possibly to be found in a Maine footnote to the discussion of *Falstaff*:

> All this is not to say that Elgar will never write an opera. At the age of seventy-five he is full of music and is continually sketching ideas. We know that he is now at work upon the Third Symphony. If, when that is finished, he found a sufficiently attractive libretto, there would still be good reason to hope for the first opera.[40]

Perhaps Maine had been told about *The Spanish Lady*, perhaps not. Certainly Elgar had found and was shaping a libretto that attracted him; for its furnishing he gathered music from many sources, including *Arthur*. Guenevere's theme as 'Rose of Britain' (Ex.5) appears among ideas for the opera's overture.[41] Perhaps the Westminster banqueting hall and Round Table were still in Elgar's mind when he thought of bringing back the music in Act 2 scene ii of the opera.[42] The new setting was a hall in the home of Lady Tailbush, described by Elgar as thirty years old and a 'lady of fashion desirous of freedom and fortune'. Instead of Arthur's knights, there are 'withered ladies, young matrons, girls, men' and so on. Here the Guenevere music is associated with a new theme that adapts its proud rhythm to more honeyed phrases. The A minor semiquavers of the 'Banquet' music (Ex.6) were copied for W. H. Reed on 5 February 1933.[43] By that date Elgar was probably planning a symphonic destination for the twelve bars; but the page is headed '*B.J.*', the initials of Ben Jonson, author of *The Devil is an Ass*, on which the opera libretto was based.

Elgar also makes use of music associated with Arthur himself. The king's trumpet call on the battle-field (Ex.8) was based on the all-pervasive 'Chivalry' motif (Ex.2). Elgar now put it to very different use in his projected Act 1 scene i. Meercraft, the 'plausible rogue', enters boisterously and launches on his schemes to coin money 'out of cobwebs'. He has with him his servant lad, Trains, 'important, a small cheeky youth'. Trains carries with him prospectuses and circulars for Meercraft's 'projects'. He also has a trumpet to attract the attention of the crowd at crucial moments. That Trains three times uses Arthur's trumpet call is perhaps Elgar's very practical demonstration that 'This is not the day I fear for big things'. There is a further ironic comment on *Arthur* when the trumpet call takes the harsh form heard in the Introduction to Scene VII. Its climb up an augmented 4th is now the hallmark of Everill's 'Blast'. It is sounded when Meercraft describes his 'venture to Virginia', where 'Gold is more plentiful than copper with us'. Everill, Meercraft's debauched cousin and seedy accomplice, seizes Trains's trumpet '& blows a fearful blast quite unnerving Meercraft for the moment'. The two rogues drive home their latest point with Everill's 'Dogs are chained with gold' and Meercraft's 'Prisoners fettered with gold'.[44]

A sketch that found no place in the completed *Arthur* music neatly links play, opera, and plans for the Third Symphony. It first appears among the *Arthur* sketches, headed 'Good friday', an indication that has no immediate connection with the play. It has a further designation, 'Sym III', but with no hint as to speed or context.[45] Its function in *The Spanish Lady* is clearer. Near the beginning of Lady Tailbush's 'Assembly' in Act 2 scene ii, Manly, a young gentleman of means and her somewhat half-hearted suitor, is appalled by the seething crowds in the hall: 'Another flood! An inundation'. When Lady Tailbush seeks to detain him, he ungallantly comments on her excessive make-up:

> Still to be powder'd, still perfum'd;
> Lady, it is to be presumed,
> Though art's hid causes are not found,
> All is not sweet, all is not sound.

She responds tartly with 'You are sharp, sir', then melts into 'a "tragic" song'. The opening words were to be 'Oh Manly'; the G minor music of play and Symphony is now marked 'Adagio' and *espressivo*. After six bars, Manly was to console her in G major.[46] The tempo indication suggests its ultimate home might have been the Adagio of the Third Symphony.

The debt of the Symphony to Arthur is most obvious in the case of the second and fourth movements. When Fred Gaisberg of the Gramophone Company heard Elgar play the Third Symphony at the piano on 27 August 1933, he noted 'an ingenious Scherzo, well designed: a delicate, feathery, short section of 32nds contrasted with a moderate, sober section'.[47] In fact the demisemiquavers were not so numerous as semiquavers, but this was again the *Arthur* 'Banquet' music, as first heard *ppp* while Gareth and Gaheris discuss the 'red sleeve' worn by Launcelot. W. H. Reed may have recalled it from the *Arthur* performance he saw; certainly he knew of Elgar's affection for it: 'He must have had the main theme for this movement (very light and rather wistful) in his mind for some years, as I have seen it scribbled in his scrap books in various forms . . . He loved this simple little theme, and we played it again and again with violin and piano'.[48] The strings were to be muted; there were now two bars of chordal introduction to the theme in the rhythm of the 1892 *Spanish Serenade*. This rhythm displaced the original *Arthur* counterpoint for three bars, and was Elgar's last glance at a country that had lent colour to much of his music. He also queried a slightly harsh progression of the *Arthur* version, modifying it with practised ease.[49] Considerable creative thought had gone into the remaking of this 'Banquet' idea.

This was not the case with the Symphony's finale. Gaisberg heard 'a spirited tempo with full resources, developed at some length'.[50] Elgar's skill as an improviser was legendary, and he seems on this occasion to have played so dextrously with his themes that he gave the impression of a completed movement. On paper the *Arthur* music that was to be incorporated in the Symphony had merely been copied out for keyboard just as it had served in Binyon's tragedy. On one sheet were fourteen bars of the 'Chivalry' music from the Introduction to Scene I.[51] Most of the music, however, came from the Introduction to Scene II. On three separate sheets the whole section was copied in sequence, but for eight bars; six of the most chromatic bars were crossed out. The 'Nobilmente' version of the 'Chivalry' theme is fully stated, as is the augmentation in the grandly sad 'Arthur' motif.[52]

Gaisberg noted Elgar's pleasure in the Third Symphony: 'he is enthusiastically satisfied with it and says it is his best work'.[53] The *Arthur* music, inspired by a subject 'whyche ought moost to be remembred emonge us Englysshemen', as Caxton put it, was to contribute largely to the Symphony. Its pivotal function in the second movement is clear, and Elgar had even begun mapping out the full score at this point.[54] Its position in the finale remains a mystery. W. H. Reed thought that the extract from the Introduction to Scene I 'looks as though it were leading up energetically to the final Coda'. But this was exactly where Elgar would say, 'Enough of this; let us go out and take the dogs on the Common'.[55]

Notes

1.   Binyon, Laurence (1923). *Arthur: a Tragedy*. London, p.3.
2.   Moore, Jerrold Northrop (1990). *Edward Elgar: Letters of a Lifetime*. Oxford, p.320.
3.   Moore, Jerrold Northrop (1984). *Edward Elgar: a Creative Life*. Oxford, pp.674–6; and Elgar Complete Edition vol.10, pp.vii–ix.
4.   Hereford and Worcester Record Office (HWRO) 705:445:6314.
5.   HWRO 705:445:6312.
6.   HWRO 705:445:6320.
7.   *Letters of a Lifetime*, p.369.
8.   ibid., pp.369–70.
9.   ibid., p.370.
10. HWRO 705:445:parcel 4.

11. Moore, Jerrold Northrop (1989). *Edward Elgar: the Windflower Letters*. Oxford, p.277; on 28 March came tidings that Meg had been killed by a car, p.280.
12. HWRO 705:445:6318.
13. Perryfield was the home of Elgar's sister, Pollie Grafton.
14. *The Windflower Letters*, p.277.
15. HWRO 705:445:6311.
16. BL Add.MS 59870.
17. HWRO 705:445:6309.
18. *Letters of a Lifetime*, pp.370–71.
19. HWRO 705:445:6310.
20. BL Add.MS 49974C.
21. BL Add.MS 58061; pp.111–14 of the full score, including the Scene VII trumpet calls, are bound in this volume as ff.16–17v.
22. *Letters of a Lifetime*, p.371.
23. HWRO 705:445:6316.
24. *A Creative Life*, pp.763–4.
25. *The Windflower Letters*, p.278.
26. *A Creative Life*, p.764.
27. Sir George Arthur had been secretary to and was biographer of Lord Kitchener.
28. HWRO 705:445:6308.
29. HWRO 705:445:6321.
30. *The Windflower Letters*, pp.279–80.
31. ibid., p.280.
32. ibid., p.281.
33. Birthplace Museum.
34. Letters of a Lifetime, p.371.
35. HWRO 705:445:6319.
36. Holroyd, Michael (1991). Bernard Shaw, vol.3: *The Lure of Fantasy*. London, p.79.
37. Atkins, E. Wulstan (1984). *The Elgar-Atkins Friendship*. Newton Abbot, pp.390–91.
38. Moore, Jerrold Northrop (1987). *Elgar and his Publishers: Letters of a Creative Life*. Oxford, p.856.
39. Young, Percy M. (1956). *Letters of Edward Elgar*. London, pp.306–7.
40. Maine, Basil (1933). *Elgar: His Life and Works*, vol.2. London, p.176.
41. Elgar Complete Edition vol.41, p.57.
42. ibid., pp.215–6.
43. ibid., p.180.
44. ibid., pp.5–8.
45. BL Add. MS. 58061, f.46v.
46. Elgar Complete Edition vol.41, pp.157–8.
47. Moore, Jerrold Northrop (1974). *Elgar on Record*. London, p.213.
48. Reed, W. H. (1936, 2/1973). *Elgar as I knew him*. London, p.176.
49. BL Add. MS. 56101, ff.29 and 27, reproduced in Reed, ibid., pp.202–3.
50. Elgar on Record, p.213.
51. BL Add. MS. 56101, f.44, reproduced in Reed, op. cit., p.222.
52. BL Add. MS. 56101, ff.45, 48, 105, the first two reproduced in Reed, op. cit., pp.219, 218.
53. *Elgar on Record*, p.214.
54. BL Add. MS. 56101, ff. 36, 73–4, 98–9.
55. Reed, op. cit., pp.178–9.

11 Elgar's Use of Literature

Brian Trowell

My title is intended to suggest an approach to Elgar's literary aspirations and achievements rather more analytical and critical than is common.[1] The usual reason for investigating a composer's reading is in order to assess the practical use he made of it in choosing texts and setting them to music, or employing them as the basis for programme music; in Elgar's case there is the additional interest of his frequent use of literary epigraphs, not all of which found their way into the published scores, and of further quotations inscribed in presentation copies or associated with particular works in private letters to his friends. In these matters Elgar has been well served by Michael Kennedy and Jerrold Northrop Moore,[2] though I am able to bring further material into the discussion in the latter part of this essay. The secondary reason is biographical and contextual: one wishes to construct an account of the growth of a composer's intellectual and spiritual development, and its relationship both with past traditions and with the world about him. It is here, I think, that in Elgarian biography we encounter certain distortions of the record, an unwillingness to proceed with care and circumspection, a readiness to accept statements and records at their face value without probing for the underlying motivation, a combination of enthusiastic hero-worship and over-protectiveness that clouds judgement and obscures the truth.[3] The questions, it seems to me, are not simply what books Elgar read or bought and when, but why he read them, what he gained from them, and how he employed his knowledge. Looked at in this way, the history of the uses that he made of his reading begins to yield further insights into his puzzling and paradoxical character. But where do the distortions that I have mentioned originate? To answer that we must turn to the end of Elgar's life, to a controversy whose only lasting effect has been to unbalance the views of Elgar's biographers on his literary attainments.

The Dent affair

Devoted Elgarians have always found the subject of E. J. Dent's belittlement of Elgar as distasteful as the composer himself must have. Perhaps that is why certain inaccuracies relating to it have been allowed to persist for so long, and why the valuable observations of the late Philip Radcliffe,[4] published in 1976, have not so far been noted in the literature on Elgar. Dent's article certainly betrays a personal dislike of Elgar's music and fails to recognize his stature at the point in time when the controversy over it erupted in the winter of 1930/31. What was peculiarly unsettling about his attack, besides its context in an authoritative and durable international monument of Austro-German scholarship, was the fact that it came from so eminent a man. Dent was by 1930 a justly famous scholar and critic, distinguished also for his tireless efforts to promote the cause of modern music. He had been Professor of Music at Cambridge University since 1926 and President of the Royal Musical Association since 1928; he was only half-way through his long term of office as founding President of the International Society for Contemporary Music, and was President-elect of the International Musicological Society. The writing of his paragraph on Elgar is therefore viewed as an act of impetuous and irresponsible malice. Even Dr Moore, normally so careful, judicious and self-effacing, prefaces his discussion of the incident by presenting unjustifiable speculation as fact. He implies that Dent had been moved to anger by some anti-academic remarks in an article praising Elgar by C. W. Orr, published in January 1931 in *The Musical Times* and followed by further correspondence supporting Elgar's claim to be recognised as a great composer: 'It was all too much for Stanford's pupil and successor as Professor of Music at Cambridge, Edward J. Dent . . . His remarks, published in Germany, quickly found their way back to England'.[5]

It is surprising, after this, to find that the second edition of Guido Adler's *Handbuch der Musikgeschichte*, in which Dent's article was discovered, had in fact been published in Berlin early in the previous year, 1930. I mention the matter, not to score a cheap point – for Dr Moore's many labours on Elgar's behalf place us immeasurably in his debt – but to show how the red rag of Dent is still liable to cause momentary blindness amongst even the most scholarly Elgarians. And my tale continues. Except for Basil Maine[6] all those who have discussed this question, and even Dent's bibliographer, Lawrence Haward,[7] say or imply that the offending article was added to the second edition of Adler's book. In fact it appears, word for word, in the first, which was published in 1924.

Knowing how long it takes for an editor to assemble a large compendium of this kind (involving international collaboration and translation), I would think it quite likely that Dent wrote the piece as much as two or three years before the date of publication. That would bring us to 1921–2, when Dent was not nearly so widely known, held none of the offices listed above, and had no association with Cambridge, but was earning his living as a music critic in London. Parry was recently dead (in 1918, aged 70); Stanford, one of

Dent's teachers, was still alive and active, also aged 70; Elgar was in his mid-sixties, not yet the lonely eminence of 73 that he was in 1930. In these circumstances it becomes easier to understand why Dent allowed Elgar only a quarter of the space devoted to Parry and only two-fifths of Stanford's allocation, and why it was harder for him, writing in the early 1920s, to perceive Elgar's true stature.

That still does not excuse the passage in his article which gave, and continues to give, most offence. Here we return to our main theme, for it appeared to be a gratuitous sneer at Elgar's intellectual standing. I quote it in the translation invariably used since Maine published it in 1933; this was the version known to Elgar, and was surely the one communicated by Philip Heseltine[8] to those who joined him in signing the well-known letter of protest sent to the Press Association early in 1931. The immediate context of the offending words is important. They follow a sentence associating Elgar with Alexander Mackenzie in that they were both professional violinists and studied the works of Liszt, 'which were abhorrent to conservative academic musicians': true enough on all counts, for Mackenzie was a friend of Liszt and an active exponent of his music, while Elgar's admiration of his symphonic poems, reported by W. H. Reed, is also attested by his praise of *Orpheus*.[9] The more interesting thing to note here is that Dent links two composers who had both won through to recognition from unprivileged beginnings (though in each case there was music in the family), and were therefore not 'establishment' figures. He then continues, speaking only of Elgar, 'He was, moreover, a Catholic, and more or less a self-taught man, who possessed little of the literary culture of Parry or Stanford'. Dent disliked Catholicism and indeed any form of religion, and Francis Toye[10] has suggested that it was this hidden factor that really determined his attitude to Elgar;[11] here, though, the matter of Elgar's religion is presented objectively as another feature that sets him apart from the prevailing orthodoxy of English musicians. 'More or less a self-taught man' is again a true statement, continuing the same idea and implying no condemnation. But to say that he 'possessed little of the literary culture of Parry or Stanford' seems a calculated insult.

Was it so intended? I suggest that it was not. The German word here is not the unequivocal 'Kultur', but the more ambiguous 'Bildung'. This may mean 'culture' – a loaded word! – but a commoner meaning, deriving directly from the stem-verb 'bilden', that is 'to form, shape, or fashion', is 'education', 'instruction' or 'schooling'. It seems rather more likely to me that Dent was simply expanding his use of the word 'Autodidakt': 'who possessed little of the [formal] literary education of Parry or Stanford'. This would have been perfectly true. It would be interesting to unearth Dent's English original[12] if indeed there ever was one, for Dent was a brilliant linguist and quite capable of writing his essay in German. Meanwhile, it seems to me that the passage was probably intended as objective comment, and that in the interests of truth and in fairness to Dent we ought at the very least to suspend judgement. The thing is implausible for another reason. Though he came of gentle stock, Dent hated the conventions of gentility, voted Labour all his life, and spent a great deal of time and effort helping to develop access to the arts for the underprivileged through his work for the Old Vic and Sadler's Wells theatres. It would have been quite out of character for him to sneer at a self-educated man for lacking advantages which were beyond his grasp.[13]

The phrase passed into circulation, nevertheless, as 'who possessed little of the literary culture of Parry or Stanford', and has always been taken as an insult. Curiously, it escaped comment or rebuttal in the Open Letter of protest, and it was left to Bernard Shaw to take up the matter in his powerful postscript. That may have been at the wish of his fellow-signatories, most of whom were musicians whose opinions would have carried little weight. Perhaps they recalled Shaw's hyperbolic praise of Elgar's reading habits in the essay he had published in 1920 in the first issue of *Music & Letters*; this had very likely been intended to console his friend after Gerald Cumberland's quizzical remarks about his literary tastes in *Set down in malice*,[14] a book which had made a considerable stir in the previous year, and which Shaw must have read. Elgar, he then wrote, 'sucked libraries dry as a child sucks its mother's breasts'.

But a thirst for reading, though a necessary prerequisite, is not in itself evidence of high cultural and intellectual attainment. Elgar had published virtually nothing to set beside the impressive number of books and articles by Parry and Stanford, who were also fluent in several modern and classical languages, which Elgar was not.[15] Shaw would have found Elgar's formal prose stiff and old-fashioned (we know that it was written with much difficulty),[16] would have regarded his letters to the *Times Literary Supplement* as mere scribblings in the margin of index-scholarship, and would have seen the Literary Society, to which Elgar had been elected in 1920, as little more than a belletristic dining-club. (And we need to remember that neither Dent nor Shaw nor anyone else had then been privileged, as we have, to see the full wealth of Elgar's principal claim to literary attainment, the marvellous informal prose of his letters, with their easy mastery of phrase and rhythm, their remarkable powers of imaginative empathy and self-dramatisation, their wit, verve and sense of fun.) We must also recall that Elgar had not always been as discriminating as Parry and Stanford in his choice of poems for setting to music, and that Ernest Newman, in Chapter 4 of his *Elgar* (1905), had adversely criticized, and with some justice, various examples of his apparent insensitivity to English prosody.

Shaw must have realised that his task was difficult, for his lordly postscript adroitly shifts the ground, and even seems to invoke yet a third meaning of 'Bildung' as 'structure'. He is really adducing Elgar's musical gifts rather than his literary ones when he points to *The Apostles* and *The Kingdom* as 'a new form of symphonic art involving a "literarischen Bildung" of which Parry and Stanford never dreamt', adding that 'Prof. Dent should not have made them ridiculous by such comparison'. This is unfair to Parry, at least, who had also written symphonic choral works to libretti entirely his own, such as *A Vision of Life*, which Elgar deeply admired.[17] It is also an ironic tribute to the persuasiveness of Elgar's musical gifts that we should here find the free-thinking exponent of the Life Force praising Christian oratorios composed by a Catholic.

Later repercussions of the Dent affair

What of later responses? Was it at Elgar's request that Maine omitted the sentences about oratorio, Parry and Stanford each time that he quoted from Shaw's postscript,[18] or because he himself found it an ineffective reply? Maine's own defence comes elsewhere: 'books are his [Elgar's] greatest treasures, and in an access of great wealth a large proportion would certainly be devoted to his library. Apart from his music, his collection of books is the most complete manifestation of that remarkable mind . . . It can safely be said that no living composer is more widely-read than Elgar'[19] The latter claim is a very large one, considering that Elgar's reading was confined to one language; to substantiate it would require investigation into the reading of such intellectually-inclined composers as Bantock, Bartók, Berg, Berners, Bruneau, van Dieren, Hindemith, Holst, Constant Lambert, Milhaud, Pfitzner, Roussel, Schoenberg, Stravinsky and Wellesz, all active when Maine was writing. But Michael Kennedy was to go even further in answering Dent's supposed slur: 'as has been amply demonstrated, Elgar was one of the most widely read men of his time, with a brilliantly retentive memory. The literary allusions and quotations in his Birmingham lectures would do credit to a professor of English literature'.[20] That is certainly the impression that Elgar intended to convey, but he did not feel confident enough to publish the lectures: we shall return to this subject later on. No-one would possibly wish to doubt that Elgar read widely (but not, I think, systematically), that he possessed an extensive collection of books, and was capable of intense application in pursuing out-of-the-way subjects. But Maine is at fault either in his logic or his use of English when he says that 'his collection of books is the most complete *manifestation* of that remarkable mind': for that to be true, Elgar would have had to write them.

William Reed was inspired by Shaw to write *Elgar as I knew him* (1936).[21] Valuable as the book is, Reed modestly disclaims any literary skill and even the ability to punctuate correctly, comforting himself with complete justification by quoting an epigraph from Ruskin (from the same passage as Elgar's 'This is the best of me'). He avoids discussion of Elgar's literary abilities, but correctly praises his knowledge: 'He had great literary knowledge too, and an omnivorous taste for it. He knew all the great poets; he loved and adored every word of Shakespeare; and he read all the modern writers of poetry with interest. He liked some light reading, but not very much; but he was very amused always with the works of O. Henry, one of whose books was generally by his bedside'. This is fair enough, though I suspect that 'modern writers of poetry' probably did not extend to any style more advanced than Belloc's.

Reed did not mention Dent or even discuss Elgar's literary tastes in his *Elgar* (1939).[22] Nor does Eric Blom, in the additional chapter that he added to the reprint of 1943, though he alludes to Dent's article.[23]

Percy M. Young's *Elgar O.M.*[24] of 1955 was the first to quote extensively from Elgar's letters and thereby to demonstrate where Elgar's literary abilities really lay. He went on to publish important collections of Elgar's correspondence in 1956 and 1965,[25] and contributed a charming essay with a deliberately ambiguous title, 'Elgar as a man of letters', to *Edward Elgar: centenary sketches*, published in 1957.[26] This contrasts the wealth of the letters with the paucity of Elgar's public pronouncements.[27] In a discussion of *Falstaff*, Dr Young quotes a sentence from Charles Lamb which is actually the chief clue to Elgar's reading habits: 'I love to lose myself in other men's minds'.[28] The essay also suggests that others besides Dent had sneered at Elgar's supposed lack of culture: 'he was sensitive to the calumny – which aggravated the more as time went on – that he was lacking in those qualities formerly thought to be as respectable as they were necessary to a middle-class "man of culture" . . . The injustice of the calumny hurt terribly'. He then goes on to point to the extraordinary outburst in Elgar's Foreword to his friend Hubert Leicester's *Forgotten Worcester*, which speaks of 'the many crudities which one of the many – why are there so many? – unbrilliant university men has used in reference to myself . . . ' He praises Elgar's command of theology and church history, in which he did indeed read intensively, though this was with the practical aim of assembling biblical texts for the later oratorios: the interest appears to have ceased with them. But then we come once more to hyperbole: 'His acquaintance with European literature, whether ancient or modern, was so extensive as to put to shame those of us who study his writings from the little eminence of a university course in English literature'.

Elgar's knowledge of foreign literature, so far as it can be demonstrated by collecting all references in the published documentation, and noting all texts that he set or sketched music for, appears to have been limited to fewer than forty authors, ten of them very small fry, and to a number of anthologies such as *The Greek Anthology*, Paley's *Greek Wit*, and Rossetti's translations of early Italian poets. Dozens of major writers are absent from the list, from Racine and Corneille to Tolstoy and Dostoyevsky. Forty foreign writers is of course a creditable score, but what interest is served by exaggeration? Perhaps Dr Young's last words quoted above give us the clue: as I know from my own first approach to this subject, a middle-class intellectual with a university education, when confronted with a meritorious autodidact, is almost bound to feel a certain guilt over his own advantages, and will tend to compensate accordingly.

One of the great virtues (among so many) of *Elgar O.M.* is that Dr Young provides a long, connected account of Elgar's reading, derived from many sources but reposing mainly on a study of the books of Elgar's that survive at the Elgar Birthplace.[29] It is presented with loving enthusiasm and is implicitly directed at Dent: 'We may . . . reflect on the injustice of the charge that he [Elgar] lacked literary culture'. The listings are understandably arranged for presentation into a reasonably classified order; a study of the dates of acquisition and bookplates suggests, however, that the order of purchase and reading of the Birthplace books was nothing like as systematic as it appears. Dr Young says many shrewd and wise things in these pages. He has looked inside most, but not all, of the books, as we shall see. He comments on the pencilled notes in the Greek Anthology volumes:[30] these must relate to the review comparing various English versions 'from the standpoint of *the very person it is intended for*' that Elgar, 'who read neither Gk nor Latin' half hoped to be invited to provide in August 1917.[31] Dr Young tends to romanticize on occasion. 'Bray's edition of Evelyn's *Diary* was a great solace in the lonely days of early marriage and the pencilled glosses of Alice Elgar still remain': this suggest serious study, but all she has done is add the dates at the top of each page, for which a loving note by her husband is duly grateful. Again, 'as a young man he admired the Tennyson *Birthday Book*, the slender poems of the Honourable Roden Noel . . .': the Tennyson is in fact one of those Victorian diaries with a quotation for each day of the year, and was a gift to his sister Lucy; Noel's poems lost their fascination, for the latter pages are uncut.[32] It is rather astonishing to see a book by Renan, *The Apostles*,[33] full of pencilled notes, amongst the theological volumes: his revolutionary thinking had once alarmed the Catholic establishment, and it would be interesting to assess what effect it had on Elgar's trilogy. A mystery surrounds the beautiful apothegm of Jean Paul Richter, 'copied from a copy of *Levana* which he [Elgar] found one day at Frank Schuster's';[34] Dr Moore also refers to this, saying that Elgar copied it into Schuster's vocal score of the German version of *The Dream of Gerontius*.[35] This suggests, and was doubtless intended to suggest, that Elgar had actually read a translation of Richter's much-praised tract on education: it was fashionable to admire Richter, a difficult and fantastic early Romantic writer. But no, Elgar's quotation is not taken from the only complete translation then available: it comes from Thomas Carlyle's rendering of just this sentence, cited in a review included in his *Critical and Miscellaneous Essays*.[36]

As Dr Young turned from his biography to undertake the task of editing Elgar's letters and lectures, he grew decidedly more cautious in his judgements. His justified enthusiasm for the spontaneous prose of the letters is tempered by more careful comment on Elgar's formal public prose. He distinguishes between the historical value of such documents as Elgar's essay on *Falstaff,* and their literary value. 'Elgar forever felt himself at heart a man of letters, and often went out of his way to polish the finery of secret ambition. The printed essay on *Falstaff*. . . is a case in point: of great interest, and evidence of the widest reading, it is almost depressingly literary and donnish.'[37] Of Elgar's Birmingham lectures he writes: 'Elgar's struggle to educate himself is indicated not only by his exercises in manipulating prose style, but also by his affection for the recondite allusion, or the impressive quotation. He was, of course, an omnivorous reader, but in the way in which he advertised the extent of his reading he was more than a little self-conscious'. 'Recondite allusions . . . illustrate a natural zest for accumulating knowledge, but also Elgar's hidden intention to out-professor the professors'.[38]

This is excellent; but Dr Young's footnotes to the lectures – often a remarkable display of his own abilities in literary detective work – sometimes give the impression that Elgar was much more learned than he really was. Why pursue Strabo and Stratonicus at such length, when Elgar had simply lifted his anecdotes from F.A. Paley's anthology, *Greek Wit,*[39] where I suspect he also found the quotation from Protagoras, equally impressively footnoted later on? It is clear from the notes that Dr Young has spotted the source from which Elgar has lifted his airy references to Jean Hardouin and Giovanni Pietro Pinamonti, namely James Mew's *Traditional aspects of hell,*[40] a distillation of material from scores of earlier writers: it would be very easy for the reader to assume, from the eighteen lines of erudite commentary on these two writers that the editor provides, that Elgar was as learned in this matter as he. Dr Young does not give us a reference when Elgar observes that certain composers, in their orchestral excesses, 'remind me of the sentence quoted by Motley from the sarcastic Padovaro, "When he finds himself SOBER he believes himself to be ill".'[41] Turning to J. L. Motley's *The Rise of the Dutch Republic,*[42] one discovers that this was said of the Germans (a dig at Strauss, therefore?), and also that Motley invariably uses the alternative spelling of Badovaro for the Venetian agent: Elgar seems to have borrowed his *trouvaille* from some other source, probably again an anthology of some kind. When Elgar talks of 'Erasmus . . . , a German',[43] we are offered a note; but it does not point out Elgar's extraordinary mistake over the nationality of the famous Dutch scholar. Neither Elgar nor Dr Young seems to be aware that the beautiful passage from Ford's *The Lover's Melancholy* cited on page 139 is itself a translation of Strada's well-known Prolusion on the Nightingale. Mr Kennedy's Professor of English Literature would certainly not have missed that.

The examples I have here adduced certainly give a one-sided picture, and it would not do to dwell on them. By introducing a certain number of highly recondite references among dozens more appositely quoted from his genuinely wide reading, Elgar was only doing what he thought was expected from a university Professor, and they are, after all, merely an extension of the love of literary allusions that characterizes his letters to like-minded friends. On occasion, it is true, the train of thought is disturbed in order to provide a cue for a 'cultural' reference; but, if he was sometimes concerned to display his own reading, he was also, by his own example, reinforcing the point to which he frequently returns here and elsewhere, that modern musicians need to develop their brains and sensibilities. The comparative paucity of references to books about music is also notable:[44] he wished to move musicians out of that hermetic, technical way of thinking. In his pursuit of the abstruse, though, he must at times have felt that he was walking a terrifying tightrope of his own creation: what if the Professor of Greek had stood up and asked him a question about Stratonicus or Mimnermus?

There is no need to pursue the after-effects of Dent's supposed attack further through the Elgar literature. Apart from the sentence quoted earlier, Michael Kennedy's comments on Elgar's literary tastes are highly judicious and sensitive.[45] Dr Moore avoids an analytical review of the subject, since his method is strictly chronological and cumulative; but he provides valuable insights by pausing from time to time to discuss the flavour and content of books and poems that were important to Elgar, such as Longfellow's *Hyperion* and Jessie Fothergill's *The First Violin*. I wish now to say a little about the compulsions that led Elgar and his wife to 'advertise the extent of his reading', in Dr Young's phrase.

Literary culture in the Elgar interviews

Elgar himself said that 'my general education was not neglected'.[46] It was no dishonour in 1872 to leave school at 15; indeed, it was a privilege that did not become general until quite recently. The Education Act of 1921 raised the school-leaving age in Britain to 14; the abortive Act of 1936 attempted to raise it to 15, though still allowing exceptions; it took the Act of 1944 to make the extra year general and compulsory. Though Elgar lacked a university education, it is worth reminding ourselves that so too did Shaw and Arnold Bennett, and that H. G. Wells' London degree was in science.[47] In an age without radio, television and cinema, and particularly in areas of

Britain which did not enjoy the cultural amenities of a large city, reading was nevertheless an exceptionally important and widespread activity among members of the stratum of society into which Elgar was born.

Elgar was a voracious reader for many different reasons. One easily perceives the intense delight in language of a sensitive and enquiring mind, early accustomed to using books and profiting from a decent general education. To this is added the need to make sense of his peculiar circumstances as a Catholic and a poor man with intimations of great things within him, which he felt might express themselves in literary form; his deep emotional frustrations in early manhood, which could discover no outlet through his music until he was middle-aged, directed his quest for a sense of artistic pattern, order and purpose into his reading; minor scientific studies offer some of the same attractions. This need continued long after he had become a workmanlike composer: the music was, I think, not enough. The quest led him into apparently safer imaginary worlds, especially of the past; but it was an escape, and he seems to have found that he had little creative literary talent. At the same time, he had started to move amongst upper middle-class people and to encounter fashionable opinion, the delights of allusion-swapping, and certain literary shibboleths. He married, without deep romantic love,[48] an upper middle-class lady with literary ambitions of her own which she largely abandoned on his behalf.

From this point Alice Elgar's conventional and belletristic tastes begin to overlay his own broader and more developed literary sense, and he tends to take over her lost ambitions. His growing artistic eminence leads to an upward social migration where comparisons with senior establishment musicians occasion, it would seem, malicious comment on his origins and his lack of a university education. He feels the need to prove himself as a 'scholar': not merely to be one, but to advertise the fact. He briefly and mistakenly becomes a university professor. He seeks out the company and friendship of men of letters, mostly of the scholarly type such as A. C. Benson and the group at the British Museum (Barclay Squire, Binyon, Colvin, Garnett and Streatfeild); his friendship flatters them, and theirs him. He wins and keeps the admiration and friendship of Bernard Shaw (they must have agreed, however, not to discuss politics). But Arnold Bennett and Siegfried Sassoon, though his music holds them in awe, quickly tire of his refusal to be considered a 'mere musician', of his eccentric behaviour and opinions.[49] As the 1920s pass, he seems to lose his zest for literature as well as for large-scale composition. His last years, however, must have been made exceptionally if needlessly bitter by Dent's supposed attack, which probably came to his notice in 1924: he wrote no further pseudo-scholarly letters to the *TLS* after 1923.

We may now trace some of the uses to which the 'man of letters' image was put in a number of interviews from the years when Elgar first achieved national fame. In one case, the interview with F. G. Edwards for *The Musical Times*, we are able to look behind the scenes at proof stage, to observe the Elgars feeding in further material and ensuring that remarks distasteful to them are cut. This was the first really long and important account of him; it appeared in the Novello house journal; but one wonders whether such control was exercised over other interviews as well.

Books figure prominently in R. J. Buckley's portrait of the Elgars at Forlì in 1896; this forms Chapter 4 of his book *Sir Edward Elgar* (1904), but reads as if reprinted from an earlier article. There is a flavour of provincial self-improvement about it, and the Grossmiths would have rejoiced in the Pooterish mention of Mrs Lynn Linton, a minor and now forgotten Victorian novelist:

> The composer revealed himself as a book enthusiast, a haunter of the remoter shelves of the second-hand bookshops, with a leaning to the rich and rare. In the sitting-room [were] . . . books, and books, and more books. He declared himself to be a devoted reader of all kinds of literature . . . Elgar spoke of a Malvern book club, a sort of literary federation, of which he was the first member, the late Mrs Lynn Linton being an enthusiastic supporter. The surrounding piles of books were expressive of the man . . . [50]

Elgar's liking for the out-of-the-way is suggested by the 'remoter shelves', and the unsystematic nature of his acquisitions is thereby underlined. If his reading was wide, that was partly because it was desultory and adventitious. One worries a little over 'rich and rare', which suggests fine bindings and first editions. This type of bibliophily is not commonly important to a man hungry for intellectual pabulum: he will not care what covers it comes in. One notes that here, as in most interviews, there is no mention that Alice Elgar was an author.

The next account of Elgar is the long article by Edwards[51] already mentioned. The interview, corrections to the first proof and accompanying letters from the Elgars all belong to September 1900. Dr Moore has recently published this interesting material.[52] Edwards begins with verses from *Piers Plowman* and Elizabeth Barrett Browning that were quite possibly suggested by Elgar himself, since they were both Malvern poets. It is in this interview that the story about the books discovered in the stable loft first surfaces. Edwards originally mentioned only Sir Philip Sydney, but Elgar added *Arcadia*, Baker's *Chronicles*[53] and Drayton's *Polyolbion*[54] to the proof. These are indeed extraordinarily unlikely books for a fifteen-year-old to read, more a test of endurance than a literary experience; I must confess that I myself have been defeated by the tedium of the first (save for its songs) and the last (British topography and local history, delivered in pounding Alexandrines, but with learned notes that may plausibly have stimulated Elgar's known interest in these subjects). Elgar's mature literary tastes are described as follows:

The composer of 'King Olaf' is a great lover of books. He not only reads and digests them, but carefully marks what seem to him to be striking points as specially worthy of his attention. Some prized first editions are in his library. Pictures of every school, and literature, especially of the last century, have a strong fascination for him . . .

Edwards brings out the scholarly habit of annotation with suitably deferential solemnity. The last two sentences, however, have been stage-managed by Alice Elgar. Edwards originally wrote 'Some first editions of Dickens are in his library'. Dickens was a vulgar taste, and has to go, and the aura of bibliophily must be polished with 'prized'. Alice's comment in her accompanying letter is 'we are not devoted to Dickens altho' we possess his best, may "Dickens" be left out, & the sentence slightly amplified as I have marked, pictures of course he is devoted to but it is the last century *literature* wh. he has so especially made his own'.[55] The proof shows that Edwards thought he had finished with literature after the word 'library'. It was his intention to move on to pictures and furniture; no doubt he knew little about art, since he suggests that Elgar's taste is simultaneously catholic and fastidious (a phrase we shall meet again). He originally wrote: 'Pictures of every school – especially that of the last century – have a strong fascination for him, as does old furniture'. The addition of literature, and emphatically eighteenth-century literature, is Alice Elgar's. (Actually, Elgar's undoubted delight in eighteenth-century English literature was largely confined to letters, memoirs and biography: he seems to have concurred in the low estimation of eighteenth-century poetry common in his time.) Edwards also mentions that at the age of 15 Elgar 'began to learn German, with a view of going to Leipzig for the further study of music'; his father's lack of means prevented this, so that Elgar 'escaped the dogmatism of the schools'.

The next important interview, with Rudolph de Cordova, was published in *The Strand Magazine* in May 1904,[56] the same year in which Buckley's book appeared, to which we shall return. Cordova, like Buckley and Edwards, mentions the early study of German, from which one might deduce that Elgar had learned the language. I would not wish to minimize the difficulties of learning German on one's own in a provincial town in 1872, but a draft letter to Fritz Volbach of 1903 surviving in the sketches for *The Apostles*,[57] presumably corrected after advice from Alice, whose German was good, suggests that Elgar never mastered its grammar and had difficulties with vocabulary and capitalization. The draft runs:

Lieber Freund: / Wo ist ihre en [deleted] Briefe in

english (abgeschafft? Gratuliren und gute [interlined] in (geschrieben?

[deleted] beg[leisterung? deleted] inspiration für (der
                                                      (den

Wagner'sche Hymnus in Berlin / Ihr getreuer Edward.

The first sentence is then corrected to 'Wo ist ihr englischer Brief ausgeblieben?' He fared rather better with later efforts to learn French, and even made a good joke in the language, though Percy Pitt had to correct his poor prosody in the song 'Quand nos bourgeons se rouvriront' in Une voix dans le désert;[58] Italian gave him trouble, as he honestly avowed to Schuster in 1903: 'I like the French now but can't get on with the Italian tongage (good word)'.[59]

The episode of the books in the stable-loft is considerably expanded in Cordova's article. There are now theological books, Elizabethan dramatists, many old poets, among whom Sydney and Drayton are presumably included, and translations of Voltaire; Holinshed and still other chroniclers now keep company with Baker:

> There were books of all kinds, and all distinguished by the characteristic that they were for the most part incomplete. I busied myself for days and weeks arranging them. I picked out the theological books, of which there were a good many, and put them on one side. Then I made a place for the Elizabethan dramatists, the chronicles including Baker's and Hollinshed's, besides a tolerable collection of old poets and translations of Voltaire, and all sorts of things up to the eighteenth century. Then I began to read. I used to get up at four or five o'clock in the summer and read – every available opportunity found me reading. I read till dark. I finished by reading every one of those books – including the theology. The result of that reading has been that people tell me I know more of life up to the eighteenth century than I do of my own time, and it is probably true.[60]

I know of no other evidence that Elgar had read Sydney's *Arcadia*, Drayton's *Polyolbion*, Baker or Holinshed; but the story, with its emphasis on the remote and its taste for serendipity, chimes convincingly enough with Elgar's later reading habits. Even if it has been romanticized, the general picture of the imaginative lad poring over his first vicarious library seems truthful enough. Cordova leaves the date of the episode vague. When Buckley gives it, in the shortened form retailed by Edwards – he must have written his account some time before Cordova – the period has shifted back into Elgar's schooldays, since two pages later a paragraph begins 'Meanwhile Edward Elgar attended school at Littleton House', that is the years 1868–72. And great names are afterwards invoked to suggest Elgar's limitless literary potential: 'There were the "Arcadia" of Sir Philip Sydney, Baker's "Chronicles", Drayton's "Polyolbion", and other volumes regarded by the shy, retiring youth as treasures of unspeakable worth. Without his musical surroundings Edward Elgar might have been a poet, might have emulated Dante or Milton'.[61] When Elgar (presumably) told the story to Basil Maine, the same three books are mentioned, but the tale is placed in the paragraph relating to Elgar's schooling with Miss Walsh[62] (that is before 1868). The dating is further confused by a reference to his apparently contemporaneous violin lessons with Frederick Spray, which Elgar himself dated to six months during 1874, when he was seventeen.[63] He seems to have been this age when a factory girl smiled up at him as he stood practising at a window, whom he later took 'to the loft where the old books were stored' and read her a passage from *Candide*. Apparently the books were left there for several years. Did Elgar's love of a good tale take the artistic licence of compressing his reading into a period shorter than was really the case?

One or two other points in Buckley's book, not relating to his Forlì interview but to recent years (1904), call for comment. Elgar stresses, as in his Birmingham lectures, that 'musicians need good education. More culture is desirable for vocalists . . . Yes, education is needed for musicians'.[64] There is a remark recalling the habit of annotation earlier described by Edwards, when Elgar 'suggests that if people would index good books instead of writing music, there would be some sense in it'.[65] This was curiously important for Elgar, who reveals one of his methods of finding good 'quotes' in a letter to Sidney Colvin of 1917, in which he somewhat presumptuously advises him, hearing that he is preparing a new book, as follows: 'We will talk over this – I always say the same thing to anyone producing a book. Do have a GOOD INDEX. It is especially desirable in such a work as you propose [*A team of eight*] – it leads to quotation, which is what I want. As how: thus: a man writing wants to fortify his opinion – he remembers that Colvin has said, etc: he wants the exact words – tumbles over the index – nothing there; then he quotes somebody else. I thought I found this, to a very heavily appreciable degree, when I was mugging at (pseudo) theology. *Farrer* [*rectè* Farrar] *& Liddon* (Bampton lectures I think) have marvellously minute indexes & get quoted out of all relation to their worth & consequence – that is my view – but I am getting out of the corral proper for fiddlers'.[66] A. J. Balfour and Sir Charles Eastlake, who presumably had good indexes, accordingly get quoted in Elgar's talk with Buckley.[67] That talk is described as 'brilliant and cultured . . . running over with enthusiasm, full of ideas about all things in heaven and earth'.[68] Among the things that Elgar told Buckley was that his astonishing mother 'had affinity with the best English literature; moreover, she read translations of the Latin classics, of the Greek tragedians, and talked in the home of what she read'.[69] Buckley explains the son by the mother: 'His boyish choice of books from the stable loft is no longer inexplicable'. It is a pity, though, that Buckley does not himself write better prose: one might then be more readily inclined to trust his judgements . . .

The next interviewer, 'Gerald Cumberland' (C. F. Kenyon) could certainly write. Though he was a journalist, his work is not mere *reportage*: he knew a great deal about music, and admired Ernest Newman's critical writings almost as much as he admired Elgar's compositions.[70] His two books of reminiscences reveal a very wide acquaintance amongst composers and performers as well as literary and theatre folk and artists. Through his friendship and collaboration with Havergal Brian, whom he first met in

1905, he would have been well informed about the musical culture of the English Midlands, which had offered Elgar his early training and first successes. Cumberland was a radical and naturally inclined to question the Elgars' Tory allegiance; he is likely to have felt uneasy that Elgar, once proud to be a provincial and not afraid to speak out against the London musical establishment, should now seem intent on joining it. That, I think, partly explains the difference in tone between the respectful approach of his two interviews with Elgar published in 1906 and 1913, and the decidedly less reverent account of the same meetings given in *Set down in malice* (1919). The first interview could perhaps have been vetted by the Elgars, but not the second; the editors of the journals in which they appeared would in any case hardly have thought it appropriate for Cumberland to explore in them the mixture of fascination and irritation that Elgar's personality evoked in reaction with his own personal chemistry. The chapter devoted to Elgar in *Set down in malice* is part of a book largely written on active service during the Great War, as the prefatory note tells us, 'in trenches and dugouts of Greece and Serbia', in Port Said, Alexandria and Marseilles: it is the work of a sharp and highly intelligent observer who wished, no doubt in the face of possible death, to leave a true record of his experiences, and to say much that he had not previously been allowed to say. Because the book is critical of Elgar the man, there has been a tendency for Elgarians to discount or neglect what Cumberland offers; but, though presented with a tart sense of comedy and a resolute determination not to efface his own personality in the presence of a genius, Cumberland's later account seems honest and true. And he was, after, very well aware of Elgar's greatness.

Cumberland's interview for *The Musical World*,[71] following a visit to Plas Gwyn on 23 December 1905, presents the composer as he would have wished to appear, as a man of broad and diverse interests, 'absorbed in the life around him, and in the literature of the past and present'. Cumberland, who had evidently studied reports of the first six Birmingham lectures, resumes one of Elgar's themes: 'To be a musician and nothing else is to work out of touch with the spirit of the age, and to make but an infinitesimal contribution to the development of thought in one's own generation'. It is however Elgar's sympathies that he stresses, and his studiousness: the influence of these, and Elgar's real intellectual attainment, are seen as demonstrated not in themselves, but through his music – an important point, and in fact the line taken by Shaw, as we have noted. 'The variety of his interests, the comprehensiveness of his intellect, the depth and breadth of his nature – all these are revealed in his music: it is because they dwell in it, suffuse it, and quicken it to life, that his work has become part of the intellectual and emotional life of the people . . . it is the outcome of today's ideas, and consequently is the intellectual food of all to whom music makes appeal'. The notion of music carrying ideas to the people sounds like authentic Elgar rather than Cumberland, the Elgar of the early works as well as the Elgar who had composed *The Apostles* and was even then writing *The Kingdom*. But not all of what Elgar thought of as 'today's ideas' were to Cumberland's taste, as his later account of this meeting shows.

The interview then moved on to the fuss created by the Birmingham lectures, which Cumberland hopes will be published. Elgar expands on his recent strictures about young composers who attempt to do precisely what has just been recommended, to put intellect into one's music. But they are too young, too inexperienced, and exercise their intellects on the wrong subject-matter: 'it was the custom for a young man in his early twenties to compose the most heavy and lugubrious music imaginable – music that was full of metaphysical subtleties and introspective questionings . . . the public has again and again refused to listen to the morbid self-revelations and mystical profundities of mere youths, who . . . are certainly not yet sufficiently mature to originate creeds and philosophies of their own'. Who will wish 'to hear the metaphysical moanings of men who are in experience little more than children?' But what are young composers to put in place of the 'unnecessary complications and neurotic rubbish', to use a phrase from the lecture on 'English composers', that surrounds them?[72] It would seem that they must turn their back on 'today's ideas', and also avoid anything obscure: they are to give up – again in the words of the lecture – 'ransacking for new titles or forgotten poems. The old re-illustrated will serve'.[73] In 'English composers', Elgar had gone on to quote Charles Kingsley at this point, slightly uneasily, it is true. Elsewhere in the article that Elgar had cited, Kingsley had called on poets to pursue a 'nobler and healthier manhood' and 'sounder philosophical and critical training' in place of the 'Atheism and Autotheism', the 'poetry of doubt' of Shelley and Keats and their imitators such as Alexander Smith. Instancing the *Marseillaise*, 'Scots wha hae wi' Wallace bled', 'Let Erin remember', Wolfe's *The burial of Sir John Moore*, Campbell's *Hohenlinden* and *Mariners of England*, with *Rule, Britannia* and Hood's *Song of the Shirt* and *Bridge of Sighs*, he went on to ask: 'Were it not better to have written any one of these glorious lyrics than all which John Keats has left behind him?'.[74] It was surely with this in mind, as well as his own earlier compositions, that Elgar said to Cumberland, 'We Englishmen have in our naval and military history, in our religious struggles and traditions, in our national temper and qualities, in our literary and social achievements, and in our legends and tales, sufficient material to inspire and hearten the weakest and most cold-blooded of men. It is impossible for us Englishmen to do great work and have a school of music of our own, until we embody in it our national characteristics.'

Cumberland seems to have been unaware that he was being treated to the views of Charles Kingsley, suitably adapted to the world of music: he would probably have aligned Elgar's opinions, no doubt contemptuously,

with the practice of a more recent Anglican poet, Canon Henry Newbolt.[75]
Kingsley's literary views may have been reactionary and his religious
thought of the 'muscular' variety, but he was also a Christian socialist and a
reformer, a left-wing thinker like Ruskin, whose name Cumberland passes
over without comment in a later interview. If Cumberland had realised the
implication of these unexpected intellectual affinities between Elgar and the
great Victorian social reformers, he might have questioned Elgar further and
elicited the fact that he read Carlyle[76] and Ibsen,[77] and also the novels of
Walter Besant,[78] with their picture of the life of the poor in London's East
End – not to mention the vulgar Dickens: these interests help to explain, at
least in part, Elgar's friendship with radicals and free-thinkers such as
Newman and Shaw, and also with men such as Parry and Lord Northampton,
whose political views were not those of their class. It is evident, nevertheless,
that Elgar talked to Cumberland about his social concerns, for the 1906
interview speaks of him as 'an ardent student of life, particularly the hidden
life of the very poor and destitute', and 'at home in the house of both prince
and peasant'. Cumberland also tells us, in a unique but neglected vignette,
that as a young man Elgar 'drove around with a baker's cart delivering bread
to the houses of the very poor, in the hope that in this manner he might see
something of the way in which they lived; and for weeks together he
accompanied a doctor in the slums, eagerly in search for anything typically
human'. Elgar may have been a Conservative,[79] both by temperament and
through his upbringing as a shopkeeper's son in a country town, but he was
a progressive one, and his thought, like his music, addressed the whole of
the people. In portraying him as an 'aristocrat', and stating in *Set down in
malice* that 'his intellect is continually rejecting the very matters that, in
order to gain largeness, tolerance, and a full view of life, it should
understand and accept',[80] Cumberland certainly underestimated this side of
Elgar. It is worth noting, all the same, that the composer himself plays no
part in the satirical portrait that Cumberland presents of Lady Elgar's
unthinking Toryism.

It was not only politics, though, that led Cumberland to the view that
Elgar's 'mind is essentially narrow, for he shrinks from the phenomena in life
that hurt him and he will not force himself to understand alien things'.
Elgar's mind was instinctive and intuitive, not objective and analytical, and
one may justly doubt whether any university course would have helped him
to marshal well-chosen facts into a logical chain of coherent and persuasive
argument. His own lectures, for all their insights and practical common
sense, frequently fail in this respect. What he sought from literature was
essentially what he sought from conversation with friends, sympathetic
communion with congenial minds. He wished to be understood, as he felt
he understood the authors that he liked to read.[81] But this kind of solitary
engagement with the pages of a book allows for no debate or questioning of

the kind that one encounters, or should encounter, amongst one's fellow-students and tutors at a university. The self-educated man, unless circumstances throw him into the public arena, is often intellectually lonely. That leads him to assert the ideas that he has formed from his reading, rather than to discuss them: the knowledge that he has acquired becomes part of his personality, of his pride in himself, and he will often regard a challenge to his ideas as a threat or a direct attack.

This was clearly the case with both Cumberland's interviews: he tells us in the first that the interviewer must 'rigidly abstain from direct questions', that Elgar seemed unable to 'consider, even temporarily, any change in the attitude he has already assumed'. Cumberland was an intellectual whose trade was ideas. He was not simply after a story when in his first interview he took Elgar up on Newman's challenge to his opinions on programme music. He presented Elgar's contradictory responses with some editorial charity in 1906 (just in time for Newman to quote them in an Appendix added to his book on Elgar);[82] but his later account in *Set down in malice* offers a very different yet completely plausible picture of Elgar tacking, dodging, stammering and at times reduced to silence or inconsequentiality in the face of Cumberland's persistent pursuit of an idea that interested him. It was clearly this unwillingness to argue or to answer perfectly valid questions, let alone concede the possibility of a different viewpoint, that led Cumberland to define Elgar's intellect as narrow, as shrinking from 'alien things'. The charge is too general, although based on just observation of Elgar's behaviour: such an approach as Cumberland's was simply not calculated to get the best out of him.

Cumberland's second interview, which took place on 17 July 1913, was for the purpose of gaining advance information about *Falstaff*, due for its first performance in Leeds on 2 October.[83] It was to be published in a paper with a predominantly Labour readership, *The Daily Citizen*, and this seems to have betrayed Elgar into adopting a patronizing attitude towards Cumberland. I suspect that Elgar's previous experience of him – which, however awkward the interview, had resulted in a most satisfactory article – had persuaded the composer that Cumberland, though misguided and perhaps lacking in manners, had his heart in the right place and might be helped along the road to a proper understanding of matters cultural and intellectual. Cumberland allowed himself to become nettled by counsel which he admits was kindly and well meant, though at first, relishing the comedy, he pretended to be grateful. Obviously, Elgar's advice that he should purify his style and enlarge his vocabulary by reading Shakespeare arose quite naturally from the subject of the interview, *Falstaff*. Ruskin was good, too; but Cardinal Newman was too much for Cumberland, who proceeded to denigrate the prose style of the *Apologia pro vita sua* as a model and to propose in its place the racy English of that inspired fellow-journalist, Daniel Defoe. He could not have offended Elgar's literary susceptibilities more deeply, for Elgar loathed Defoe's truculent protestantism and once suggested that 'Defoe' was 'a fine and wholesome name for a pig'.[84] Cumberland made matters still worse, no doubt, by his praise of *Moll Flanders*, the story of a prostitute. Elgar's reply, '*Moll Flanders?* I do not know the book', however, must surely be taken as an expression of lordly disgust, not as a confession of ignorance.

I have dwelt at some length on the Cumberland interviews because they show Elgar in dialogue with an intellectual who was not afraid to stand up to him, and because their interesting evidence has been rather neglected. Cumberland was not alone in questioning Elgar's stance in intellectual matters, or at least in setting some limit on the claims that others made.[85] Though he did not know Elgar well, two at least of those who did were cautious in their judgements. Dora Powell, in an essay of 1957, says rather carefully that 'he had a considerable command of words and he was fairly widely read'.[86] Rosa Burley, besides criticizing his choice and sometimes his setting of English texts, gives us a valuable insight when she points to Alice Elgar's determination to place her husband on a high intellectual pedestal as a factor governing his conduct. Sometimes he reacted by teasing her with pretended vulgarity, but usually he played up to her expectations: 'she seemed to feel that on every occasion he should act as general guide and mentor. Often of course he could live up to all that was expected [as in discussion of music] . . . At other times one felt that he was *having to pretend to know far more than he actually did* to maintain this persona'[87] [my italics]. This trait, as I have said, probably had its origins in the bright boy's desire to surprise his family and friends with a good 'jape'; but it could easily spread beyond the family into his public persona. One of the two letters to the *Times Literary Supplement*[88] that have so far not been republished concerns the Greek word *poluphloisbos* ('loud-roaring', said of the sea); Elgar notes that Tennyson, who referred to it, may have read it in an obscure essay on his poems by George Brimley, and ends his letter, characteristically, 'I am prepared to hear that there are few readers of Brimley in these days'. In fact, Greek scholars tell me, the epithet is well-known. But Elgar decked out the letter with the correct quotation from Homer, copied no doubt in the elegant Greek characters that he had taught himself as a young man,[89] and his friend Speyer was taken in: 'I saw your letter . . . & your bursting out as a Greek scholar. I never had any suspicion of this, & must declare that you are the most many sided musician that ever lived'.[90] A jape, no doubt, but did Elgar take the trouble to reveal the truth to him? And would not a great many other readers have been similarly misled?

The later interviews with Elgar need not detain us long. The anonymous visitor to Severn House in 1912[91] duly noted the cosy bookroom, whose shelves revealed a 'catholic and most fastidious taste in literature' – a contradiction in terms, but Elgar was still to be presented as simultaneously omnivorous and discriminating. He was also proposing to solve a mystery that had defeated professional literary critics and historians since the 1760s and continues to baffle them today: 'He is devoting time at the present moment to the unravelling of certain literary problems, of which the authorship of *The Letters of Junius* is apparently uppermost in his thoughts.' One wonders what the others were. Before moving on to the question of Elgar's scholarly activities, though, we should perhaps note that Elgar's reading and learning was put to important use as a skill to be deployed in conversation. This might be in earnest or in jest. Percy Scholes, in our last interview (for *The Music Student*,[92] in 1916) was evidently fascinated: 'It is a pity Sir Edward does not write books as well as music, for he has much to say . . . is it not time we had a volume of reminiscences . . . ?'[93] Adrian Boult gives an account of a literary joust, perhaps only half humorous, that took place at Severn House when Elgar and Ernest Newman 'spent some time capping each other's knowledge of out-of-the-way books, mainly novels'.[94] Fair enough; but a man who wishes to display his knowledge of recondite literature in conversation will often indulge in irrelevance, or attempt to twist the talk to his purpose: was this why Bennett and Sassoon came to find Elgar tiresome?[95]

Elgar's literary scholarship

'This grubbing delights me', wrote Elgar to Sidney Colvin in January 1915.[96] He had been at the British Museum, where he had enlisted Laurence Binyon to help him in an unsuccessful search for a print of the obscure poet Edmund Smith (1672–1710). He had also been examining two copies of the once notorious Mrs Manley's *The New Atlantis* (1709) which contained MS notes identifying the subjects of her slanders; these he wished to compare with a printed leaf of identifications bound into his own copy. We hear no more of these particular endeavours, though he wrote at least four letters to the *Times Literary Supplement* between 1919 and 1923 on similarly unimportant matters.[97] It appears to have been the sensation of doing original research, the quest, not the result, that mattered to him. There is a romantic delight in handling old material – particularly unique manuscript material, though Elgar seems not to have owned or researched among manuscripts – and any university supervisor of historical research students will tell you that there are those who never progress beyond this delight into a productive assessment of their discoveries. For Elgar, his 'grubbing' seems to have been a way of getting in touch with the lost past, like his interest in heraldry; along with his growing passion for microscopy, it was also a harmless pursuit with which to fill his empty hours after the death of his wife, in the years when he could not summon the courage or the inspiration to compose large-scale works for a world which had grown unsympathetic to him. As he said to Compton Mackenzie, who first met him in 1921: 'I take no more interest in music. You'll find as you grow older that you'll take no more interest in literature. The secret of happiness for an artist when he grows old is to have a passion that can take the place of his art'.[98]

Each of Elgar's letters to the *Times Literary Supplement* is intended in the first place as a display of remarkably obscure bibliographic knowledge. The subject matter in each is equally remarkably slight. In the first, Elgar tries to suggest sources for the pseudonyms adopted as schoolboys by Horace Walpole, Thomas Gray and two friends. Elgar does not seem to realize that his ingenious arguments for other derivations than the accepted one for Gray's nickname, 'Orosmades' or 'Orozmades', thought to be a mis-spelling of 'Oromasdes', are in fact negated by Walpole's mis-spelling, which he mentions, of 'Orozmades' and 'Arimanius' for 'Oromasdes' and 'Arimanes' (the good and evil principles of light and darkness in Persian cosmology): the man who could mis-spell a name in 1770 would no doubt have made the same mistake in the 1730s. Elgar also refers in the same letter to Bayle's *Dictionnaire*,[99] saying, as if to reprove an editor at fault, 'There is an earlier edition . . . than the one mentioned, 1735; my own folio is dated 1710'. This let the world know that he owned a first edition; but its date would hardly have been news to a literary scholar, who would have cited the famous edition of 1734–41 because the book had then been greatly enriched and expanded under the editorship of Thomas Birch. Bayle leads us back to Elgar's 'grubbing': he presented a copy of the *Historical and critical dictionary of Mr Peter Bayle* to Ivor Atkins in 1915, interjecting, in the course of a letter about the gift, 'Oh! the notes'.[100] Notes were what he liked, more, really, than the main text. Though he parodied scholarly practice in a letter to Troyte Griffith, interlarding it with comic footnotes,[101] his letters to the *TLS* are themselves little more than tiny footnotes (though sometimes entertaining) to minutiae of literary history.

The second letter is concerned with Shakespearean borrowings and echoes in Walter Scott, but he never asks the one question of interest: why did Scott do it? The third letter has been mentioned earlier. The fourth cost him a hunt through no less than seventeen books, works on London topography, literary histories and editions of Swift, in order to scent out the track of a single small mistranscription. This was not difficult to do, but his application was certainly extraordinary. In fairness we should remember that the same powers of application enabled him to produce the libretti for the oratorio trilogy and Ivor Atkins' *Hymn of Faith*,[102] and the scenario around which *Falstaff* is built: here his scholarship was harnessed to important practical ends. At the same time, he could on occasion evince an unscholarly carelessness in transcribing and proof-reading the words that he set to music. In 'A Song of Union' (*Pageant of Empire*, 1924), did the massed choirs at Wembley really sing 'No more the dreams of war shall sound' (for 'drums')?[103] Anyone puzzled by the line 'We come, our life's work and its brevity feeling' ('How calmly the evening', 1907), may like to know that T. T. Lynch actually wrote 'our life's worth and its brevity feeling'.[104] Perhaps Elgar attached little importance to these compositions; it is rather more surprising to discover that mezzo-sopranos have been happily singing nonsense all these years in so well-known a piece as the last song of the cycle *Sea-Pictures*, Gordon's 'The Swimmer'. What on earth are 'strifes forbidden'? The poet wrote 'To gulfs foreshadow'd through straits forbidden',[105] but all Elgar's sketches, and the MS and published scores, have 'strifes'. Elgar often made minor alterations in literary texts when he lifted them into the sphere of song, but the above examples are plainly due to slap-dash copying.

In considering Elgar's scholarly proclivities, there are a few more points to be made about his other publications and his Birmingham lectures. At times he seems hardly to have been able to write a paragraph without the prop of quotation.[106] Sometimes the allusion chimes aptly with his thought and expresses his meaning more tellingly and concisely than could any phrase of his own, which is surely one proper use of quotation – as when he recalls, in his Foreword to *Forgotten Worcester*, a line from Vaughan that he had set to music many years before, 'The unthrift sun shot vital gold'.[107] But the phrases from Keats and Milton (unattributed, like the previous example) sit far less comfortably in their context.[108] Elgar does not use Milton's line about the names 'That would have made Quintilian stare and gasp' in the poet's sense at all (which is that names which are easy to a British tongue would have proved difficult to a Latin-speaking Roman); but he evidently feels that he has somehow acquired merit by claiming acquaintance with both Milton and, by implication, Quintilian.

Other legitimate uses of quotation are to strengthen one's argument by reference to established authority, or to give an example. Several of the citations in Elgar's Preface to H. Elliott Button's *Musical notation* (written in 1919)[109] come into these categories, but in such cases it is usual scholarly practice to give a proper reference, or at least to attribute an unfamiliar extract to its author. Elgar does not always do this. It is easy enough, knowing his penchant for collections of correspondence, to trace his sentence from Gray to a letter of 28 February 1762;[110] and not too difficult to run Swift down, since he is young and uncharacteristically obsequious, to a letter accompanying his first (and worst) printed poem.[111] But who will hunt through Roger North? And what is the source of the two fine phrases given without attribution? – 'knowing and conversable men, with whom, for the sake of knowledge, the greatest wits were pleased to converse', and 'those who can look "unappalled upon the spears of kings, and undisdaining, upon the reeds of the river"' (the latter does not seem to be Johnson). These are challenges to the reader, not the common coinage of discourse between men of culture. They are a form of play, of a kind that Elgar also sported with in his letters, though it is often an unpremeditated mannerism of one whose head is continually buzzing with the echoes of other men's thoughts. How was Jaeger, a German, to know what Elgar meant when he wrote that 'the fiddles could then draw "three souls out of one weaver"'[112] (Sir Toby Belch in *Twelfth Night*, II, iii, 59)? Or '"Am I subtle? Am I [a] Machiavel?" Where's that from? Yah!'[113] (Mine Host of the Garter in *The Merry Wives of Windsor*, III, i, 104)?

There are a number of still untraced quotations in Elgar's Birmingham lectures, on which a few observations may assist further research. The curious and presumably incomplete reference to 'the soul, of which Plato speaks' on p.41 of Dr Young's edition[114] must surely relate to the sentence from Jowett's translation of the *Phaedrus* placed at the head of Elgar's Preface to David Ffrangcon-Davies' *The singing of the future* (London, 1904), published in the previous year and mentioned on p.137 of the lectures. From the bottom six lines of p.47 to the fifth line of p.49, Elgar is quoting without attribution from a passage copied on a leaf inserted by Dr Young on p.155, where it stands among material taken from Leslie Stephen: since the passage ushers in the most famous statement in the lectures ('English music is white, and *evades everything*'), it will be important to trace its origin. On p.123, to whom do we owe the splendid but unattributed phrase, said of the artist and his art, 'It darkens with his eye, stiffens with his hand, freezes with his tongue'? On p.187 the unusual word 'tryginonic' presumably derives from the Latin *tryginon*, 'black colouring matter made from the lees of wine' (which ought however to yield 'tryginic'); the context, however, suggests that Elgar is pointing to the anonymous critic's malice rather than his drunkenness, which would suggest that he associated the word with the Greek 'trygon', a fish with a sharp spine in its tail, or sting-ray (see *O.E.D.*, quoting 'the pois'nous Trygon's bone'). Elgar spared his hearers the word 'microglophany', copied in his notes on p.208, which presumably should have read 'microglyphany', small-scale carving, in view of the 'little leaden images' mentioned at the foot of p.209.[115] The citations from Bentham on p.205, which Elgar dates to his days in the solicitor Allen's office, are of great interest: see the discussion in Appendix 4. Sterne's ass is to be found eating his macaroon at the end of chapter xxxii of book VII of *Tristram Shandy*, but Elgar has presumed to improve the order of the words. The quotations from J. A. Symonds on pp.215–6 pose problems. I have been unable to trace the first, and the second agrees with neither the original nor the second publication of Symonds' essay on Pindar, though it resembles them.[116] Noticing that Elgar had visited Greece in the autumn of 1905, one suspects that when he says 'I have seen this land and remembered Symonds' prose', he may in fact have been remembering a passage excerpted and altered in a guidebook, though his notes give a correct page-reference to the 1873 edition of *Studies of the Greek poets*. Reading p.219 of the lectures, the modern student may not know Macaulay's New Zealander quite so well as Elgar's hearers did, who were, it seems, tired of him: at the end of the third paragraph of his essay on von Ranke, Macaulay says of the Church of Rome: 'And she may still exist in undiminished vigour when some traveller from New Zealand shall, in the midst of a vast solitude, take his stand on a broken arch of London Bridge to sketch the ruins of St. Paul's'.[117] The quotation on p.221 comes from Rosa Newmarch's *Tchaikovsky* (London, 1900), pp.280–1; the Emerson on p.222, from the essay 'On writing poetry', though Elgar has apparently adapted the passage.[118] Emerson, with his doctrine of self-reliance and his mistrust of the homogenizing tendencies of universities, was a most important mentor for Elgar's self-education. Finally, the information about Beckford's *Dreams, waking thoughts and incidents* is taken with slight changes from G. T. Bettany's Introduction to his edition of Beckford's *The History of the Caliph Vathek and European travels* (London, 1891), pp.iv–v.

Further biographical implications of Elgar's reading

It would be tedious to pursue here every literary reference in Elgar's published letters (though I have indexed them).[119] The most literary in tone are those to Sidney Colvin, biographer of Keats and recipient and editor of R. L. Stevenson's *Vailima Letters*: Elgar's letter to him of 17 April 1917 starts off, indeed, with what appears to be an imitation of Stevenson's manner. Elgar's letters to Troyte Griffith and Ivor Atkins[120] abound in enthusiastic references to books recently read, memorable phrases culled from them, and stylistic parody, a trick that Elgar may have learned from F. S. Mahony's *The Reliques of Father Prout* ('Oliver Yorke'), since there is a London edition of 1881 in the Birthplace Library. Parody and riotously comical mis-spellings also characterize Elgar's letters to Augustus Jaeger,[121] though the latter feature is liable to erupt with other correspondents whom Elgar knew well or wished to tease, such as Dorabella.[122]

It has not hitherto been noticed that this characteristic has its origins in Elgar's love for the writings of 'Artemus Ward', namely the American humorist Charles Farrar Brown (1834–67), who would also have endeared himself to Elgar in that, like Samuel Richardson and Restif de la Bretonne, he was a compositor by trade. Readers of Elgar's letters will recognize many phrases, examples of tortured grammar, and phonetic manglings of English orthography among the following, from *Artemus Ward his book*[123] (Alice Elgar would certainly not have approved):– 'I've bin nussin a Adder in my Boozum. The fax in the Kase is these here' (p.41); 'the perlittercal ellermunts are overcast with black klouds, 4boden [foreboding] a friteful storm' (43); 'arrove' [arrived] (51); 'the fires which was rajin in my manly Buzzom' (56); 'pussylanermus' [pusillanimous] (73); 'take a little old Rye for the stummuck's sake' (75);[124] 'Injins is Pizen, whar ever found (N.B. This is rote Sarcasticul)' (77); 'Cotashun' [quotation] (102); 'Things came to a climbmacks' [climax] (156); '"the swings and arrers of outrajus fortin"', alluded to by Hamlick' (162); 'Grate applaws' (170); 'awjince' [audience] (171); 'I must forth to my Biz' (180). In *Artemus Ward his travels* (New York, Carleton, and London, Sampson Low, 1865) we find: 'centsibly' [sensibly] and 'goak' [joke] (35); Artemus, we learn, was a meticulous editor, 'very careful to expunge all ingramatticisms and payin' particler attention to the punktooation' (51), and a careful proof-reader – 'You have to watch these ere printers pretty close, for they're jest as apt to spel a wurd rong as anyhow' (33).

Elgar shared a special form of private language with his wife Alice, e.g. 'For my Beloved's booful music . . . Pease not beat. Will dis do?' One of his replies reads 'if zu smells sis, zu'll find it not fesh!'.[125] It is conceivable that this babytalk derives from the partly coded 'little language' used in Swift's *Journal to Stella*, which Elgar certainly knew, for example 'Nite deelest Sollahs; farwell deelest Rives; rove poopoopdfr farwell deelest richar MD', that is: 'Night, dearest Sirrahs; farewell dearest Lives; love PDFR [Swift], farewell dearest little MD [Stella and her companion]':[126] an enigmatic utterance which would surely have appealed to Elgar.

There are in Elgar's surviving books a number of items which he underlined, ticked or otherwise marked in the margin or index; and sometimes he himself made an index on a flyleaf. Some are marked for the purpose of copying or later quotation. Some contain scholarly cross-references or comment. Some are humorous, some pathetic or gloomy. Among the poems so marked are many which he set or thought of setting to music, and these often bear indications of verses to be omitted, re-ordered or in some way altered; there are also little musical plans showing repeats or the return of the main key. In some cases the poem is simply ticked or marked 'good', and if the book contains no other poem which he set to music, one may surmise – perhaps wrongly – that he liked the poem without wishing to turn it into a song. And, as already noted, he occasionally copied poems and other literary matter on to separate sheets, or into blank spaces in his musical sketchbooks. Some of this material appears to have been singled out because he saw it as referring particularly to his own condition, like many of the literary quotations he used to include in letters to friends. While his motives must remain conjectural, it will be interesting to list a number hitherto undiscussed examples here, and to comment on certain others to which his biographers have already drawn attention.

Elgar marked several poems in his copy of the now unfashionable Adelaide Ann Procter's *Legends and Lyrics*, 4th edition (London, 1865), volume ii (it survives in the Birthplace Library, like all the books alluded to in this section). Miss Procter was at times a much better poet than 'The lost chord' would lead one to expect. The daughter of 'Barry Cornwall', she was much interested in social questions affecting women, and her work was first published in Dickens' *Household Words*. She became a Catholic in 1851. Elgar – for one must presume it was he – put a dash or asterisk against fifteen of her poems in the index, and here and there marked particular verses on the page. Several of the poems tell of the early death of loved ones or other forms of lost love, and he would have related them to his dead brothers or to his first fiancée, Helen Jessie Weaver, who broke their engagement and emigrated to New Zealand in 1885, a consumptive in quest of a kinder climate. Other poems are mildly sentimental guides to behaviour. Those marked (easily found in the Everyman edition) are: 'Maximus', stanzas 4 and 6. 'Optimus', last four stanzas. 'Too late', about a betrayed girl whose lover's long-expected letter came a day too late to save her. 'Two worlds', stanza 8: 'Beauty and Joy are cankers/That eat away the soul'. 'King and slave': 'He [Love] counts it dishonour/His faith to recall;/He trusts; – and for ever/He gives – and gives all!'. 'Dream-life'. 'Sent to Heaven', about a lover whose thoughts cannot reach his dead love except through music – surely most relevant to our reading of Elgar, however mawkish and undistinguished the poet's words. The poem ends:

> Then I heard a strain of music,
>   So mighty, so pure, so clear,
> That my very sorrow was silent,
>   And my heart stood still to hear.
>
> And I felt, in my soul's deep yearning,
>   At last the sure answer stir:–
> "The music will go up to Heaven,
>   And carry my thought to her."
>
> It rose in harmonious rushing
>   Of mingled voices and strings,
> And I tenderly laid my message
>   On the Music's outspread wings.
>
> I heard it float farther and farther,
>   In sound more perfect than speech;
> Farther than sight can follow,
>   Farther than soul can reach.
>
> And I know at last that my message
>   Has passed through the golden gate:
> So my heart is no longer restless,
>   And I am content to wait.

'Borrowed thoughts, no.IV', warns a new love not to question the memory of the old, and seems to be highly relevant to Elgar's marriage.[127] It is apparently a translation. From stanza 2 on, Elgar has drawn a line in the margin:

> Within the kingdom of My Soul
> I bid you enter, Love, today;
> Submit my life to your control,
> And give my heart up to your sway.
>
> My Past, whose light and life is flown,
> Shall live through memory for you still;
> Take all my Present for your own,
> And mould my Future to your will.
>
> One only thought remains apart,
> And will for ever so remain:
> There is one Chamber in my heart
> Where even you might knock in vain.
>
> A haunted Chamber:– long ago
> I closed it, and I cast the key
> Where deep and bitter waters flow
> Into a vast and silent sea.
>
> Dear, it is haunted. All the rest
> Is yours; but I have shut that door
> For ever now. 'Tis even best
> That I should enter it no more.
>
> No more. It is not well to stay
> With ghosts; their very look would scare
> Your joyous, loving smile away –
> So never try to enter there.
>
> Check, if you love me, all regret
> That this one thought remains apart:–
> Now let us smile, dear, and forget
> The haunted Chamber in my Heart.

'Light and shade' urges the sufferer to accept his grief and to work for the greater good of man: 'The cry wrung from the spirit's pain/May echo on some far-off plain,/And guide a wanderer home again'. Stanzas 14–15, with their special application to music, have a line against them:

> Thy heart should throb in vast content,
> Thus knowing that it was but meant
> As chord in one great instrument;
>
> That even the discord in thy soul
> May make completer music roll
> From out the great harmonious whole.

'The warrior to his dead bride' speaks of the protection and humanizing influence that the dead love affords the living. 'A letter' is a poem of absent love, and stanza 8 is marked:

> And I thought: "Love's soul is not in fetters,
> Neither space nor time keep souls apart;
> Since I cannot – dare not – send my letters,
> Through the silence I will send my heart".

'A comforter' is a poem to a child, about wanting impossible things. 'Our dead' tells of dead children; our joy in them during their short lives is preserved in our memories by their early death, whereas the others who survive grow up, 'and in their places,/Weary men and anxious women stand'. 'A woman's answer' refers to that long under-rated poem, Mrs Browning's *Aurora Leigh*, and Elgar has marked the line, 'I love all good and noble souls'. 'A contrast' is about a casket containing some old letters and a portrait, returned by a faithless lover; it contrasts the present 'quiet and weary woman' with the radiant, confident face in the picture, whose 'blue eyes seem to gaze' . . .

> With that trust which leans on the Future,
> And counts her promised store,
> Until she has taught us to tremble
> And hope, – but to trust no more.

The general theme of loss and disappointment is reflected in the epigraph to one of Elgar's favourite books at this period of his life, Jessie Fothergill's *The First Violin*, taken from Goethe's *Faust* (Part I, *Studienzimmer*, line 20): 'Entbehren sollst du; sollst entbehren!' – 'You shall do without!'. It is further emphasized by the epigraph to a book which Elgar loved even more, Longfellow's *Hyperion*, written when the poet had recently lost a young bride. Elgar underlined these words in the copy he presented to his sister Lucy on 4 May 1889 ('In memory of our six years companionship', when he had lodged in her house): 'Look not mournfully into the Past. It comes not back again. Wisely improve the Present. It is thine. Go forth to meet the shadowy Future, without fear, and with a manly heart'. This, essentially, is the message accepted by 'E.D.U.' in the finale of the *Variations*, op.36.

Moving on over a quarter of a century, it is hard to see why Elgar should have marked the following epigrams in his copy of W. R. Paton's translation of *The Greek Anthology*,[128] published in 1916 when he was approaching 60, unless he felt that they referred in some way to himself. (He has not in these cases scribbled complaints about the English rendering, as he did elsewhere; nor did he ever set prose versions to music.) Here is no.58, on p.329 of vol.i, by Isidorus Scholasticus of Bolbytine:

> Thy friend Endymion, O Moon, dedicates to thee, ashamed, his bed that survives in vain and its futile cover; for grey hair reigns over his whole head and no trace of his former beauty is left.

And here is no.239, on p.249, 'Love in age', by Paulus Silentiarius:

> The raging flame is extinct; I suffer no longer, O Cypris; but I am dying of cold. For after having devoured my flesh, this bitter love, panting hard in his greed,

creeps through my bones and vitals. So the altar fire, when it hath lapped up all the sacrifice, cools down of its own accord for lack of fuel to feed it.

Finally, no.118, on p.69 of vol.ii, by Diogenes Laertius on Zeno, dying:

Some say that Zeno of Citium, suffering much from old age, remained without food, and others that striking the earth with his hand he said, 'I come of my own accord. Why [Death] dost thou call me?'

We shall meet other self-references among the epigraphs and poems that Elgar associated with his music, to which I shall shortly turn. But I must end this section with two passages that he excerpted. First, the latter part of a sonnet by Cino da Pistoia, as translated by D. G. Rossetti, to which I have already referred.[129] It is copied on a blank half-page in British Library Add. MS. 63161 (f.15v). The first part of the poem answers a charge of plagiarism made by Guido Cavalcanti. Elgar has marked the final tercet with a double line (here shown by italics):

> From whose rich store my web of songs I weave
> Love knoweth well, well knowing them and me.
> No artist I, – all men may gather it;
>   Nor do I work in ignorance of pride,
>   (Though this would reach above the coarser sense;)
> *But am a certain man of humble wit*
> *Who journeys with his sorrow at his side,*
>   *For a heart's sake, alas! that is gone hence.*

This was copied at Careggi in 1909, but the twenty-year-old memory of what might have been haunted him still. Yet later, a certain mystery surrounds the four opening lines of Swinburne's beautiful poem 'A leave-taking'[130] that Elgar copied out at some unspecified time, and to which he added the date of Alice Elgar's death, 7 April 1920:

> Let us go hence, my songs; she will not hear.
> Let us go hence together without fear;
> Keep silence now, for singing-time is over,
> And over all old things and all things dear.

On the face of it, Dr Moore seems to be quite correct in describing this as 'the epigraph to a left-over life'.[131] But the poem is not an elegy for a dead partner. Swinburne is complaining that he has been deserted by a mistress who would not or could not understand him, and the first stanza continues (with some loss of poetic quality):

> She loves not you nor me as all we love her.
> Yea, though we sang as angels in her ear,
> She would not hear.

The second stanza ends:

> And how these things are, though ye strove to show,
> She would not know.

What are we to make of this? Did Elgar choose or recall his four lines quite independently of their actual context? They are certainly the most memorable in the poem; and he once stated in regard to the *Apostles* libretto that the biblical quotations from which it is constructed were to be interpreted according to their placing in the oratorio, without any particular consideration of their meaning in their original contexts in the Bible. Elgar's mind was elusive as well as allusive, and it is often hard or impossible to pin him down with precision. (For similar reasons it is always dangerous to speculate naively about biographical connections between his life and his music; though Ernest Newman rightly observed that 'his music had come straight out of some highly vitalized experience or other',[132] we have also to remember Elgar's words written to Alice Stuart Wortley in 1917: 'Well, I have put it all in my music, *& also much more that has never happened*'[133] [my italics].) Nevertheless, the context of Swinburne's poem, which presumably had registered with Elgar when he first read it and may have remained in his subconscious mind, recalls Dr Young's wise words on Alice's inability to follow her husband's deeper thoughts: 'From some of the errors which crept into her transcriptions of her husband's rough notes [for the Birmingham lectures] it becomes clear that he was from time to time talking of things that were some way beyond her comprehension. But this only serves to make the fact of her faith in his genius the more moving'.[134]

Elgar's epigraphs and other quotations associated with his music

Among the writers of the nineteenth century, the use of epigraphs was common enough; less so among composers. It may be seen as an extension of the use of descriptive or programmatic titles. It was a device more gnomic, more condensed, less specific and therefore more mysterious than a fully-fledged programme-note in Berlioz' manner; and thus it appealed to Elgar, who was also in the habit of privately attaching similar literary quotations to his works in letters to his friends or in presentation copies. He included literary references in some of his programme-notes, too.

That is what he did in his programme-note for *Sevillana* (1884),[135] where a number of unnecessary French words build up to an unnecessary use of everyone's first Molière line: 'Çela était autrefois ainsi, mais nous avons changé tout çela'. This, with its incorrect cedillas under the 'c' of 'cela', in fact betrays his ignorance of French (he also used a supernumerary *tilde* over the 'n' of *Sevillana*). The music is, of course, 'foreign', if rather more French than Spanish in style, but here, surely, Elgar was not so much trying to suggest exotic colourings as trying to fall in with the 'smart' middle-class taste of spattering one's conversation with French words and phrases.

Froissart (1890) is the first work to bear an epigraph: 'When *Chivalry*/Lifted up her lance on high', from Keats. The work's main inspiration was the chronicles of Froissart, though perhaps seen at one remove through the eyes of a character in Walter Scott's *Old Mortality*.[136] The couplet from Keats is taken from his lines 'To ****', apparently Miss Georgiana Wylie, whom the poet's brother was to marry.[137] The poem depicts the lady twice, first sensuously, as a naked Grecian nymph, then heroically as a medieval amazon, a Bradamante or Britomart, and the quoted lines usher in this second portrait. I have sometimes wondered whether Elgar was intending a private reference here, a tribute to the heroic qualities of his wife. Thirty years later he recorded in his diary his 'Thoughts of the 30 (weary fighting) years of her help and devotion'.[138] The MS full score of *Froissart* bears on its cover a drawing of a knight in full armour and a girlish-looking squire,[139] which explains Elgar's wish, when the work was eventually published, for an illustrated title-page showing 'a Knight in full armour with gonfalons all round & shields & trumps of war'.[140] It has been asserted that he himself did the drawing, but it must have been the work of Edith Lander, the wife of a London solicitor who befriended the Elgars during their early years in London:[141] Elgar has circled the drawing in pencil and added her name beneath. He himself was no draughtsman, save in a comic and Thurberish vein.

The *Imperial March* (1897) was originally to have borne a motto from Edwin Arnold's *The Queen's Song A.D. 1897*, probably a couplet from the refrain, 'So true a Sovereign Lady/Ne'er ruled all hearts before!'.[142] This is of little interest in itself; but if Elgar's knowledge of Arnold extended beyond the pages of *The Musical Times*, where the poem had been published, he may well have read this once admired poet's *The Light of the World* (1891), which would have afforded another source of ideas for the oratorio trilogy, particularly in regard to Mary Magdalene.

Elgar considered adding an epigraph to *The Banner of St George* (1897). On f.52 of British Library Add. MS. 47901A, the work's title-page, we find 'Captaines Couragious Percy vol.II p 240 ("Inne december, when the dayes grow [deleted] draw to be short / *I sawe one sit by himself making a Songe*") Percy'. I have not yet succeeded in tracing the edition of Bishop Thomas Percy's *Reliques of ancient English poetry* to which this refers, but Elgar's note points to two separate poems. The 'captaines couragious', on whom the eye of Kipling also lit, appear in the first line of the ballad 'Mary Ambree',[143] another Amazon, who fought at the siege of Ghent in 1584. It can hardly relate to St. George. The couplet about the song-maker, with whom Elgar evidently identified himself, opens a satirical Catholic poem on the Reformation of *c*.1550.[144] Each stanza ends with a description of the author as 'little John Nobody, that dare not once speake', and the final verse runs:

> Thus in NO place, this NOBODY, in NO time I met,
> Where NO man ne NOUGHT was, nor NOTHING did appear . . .

> For I would no wight in this world wist who I were,
>> But little John Nobody, that dare not once speake.

The first stanza has the poet complain 'That few were fast i'th'faith', and his interlocutor enquires:

> Whether he wanted wit, or some had done him wrong.
> He said, he was little John Nobody, that durst not speake.

This lonely image recalls the Elgar who was to write to Jaeger in 1905 that 'I have no news of myself as I have for ever lost interest in that person – he ceased to exist on a certain day when his friends interfered & insisted on his – It is very sad'. The self-pity of the forlorn, neglected Elgar plays no part, of course, in the tub-thumping *Banner of St George*; but Elgar must have had in mind that he was writing music for a Catholic saint who now protected a protestant land.

The *Te Deum and Benedictus*, also of 1897, has at the end the words 'Inter spem et metum', which I have not been able to trace.

The early printed vocal parts of *Caractacus* (1898), as the editors of the full score in the Complete Edition point out,[145] bore a motto from Virgil's *Aeneid*, which helps to explain Elgar's quotation of the phrase 'belloque frementem' in a letter to Jaeger of 21 June 1898. The editors would have been able to discover whose translation of the *Aeneid* had been used if Dr Young had not placed Elgar's letter to Griffith of May 25 [1898][146] in the wrong year, 1903, where Griffith had thought it belonged: the letter does not refer to *In the South*, as Dr Young assumed, but to *Caractacus*. It shows that, although Elgar considered using Dryden's Virgil, he settled in the end for Kennedy's (book iv, lines 264–7).

The *Variations*, op.36 (1899) have a veritable constellation of quotations clustered around them, three literary and two musical (counting the mysterious unknown countersubject).[147] At the end of the score, Elgar copied the most famous line from Tasso's *Gerusalemme liberata* (Book ii, stanza 16), but altered from the third person singular to the first. Tasso wrote 'Brama assai, poco spera, nulla chiede'. This appears as '"*Bramo assai, poco spero, nulla chieggio*" (*sic*, 1595)', to which Elgar later added, in square brackets, '[Tasso]'. For the moment this remains an enigma. Elgar was certainly sufficiently aware of scholarly practice to know that 'sic' is employed to mean 'this looks like a mistake, but that is how it reads'. He had evidently come across this deformation of the line in a version dated 1595, which is not the year of publication of Tasso's epic, nor of its revision, in which in any case the second canto is excised; a further complication is that 'chieggio' would upset the rhyme-scheme;[148] 1595 was the year of Tasso's death, and it is conceivable that on that occasion someone observed that the poet might well have applied the line to himself; but none of the known funeral orations and speeches and writings in Tasso's memory quotes the line, and his grave was marked by no headstone or tablet which might have carried an inscription. Three leading Tasso scholars have been unable to help me. A secondary enigma is that on the next leaf there appears a mistranslation: 'I essay much, I hope little, I ask nothing'. 'Bramo assai' means 'I desire much': could Elgar, a musician who ought to have known the meaning of 'assai', possibly have confused it with the verb 'assaggio' (I essay)?

The line in its original form refers to Olindo, a Christian youth who loves a beautiful maiden, Sophronia, also a Christian. In pagan-occupied Jerusalem, an unknown hand defiles the Mahometan temple, and the governor, unable to discover the culprit, resolves to take hostages and decides that Sophronia shall be burned at the stake. In the hope of saving her, Olindo falsely confesses that he was responsible for the crime, and the governor obligingly arranges for him too to be burned at Sophronia's side. Olindo declares his love as the torch is put to the faggots, whereupon the warrior-maiden Clorinda rides in and puts a stop to the threatened atrocity. The stanza containing Elgar's line was translated thus by Edward Fairfax in 1600:[149]

> *Sophronia* she, *Olindo* hight the youth,
> Both of one Town, both in one Faith were taught;
> She fair, he full of Bashfullness and Truth,
> Lov'd much, hop'd little, and desired nought;
> He durst not speak by Suit to purchase Ruth,
> She saw not, mark'd not, wist not what he sought:
> Thus lov'd, thus serv'd he long, but not regarded,
> Unseen, unmark'd, unpity'd, unrewarded.

It was long believed, and was still believed by some in Elgar's time (but not by serious scholars) that in the story of Sophronia and Olindo Tasso was covertly alluding to his own alleged love for a high-born lady, Leonora d'Este, sister of his patron the Duke of Ferrara. This is the subject of Goethe's play *Torquato Tasso*, and of many another play and opera. We may take it that Elgar knew the legend, though we cannot say whether he believed it. He can hardly have been unaware of some of the fictional treatments just mentioned, which include Donizetti's opera 'Torquato Tasso' (1833); he would have seen similar references in the poems of Byron and Shelley; and he would almost certainly have read an article by one Poole, published in 1871 in a magazine evidently familiar in his childhood home, *Temple Bar*,[150] which asserted that Leonora loved Tasso in return. Did he know the poem itself, and the context of the celebrated line that he borrowed, or had he simply plucked it from a critical work such as Leigh Hunt's *Studies from the Italian Poets*,[151] where it is correctly quoted in Italian with the comment 'A line justly famous'? I think he knew the poem. Tasso's epic seems to have been standard reading in nineteenth-century England, where no fewer than nine new translations were published between 1818 and 1874, to add to those by Carew and Fairfax and the three eighteenth-century versions, of which Hoole's was the most famous. And Elgar's '*sic*, 1595' must surely mean that he was familiar both with the original version of the line and the correct date of the poem. In choosing to employ the altered version in the first person singular, he plainly intended the thought to be taken as referring to himself; but was he going further and seeing himself in Olindo's situation? I doubt it. It would be very easy to fantasize at this point about the only high-born candidate for an undeclared passion of Elgar's at this period, the 'angelic'[152] Lady Mary Lygon, she of the mysterious 'Romanza' (Variation XIII). But although she was living in the locality, was associated with Elgar in local musical enterprises and apparently helped with his work, she was not, like Elgar, a Catholic ('Both of one Town, both in one faith were taught'). There is no known evidence to support such a romantic association, and common sense tells us that Elgar would never have hinted at such a thing on a score which his wife had helped him to copy. Even though the Tasso quotation was omitted when the *Variations* were printed, he added it again to the score of *The Music Makers*, saying in a published note[153] that 'at the end of the full score of the "Variations" I wrote: "Bramo assai, poco spero, nulla chieggio" (Tasso): this was true in 1898 and might be written with equal truth at the end of this work in 1912'. His comments follow on from a passage justifying the re-use of the Enigma theme in the later work, 'because it expressed when written (in 1898) my sense of the loneliness of the artist as described in the first six lines of the Ode and, to me, it still embodies that sense'. It remains a very remote possibility that Elgar may have projected on to the charming Lady Mary some tiny fraction of his suppressed feelings for his lost love; but the quotation itself seems to refer only to his situation as an artist: his ambition was great, but he had few illusions about his chances and meant to ask no favours. The use of Tasso's words in their subjective form evidently betokens some new resolve; and the 'programme' of the *Variations*, as all authorities now agree, does indeed move from the lonely melancholy of the Theme (with its fleeting glimpse of happiness) to the almost military determination of the Finale – from the isolated, inactive 'E.E.' to 'E.D.U.', Edoo, Alice's Edward.

I have much more to say about all this, but for the moment I must confine myself to one further observation, since it shows a quite unexpected aspect of Elgar's use of literature. In the surviving drafts for the note on *The Music Makers* quoted above,[154] Elgar at first said, referring to the Enigma theme (my italics): '*under this theme of the Variations* I wrote "Bramo assai, poco spero, nulla chieggio'. He corrected this to 'at the end of the full score', where indeed he copied Tasso's words, but I do not think his original draft was an error. The words fit the theme very well, and it is interesting to note in the manuscript full score that Elgar brought out the typical cross-accentuation of 'poco' by adding the direction 'tenuto' to the d in the second bar, at a later stage (Ex.1 below). In his first sketch, now lost, did he write

Tasso's words 'under this theme of the Variations' because they had inspired it? If so, it is possible that all six bars originally had the same rhythm as the first. Ex.1 shows the theme starting off with the Tasso quotation underlaid to the familiar phrases, and invites the question 'how did the words continue?'[155] Ex.2 shows a hypothetical first version, repeating Olindo's words to the same monotonous ostinato that they might easily have suggested; if this were indeed the genesis of the idea, the subsequent alteration to a rhythmic palindrome, though the pattern is still limping and repetitive, makes the tune arresting instead of obvious.

Ex. 1

Ex. 2

The hexameter by his early favourite Longfellow that Elgar copied at the close of the full score of the revised coda to the *Variations*, 'Great is the art of beginning, but greater the art is of ending', is taken from *Elegiac Verse* no.xiv. It is possible that Elgar copied it with some misgivings, or at least with a backward glance at his own initial unwillingness[156] in the face of Jaeger's insistence that he should lengthen the Finale; for the couplet continues with the pentameter 'Many a poem is marred by a superfluous verse'.

In the material that Elgar contributed to the programme-note for the first performance of the 'Variations', there are references to two one-act plays by the Belgian dramatist Maurice Maeterlinck, only the first of which he could have read in English: 'So the principal Theme never appears, even as in some late Dramas – for example Maeterlinck's "L'Intruse" and "Les sept Princesses" – the chief character is never on the stage'. It is not really true to say, as Dr Moore does, that 'The chief character who is never on the stage in both the Maeterlinck plays was Death'.[157] In *L'Intruse* (1890), translated in

1892 by W. Wilson as *The Intruder*, it is an unnamed wife, dying after childbirth, who lies in the next room and is 'never on the stage': Death, it is implied, walks invisibly across the stage and forces his way in to her. In *Les Sept Princesses* (1891), which was not translated until 1905 (by William Metcalf, as *The Seven Princesses*), the princess Ursule has waited seven years for Prince Marcellus [Pelléas' father?] to return to her. She lies apparently asleep among her six sisters, in an inner room, visible but cut off from and inaccessible to the main stage. All of them, we learn, are sick, but Ursule is mortally ill and does not move: 'Il y a une ombre sur elle . . . On dirait qu'elle se cache . . . Le visage est presque invisible'. Alarmed, they break into the room through the vaults, but too late: her sisters awaken, but Ursule is already stiff in death. Though the atmosphere is certainly menacing, the character of Death is not mentioned and does not appear.

The missing character, then, is in both cases a stricken woman, one a bride who dies, the other a lover who is already dead. This can only relate to Helen Jessie Weaver, Elgar's early love. From revelations in recent books about Elgar[158] it is clear that she was the lady so mysteriously mentioned by Ernest Newman and Rosa Burley[159] as the true subject of the unlucky thirteenth Variation (and, Wulstan Atkins suggests, of the Violin Concerto as well). She was three years younger than Elgar, the daughter of a well-to-do family of Worcester shop-owners, who could afford to send her to Leipzig Conservatory for three years to study the violin. Elgar visited her there and they became secretly engaged, apparently in the New Year of 1883. They promised not to make the matter public for two years, ostensibly so that Helen could finish her studies in Leipzig, and in the hope of resolving the religious difficulty caused by the fact that she was a Unitarian and Elgar a Catholic; but one may readily imagine that the Weaver family may have thought the penniless Elgar a poor match and hoped that the relationship would not endure.

It did not. The engagement was broken off, probably in June or July 1884, 'mainly', thought Ivor Atkins, 'because of their different religions'. I think it possible that Miss Weaver's extremely poor health may have played some part in the matter, and this brings us back to Maeterlinck's dead and dying heroines. She interrupted her studies and returned to Worcester in autumn 1883 in order to nurse her stepmother, who died of consumption (tuberculosis, which later was to claim another of Elgar's great friends, Jaeger) around the turn of the year 1883/4. A letter of Elgar's informs us that Miss Weaver's own lungs were affected.[160] After breaking with Elgar she went to stay in Bradford with her friend Edith Groveham, a fellow-student in Leipzig who also knew Elgar, and to teach the violin (presumably also in Bradford). At this time, or perhaps earlier on, she contracted smallpox. This may, of course, have affected her looks. It left her with asthma. If these accumulated disabilities did indeed help to persuade her to renounce marriage, the parting must have been even harder for Elgar to bear. There was probably no clean break, no outright rejection, of the kind which leaves a man free to summon his pride and recover his self-reliance.

Miss Weaver embarked for New Zealand in late October 1885, a land still justly famous for its clean and healthy air. Though Elgar must have expected news of her early death, she recovered and survived until 23 December 1927, having married on 9 August 1890 and borne a daughter, Joyce, who predeceased her, dying in 1925 at the age of 28. That would place her birth in 1897; Frank Weaver would have told Elgar about it.[161]

It is generally believed that Elgar made a mistake when he added the date 'Feb. 18. 1898' just beneath the Tasso quotation at the end of the autograph full score of the *Variations*. The correct date of completion is given on the title-page, 'Feb. 19 1899'. I can think of no other Elgar MS containing a mistake over the date of completion,[162] or, among the larger works, of any which repeats the date of completion. What is more, it is evident even from a glance at plate xii of the new edition of the *Variations* by Robert Anderson and Jerrold Northrop Moore (Elgar Complete Edition, vol.27, London, 1986) that Elgar did not sign and date the last page of the original ending immediately he completed the score. The music and the Tasso quotation are in the same dark ink, but the word 'Tasso' (in square brackets), the signature, date and place have been added in a lighter ink. He may, I suppose, have changed over immediately to a fountain pen at this point (we know that he preferred to use a dipped pen for copying music, to change his arm-position and avoid cramp); but in that case why not change before writing the quotation? It seems implausible that he wrote the wrong date because he was over-tired after a long day's work finishing the score and could not be bothered to check. In any case, he or his wife or Winifred Norbury (for the initials on the title-page are 'W.N.', not the 'W.E.E.' of the Complete Edition, p.xviii) would have been bound to notice the wrong date at some point, and Elgar could easily have corrected it. His note for *The Music Makers* also places the quotation in 1898. February 18 must record some significant event which led him to adopt the Tasso line as his personal motto: he would work on, hoping for little and asking for nothing. The news that Helen Weaver, now Mrs Munro, had borne a daughter in 1897 must have led to the incipient mid-life crisis traceable in Dr Moore's biography from March 1897 (from p.221): ill-health; a sudden escape to Bavaria; misery at a time of success and a wish to abandon composition; twice, a desire to move house. It must have come to a head in February 1898. Its musical possibilities did not crystallize in his mind until the autumn. Meanwhile, he threw himself into *Caractacus* and thought of other, greater works.

We are now in a position to discuss the final quotation in the score of the *Variations*, the phrase three times placed in inverted commas in Variation XIII. There can be little doubt, I think, that Elgar took it from Mendelssohn's overture *Meeresstille und glückliche Fahrt*. Why should he gratuitously have lied about it in a private letter of 2 May 1899 to Jaeger, who had by then become a close friend?[163] Rosa Burley brings the Schumann Piano Concerto into the question, and also Beethoven's overture *Leonora* no.3 (that is Florestan's aria).[164] But Elgar's source was in the major mode, or he would not have omitted the inverted commas from the statement in F minor: this, I think, knocks the Schumann idea on the head, while the Beethoven does not have the same rhythm. Mendelssohn is the prime and obvious candidate, and it was evidently not Elgar who suggested the others to Miss Burley. In any case, it can only have been this primary and obvious reference that he was seeking to obliterate when in May 1899 he panicked for a moment and asked Jaeger to alter the second note of the quoted phrase each time it occurred in the pianoforte arrangement (where it was not yet placed in inverted commas).[165]

The 'Meeresstille' overture is itself based on literature, two matching poems by Goethe that were also set to music by Beethoven in 1815 (for chorus and orchestra). It is perhaps worth reminding ourselves that they were written in the age of sailing-ships, when a calm sea, which meant a lack of wind, ensured that one's voyage did *not* prosper. Mendelssohn's phrase is taken from his music for the 'prosperous voyage', a picture of the buoyant, speeding ship with its passengers yearning towards the fast-approaching shore, towards new life and new friends, or perhaps tenderly thinking of reunion with old ones.[166] Elgar takes the phrase and envelopes it, ironically no doubt, in a flat and motionless calm. The liner's engines (for Miss Weaver would have travelled on a steam-powered boat in 1885) may throb in the long pedal bass and the ghostly timpani, but the Enigma rhythm, uselessly, aimlessly rocking, shows us that it is the mournful composer, obsessed with his thoughts of the person voyaging further and further away from him, who is afflicted with the numbness and torpor of the dreaded Sargasso calm depicted in Coleridge's *The Ancient Mariner*, or, as Goethe expresses it, 'Todesstille fürchterlich!' – 'the terrible stillness of death!'

Why should this image of heartbreak and mental and emotional paralysis alternate so strangely with what appears to be a charming portrayal of the gracious and lovely Lady Mary Lygon? For, as recent research has shown, she is unquestionably associated from the first with the 'Romanza'. The earliest sketch for it, hitherto unremarked, is headed 'Lml's' (see below). The Variation's incipit is marked 'L' in the thematic Table among the sketches, and there is a draft showing how Elgar at some point thought of introducing the Mendelssohn quotation into the finale, with the note 'introduce LML';[167] this would of course have ranked L.M.L. with C.A.E. and Nimrod, 'two great influences on the life and art of the composer', in Elgar's own words, whose appearance in the Finale was 'entirely fitting to the intention of the piece'.[168]

If that is granted, Variation XIII would surely have been among the earliest to be conceived, and such indeed appears to be the case. The very first outline of its opening phrase is scribbled upside-down on the back of some sketches for Variation X (Dorabella),[169] on f.8v of British Library Add. MS. 58003, and is headed 'Lml's'. The editors of the new edition have not mentioned this, so I give it below as Ex.3(b). The melody is in the key of E minor (though moving to G major), which perhaps supports my view that Elgar conceived the Enigma theme in 'his' key of E minor. It derives from the second, G major part of the Theme, but Elgar decided not to use the first six notes, transferring that part of the idea to Variation VI (Ysobel). The remainder, in the major mode, is clearly the origin of the dipping sequence of descending fourths (very common in his music) that opens Variation XIII. This I have added as Ex.3(a), transposed into D major for comparison. Elgar's alterations of the time-signature show that he first thought of the music in 3/4, obliterated the '3' with a '4', then wrote '4/4', then added '2' (for 2/4) above the stave, and finally 'C'. In the Variation, he turned it back into 3/4 by removing the crotchet appoggiaturas, but an ambiguous rhythm survives, since the falling fourths are placed across the triple beat. The accompaniment, which one may easily imagine proceeding on down the scale in crotchets from the *c* note-head, offers no hint of the figure that he eventually used.

Ex. 3

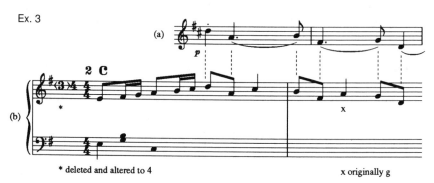

* deleted and altered to 4   x originally g

Variation XIII is one of the eight marked as 'finished' in the thematic Table among the sketches; it was probably, in fact, one of the first three, since like R.B.T. (III) and W.M.B. (IV) it bears the annotation in ink, apparently the same ink used for the Table itself (the others have it in pencil). The incipit given is perfectly accurate, and is headed 'L'. There seem to be no grounds for the editors to have distinguished it from the others by asserting that it represents 'a version of what was eventually to become XIII'.[170] This must stem from Dr Moore's theory that the music was substantially altered at the last moment, and that the Mendelssohn quotations were introduced in late January 1899: Elgar's imagination, he thinks, suddenly flared up when it was then announced that Lady Mary was to sail for New South Wales with her brother, and very intense feelings flowed into the new music. It therefore became impossible for Elgar to place Lady Mary's initials at the head of a 'Romanza' containing such a high charge of emotion.[171] The feelings are there all right, and the reason for omitting L.M.L.'s initials is believable and I think correct, though it is not the only reason; but, unless Dr Moore can produce documentary proof, his theory encounters a very considerable difficulty in Rosa Burley's statement that she heard Elgar play this Variation 'before the end of 1898'.[172] Since she was musical, and since she was particularly concerned with the question of the Mendelssohn quotations (which occupy three-fifths of the music) and of their connection, or lack of it, with Lady Mary's departure, it seems hardly conceivable that she would not have noticed such a remarkable and extensive reworking of the music as Dr Moore posits; she would have been bound to comment on such a thing.

The full sketch for Variation XIII, like much of the working-out of the Finale, is missing. This material may be among the leaves that have been stuck together inside the bifolium bearing the first draft of Variation V (R.P.A.), which Jaeger inserted into his copy of the full score of the *Variations* (Elgar Birthplace Library, no.1145, after p.18). The only other version of the music that we at present possess is the short notation in 3/2 time of the accompaniment figure, in E flat like the last statement of the Mendelssohn theme in Variation XIII. It is with the Finale sketches, among the early drafts, and was therefore not part of Elgar's response to Jaeger's request that he should lengthen the Finale. It remains possible that Jaeger had in mind the re-introduction of 'L.M.L.', since he knew the secret of the Enigma; but Elgar must originally have decided against the idea of a simple repetition because it would have been impossible, even for him, to repeat in a different context the magical ending of the variation. Instead, as Dr Moore has shrewdly observed,[173] he converted the Mendelssohn theme, by adding an extra note and displacing the rhythm, into a new figure, full of purpose and vigour, which dominates the Finale. Its rhythm, writ large, forms the basis of the opening. After the first appearance of its basic form, curiously enough, Elgar disguised it by crossing the parts among the upper strings (a trick he learned from the last movement of Tchaikovsky's *Pathétique* Symphony):

Ex. 4

This, I think, is the 'one phrase which I can use again' mentioned in Elgar's letter of 7 July 1899: it combines with fragments of the Enigma theme to provide the first climax of the excursion from and back to the tonic at figures 78–9; the three-note descent of the original Mendelssohn provides the bass between figures 79 and 81, very obviously so from bar 732; it extends itself again to the four-note descent of Ex.6[174] by the addition of a chromatic step at figure 81; and at 82 this leaps into the first violins in huge augmentation, its fifth note grasping upwards to a high *d* to end the work. W. H. Reed noticed that this last passage (which he did not recognise as a development of Ex.4) turned into the opening theme of the First Symphony nine years later.[175] Elgar said that he was quite unaware of the connection, but it is interesting to note that in the later work the tune appears in the same key as its ultimate source, the first two statements of the 'Meeresstille' theme in Variation XIII.

'L.M.L.', then, through these ingenious, partly hidden but typically Elgarian transmutations of the Mendelssohn phrase, is an important presence in the Finale to the *Variations*. But we are still left asking what all this has to do with Lady Mary Lygon. There must be a rational explanation for the fact that, after her death in 1927, Elgar contemplated restoring her initials to the public gaze in the notes he prepared for issue with the pianola rolls of the Variations in 1929[176] (though in the end he did not include them). His private draft states quite definitely that 'The asterisks take the place of the name of Lady Mary Lygon', but continues, with the untruth which has caused so much speculation, 'who was, at the time of the composition, on a sea voyage'. The first, deleted version of this sentence, however, shows that he originally set out in a more cautious and roundabout way to present the whole idea impersonally as the speculation of others: 'The asterisks have been identified as replacing the name of Lady Mary Lygon, who was, at the time of the composition, on a sea voyage'. The relative clause was the reason for the identification, which was not initially presented as Elgar's own. By accident or design, after changing the beginning, he omitted to alter the end of the sentence.

And yet, as we have seen, the first part of it was true: it was indeed Lady Mary's Variation. But because it was called a 'Romanza' and contained highly emotional music that was not 'hers'; because it was not, like all the other variations, a depiction of its subject looking at Elgar;[177] because it referred to a tragic, hidden episode in his life that Ernest Newman and Rosa Burley chose never to reveal, while Ivor Atkins made his son Wulstan promise to keep it secret until Elgar had been dead for fifty years, there was nothing that Elgar could do to explain matters. And how did the emotional core of the work come to be located in 'her' variation? I can think of only one explanation that fits all the facts. He must have told Lady Mary about Helen Weaver, and she must have brought him comfort.[178] He told others:

Rosa Burley, Jaeger, surely, and his very dear friend Ivor Atkins, who saw to it that Variation XIII was played last, after the Enigma theme itself and 'C.A.E.' and 'Nimrod', at the national memorial service held in Worcester Cathedral after Elgar's death, on 2 March 1934.[179] Was this the composer's wish?

The 'Romanza' is not merely an 'olden tale', to use a phrase of Elgar's, but a colloquy. The first statement of the 'Meeresstille' phrase quietly but arrestingly interrupts the charming G major of L.M.L.'s opening music with a Neapolitan sixth chord (originally a tragic cadential inflection and here also reminding us of the typical beginning of a recitative). A move through C minor brings a more contained repeat of the quotation, still on a chord of A flat, but with the keynote sounded in the bass. The end is then transformed, by means of the quietest yet most piercing of augmented sixths, to lead through C to a terrible pianissimo F minor, unexpected both in tonality and mode, where the third statement of the Mendelssohn expresses the full depth of the tragedy. It must have been the simple yet unprecedented scoring of this particular passage, with the brass octaves at first grieving, then swelling in an indescribable mixture of questioning resentment and ultimate despair while the five-deep strings turn and turn around a pedal C, locked inescapably on their minor third, that led Newman to say that Elgar 'was here dwelling in imagination on somebody and something the parting from whom and which had at some time or other torn the very heart out of him'.[180] After that, Lady Mary's voice returns, in music note for note the same, sweetly but firmly refusing to accept the tragic F minor and pulling the tonality back to G major (via the Phrygian step A flat to G, which has a long tradition of pathos behind it). The final statement of the Mendelssohn phrase, the most hushed of all, still surprises us, for we expect the music to move to A flat as it did before; but the chord shifts to E flat instead, a nearer, warmer relationship to the home tonic, G, which remains as the bass note, so that the last bar may find relief after confession, if not peace, and a kind of benediction, if not comfort, by gently easing on to a chord of G major.

The close of Variation XIII seems exactly to mirror, but of course with infinitely greater art, the last two lines of A. A. Procter's 'Sent to Heaven', already quoted as a poem marked for remembrance by Elgar:

> . . . my heart is no longer restless,
> And I am content to wait.

If I am right about the meaning of Variation XIII, Lady Mary must indeed have seemed worthy of Elgar's description of her as 'a most angelic person': this was written by a Catholic, and very probably we should understand 'angel' in its primary meaning of a 'ministering spirit' or 'divine messenger', a sense to which Elgar elsewhere alludes. Does not Lady Mary's poised yet gently descending theme, with a flutter of drapery about its feet, suggest an angel hovering and alighting in the manner, perhaps, of that painter of angels, Melozzo da Forlì, so admired by the Elgars? A rather similar confidante was to enter Elgar's life a few years later in the person of Alice Stuart Wortley. Such confessors were needed. Elgar's hidden grief, the 'haunted chamber of his heart' (to quote Procter again) was not a subject on which he could easily talk to his wife: how could he have asked her to bear it? He may have thought that after his marriage he would be able to 'shut that door forever now', but I think it proved impossible. I have speculated that news of Helen Weaver's baby may have made the forty-year-old Elgar's misery ever more acute; confessing the cause of his misery to Lady Mary, perhaps on 18 February, when he must have come to his new resolve, cannot immediately have helped. He and Alice were often ill. His obsession with thoughts of suicide, mentioned by Alice to Ernest Newman at their very first meeting(!) in 1901, presumably has its roots in this slightly earlier period.[181] The renting of Birchwood Lodge and the move from Forlì to Craeg Lea must have been initiatives encouraged, if not taken, by Alice in the hope that new surroundings might ease his difficulties. As he laboured at the composition of *Caractacus*, he became aware of new powers stirring inside him: 'Caractacus', he wrote on 1 March 1898, 'frightens me in places'.[182] Jaeger's comment in reply no doubt prefigured what he was to say to Elgar in the long and intimate talk that won him immortality as Nimrod, and also what Lady Mary would have told him: that Elgar was frightened 'is a *good* sign; for directly you become familiar with the "visions" that now "frighten" you, they will inspire you and become your friends'.[183] That is how Elgar learned to make 'something' out of the 'nothing'[184] that was the Enigma theme and, by facing and transmuting his terrible experience, turned himself into a great composer.

My pursuit of the quotations associated with the *Variations* has led me into a regrettably long digression; but, even though we cannot yet point to the intermediate source where Elgar found his version of the line from Tasso, nor to the exact meaning of the date he seems to have attached to it, the importance of this and the other quotations for elucidating his musical intentions must surely be granted. From this point onwards he 'shows himself' in his major works, though darkly, and moves into a higher sphere of art. His habit of gathering allusions from literature which in some way reflect his view of himself therefore assumes a deeper significance for his music, offering us potential insights which we cannot afford to neglect.

On 12 November 1897 he had acquired a copy of William Langland's *The Vision of Piers Plowman*, now in the possession of the editor of this volume, Raymond Monk.[185] This fourteenth-century allegory – which unlike most such poems is full of highly realistic detail – rapidly took on a symbolic importance for him. The frequent puns and linguistic games would have appealed to Elgar, as Dr Moore suggests;[186] and so would the many obscurities and consequent footnotes. But the main attraction would have been the dim figure of the West Midland poet himself, a poor man and a priest, falling asleep on Malvern hills, dreaming a vision which took him to a corrupt London, and awakening again in Malvern. It was doubtless Elgar who suggested the analogy with himself that led F. G. Edwards to quote from *Piers Plowman* at the beginning of his *Musical Times* article already cited,[187] and who directly or indirectly drew it to the attention of the Public Orator of Cambridge University, John Edwin Sandys: the latter's speech at the honorary degree ceremony on 22 November 1900 could have had only Langland in mind in referring to the Malvern hills as 'prope ipsa Musarum Britannicarum incunabula' – 'near the very cradle of the British Muses'.[188] A month later Elgar inscribed some lines from the poem in Jaeger's copy of *Sea Pictures* (1899), his Christmas present for 1900, adding in his letter 'that's my Bible, a marvellous book!'[189] Jaeger must have been intrigued, at least by the quaint medieval spelling, for in late January Alice Elgar sent him a copy of the poem. He pronounced it a '*Delightful* Book', perhaps out of politeness, for the middle English must have seemed impenetrable to a German, and alleged that he read it on the underground travelling to and from his work.[190]

It was around this time that Elgar conceived the overture *Cockaigne*. At the end of the full score he added in March 1901 a line from *Piers Plowman* (carefully including the editorial dot which indicates the alliterative division of the verse): 'Metelees & monelees ? on Maluerne hulles'.[191] Was this intended to suggest anything more than an ironic parallel with Langland's own awakening after his visions, 'meatless and moneyless on Malvern hills'? I think not, for the poet's picture of London, home of the Seven Deadly Sins, is bitterly satirical, whereas Elgar's is affectionate, genial and even noble. I know of no evidence, in fact, that Elgar penetrated at all deeply into the allegory of *Piers Plowman*; but, if he did sympathise with this critique of decadent catholicism, Langland must be counted with two other poets, Shelley and Morris, among the 'left-wing' sources that interested him.

After the successful first performance of *Cockaigne*, the critic Joseph Bennett noted that 'There is no suggestion here of a city of dreadful night'.[192] Elgar seems at first to have treated this reference to the Victorian James Thomson's gloomy and nihilistic *The City of Dreadful Night* (1874) as a kind of joke, perhaps because Bennett went on to assert that 'the composition of street scenes is not activity on the highest plane of music'. At all events, the composer's first reaction was to sketch a Tchaikovskian parody of a tune from *Cockaigne*, aping the manner that he had condemned in his Birmingham lectures:[193]

Ex. 5

He later came to take the idea of a second 'Cockaigne' overture seriously, and it inspired one of his most striking themes.[194] Presumably he had meanwhile studied or re-studied the poem, and found out more about Thomson, who was, I suspect, more talked of than read, for he was not only a melancholic and a dipsomaniac but also an atheist and a friend of Charles Bradlaugh. He was, however, a member of a group of poets friendly with the Rossettis, all short-lived, at least two of whom were admired by Elgar: Arthur O'Shaughnessy and the blind Philip Bourke Marston, from whose house Thomson was taken to University College Hospital to die. Thomson came of a poor family; a stroke left his father feeble-minded, and his mother died when he was eight. As a youth of 18 he had fallen deeply in love with a girl of 14 whose death, a year or two later, combined with an inherited strain of weakness to plunge him into a lifetime of depressions and despair.[195] His most famous poem, though widely supposed to be a Dostoievskian portrait of London, is not really anything of the kind. The fog-enshrouded, mouldering metropolis through which the poet wanders might be any large city, and serves only as a sombre and anonymous background to his nihilistic quest for extinction and oblivion. The city is Dante's Hell, the 'città dolente' of the *Inferno*, as an epigraph makes clear. Faith, Love and Hope are dead. In a vast cathedral, silent and unlit, the narrator hears an organ-voiced preacher deliver a Lucretian anti-sermon, bringing

> Good tidings of great joy for you, for all:
> There is no God: no Fiend with names divine
> Made us and tortures us;

and his message of Leopardian despair ends by praising the act of suicide.[196] The poem as a whole concludes with a picture of the titanic statue of the city's Patroness and Queen, an image of Durer's 'Melencolia':

> Baffled and beaten back she works on still,
>   Weary and sick of soul she works the more,
> Sustained by her indomitable will . . .

Like the poet, she must endure

> The sense that every struggle brings defeat
>   Because Fate holds no prize to crown success;
> That all the oracles are dumb or cheat

Because they have no secret to express; . . .
That all is vanity and nothingness.

It is easy to see how this powerful but roughly-finished poem must have appealed to Elgar. Like Thomson he was a melancholic, subject to prolonged fits of depression; like him, he had lost his first love, and his unprivileged origins had denied him any easy advancement in his profession; success, when it came, came too late, and even his best work, *The Dream of Gerontius*, had at first seemed a heroic failure. Thomson's phrases echo some of his own bitter comments after that experience, which led him to rail against providence and even, it seems, to lose his religious faith for a time. But his art offered a kind of relief through action (although he often felt drained and miserable on completing a major work). It is notable, however, that when he turned for inspiration around this time to Matthew Arnold's *Empedocles on Etna*, which deals with a famous and philosophically justified suicide in antiquity, it was only the closing song of Callicles that he chose to set:[197] an ecstatic and optimistic hymn which leads us away from the brink of the vortex to rejoice in the acceptance of natural beauty and the divinity of art. Elgar would have understood very well the reasons that led Matthew Arnold to withhold the full version of *Empedocles on Etna* from publication in 1854: it described a situation,

> from the representation of which, though accurate, no poetical enjoyment can be derived . . . in which the suffering finds no vent in action; in which a continuous state of mental distress is prolonged, unrelieved by incident, hope, or resistance; in which there is everything to be endured, nothing to be done. In such situations there is inevitably something morbid, in the description of them something monotonous. When they occur in actual life, they are painful, not tragic; the representation of them in poetry is painful also.[198]

This is precisely the case with Thomson's *The City of Dreadful Night*. If Elgar had attempted a 'Cockaigne No.II' based on the poem, it would not have been a parallel portrait of the dark side of London, but a portrait of Elgar's own despair and threatened loss of faith. No wonder that he did not proceed with the idea. But to read Thomson, or indeed Empedocles' speeches, gives us an insight into Elgar's own 'dark night of the soul', a state through which all religious mystics are said to pass. It enables us to understand what he meant when he said of *The Apostles* that

> To my mind *Judas*' crime & sin was *despair* . . . .In these days, when every 'modern' person seems to think 'suicide' is the actual way out of everything my plan, if explained, may do some good: I end Part I with 'Turn ye to the stronghold' – including 'Blessed is he who is not *fallen from his hope in the Lord*'. This has much point in connection with the subsequent Judas scene.[199]

My discussion of the practical mysticism of *Piers Plowman* has led a little off the chronological track into a consideration of the personal despair of Thomson and the philosophical pessimism of Arnold; but it was necessary to set the scene for a discussion of Elgar's major religious works. If one is not a believer it is all too easy to regard the oratorio trilogy as an aspect of Elgar's art that is somehow less important. It is seen as a dead end because he left it incomplete; and the under-attentive ear allows its response to be further dulled by the oratorios' historical associations with the easy-going, summer-afternoon world of Edwardian Anglicanism. But the voice of Judas echoes Elgar's individual experience of despair; and Elgar's reaffirmation of his faith at this time was achieved only after much doubt and anguish.

The Dream of Gerontius (1899), a work crucial to Elgar's development as a composer and a turning-point in his career, matured slowly in the composer's mind. He must have wondered, as he elaborated the music, at the new and powerful imagery and the greater architectural scope that Newman's fine poem was evoking within him. A composer of Elgar's character does not suddenly achieve high art, still less high religious art, without pondering deeply on what is happening to him and on the purpose and effect of his music. Two principal influences seem to have operated on him. One was Ruskin, from whom he took the well-known epigraph copied at the end of the autograph full score. The other must have been Newman himself, whose views on sacred music Elgar would surely have read, and possibly discussed with the priests who had known the Cardinal at the Birmingham Oratory. Before dealing with these influences, we should mention two other quotations connected with *The Dream of Gerontius*. First, the beautiful sentence from Richter's *Levana* that Elgar found in Carlyle (already discussed);[200] it describes Belief as the last comfort left to the dying Christian, but, as we have seen, Elgar probably did not know its original context. Second, the phrase from Virgil's *Aeneid* (Book vi, line 721) that Elgar entered on the title-page of the autograph full score, together with the version offered by John Florio in his English translation of Montaigne's *Apologie de Raimond Sebond*, where Elgar evidently found it: 'Quae lucis miseris tam dira cupido' – 'Whence doth so dyre desire of Light on wretches grow?'[201] I must confess that I find this puzzling. In both Virgil and Montaigne the line refers to the pagan doctrine of metempsychosis. Aeneas, standing on Lethe's banks with the shade of his father Anchises, asks why it is that the souls whom he sees happily thronging to drink the waters of forgetfulness should wish to return to the upper air and the light of day, to live once more in heavy mortal bodies. In the context of the dying Gerontius, Elgar seems to be distorting the speech's original meaning so that it refers to a sinful Christian's unwillingness to die; but anyone unfamiliar with Virgil and Montaigne might be forgiven for thinking, as I at first did, that the line referred to Gerontius' desire, mingled with fear, to come into the presence of God, into the blinding light that surrounds his Maker and Judge – this is, after all, an important theme in Newman's poem.

The Dream of Gerontius was not the only work to which Elgar applied Ruskin's phrase 'the best of me'. He used it of *Caractacus*[202] and also, much later, of the Violin Sonata,[203] though it is only in *Gerontius* that he advances it to the dignity of an epigraph and cites the whole sentence from *Sesame and Lilies* (1865) that had so impressed him. The words are printed in quotation marks by Ruskin himself, in a passage in the lecture 'Of Kings' treasuries' where he distinguishes between two kinds of good books, 'the books of the hour, and the books of all time'. A book of permanent value, he says,

> is written, not to multiply the voice merely, not to carry it merely, but to preserve it. The author has something to say which he perceives to be true and useful, or helpfully beautiful. So far as he knows, no one has yet said it; so far as he knows, no one else can say it. He is bound to say it, clearly and melodiously if he may; clearly, at all events. In the sum of his life he finds this to be the thing, or group of things, manifest to him; – this the piece of true knowledge, or sight, which his share of sunshine and earth has permitted him to seize. He would fain set it down for ever; engrave it on rock, if he could; saying, 'This is the best of me; for the rest, I ate, and drank, and slept, loved, and hated, like another; my life was as the vapour, and is not; but this I saw and knew: this, if anything of mine, is worth your memory.'[204]

The context makes it clear that Elgar meant to imply a good deal more than that *The Dream of Gerontius* was his best, most individual or most durable work. His comment to Canon Gorton cited above, hoping that, in an age of despair, *The Apostles* would 'do some good',[205] also suggests that he thought his best work would be 'true and useful, or helpfully beautiful' – in other words, that he would have subscribed wholeheartedly to Ruskin's views on the morality of art. Whether he would have agreed with Ruskin's very original and indeed revolutionary opinions about political economy and social reform is doubtful, but these are so closely bound up with the critic's theory of artistic value that, if Elgar read Ruskin at all, he cannot have avoided confronting them. Since he owned an early edition of *Sesame and Lilies*,[206] he could hardly have missed, towards the end of this same lecture, a passage that the great reformer had printed in red, an account of a poor honest cobbler who had chosen to die of starvation rather than go to the workhouse. Few people read Ruskin today, and it is curious how superficial our notions of 'Ruskinian aestheticism' have become. In his own time, Ruskin was considered by many to be an unsettling and dangerous writer, or at best an unpractical visionary. Although Elgar is quite close to him in his view, expressed in the Birmingham lectures, that good music might play a worthier and more valuable part in our national life if it were subsidized and made more accessible to the masses,[207] Ruskin's name is resoundingly absent from the parade of authorities invoked. Even in the heart of non-conformist Birmingham, the municipality which was the first to implement some of Ruskin's more practical suggestions for social reform, and even in the passages where Elgar turned for illustration to art and architecture, there is no mention of Ruskin. This is not merely odd, but disappointing. One could understand Elgar fighting shy of Ruskin's powerful anti-*laissez-faire* propaganda, which led to the socialism of William Morris; but there is another strain in Ruskin's thought which dwells, in the manner of Carlyle, on the social responsibility of the aristocrat, the lord or 'law-ward', who must take care of those who are placed in his charge. One would have expected Elgar to respond to this one-nation view of Toryism; but no, his politics were instinctive and emotional, not intellectual, and appear to have sprung from a romantic and escapist identification with the great Tory families of Queen Anne's reign, many of whom were Catholic and even Jacobite in their sympathies.

At the same time, the Elgar who advised English composers to draw inspiration from our national 'naval and military history, . . . our religious struggles and traditions, . . . our legends and tales',[208] the singer of St George and Caractacus, who wrote idealized military marches and planned a symphony to commemorate General Gordon, would surely have responded to much of what our leading critic of the arts had to say about the role of 'Admiration . . . the Faculty of giving Honour' in a national system of education: the children, wrote Ruskin in *Fors clavigera* (1871, Letter IX),

> shall learn, so far as they can understand, what has been bravely and beauti-fully done; and they shall know the lives of the heroes and heroines . . . ; so that the year shall have its full calendar of reverent Memory . . . , on every day, part of their morning service shall be a song in honour of the hero whose birthday it is; and part of their evening service, a song of triumph for the fair death of one whose death-day it is: and in their first learning of notes they shall be taught the great purpose of music, which is to say a thing that you mean deeply, in the strongest and clearest possible way; and they shall never be taught to sing what they don't mean. They shall be able to sing merrily when they are happy, and earnestly when they are sad; but they shall find no mirth in mockery, nor in obscenity; neither shall they waste and profane their hearts with artificial and lascivious sorrow.

Elgar would have found Ruskin's proposal to erect a kind of lay liturgy on the lines of the Catholic church's celebration of its saints very striking. At the age of seventy-five, England's greatest composer was to start on the humble task of providing music for no less than twenty-four unison songs for schoolchildren to sing, both merry and earnest.[209] He wrote for the whole nation. In the next extract, while the mention of 'superstition' might not have pleased Elgar, the attack on 'sensuality' and the misuse of music for unworthy ends would have met with full approval from a man who hated 'commercial brutalities' and rejected the advice of his friends that he should write for profit.[210] Elgar, I think, fully shared Ruskin's resolutely Platonic view of music as an art of great ethical power (particularly when associated with words), potent alike to ennoble or degrade. This sharply contrasts with the traditional English view, common since the time of Burney, that music was an 'innocent pleasure', the only gratification of the senses involving no sin.[211] Music, Ruskin wrote (in *Time and Tide*, 1867, Letter XI)

> is the nearest at hand, the most orderly, the most delicate, and the most perfect, of all bodily pleasures; it is also the only one which is equally helpful to all the ages of man, – helpful from the nurse's song to her infant, to the music, unheard of others, which often, if not most frequently, haunts the deathbed of pure and innocent spirits. And the action of the deceiving or devilish power is in *nothing* shown quite so distinctly among us at this day, – not even in our commercial dishonesties, nor in our social cruelties, – as in its having been able to take away music, as an instrument of education, altogether; and to enlist it almost wholly in the service of superstition on the one hand, and of sensuality on the other.

And in *The Queen of the Air* (1869, section 42), while explaining the ancient Greek view of Music, he associates the art even more specifically with religion:

> this, which of all the arts is most directly ethical in origin, is also the most direct in power of discipline; the first, the simplest, the most effective of all instruments of moral instruction; while in the failure and betrayal of its functions, it becomes the subtlest aid of moral degradation. Music is thus, in her health, the teacher of perfect order, and is the voice of the obedience of angels, and the companion of the course of the spheres of heaven; and in her depravity she is also the teacher of perfect disorder and disobedience, and the Gloria in Excelsis becomes the Marseillaise.

Elgar also read and quoted from Hanslick, who took a similarly moral view of the 'healthiness' or 'morbidity' of the emotions aroused by music, though he was uneasy (like Elgar) about its 'poetic-pictorial' associations.[212] But Hanslick was mainly concerned with high-art music, and Elgar also composed popular music. Ruskin saw that popular music too might be good or bad, and Elgar might have invoked the following antitheses, also from *The Queen of the Air* (section 141), both to justify his marches, minuets, gavottes and other 'light' pieces, and perhaps also to account for his greater care, as he grew older, over his choice of literary texts for setting:

> music for the multitude, of beneficent, or of traitorous power, – dance-melodies, pure and orderly, or foul and frantic, – march-music, blatant in mere fever of animal pugnacity, or majestic with force of national duty and memory, – song-music, reckless, sensual, sickly, slovenly, forgetful even of the foolish words it effaces with foolish noise, – or thoughtful, sacred, healthful, artful, for ever sanctifying noble thought with separately distinguished loveliness of belonging sound . . .

It is most unlikely that the Elgars had not read and discussed the works of Ruskin, for Alice wrote at least one essay in art criticism at a time when he was still regarded as supreme in that field. Elgar also admired the pre-Raphaelite painters and poets, whom Ruskin had defended (his association with them cost him his wife, Effie Gray, who eloped with the painter Millais; Alice Stuart Wortley, Elgar's 'Windflower', was their daughter). I end with one further extract from *Sesame and Lilies*, which Elgar himself owned and quoted from. In the lecture 'Of Queens' gardens', Ruskin applies his three criteria of 'the truest, simplest, usefullest' to the art of music, 'where you might think them the least applicable'; again he implies the primacy of vocal music:

> I say the truest, that in which the notes most closely and faithfully express the meaning of the words, or the character of the intended emotion; again the simplest, that in which the meaning and melody are attained with the fewest and most significant notes possible; and, finally, the usefullest, that music which makes the best words most beautiful, which enchants them in our memories each with its own glory of sound, and which applies them closest to the heart at the moment we need them.

Elgar certainly deployed large forces in *The Dream of Gerontius*, but he was no spendthrift: his setting displays great powers of compression, concentration and, thanks to his use of Wagnerian *Leitmotiven*, great economy of means ('the fewest and most significant notes possible'). Though his command of *Sprechgesang* still leaves something to be desired – for the prosody is liable to suffer when a motive finds its way into the vocal line, a difficulty that he learned to overcome in *The Apostles* and *The Kingdom* – no-one can doubt that he took unusual pains to 'faithfully express the meaning' of Newman's text. And his music has done more than beautify the poem and make it dwell in our memories: it has applied the words 'closest to the heart' of thousands of listeners who would never otherwise have read them.

The didactic and theological content of Newman's poem were of great importance to Elgar. It is well known that he received a copy from Father Knight of St George's Church, Worcester, as a wedding gift, though Dr Moore has pointed out that he must have possessed another copy, also with General Gordon's markings copied into it, as early as June 1887.[213] Gordon was a kind of evangelical Anglican, though never confirmed and of a decidedly eccentric cast of mind: Elgar must have noted this evidence that the appeal of *The Dream of Gerontius* was not limited to those of the Catholic faith. His own interest extended beyond the poem into a veneration for its author. He was very friendly with Fr Henry Bellasis, one of the two sons of Newman's great friend Serjeant Edward Bellasis; they had been among the first pupils at the Birmingham Oratory school, had later become priests under the Cardinal and had shared his interest in music.[214] Henry must have discussed Newman and his poem with Elgar, who also consulted at the Oratory with Newman's friend and executor Fr Neville about the cuts he proposed to make, a discussion which can hardly have been conducted on a purely literary basis;[215] as late as 6 April 1900, when the proofs of Part I of *Gerontius* had been sent to him, he was 'with Fr Blakelock [another of Newman's executors?] to go through *Dream of Gerontius*'.[216] He also knew and admired Newman's prose and later, as we have seen, recommended it to Gerald Cumberland as a model. Presumably he had read both of Newman's major works, not only the *Apologia pro vita sua*,[217] but also one or more of the different versions of *The idea of a University defined and illustrated*,[218] which Newman himself described as one of his 'two most perfect works artistically'. I suspect that Elgar read these books, or more likely re-read them with added attention, when the task of composing *The Dream of Gerontius* aroused in him a deeper curiosity about England's most famous and controversial Catholic,[219] who had until 1845 been an Anglican priest. It seems to me likely that in his reading of Newman, founder of the Oratorian movement in Britain, he came across two streams of thought which were important for the conception and the general tone of *The Apostles* and *The Kingdom*; they help to explain why the unfinished oratorio trilogy differs so markedly from *The Dream of Gerontius*, a work whose characteristics were probably fixed in Elgar's mind before he had fully absorbed Newman's ideas.

Elgar would surely have been interested in the musically sensitive Newman's opinions on music in the service of the church. These are to be found in Discourse IV of *The idea of a University defined and illustrated*,[220] which is concerned with the bearing of other branches of knowledge on theology. Like St Augustine, whose writings Elgar also knew,[221] Newman saw that, while music might beautify and dignify a liturgical text, there was a danger that its autonomous artistic power might distract the hearer from the sacred words. 'For sometimes', says Augustine,

> I seem to myself to give them [the notes of the chant] more honour than is seemly, feeling our minds to be more religiously and fervently raised unto a flame of devotion, by the holy words themselves when thus sung, than when not . . . .this gratification of the flesh, to which my mind ought not to be resigned to its weakening, doth oft beguile me, the sense not so waiting upon reason, as patiently to follow her; . . . it attempts to outrun her, and to take the lead . . . Yet again, when I remember the tears which I poured forth at the chants of Thy church, in the beginnings of my recovery of the Faith, and how even now I am moved, not with the singing, but with the things sung, . . . I realise again the great advantage of this institution. Thus I hesitate between the danger of mere enjoyment, and my experience of their wholesomeness; . . .

He finally decides to approve the custom of chanting in church, moved by the thought 'that so by the delight of the ears, the weaker minds may rise to the feeling of devotion', and recalling, no doubt, the part that the music played in his own return to the faith. 'Yet when it befalls me to be more moved with the singing, than with the words which are being sung, I confess that I sin grievously . . . '

Newman's attitude is very similar to this. He discusses music along with the fine arts: 'These high ministers [servants] of the Beautiful and the Noble are, it is plain, special attendants and handmaids of Religion; but it is equally plain that they are apt to forget their place, and, unless restrained with a firm hand, instead of being servants, will aim at becoming principals.' He sees no threat in ancient and medieval art and plainchant, since these 'rudimental' or 'inchoate sciences' have 'little innate vigour and life in them' [!]. 'But the case is very different when genius has breathed upon their natural elements, and has developed them into what I may call intellectual powers'. He points to the particularly strong dangers associated with Painting, both in its use of realistic models to portray things unseen, and in its domination, since the Renaissance, by ideas from pagan antiquity. 'Music and Architecture', however, 'are more ideal, and their respective archetypes, even if not supernatural, at least are abstract and unearthly'. Yet he sees dangers, analogous to the threat posed by Painting,

> in the marvellous development which Musical Science has undergone in the last century [that is the eighteenth]. Doubtless here too the highest genius may be made subservient to Religion; here too . . . the Science has a field of its own, perfectly innocent, into which Religion does not and need not enter; . . . Music . . . has an object of its own . . . If then a great master in this mysterious science . . . throws himself on his own gift, trusts its inspirations, and absorbs himself in those thoughts, which, though they come to him in the way of nature, belong to things above nature, it is obvious he will neglect everything else. Rising in his strength he will break through the trammels of words, he will scatter human voices, even the sweetest, to the winds; he will be borne on upon nothing less than the fullest flood of sounds which art has enabled him to draw from mechanical contrivances; he will go forth as a giant, as far as ever his instruments can reach, starting from their secret depths fresh and fresh elements of beauty and grandeur as he goes, and pouring them together into still more marvellous and rapturous combinations; – and well indeed and lawfully, while he keeps to that line which is his own; but, should he happen to be attracted, as he well may, by the sublimity, so congenial to him, of the Catholic doctrine and ritual, should he engage in sacred themes . . . – is it not certain, from the circumstances of the case, that he will be carried on rather to use Religion than to minister to it, unless Religion is strong on its own ground, and reminds him that, if he would do honour to the highest of subjects, he must make himself its scholar, must humbly follow the thoughts given him, and must aim at the glory, not of his own gift, but of the Great Giver?

Elgar may have had this in mind when he quite rightly sought to resist Jaeger's request – from an agnostic of Protestant antecedents, whose wife kept a picture of Luther in her bedroom[222] – that he should alter *The Dream of Gerontius* by introducing a tremendous climax at the moment when the Soul appears before its maker. His revision certainly produced the 'fullest flood of sounds' in all his music; the restraint and relative impersonality of the two later oratorios may well stem from a more careful consideration of Newman. Elgar surely 'made himself Religion's scholar' in the long course of reading and consultation with experts that went into the making of the libretti for his later oratorios. Was he also recalling Newman and humbling himself before 'the glory . . . of the Great Giver' when he added 'A.M.D.G.' as a superscription at the head of each of his oratorios? 'Ad majorem Dei gloriam', 'To the greater glory of God', was, of course, the motto of the Society of Jesus, whose founder, St Ignatius Loyola, was a great friend of Newman's 'own special Father and Patron, St Philip Neri'. I shall return shortly to the theme of Elgar's oratorios as ecumenical 'propaganda' (in the word's original sense). For the moment, it is interesting to note that Newman ends his *Discourses* with a long paean to the memory and ideals of St Philip, the first Oratorian, and stresses his musical connections. 'Palestrina', he writes, 'had Father Philip's ministrations in his last moments. Animuccia hung about him during life, sent him a message after death, and was conducted by him through Purgatory to Heaven'. Just as the Society of Jesus took on the task, amongst others, of mastering and combating the exciting but dangerous ferment of new intellectual ideas that erupted during the Renaissance, so did St Philip Neri seek to bring into the church's treasury the astonishing new wealth of developments in the secular arts, not condemning them like Savonarola, but welcoming them into the service of the faith. It was an age

> when a new world of thought and beauty had opened upon the human mind, by the discovery of the treasures of classic literature and art. He saw the great and the gifted, dazzled by the Enchantress, and drinking in the magic of her song; he saw the high and the wise, the student and the artist, painting, and poetry, and sculpture, and music, and architecture, drawn within her range, and circling round the abyss: he saw heathen forms mounting thence . . . and he perceived that the mischief was to be met, not with argument, not with science, not with protests and warnings, not by the recluse or the preacher, but by means of the great counter-fascination of purity and truth . . . he preferred to yield to the stream, and direct the current, which he could not stop, of science, literature, art, and fashion, and to sweeten and sanctify what God had made very good and man had spoilt.

Newman had framed these words in the hope of founding a Catholic university in Dublin, an 'universitas' which might embrace the new arts and ideas of the nineteenth century as St Philip's oratory had embraced those of the sixteenth. The venture failed, and this lecture was never in fact delivered. But Elgar, in harnessing the language of Wagnerian music-drama to the service of the oratorio, seems to have been carrying into practice, in his own sphere, the ideals of Newman and St Philip.

One of the original purposes of the Society of Jesus was ecumenical, the reconciliation of new ideas with the central faith of the church, and one way to achieve the 'greater glory of God' was to increase the number of true believers. There can be no doubt that Elgar saw his oratorios, in particular *The Apostles* and *The Kingdom*, as propagating aspects of the faith, as an attempt to exercise the 'fascination of purity and truth', and to 'sweeten and sanctify what God had made very good and man has spoilt'. In telling Jaeger in 1908 that he could not afford to complete his oratorio cycle, he wrote: 'I am not allowed to beg a dispensation of a benevolent providence who objects to the world being saved or purified or improved by a mere musician'.[223] The depth of his disappointment is in proportion to the height of the ideal that had originally exalted him. During the composition of *The Kingdom*, Jaeger apparently wrote to say that he found the chorus 'O ye Priests' cold and doctrinaire. Alice Elgar angrily responded with an analogy that even the agnostic Jaeger might understand: 'If you cannot feel the Sacerdotalism of any Church, there is the eternal priestdom of elect souls in all ages, who have stood above the lower minds & dragged them up; to those who believe by religion, & to others by art, literature & pure & noble character & aspirations. So instead of "Matthias" meaning nothing to us, it is the type of everything wh. can infuse heroism, self-sacrifice & great thoughts into all who are not dead to such things'.[224] Elgar the artist, then, was to be seen as one of the 'eternal priestdom'. The calling of humble and otherwise ordinary men to the vocation of priestdom is also a central theme of *The Apostles*, as the motto from Jeremiah (iii,15) that Elgar copied into a sketchbook suggests: 'I will give you pastors according to my heart, which shall feed you with knowledge and understanding'.[225] He sent the godless Jaeger commentaries on the Acts of the Apostles for his analyses of the oratorios;[226] and in suggesting that an Anglican friend, Canon Gorton, who had helped him assemble texts for *The Apostles*, should write a booklet 'interpreting' its libretto, he was surely doing more than protect himself against anti-Catholic suspicion.[227] He later said of Gorton's work: 'his book has done more real good – if you know the people it has reached – than anything else'.[228]

The performance history of the two later oratorios seems to me to underline their ecumenical purpose. In producing sacred works on the subject of the early church which Anglicans might sing in their own cathedrals without religious misgivings, Elgar may well have had in mind the long and interesting account that Newman gave in the *Apologia* of his years as an Anglican priest before 1845.[229] One of his principal concerns was the so-called *Via media*, the middle way. He tried, while still a sincere believer in the Church of England, to emphasize the very large area of common ground between the Anglican and Roman traditions, and, setting to one side the sometimes very cruel historical circumstances of the Reformation, to distinguish the doctrinal extremes from which the two catholic traditions (for the Church of England is a catholic church) might need to retreat in order to come to an understanding. The attempt was cut short in 1841 by the outcry that greeted the ninetieth of the *Tracts for The Times*. But Newman's thought, and his discussions of the early history of the as yet undivided Church (also a primary interest of Ernest Renan)[230] seem very much to underlie Elgar's purposes in his trilogy.

In *The Dream of Gerontius* there were certain phrases that had to be omitted and replaced by less contentious words when the work was performed in Anglican places of worship. With the later oratorios, Elgar took good care to avoid the problem. How far was he trying to achieve Newman's common ground? Vaughan Williams, a sensitive but from the doctrinal point of view a disinterested observer, thought that in *The Apostles* Elgar 'was writing for the Church of England', and that he was 'oppressed by the fact'. This was in a letter to Michael Kennedy, who published the phrase with the comment that V. W. was 'mistaken'.[231] Few will wish to disagree with Kennedy so far as the artistic quality of the work is concerned, but I feel that he is a little too quick to dismiss the possibility of Elgar's ecumenism when he says that 'In setting the verses from St. Matthew upon which the papacy founds its claim to infallibility – "Thou art Peter, and upon this rock I will build My church" – he knew he was stating a Catholic belief'. For Elgar was also stating a belief of the Anglican communion, which is catholic and believes firmly in the apostolic succession. It is true, as Geoffrey Hodgkins has pointed out, that Elgar knew that the inclusion of the text (Matthew xvi, 18) might prove contentious to some, 'because the Papacy builds upon it its high claims to infallibility and supremacy';[232] but not to all. Hodgkins, like Kennedy, goes rather too far in stating that the text 'could mean only one thing to Protestants: the everlasting Gospel of Roman Catholicism', for we have to remember that the libretto of *The Apostles* had received 'a full approval'[233] from two Church of England divines, Canon Gorton and Dr Armitage Robinson, Dean of Westminster Abbey, and was performed as it stood in Anglican cathedrals. The clearest statement of Elgar's ecumenism, remarkable both for its explicitness and for the fact that he was under absolutely no compulsion to provide it, comes in the extraordinary letter that he wrote to the Anglican Archbishop Randall Davidson on the twenty-fifth anniversary of his succession to the see of Canterbury:

> Bred in another form of religious observance I stand aside, unbiased, from the trivialities with which controversies are mostly informed; whatever differences exist there remains the clear, wide & refreshing Christianity, desired by all men, but obscured by the little darkness of their own imperfect vision. To the better understanding of such broad Christian feeling I am thankful to have been permitted, in a small way it is true, to exercise my art . . . [234]

He ends by describing the Primate as 'an embodiment of all that is good & true in Christianity past mere forms and observances'.

The autograph scores of the two oratorios bear epigraphs taken respectively from William Morris and the Canadian poet Bliss Carman. Morris, a socialist 'careless of metaphysics and religion',[235] had died only seven years before the completion of *The Apostles*. Though a late convert to parliamentary Fabianism, he had publicly avowed, not long before his death, 'I do declare that any other state of society than Communism is grievous and disgraceful to all belonging to it'.[236] Earlier, he had twice been arrested in street demonstrations. An odd choice, you may think, to introduce a sacred oratorio. Had Elgar really read him, or did he know only the narrative poems and translations, admiring the poet and the craftsman but ignoring his creed? Did he mean to show, by invoking Ruskin and Morris, that he approved of their condemnation of Victorian society? The quotation that Elgar uses is to be found in *The Earthly Paradise*, from which Elgar also borrowed a famous phrase in 1905 when he ruefully said, 'And so I, the idle singer of an empty day, became a Professor of Music'.[237] For the epigraph to *The Apostles* he turned to the last three lines of Apollo's song in 'The love of Alcestis'. The two verses are in fact central to Morris's view of the Earthly Paradise, and present a pagan outlook. Though it is a god that sings, he has been exiled from heaven (for killing the Cyclopes), and, living in Thessaly as a shepherd-musician, he finds the world fair. In the first stanza, singing alone to himself, Apollo addresses the race of men, telling them that their prayers to the gods are fruitless, since the gods do not care for them, and that they should take no thought for the future or for fame, or even for romantic love, but play their parts contentedly (if vegetatively) amid the beauties of the world. In the second stanza he addresses Zeus, who has forgotten his creation, or has become blind, because of human fears, doubts, sorrows and mortality, to the great possibilities for happiness offered by the earthly paradise. Again, this is an odd context from which to choose an epigraph for sacred music.

> Why will ye toil and take such care
> For children's children yet unborn,
> And garner store of strife and scorn
> To gain a scarce-remembered name,
> Cumbered with lies and soiled with shame?
> And if the gods care not for you,
> What is this folly ye must do
> To win some mortal's feeble heart?
> O fools! when each man plays his part,
> And heeds his fellow little more
> Than these blue waves that kiss the shore
> Take heed of how the daisies grow.
> O fools! and if ye could but know
> How fair a world to you is given.
>
> O brooder on the hills of heaven,
> When for my sin thou drov'st me forth,
> Hadst thou forgot what this was worth,
> Thine own hand made? The tears of men,
> The death of threescore years and ten,
> The trembling of the tim'rous race–
> Had these things so bedimmed the place
> Thine own hand made, thou couldst not know
> To what a heaven the earth might grow
> If fear beneath the earth were laid,
> And hope failed not, nor love decayed.

A Christian reader, seeing the last three lines without knowing their context, will quite naturally take them as referring to the Christian vision of paradise on earth. But that was far from Morris' intention, and I suspect that Elgar was originally attracted to this whole passage during the period after the first performance of Gerontius when his faith came under severe strain and he began to rail against providence (at a later moment, during World War I, he even went so far as to curse God).[238] If romantic love had failed him, if faith was beginning to fail him, one can see how he might be tempted to adopt Morris's belief that one should not waste time on such things but find one's happiness through hard work and helping one's fellows. When he copied out his epigraph, Elgar underlined the words 'hope' and 'love'; by 'love' he evidently understood the Christian 'caritas', and this, no doubt, helped to restore his faith. He used the words again when writing to Walford Davies in 1908 about the First Symphony: 'There is no programme beyond a wide experience of human life with a great charity (love) and a *massive* hope in the future'.[239]

The effect of Morris' philosophy may be operating in *The Kingdom*, which was begun at the same time as *The Apostles*: 'the whole thing is intentionally less mystic than the A[postles]', Elgar wrote to Jaeger in July 1906: – 'the men are alive & working & the atmosphere is meant to be more direct and simple'.[240] On the title-page of the autograph full score[241] he copied two lines from the Canadian poet Bliss Carman, saying:

> I would write
> 'A Music that seems never to have known
> Dismay, nor haste, nor wrong–'

These lines had been in his mind for some time, for he had added them to his own printed score of *The Apostles*, which is dated 'Oct 7:03', heading them 'An *Aspiration* E.E.'[242] The verses evidently reflect the calmer, unforced nature of the musical narration in *The Kingdom*; a study of their context in Carman's *The Pipes of Pan*, published in London in 1903, underlines this, for the poet, a gentle nature-mystic with a fine eye for detail, is referring to birdsong. His volume is subtitled 'from the book of myths', and Elgar found his epigraph in a poem entitled 'Daphne',[243] which begins:

> I know that face!
> In some lone forest place,
> When June brings back the laurel to the hills,
> Where shade and sunlight lace,
>
> Where all day long
> The brown birds make their song–
> A music that seems never to have known
> Dismay nor haste nor wrong–
>
> I once before
> Have seen thee by the shore,

> As if about to shed the flowery guise
> And be thyself once more.

Daphne, transformed to a laurel and lost to Apollo; in Morris's *The Earthly Paradise* the story of Alcestis, who had no fear, whose hope did not fail, nor her love decay, but who in dying for her husband was lost to him – was the loss of Helen Weaver still in Elgar's memory as he fastened on these passages?

It is time now to return to the epigraphs and quotations associated with certain of Elgar's instrumental works, starting with the *Pomp and Circumstance* marches, of which the first two were produced in 1901. They are 'music for the multitude', in Ruskin's phrase, and certainly 'majestic with the force of national duty and memory'. But I feel that Michael Kennedy is right to sense in No.1 – to which I would add No.3 – a 'note of recessional', a 'heroic melancholy . . . rather than self-confident assertiveness'.[244] A year before, Elgar had wished to compose music for Kipling's 'Recessional' (1897), a poem which predicts national humiliation and the loss of empire.[245] It is easy to forget that the title 'Pomp and Circumstance' is taken from Othello's farewell to his occupation as a soldier (III, 3).[246] The epigraph that Elgar chose for the Marches as a whole, however, lends no support to the idea that they look back nostalgically to lost greatness. Dr Young tells us that the motto comes from Lord de Tabley's 'The march of glory', commenting that the poem is 'an oddly fiery piece from a poet who was a scholar and recluse'.[247] So it is. But Elgar's epigraph has been taken from some early version, no doubt published as an occasional piece in a magazine. Since only Newman[248] gives the lines in full, I repeat them here in the hope that some other scholar may be more successful in tracing their origin than I have been:

> Like a proud music that draws men on to die
> Madly upon the spears in martial ecstasy,
> A measure that sets heaven in all their veins
> And iron in their hands.
> I hear the Nation march
> Beneath her ensign as an eagle's wing;
> O'er shield and sheeted targe
> The banners of my faith most gaily swing,
> Moving to victory with solemn noise,
> With worship and with conquest, and the voice of myriads.

The finer version that Lord de Tabley[249] wished to be remembered preserves only the opening two lines and the fifth (see lines 1, 5 and 9–10 below); it was first collected into *Poems dramatic and lyrical* (Second Series, London, 1895, pp.37–40) and was repeated in *The complete poems of Lord de Tabley* (London, 1903, pp.371–2):

> I hear the nations march,
>   As sweeping autumn rain,

By laurel-garnished arch,
    And trophies of the slain.
To music proud and high
    By Glory led,
The stern-eyed ranks go by
    To her battle-fields of dead.
Her heroes and her soldiers rush to die
Madly upon the spears with martial ecstasy.

The significance of the epigraph to *Dream Children* (1902), taken from the end of Lamb's essay of the same name in *Essays of Elia* (1823), may have been obscured by Rosa Burley's comments: 'Lamb's use of the name "Alice" gave the passage a deep and special significance for Edward, and I always understood that the two pieces were to be dedicated to a certain lady who was a friend of the Elgars. When the work was published, however, her name did not appear ... '[250] Michael Kennedy accepts this unmistakable reference to Alice Stuart Wortley, adding that 'Elgar, perhaps for obvious reasons, put no dedication on the score'.[251] In the present state of knowledge about Elgar's relationship with 'Windflower', however, Miss Burley's speculation does not seem to hold water. Mr Kennedy himself says elsewhere in his book that, although Elgar had met Mrs Stuart Wortley as early as 1897, it was not until 'about 1906' that 'their friendship ripened from formality'.[252] Miss Burley seems to have been extrapolating backwards with no apparent justification; perhaps her memories became foreshortened with the passing of time.

Dr Moore, with his usual care and restraint, observes after citing the epigraph that 'The dreams were brought close to home by the name of Alice'.[253] I take this to imply no more than that Elgar's eye happened to light on the passage in Lamb because it contained his wife's name. But he already had a child by Alice Elgar: why should he father dream-children on to her?

Lamb's essay, subtitled 'a reverie', portrays Elia, his adopted persona and a childless old bachelor like himself, musing on what might have been. His two dream-children, Alice and John, are at first presented as real, reacting to his story and interrupting it. Elia tells them first about the great country mansion in Hertfordshire where his grandmother was housekeeper and where he used to visit her as a boy, and then about his brother John, their uncle, who has recently died. But they ask him to 'tell them some stories about their pretty dead mother'.

> Then I told how for seven long years, in hope sometimes, sometimes in despair, yet persisting ever, I courted the fair Alice W–n; and, as much as children could understand, I explained to them what coyness, and difficulty, and denial meant in maidens, when suddenly, turning to Alice, the soul of the first Alice looked out of her eyes with such a reality of re-presentment, that I became in doubt which of them stood there before me, or whose that bright hair was; ...

Alice W–n is mentioned in no less than four of Lamb's essays, lightly disguised like other real figures from the author's tragic life. Elgar would surely have noted all her appearances, for that is exactly the kind of tracing of minute correspondences that he delighted in. She was evidently the 'Anna', the 'fair-haired maid' of the sonnets that Lamb wrote in or before 1795–6,[254] who lived in a cottage in Islington; they broke off their relationship, perhaps after his attack of madness in the winter of 1795–6, certainly and permanently after his sister Mary's fit of insanity in September 1796, when she murdered her mother. Lamb eventually allowed Coleridge to publish his early poems, 'but do not entitle any of my *things* Love Sonnets, as I told you to call 'em; . . . for 'tis a passion of which I retain nothing. 'Twas a weakness . . . Thank God, the folly has left me for ever.'[255] A year later, he wrote of his 'Vain loves and wanderings with a fair-haired maid',[256] whom he also remembered in the third stanza of his best-known poem, 'The old familiar faces' (January 1798)[257]:

> I loved a love once, fairest among women.
> Closed are her doors on me, I must not see her–
> All, all are gone, the old familiar faces.

Elgar would assuredly have known this touching story. He must have read the following in 'New Year's Eve', since he quoted a phrase from the essay to Ivor Atkins in 1913.[258] 'Methinks it is better that I should have pined away seven of my goldenest years, when I was thrall to the fair hair and fairer eyes of Alice W–n, than that so passionate a love adventure should be lost'; later on Lamb says, of the supposed comfort that we shall meet our loves after death, 'why, to comfort me, must Alice W–n be a goblin?' In 'A chapter on ears' he writes of a singer he had heard as a boy, 'who had the power to thrill the soul of Elia . . . and to make him glow, tremble, and blush with a passion that not faintly indicated the day-spring of that absorbing sentiment which was afterwards destined to overwhelm and subdue his nature quite for Alice W–n'. In *Last essays of Elia* (1833), when he resumes the theme of the great house at Gilston in the essay 'Blakesmoor in H–shire', the lady returns to haunt him in a parenthesis as he gazes at an old portrait of a flaxen-haired, blue-eyed beauty, 'with the bright yellow H–shire hair and eye of watchet hue – so like my Alice!–'.

Though Alice Elgar's eyes were blue, her hair was light brown. I doubt whether the colours were significant; but the sentence which Elgar omitted from his epigraph to *Dream Children* may have been, and it points elsewhere. I restore the lacuna in square brackets below; the passage follows on directly from my previous quotation from Lamb's essay:

> And while I stood gazing, both the children gradually grew fainter to my view, receding, and still receding till nothing at last but two mournful features were seen in the uttermost distance, which, without speech, strangely impressed

upon me the effects of speech:–'We are not of Alice, nor of thee, nor are we children at all. [The children of Alice call Bartrum father.] We are nothing, less than nothing, and dreams. *We are only what might have been.*[259]

'The children of Alice call Bartrum father': reality impinges on the dream. After breaking off with Elia/Lamb, Alice W–n married another man and mothered his children. Those seven words make the fantasy almost unbearably poignant, and offer a further reason for Elgar's identification of himself with Elia. Dr K. E. L. Simmons has discovered, as we have seen, that Helen Weaver married in August 1890, aged 29, and had a daughter, christened Joyce, in 1897.[260] Her husband, Elgar's Bartrum, was a Glaswegian-born bank officer named John Munro. Was it because of these early memories that Elgar delved back into his old sketchbooks for the music of *Dream Children*?[261] This was, I believe, the first time that he produced a small masterpiece by revisiting the past with the maturer feelings and technical ability of a great composer. When F. G. Edwards asked him about *Dream Children* in 1907, he hedged: 'I really can tell you *nothing*! . . . They were (or it was) written long ago, or rather sketched long ago & completed a few years back'.[262]

There is little new to say about the literary connections of *In the South*, which have been admirably handled by Michael Kennedy.[263] I have already pointed out the mis-dating which caused an incorrect association of the 'Romans' music with the fourth book of the *Aeneid*.[264] The context of the phrase from Sir Thomas Browne which Elgar applied to the same music is of some interest. The 'drums and tramplings' come from the beginning of the fifth chapter of *Hydriotaphia, Urn Buriall; or, a discourse of the sepulchrall urnes lately found in Norfolk* (1658); speaking of the ancient remains found shallowly buried in urns, Browne says:

> Now since these dead bones have already out-lasted the living ones of *Methuselah*, and in a yard under ground, and thin walls of clay, out-worn all the strong and specious buildings above it; and quietly rested under the drums and tramplings of three conquests; what Prince can promise such diuturnity unto his Reliques . . . [?]

This burial in a clay urn has proved a safe and quiet rest; but the fact that it is 'a yard under ground', and the image of 'drums and tramplings' overhead, not to mention the threatening tread of the music itself, curiously resemble the terrible picture of the shallow grave in Tennyson's *Maud* that Elgar associated with the pounding climax in the third movement (Rondo) of the Second Symphony: 'Only a yard beneath the street,/And the hoofs of the horses beat, beat . . . ' I shall return to this later (p.259).

The quotations from Tennyson's *The Daisy* and Byron's *Childe Harold* copied into the score of *In the South* are of topographical rather than biographical interest. The remaining literary connection is Shelley's *To Jane: 'The keen stars were twinkling'*. ('Jane' was the wife of Edward Williams, who drowned with Shelley a month or two after this little poem was written.) Elgar fitted the second and fourth stanzas to the melody of the 'canto popolare', but although he was as proud of the result as he had been cavalier in changing and repeating Shelley's words, one has to confess that he produced a botched job.[265] His excuse for the 'parody' (that is the fitting of words to existing music) lies in stanza 1: 'The guitar was tinkling,/But the notes were not sweet till you sung them/Again'. In stanza 4 he would have recognized, as he copied the words 'Where music and moonlight and feeling/Are one', the source of the title that Arthur O'Shaughnessy chose for the collection in which he published 'The Music Makers', *Music and Moonlight* (1874).

The dedication of the Violin Concerto, Op.61 (1910) has occasioned much comment, because Elgar left it incomplete: 'Aquí está encerrada el alma de . . . . ' These are the opening words of a phrase quoted in Spanish in the address 'Gil Blas au lecteur', 'Gil Blas to the reader', with which the French writer Alain René Le Sage had introduced his well-known picaresque novel, *L'histoire de Gil Blas de Santillane* (1715, 1724, 1735). Elgar would have read it in the English translation made or revised by Tobias Smollett (1748), where the full quotation, 'Aquí esta encerrada el alma del Licenciado Pedro Garcias', is followed by the rendering 'Here is interred the soul of the Licentiate Pedro Garcias'. Elgar's own published translation was 'Here is enshrined the soul of . . . . .'; but he had earlier explained the phrase in the postscript to a letter of 5 November 1910 to Nicholas Kilburn:[266]

> Aqui esta encerrada el alma de . . . . Here, or more emphatically *In here* is enshrined or (simply) enclosed – *buried* is perhaps too definite – *the soul of* . . . ? the final 'de' leaves it indefinite as to sex or rather gender.
> Now guess.

A month before that, on 9 October, as Dr Moore has discovered, he had written to a Spanish friend, Antonio de Navarro, asking a question which shows that he was still undecided as to the exact wording of his dedication: 'If I want it to refer to the soul of a feminine shd. it be – de la . . . ?'[267] Basil Maine, after asking (on his own account) 'What spirit is enshrined here if it is not that of the violin itself?', informs us that 'The composer once went so far as to tell the writer that it was a feminine spirit he had in mind when he wrote those words at the beginning of his work', and concludes 'if not the violin, then perhaps a woman who played upon it surpassingly well, is the solution of this typically Elgarian puzzle'.[268] This latter suggestion, which may conceivably repose on a hint from Elgar himself, would lead us to the violinist Helen Weaver, as Wulstan Atkins has pointed out.[269] But even if that is right, we must still keep in mind that there is rarely a single, simple solution to any Elgarian mystery: it would have been a Helen Weaver 'seen through the personalities' of two other ladies dear to Elgar, for he very likely confided his secret to each of them: Julia ('Pippa') Worthington, and above all Alice Stuart Wortley, whose 'Windflower' themes are so important throughout the work, and who became ever closer to Elgar as he completed it. She was a sensitive musician, and Elgar seems to have transferred to her many of his suppressed feelings for his first love. By 1910, I think, turning to this Alice, Elgar may well have felt that the soul of Helen Weaver, in Lamb's words, 'looked out of her eyes with such a reality of re-presentment, that I became in doubt which of them stood there before me'. The earliest known mention of the Spanish dedication of the concerto, in fact, occurs in a telegram that he sent to Mrs Stuart Wortley on 22 September 1910, where he used it (perhaps furtively?) in place of the sender's name. It puzzled the Post Office clerks, who checked it but had to give up on 'Aqui' and still got the last word wrong: 'Missed train [Aqui] Esta Encerrada El Almt'.[270]

In printing his dedication, Elgar used five dots to indicate the omission in place of the usual three. Newman thought that this might be some kind of clue, and much has been made of the dots ever since[271] – but to no avail, for all three possible dedicatees have five-letter names. Since Elgar appears to have used three dots after the Spanish phrase in his letter to Navarro, four in his letter to Kilburn, and three after the English translation in the same letter (which invited Kilburn to guess the secret), this is very likely a false trail.[272] In any case, the fifth dot may by the usual convention be a full stop. The curious wording of Elgar's question to Navarro, 'the soul of *a feminine*', and his comment to Kilburn that 'The final "de" leaves it indefinite as to sex *or rather gender*' (my italics) seem to me to show that what is missing is not a female name but a feminine noun. The obvious candidate is 'la anímona' or 'la anímone' (Spanish for 'windflower').[273]

Le Sage's *Gil Blas* was much better known in Elgar's time than it is today. There is no need, I think, to assume that Elgar took his motto from some intermediate source.[274] He mentions *Gil Blas* in a letter to Griffith of August 1917,[275] and it is in any case unlikely that a man who 'spent some time' with Ernest Newman 'capping each other's knowledge of out-of-the-way books, mainly novels'[276] would not have read so famous an example of the genre, particularly when it had been translated by a well-known English novelist. The witty tale of Le Sage's 'Gil Blas to the reader' appears to have been admired even more than the novel itself. Since it offers an instructive moral that reflects valuable light on to Elgar's own love of mysterious quotation and buried emotional treasure, I make no apology for repeating the whole thing here, in Smollett's version. (A Licentiateship, by the way, is a degree between a Bachelor's and a Doctor's, and/or a license to preach, or to practise law, etc.; in the novel, Licentiates are usually priests).

> Before reading the history of my life, listen, friendly reader, to a tale I am about to tell thee. Two students were travelling together from Pennafiel to Sala-manca. Being thirsty and fatigued, they sat down by a spring they met with on the road. There, while they rested themselves, after having quenched their

thirst, they perceived, by chance, near them, upon a stone that lay even with the surface of the earth, some letters, already half effaced by time, and by the feet of flocks that came to water at the fountain. They threw water over the stone and washed it, and then read these words in the Castilian tongue: *Aquí está encerrada el alma del Licenciado Pedro Garcías:* 'Here is interred the soul of the Licentiate Peter Garcias.' The younger of the two students, being lively and thoughtless, had not quite finished reading this inscription, before he cried with a loud laugh, 'A good joke! here is interred the soul – a soul interred! I should like to know what original has been capable of writing this ridiculous epitaph!' So saying, he rose to go away. His companion, more judicious, said to himself, 'There is certainly some mystery in this affair: I will stay here in order to un-riddle it.' He allowed the other to depart therefore, and then, without loss of time, he began to dig with his knife all round the stone. He succeeded so well that he raised it up, and found beneath a leather purse, containing a hundred ducats, and a card, on which was written the following sentence in Latin, 'Thou who hast had wit enough to discover the meaning of the inscription, inherit my money, and make a better use of it than I have.' The student rejoiced at his good fortune, replaced the stone in its former situation, and resumed his route to Salamanca, with the soul of the licentiate. Whoever thou art, friendly reader, thou art about to resemble one or the other of these two students. If thou perusest my adventures without perceiving the moral instructions they contain, thou wilt reap no harvest from thy labour; but, if thou readest with attention, thou wilt find in them, according to the precept of Horace, profit mingled with pleasure.

In chasing the identity of the unnamed 'Soul', it is easy to forget that Elgar was also inviting us to reflect on the lesson that Le Sage was offering us in the person of his hero – for it is Gil Blas himself who is speaking. He is the prototype for Beaumarchais's Figaro, but ultimately more successful. Born of humble parents, he sets off on a mule at the age of 17 for Salamanca University, just like the students in his little tale. Like Elgar, he fails to get there. He falls in with robbers and thereafter is carried by circumstance through a long series of adventures, living by his wits and personal charm. He becomes a quack physician, a valet, manservant to an actress, adviser to an archbishop, secretary to a duke, confidant of the prime minister, and finally a wealthy man with a patent of nobility. He certainly discovers, as Elgar did, that bags of ducats are important: while appreciating the allegory, Elgar would have smiled ruefully at the choice of image. But in selecting his motto from Le Sage, Elgar invites us, like Gil Blas, to look deeper than the surface of things, to have 'wit enough to discover the meaning of the inscription', to listen to his works 'with attention', in short to 'understand' him and his life and the language of his music, which the discerning may 'inherit . . . and make a better use of it than I have'.

There are further buried treasures associated with the Violin Concerto, in the form of literary quotations associated with themes sent or given to Alice Stuart Wortley, or copied in the piano score of the first two movements, which he also sent (to her and her husband Charles, respectively); all this material she left, with her father's portrait of her, to the town of Worcester 'as a *sacred* request' to her executors,[277] and it is now in the Elgar Birthplace Library. We must rejoice that Dr Jerrold Northrop Moore has edited for publication her entire correspondence with Elgar, though I fear that the material does not contain the whole story: there are unmistakable signs that some of it was tampered with, presumably by her daughter Clare, anxious for her mother's posthumous reputation.[278] Some of the fragments with musical themes on them bore inscriptions that have been erased or trimmed off with scissors, and from one of them, as we shall see, a newspaper clipping has been torn away.

The first of the Violin Concerto quotations remains a mystery, for it has so far eluded identification. Copied on the back of the first leaf of the piano sketch is:

> 'This is going to be good!
>
> "Where Love and Faith meet
> There will be Light"
>
> Feby 1910
> Queen Anne's Mansions'

Dr Moore observes that Elgar left Queen Anne's Mansions on 9 February.[279] The Love was evidently Elgar's; the Faith – in his ability to complete the work – Mrs Stuart Wortley's. The two lines of verse appear to employ an adaptation of the metre of the couplets that end Goethe's *Faust*, part II ('Das Ewig-Weibliche/Zieht uns hinan'), but are not a translation of anything in the poem. The only poet dear to Elgar whose works I have not yet had time to search thoroughly is the voluminous William Morris.

Dr Moore has drawn attention to the theme conceived 'in dejection' on 'Feb 7 1910 6 30 p.m.'[280] In the sketch of the first movement, the sixth bar after fig.19 bears the note 'Bar added May 29', with 'in dejection' deleted, followed by two or three further illegible words. Elgar's letter to Alice Stuart Wortley of 10 February 1910 alludes to a poetic source: 'written in dejection as Shelley says'. This can refer only to Shelley's 'Stanzas written in dejection, near Naples' (1818). Like Coleridge, in his much finer 'Dejection: an ode', Shelley sees natural beauty all round him, but cannot feel any pleasure in it:

> Alas! I have nor hope nor health,
> Nor peace within nor calm around,
> Nor that content surpassing wealth
> The sage in meditation found . . .
> Nor fame, nor power, nor love, nor leisure.
> Others I see whom these surround –
> Smiling they live, and call life pleasure; –
> To me that cup has been dealt in another measure.

He wishes to die, like a tired child falling asleep:

> Some might lament that I were cold,
> As I, when this sweet day is gone,
> Which my lost heart, too soon grown old,
> Insults with this untimely moan;

and finally nods off into incoherence (which Elgar never does):

> They might lament – for I am one
> Whom men love not, – and yet regret,
> Unlike this day, which, when the sun
> Shall on its stainless glory set,
> Will linger, though enjoyed, like joy in memory yet.

We may readily understand why Elgar should have been attracted to these Keatsian thoughts of death in springtime, when 'The breath of the moist earth is light,/Around its unexpanded buds', even though their melancholy is that of a young man. With the fifty-two-year-old Elgar, the case was reversed: he was condemned, in the autumn of his life, to feel emotions which took him back to relive the years of his early manhood.

Two further quotations underline the fact that the Violin Concerto and *The Music Makers* take their origin from the same matrix of thoughts and feelings. On 13 January 1911 he sent Alice Stuart Wortley a quotation from the Concerto with the line '"Musicians think our soules are harmonies": Sir John Davies (15–)', which he also copied into W. H. Reed's copy of the Ode.[281] The line is from the ninth stanza of the second part of Davies' *Nosce teipsum* ('Know thyself'), and refers to the Platonic idea that *musica humana* vibrates sympathetically to the same numerical proportions observed by the heavenly spheres singing in their courses. Elgar seems to have considered writing a symphony around Davies' poem (see n 271), which evoked musical ideas similar to, and sketched among, themes for *The Music Makers*. On f.25v of the piano score for the first movement of the Concerto, apparently associated with the music from figs.33–4, he copied lines 5–7 of William Watson's poem 'The Sovereign Poet' (1894), as Dr Moore has noted;[282] he underlined 'the immemorable' (that is, not worth remembering) with the note 'I do not like this word'. Alice Stuart Wortley copied out the whole poem: unfashionably grandiloquent but successful in its way, it presents a view of the lonely mystery of the creative artist very close to that of O'Shaughnessy in *The Music Makers*:

> He sits above the clang and dust of Time,
> With the world's secret trembling on his lip.
> He asks not converse nor companionship
> In the cold starlight where thou canst not climb.
>
> The undelivered tidings in his breast
> Suffer him not to rest.

He sees afar the immemorable throng,
And binds the scattered ages with a song.

The glorious riddle of his rhythmic breath,
His might, his spell, we know not what they be:
We only feel, whate'er he uttereth,
This savours not of death,
This hath a relish of eternity.

Two minor mysteries among the Stuart Wortley material at the Elgar Birthplace relate to newspaper cuttings. I drew attention to them many years ago in a talk for BBC Radio. The first is a nature article by 'a correspondent' entitled 'The Vernal Anemones' (Windflowers) that Elgar sent to the living Windflower with the MS heading '*The Times* Ap. 28 1923'. Dr Moore prints most of it, saying that Elgar wrote it himself and that it was published in *The Daily Telegraph* for 28 April 1924, though on another page he places it in 1923.[283] Whatever the truth of the matter, it reminds us of the days when Elgar coined the nickname for his second Alice. I suspect that he invented it before composing the first movement of the Violin Concerto, though the earliest traceable use is in association with themes in that movement, which even bears, on f.32v of the sketch, a drawing of what must be a windflower, bearing the legend 'rich foliage', no doubt referring to the lady's hair. In the sketch for the second movement, which was composed first in January 1910, during a period when Elgar was living alone in London, there are erased inscriptions in the manuscript at two points, ff.7A and 13. They accompany the second theme at the fifth bar after fig.55 (marked 'ardente') and at its last appearance in the first and second bars after fig.64. The first of these instances bears the legend 'for Caterina', followed by a deletion of a few pencilled words which may perhaps have read 'from . . . . Elgar'; over this the date 'January 24th 1910' has been written. A similar pencilled entry has been deleted in the second instance, which may read 'Caterina cariss[ima] . . . ' In each case the facing verso has on it what appears to be the stem of a flower whose blossom has been broken off, stuck to the page with stamp-edging.[284] It is fairly obvious, even without botanical analysis, that these must have been specimens of the *anemone nemorosa*, that 'Windflower' must originally have been called 'Caterina', and that Elgar's affection for her played an important part in the very beginnings of the Concerto. 'Caterina' must have been shortened to 'Cat' on occasion, for there are child-like drawings of cats here and there in the sketches.

The second mystery, which I was fortunate enough to solve, relates to the torn-off newspaper cutting already mentioned. On the second of the two 'Windflower' themes that precede the first-movement sketch (f.2), namely the melody at fig.16, dated 'Feb 1910', there is a space surrounded by a pencilled line (which gives its dimensions, therefore), and below it the words 'Claude Phillips'. In the dab of gum or paste which originally secured the cutting, a few words from its reverse side remain. By photographing these and printing them backwards, it proved possible to read the words 'Music Hall, . . . / . . . am Je . . . was sentenced to de . . . / . . . Justice A.T. Lawrence at the Old . . . / — / MISCELLANEOUS / . . . contents of . . . Page for V . . . / . . . men work . . . '. Since we know that Claude Phillips, Keeper of the Wallace Collection and a friend of the Elgars and Stuart Wortleys, wrote art criticism for *The Daily Telegraph*, and since, luckily, the careful Windflower noted on the leaf the words 'given to me May 1–1910/Sunday', it was no difficult deduction that led me to the British Library's Newspaper Library at Colindale, where I ordered up copies of that newspaper for the period in question. In the first issue that I examined, for Saturday 30 April, I found what I wanted in the sixth column on p.10. The unfortunate fate of Thomas William Jesshope, sentenced to death at the Old Bailey for murdering an attendant at the Camberwell Empire Music Hall, led me in turn to the closing paragraph, on the reverse of the page (p.9), of Claude Phillips' article 'Love in Art', which has the epigraph 'Love is strong as Death'. He ends his Art Notes with a description of what is believed to be Titian's last mythological painting, now identified as *Paris and Oenone*, and Elgar saw in it, evidently, an analogue in which both he and Alice Stuart Wortley might recognize their own relationship. Here is the extract; the cutting probably began with the second sentence, at 'It is twilight':

> But the most wonderful love-poem of Venetian sixteenth-century art is perhaps the 'Nymph and Piping Shepherd' of the Imperial Gallery at Vienna – Titian's farewell, in extreme old age, to life and love. It is twilight, and soon will be night, with the lovers, who dally still in the sombre air shot with silver. The poetry of the earlier years has come back, intensified by something of added poignancy, and of foreboding that is tinged, it may be, with remorse. This last passion has something that the earlier passion had not; in one sense it is nearer to earth and earthiness; in another it is infinitely higher and more far-reaching, more typical of the love that in its heights and depths, in its tender light and sombre, fitfully illumined shadow, is truly that which to the end of all things must hold and possess Man.

At the time when Elgar sent this to his Windflower, he was nearly 53, and she 48, two years younger than Helen Weaver.

One further literary connection suggests that Elgar's deeper relationship with 'Windflower' extends further back in time than anyone has yet been prepared to state explicitly. When her husband received a peerage in the New Year's Honours of 1916–17, Elgar wrote to congratulate her, saying 'I gave you a coronet long ago – the best I had but you may have forgotten it'.[285] This can refer only to No.5 of the Songs, Op.59, 'Was it Some Golden Star?':

> Once in another land,
>   Ages ago,

You were a queen, and I,
  I loved you so . . .

But you were a queen, and I
  Fought for you then:
How did you honour me –
  More than all men!
Kissed me upon the lips;
  Kiss me again.

Op.59 was to have contained six songs for voice and orchestra, all to texts by Gilbert Parker, the Canadian novelist; he was a friend of the Stuart Wortleys, and had sent Elgar a copy of his *Embers* in October 1908, when it was privately published, with his 'admiring good wishes'.[286] According to Dr Moore, he conceived the idea of the cycle in late November or December 1909.[287] Three months before that he had been 'possessed', according to Alice Elgar's diary, 'with his music for the Violin Concerto', but it seems to have made little progress, as did his efforts towards a second symphony that October. Festivals and conducting engagements may have kept him too busy; but something was fermenting inside him, and he seized on Parker's volume of poetry – mostly sentimental and amorous, though with some songs of adventure and empire-building – and marked no less than twenty-four poems that interested him, leaving indications in eight cases that he thought of setting them to music.[288] Six of the latter were to form Op.59, all love-songs except for 'Proem', which is a poetic prose introduction (p.xi). The whole set was presumably to form the musical coronet with which Elgar proposed to crown his queen, and there are sketches for all in British Library Add. MS. 63157;[289] he completed only the three that Muriel Foster was to sing at the memorial concert for Jaeger on 24 January 1910. These, nos.3, 5 and 6, are the finest Elgar; we must regret that they are not better known, and even more that he did not finish the cycle. Fair copies in the Birthplace Library have numberings which suggest some uncertainty as to the sequence: 'Oh, Soft was the Song' is correctly labelled III, but 'Was it Some Golden Star' has the number IV, with the note (to the engraver) 'Do not print these numerals at present!'; it eventually became no.5. 'Twilight' bears the last-minute pencil addition 'Op.59, no.6', again correctly.[290]

Of the songs that he completed, he omitted stanza 4 of 'The Twilight of Love', which is of poor poetic quality. And propriety forbade the inclusion of the first stanza of 'At Sea' ('Oh soft was the song'):

Through the round window above, the deep palpable blue,
  The wan bright moon, and the sweet stinging breath of the sea;
And below, in the shadows, thine eyes like stars,
  And Love brooding low, and the warm white glory of thee.

Of those that remained unfinished, if 'Proem' was to have been no.1, which seems plausible, then it would have been preceded by an orchestral prelude: the sketch is in E minor, beginning with a D sharp, but is annotated 'after E flat (or C m[inor)]'. It is a dialogue between an Angel and a man, speaking alternately, but Elgar omitted the lines identifying each:

> And the Angel said:
> "What hast thou for all thy travail –
> What dost thou bring with thee out
> of the dust of the world?"
>
> "Behold, I bring one perfect yesterday!"
> "Hast thou then no to-morrow?"
>
> Hast thou no hope?"
>
> "Who am I that I should hope?
> Out of all my life I have been granted one
> sheaf of memory."
>
> "Is this all?"
>
> "Of all else I was robbed by the way,
> but Memory was hidden safely
> in my heart – the world found it not."

'There is an Orchard' would perhaps have been no.2. This is a poem of lesser quality, though it offers formal opportunities to the composer. I omit the third stanza, as Elgar indicated:

> There is an orchard beyond the sea,
> And high is the orchard wall;
> And ripe is the fruit in the orchard tree –
> O my love is fair and tall!
>
> There is an orchard beyond the sea,
> And joy to its haven hies;
> And a white hand opens its gate to me –
> O deep are my true love's eyes!
>
> There is an orchard beyond the sea,
> Where the soft delights do roam;
> To the Great Delight I have bent my knee –
> O good is my true love's home!
>
> There is an orchard beyond the sea,
> With a nest where the linnets hide;
> O warm is the nest that is built for me –
> In my true love's heart I bide!

'The Waking', perhaps intended as no.4 (or 5, if 'Was it Some Golden Star' had been no.4), shows the hardened, grizzled man of action restored by love to the dreams of his youth:

> To be young is to dream, and I dreamed no more;
> I had smothered my heart as the fighter can:

> I toiled, and I looked not behind or before –
> I was stone; but I waked with the heart of a man.

> By the soul at her lips, by the light of her eyes,
> I dreamed a new dream as the sleeper can,
> That the heavenly folly of youth was wise –
> I was stone; but I waked with the heart of a man.

> She came like a song, she will go like a star:
> I shall tread these hills as the hunter can,
> Mine eyes to the hunt, and my soul afar –
> I was stone; but I waked with the heart of a man.

The soul and the dream are favourite Elgarian images. Why did he not finish these settings? Did he resume work on them, and were they the 'other wonderful things' that he played to Windflower with the Second Symphony when she visited the Elgars at Brinkwells in late August 1919?[291] Did she feel unable to accept so public a tribute? Why did he write to her so mysteriously a month later, saying 'the Studio is sad sad & I feel I have destroyed the best thing I ever wrote & that it had to be so'? The other uncompleted work that we may associate with her (besides the Pianoforte Concerto) was begun just after the Op.59 Songs were drafted: the cycle planned as four Songs, Op.60, which he later orchestrated. These had texts by Elgar himself, allegedly paraphrases of 'folk-songs from Eastern Europe'[292] by 'my confidant & adviser Pietro d'Alba' (the pet Peter Rabbit).[293] Elgar started on no.1, the ardent 'Come, oh my love!' ('The Torch'), with its image from Act II of *Tristan und Isolde*, the very next day after writing to Alice Stuart Wortley in these terms: 'I would write a sonnet to you but it would not rhyme & if it did, it would not be good enough for you otherwise. Anyhow I can *think* sonnets to you & America which had probably better not be scanned'.[294] 'America' must mean Julia Worthington, and mention of her in the same breath indicated playfulness rather than passion. But the words of stanza 1, repeated with small variations in stanzas 2 and 4, are passionate enough:

> Come, O my love!
> Come, fly to me;
> All my soul
> Cries out for thee:
> Haste to thy home, –
> I long for thee,
> Faint for thee,
> Worship thee
> Only, – but come!

When published in 1910, this was dedicated to 'Yvonne' a name baffling to all commentators on Elgar's life. I can only conjecture that, as the feminine form of Ivo, it has something to do with St Ives: Elgar must have visited the lovely seaside village on his tour of Cornwall in March and April 1910, just after visiting the Stuart Wortleys in Tintagel: did Windflower go with them? –

for her husband went to London on 4 April.[295] The other completed song of Op.60 was 'The River', a patriotic effusion whose verses date from 1909. The others were to have been 'The Shrine' (no.2) and 'The Bee' (no.3), but I have not seen these texts, if indeed they survive.

I end this section with comments on the two Symphonies, taken together because in regard to their associated epigraphs and literary quotations they form a striking contrast. The music of the First Symphony (1908) is no less intimate and personal than that of the Second, and has evidently, in Newman's words, 'come straight out of some highly vitalised experience or other';[296] but the work bears no epigraph, unlike its sister, and I know of only one literary connection, which was not made public, though it may have been confided to a friend. Significantly, it is the dying Hamlet's last words, 'The rest is silence', copied in a sketch over the beautiful theme at fig.104 that ends the slow movement.[297] This, and the general emotional progression of the work, would suggest that it reflects Elgar's favourite cycle of a life interrupted by loss and even self-extinction, but regenerated by hope, by faith, by a determined resumption of artistic activity, forward-looking if not always happy. Such a cycle may be traced in the *Variations*, in *The Dream of Gerontius*, in the Concertos, and in the Second Symphony, of which Alice Elgar wrote: 'It resumes our human life, delight, regret, farewell, the saddest word & then the strong man's triumph'.[298]

Whatever programmatic ideas may have been in Elgar's mind as he composed the First Symphony, he was not going to reveal them to anyone. It was to be his first major essay in what he regarded as the highest form of the art, absolute music. In his Birmingham lecture of 8 November 1905, he had described Brahms' Third Symphony as 'a piece of absolute music. There was no clue to what was meant, but, as Sir Hubert Parry said, it was a piece of music which called up certain sets of emotions in each individual hearer. That was the height of music . . . '.[299] Elgar is also reported as protesting about those who, listening to a Beethoven symphony, indulge themselves by 'calling up all sorts of pictures, which might or might not have existed in the composer's mind'.[300] The listener may imagine emotions, then, but not pictures: when music is 'simply a description of something else it is carrying a large art somewhat further than he cared for', music 'as a simple art' being at its best 'when it was simple, without description'. These words had evoked a major explosion from Ernest Newman in *The Manchester Guardian* next day, a Wagnerian ever on the alert for absolutist statements by 'Brahmins'. He cited Max Kalbeck's *Johannes Brahms*[301] to show that some of that master's 'ostensibly non-descriptive' works 'had a poetic or pictorial basis', and pointed to his private practice of hinting at extra-musical meanings to a restricted circle of intimates: 'if the composer did not give the "clue to what was meant" to every purchaser of a copy, he certainly gave the clue to private friends' (this was a practice which Elgar himself was to adopt). Newman carried the war into Elgar's camp by alluding to descriptive music that he himself had written, and rammed home his triumph by citing the 'Gordon' symphony: ' . . . for the symphony upon which he has been engaged for so long, has *it* not a title? Has he not already given his friends the "clue" to it?'

Elgar tried to meet Newman to explain what he felt, but no discussion could quickly be arranged.[302] All the same, he abandoned the idea of a programmatic symphony in Gordon's memory. Three years later, when it turned out that Newman had been chosen to write the introductory note for the première of the First Symphony, Elgar found it necessary and opportune, in writing to brief him, to set out his more considered views on the subject of their earlier controversy. He denied any overt programmatic aims:[303]

> As to the 'intention': I have no tangible poetic or other basis: I feel that unless a man sets out to depict or illustrate some definite thing, all music – absolute music I think it is called – must be (even if he does not know it himself) a reflex, or picture, or elucidation of his own life, or, at the least, the music is necessarily coloured by the life. The listener may like to know this much & identify his own life's experiences with the music . . . but . . . I prefer the listener to draw what he can from the sounds that he hears.

Nine days later, as already noted, he told Walford Davies, who was also writing a piece on the new Symphony, that 'There is no programme beyond a wide experience of human life with a great charity (love) and a *massive* hope in the future'. To save time, he sent Davies copies of his letters to Newman – it sounds as though there had been much questioning and answering – and added: 'I think these explain my feelings and partly my views regarding absolute music'.[304] We must hope that the indefatigable Dr Moore will publish this whole sequence of letters to Newman, for they appear to mark a conscious stage in Elgar's development – 'my latest phase', as he wrote to Griffith[305] – when he abandoned the oratorio trilogy and started to produce a stream of 'absolute' symphonic works. But it is plain from Elgar's statement to Newman that 'absolute' is no longer a term that he himself applauds; he uses it simply because it is current: 'absolute music, I think it is called'. He would have approved of the word in its meaning of 'complete in itself', but he knew that his own music was necessarily connected or related to his life (even agonizing over the fact that he had 'shown himself'[306] in his works), and that his power over the listener lay in his ability to conjure forth, by means of musical imagery, emotional responses drawn from the listener's own experience of life that were in some way similar to his own. But the general audience – in spite of his penchant for mystification – were not to try and elucidate his works by reference to his life, still less use the works to interpret his life (both of which sins I have committed). As in the case of Brahms, only his intimate friends were to be favoured with glimpses of the psychological motivations that underlay the perfect finish of his self-sufficient art.

After the unprecedented success of the First Symphony, Elgar evidently felt that he had proved his point about the way in which 'absolute' music operates, and began to relax his guard. With the Violin Concerto – admittedly because of the peculiar circumstances of its composition – he felt free to associate poetic quotations and emotional developments in his own life with various moments in the music, though most of this had necessarily to remain a private matter. He attached private literary and personal references to the music of the Second Symphony too, but several friends were now admitted to the charmed circle; and he went so far as to append a public 'motto' to the score, the opening lines of Shelley's *Song*, 'Rarely, rarely comest thou,/Spirit of Delight!'. In the observations that Elgar jotted down as a guide for Mrs Rosa Newmarch, who was to write the programme note for the first performance, he said: 'To get near the mood of the Symphony the whole of Shelley's poem may be read, but the music does not illustrate the whole of the poem, neither does the poem entirely elucidate the music'.[307] The only specific connection that he makes between poem and music relates to the slow movement, which is not, he says, a memorial tribute for Edward VII, the Symphony's dedicatee: 'it is elegiac but has nothing to do with any funeral march & is a "reflection" suggested by the poem'. To this Dr Moore has been able to add the following, from a letter to Ernest Newman: 'My attitude toward the poem, or rather to the "Spirit of Delight" was an attempt to give the reticent Spirit a hint (with sad enough introspections) as to what we should like to have!'[308]

All this is surprisingly vague. It would be naïve to expect precision; but Elgar is quite as reticent as the Spirit he wishes to invoke. Was he simply treading warily because of the earlier controversy with Newman, and avoiding too strong a suggestion that there were programmatic elements in his 'absolute' Symphony? Turning to the poem, one finds that it was posthumously published and would doubtless have been improved had Shelley lived, for it is far below his best.[309] Elgar seems to have taken nothing from it except the basic notion of a sad, quiet, sensitive, weary man trying to find his way back to some feeling of delight in life: the theme of the poem is not unlike that of the *Stanzas written in dejection, near Naples*, which Elgar had quoted in connection with the Violin Concerto. Apart from the general opposition of delight and sorrow, and the equating of the Spirit of Delight with 'love and life' ('O come,/Make once more my heart thy home'), there is little to connect with the Symphony. The 'starry night' and 'autumn evening' of the fifth stanza are sources of joy and can hardly have suggested the elegy of Elgar's slow movement. It would be fanciful indeed to think of the 'Rondo' as a portrait of 'Love – though he has wings,/And like light can flee'; though it is just possible that the movement sets a 'mournful ditty/To a merry measure' as Shelley's poem does (but the experimental dissociation between the mournful feelings and the tripping trochees of the metre is the main cause of the song's failure).

Other evidence suggests that the Symphony's epigraph is of little real relevance, and may even be partly intended to divert the general listener away from the true scent. The emotional experiences behind the music are those of the year of the Violin Concerto, 1910, for on 29 January 1911 Elgar wrote to Alice Stuart Wortley: 'I have recorded last year in the first movement [of the Symphony] to which I put the last note in the score a moment ago . . . I have worked at fever heat & the thing is tremendous in energy'.[310] Among Elgar's suggestions for Mrs Newmarch, which he said she might quote, there are references to images and romantic feelings not to be found in Shelley's poem:

> note the new 'atmosphere' at [fig.] 27 . . . with the added Cello solo at 28 – remote & drawing some one else out of the everyday world: note the *feminine* voice of the oboe, answering or joining in, two bars before 30[;] note the happiness at 30 – real (remote) peace: note the atmosphere broken in upon & the dream 'shattered' by the inevitable march of the Trombones & Tuba pp. In the 2nd movement at 79 the feminine voice *laments* over the broad manly 1st theme and may not 87 be like a woman dropping a flower on the man's grave?

The flower was evidently a Windflower, and Alice Stuart Wortley the 'some one else', the 'feminine voice' of the first movement, and the 'woman' standing at the graveside in the second.[311] The pair, we should note, are 'drawn out of the everyday world', and the man alone dies: this is not, then, a Tristanesque extinction of both lovers in their mutual passion, but the emotional 'death' of one partner, presumably through renunciation; or was it because Elgar had told Alice Stuart Wortley of his 'death' in 1885, when he parted from Helen Weaver? The new love would thus have enshrined the image of the old. His letters to 'Windflower' of 1910 contain such frequent exhortations to visit him, because the themes 'stick' and need her presence and encouragement, that it seems plain that she herself was the 'reticent Spirit' who came to see him too rarely: is not the epigraph a coded appeal? – 'O come,/Make once more my heart thy home'.

Or does the movement represent the death of feeling, the death of Love, the death of Music itself, in Elgar's Orphean mythology? No-one has yet pointed out that the solemn opening music of the Larghetto was originally conceived as a setting for six or eight voices of the opening stanza, 'In heaven a spirit doth dwell', of Edgar Allan Poe's *Israfel*.[312] The poem describes the tutelary genius of Music in Arabian theology, 'the angel Israfel, whose heart-strings are a lute, and who has the sweetest voice of all God's creatures' (according to Poe's epigraph, which quotes the Koran). Israfel's whole being is music, therefore, and at the sound of his voice the starry choir itself falls silent in wonder. But the Love that he sings of is heavenly, for he treads the skies 'Where deep thoughts are a duty – /Where Love's a grown-up God':

> The ecstasies above
>   With thy burning measures suit –
> Thy grief, thy joy, thy hate, thy love,
>   With the fervour of thy lute –
> Well may the stars be mute!
>   Yes, Heaven is thine; but this
> Is a world of sweets and sours;
>   Our flowers are merely – flowers,
> And the shadow of thy perfect bliss
>   Is the sunshine of ours.

Poe finished, however, by imagining that he, a mortal, might change places with Israfel, when 'a bolder note than this might swell/From my lyre within the sky'.

It is of course impossible to show whether Elgar, in borrowing the theme, also wished to transfer something of its original connotation. But in 1910, when composing the Violin Concerto, he had associated his music with the remote divinity, the apartness, of Watson's poet, singing 'In the cold starlight where thou canst not climb', and, as we have seen, we find the same 'apartness' in the poem for *The Music Makers*, whose sketches span this period. The music from *Israfel* certainly makes a hieratic and elevated introduction to the Larghetto of the Symphony, which like the first movement develops into a dialogue, 'a wistful colloquy between the two people'[313] as Elgar hinted to Newman, one a woman, the other evidently Elgar the artist, who imagines himself dying. A phrase relating to the first movement in Elgar's observations to Mrs Newmarch, cited above, suggests that in this earlier dialogue at figs.27–30 the artist lifts up his feminine partner into some far-off, mystical region, the 'remote' cello melody 'drawing some one else out of the everyday world'. This is not the self-absorbed, private retreat of the lovers who flee the 'Alltag' in Act II of *Tristan und Isolde* (much as Elgar admired that work): the woman is called upon to climb up to the idealized, visionary heights that are the home of the artist 'whose heart-strings are a lute'.

Elgar twice characterized this passage with images rather different to those that he communicated to Mrs Newmarch for public use. To Newman he said it 'might be a love scene in a garden at night when the ghost of some memories comes *through* it; – it makes me shiver'.[314] To the woman he then loved, Alice Stuart Wortley, he described it as 'the *most extraordinary* passage I have ever heard – a sort of malign influence wandering thro' the summer night in the garden'.[315] The wording shows that he is not recalling an experience that they have shared: it is plainly new to her. Where was the garden, and what was the malign influence?

The cello tune from this episode returns in the third movement to form its terrifying climax. Basil Maine says of the passage that 'the composer is here reflecting the mood of . . . "Dead, long dead,"' from Tennyson's *Maud*, and cites lines 8–10 of the poem:

> And the hoofs of the horses beat, beat,
> The hoofs of the horses beat,
> Beat into my scalp and my brain
> With never an end to the stream of passing feet.

He adds a cautiously worded footnote which leaves one in slight doubt as to whether Elgar had volunteered this information, or whether someone else had told Maine about it, and he had then asked the composer to comment: 'Whether Elgar was consciously influenced by those lines or not, he once told the present writer that they conveyed a true impression of the emotional significance of the episode in the Symphony'.[316] He may conceivably have read about the Tennyson connection in a letter by Canon W. H. T. Gairdner quoted in his wife's compilation *W. H. T. G. to his friends* (London, [1930]), first noticed by Dr Diana McVeagh.[317] Gairdner (1873–1928) had written an appreciation of the Second Symphony, 'a guess at its inner meaning', which he probably sent to Elgar, who met him and made admiring comments (we do not know when). He called his piece 'The Passionate Pilgrim', a literary title with Shakespearean connections, which Elgar approved but did not originate. Elgar volunteered the following information, however, and it is certainly worth reprinting here (I interpolate the lines from *Maud* (1–4), placed by Mrs Gairdner in a footnote; they are not those chosen by Maine):

> He told me that the fff passage in the second episode of the Rondo is the most 'horrible' thing he ever did. It is the *madness* that attends the excess or abuse of passion.
> He pointed out to me a passage in *Maud*, where the hero imagines he has gone mad, and that he is lying under a street with the horrible traffic roaring over his head. (*Maud*, Part II, V.1):
>
> > Dead, long dead,
> > Long dead!
> > And my heart is a handful of dust,
> > And the wheels go over my head.
>
> In the music he represents this by an incessant maddening hammering on the big drum, rising at the climax to a hideous din. He said that he had been closely associated at Worcester with a lunatic asylum, and had seen a lot of the patients, and knew their histories and symptoms. He thinks that all great music ultimately rests on experience of life. Where the young moderns are so lacking, he thinks, is in their *in*experience in this respect. When they try to write great music they only succeed in setting up a big frame, and have not the life experience to fill that frame really. For the same reason, they excel only in slighter works.

I shall return to the question of madness and lunatics later. For the moment let us stay with *Maud*, whose hero is certainly mad at this point in the story.

Dr Moore rightly observes that in this passage 'the hero's frustrated love turns into a fantasy of his own burial'.[318] He silently completes the passage, as also does Michael Kennedy, by adding the three lines (5–7) which Elgar perhaps avoided quoting, since both Gairdner and Maine contrive to omit them:

> And my bones are shaken with pain,
> For into a shallow grave they are thrust,
> Only a yard beneath the street, . . .

A shallow grave, beneath the street, horses and carts trampling and rumbling over the corpse's head: this can only be the grave of a suicide – for in England, until as late as 1823, a suicide was buried on the highway with a stake driven through his body.

There is even more to this passage, I think, than 'the agonized reaction of Elgar to sudden death' that Mr Kennedy sees in it.[319] He and Dr Moore each adduce one of the slightly different accounts by Bernard Shore telling how Elgar explained the music to an orchestra as the 'dreadful beating that goes on in the brain', the 'horrible throbbing in the head during some fever. It seems gradually to blot out every atom of thought in your brain and nearly drives you mad'.[320] Elgar was surely remembering in this music his illnesses and insomnia of the years at the turn of the century, when we know he thought of suicide. His comments to Gairdner – which are not prompted by the latter's brief comment in his appreciation on this passage of the 'Rondo' – reinforce the idea that Elgar may at times, during his long ordeal, have feared for his sanity. It must be his own experience that led him to describe this most 'horrible' music as 'the *madness* that attends the excess or abuse of passion': the excess sprang from his ardent, emotional nature, and the abuse from its frustration, his inability (then) to express his feelings through his music, or in any other form, so that for a time he turned them inwards, destructively, upon himself. That is a common cause of suicide.

All suicide is 'horrible', not least for those who survive the deceased and are left wondering whether they might have saved him. Among Catholics it is fairly uncommon, for it is a heavy sin indeed, both formal and mortal: repentance is obviously impossible. *Felo de se* (the correct legal term, as Elgar would have known, for suicide while of sound mind) was also a crime, in Great Britain, until 1961. I am not sure whether Elgar, had he made away with himself, would 'in ground unsanctified have lodg'd Till the last Trumpet'; but there is evidence that one of his fairly recent ancestors may have been interred in regulation quicklime without the proper rites, and that Elgar worried about it. When staying at Lady Maud Warrender's house at Leasham, near Rye, at some period before 1916, he asked his fellow-guest E. F. Benson, the novelist brother of A. C. Benson, to help him examine all the tombstones in the church cemetery at Winchelsea: 'Some forebear, his great-grandfather, I think, had been hanged there for sheep-stealing and Elgar's piety prompted him to search the churchyard to see if he could find his grave, thus establishing that he had received Christian burial: two searchers

9   *Arthur.* Original Old Vic Theatre programme, 1923

10   George Bernard Shaw by Sir Bernard Partridge, c. 1925

11   Elgar with Alan Kirby (left) and Fred Gaisberg, 1932

12   Original drawing of Elgar by Adrian Cope

13   Elgar with Dr Adrian Boult at HMV's Abbey Road Studios, May 1932

14 Elgar at Lawnside, Malvern, in August 1932 with Mrs Claude Beddington
and Mr and Mrs J B Priestley

15   Elgar with Fred Gaisberg (left) and Richard Mountford (right) arrive at Le Bourget aerodrome, 29 May 1933

16 Elgar with Carice Elgar Blake and Fred Gaisberg, Croydon, 2 June 1933

would make quite a short job of it.'[321] The search was fruitless. Although Benson specialized in light, comic novels, and in telling this anecdote draws an elegant parallel with the equally fruitless search after Elgar's death for the 'Air songs' (1919) for which he had provided the words, he was the son of an archbishop and would not, I think, have spoken lightly about Elgar's piety. If, having heard (no doubt) as a boy about his great-grandfather's unhappy end, Elgar could show concern fifty years later about the fate of his relative's non-Catholic soul, he would have thought deeply about the consequences of his own possible suicide. He had looked over the brink, and the death that he had imagined remained a powerful image in his musical iconology; but he knew that despair was a sin, and depicted its effects in the figure of the suicide Judas.

The welcome oblivion of death figures in another literary source connected with the Second Symphony, Shakespeare's Sonnet 66, 'Tir'd with all these, for restful death I cry' (admittedly, the poet's image is perhaps more a literary conceit than a depiction of genuinely suicidal intentions). Dr Moore reports that Elgar copied its ninth line over the second draft of the theme that begins the last movement, '[And] Art made tongue-tied by authority', and places the sketch in October 1903, very early in the history of the work.[322] The sonnet catalogues eleven examples of merit oppressed by the unworthy, of good turned to ill, of the strong and able kept down by the weak and incompetent, ending with the couplet:

> Tir'd with all these, from these I would be gone,
> Save that to die, I leave my love alone.

The sketch is on two staves, which is how Elgar drafted his partsongs; the upper theme fits the rhythm of the first line of the sonnet very well; if it is not actually a setting, the opening words seem at least to have suggested the music.

The unnamed hero of *Maud*, like Elgar himself, did not commit suicide. After the crazed imaginings of 'Dead, long dead' in the fifth and final section of Part II, he recovers in Part III after seeing his lost love in a dream among 'a band of the blest'.

> And it was but a dream, yet it yielded a dear delight
> To have look'd, tho' but in a dream, upon eyes so fair,
> That had been in the weary world my one thing bright . . .

But my main purpose in returning to *Maud* is to note that it provides a source, or at least a striking parallel, for Elgar's image of a love-scene in a haunted garden and, beyond that, offered Elgar further analogies with his own experience of the anguish of loss and separation. The garden in question is of course the one into which Maud was invited so memorably to come, the scene of her wooing by the hero of the poem.

The garden is doubly haunted. It is bordered by a wood, behind which is a 'dreadful hollow' where the hero's father had thrown himself down to commit suicide (he had been financially ruined by the double-dealing of Maud's father, who owns the Hall and its garden). The hero begins his narration by recalling the horror of his dead father's homecoming:

> I remember the time, for the roots of my hair were stirr'd
> By a shuffled step, by a dead weight trail'd, by a whisper'd fright
> And my pulses closed their gates with a shock on my heart as I heard
> The shrill-edged shriek of a mother divide the shuddering night.

The hero loves Maud, the millionaire's daughter, whom he has admired since childhood; against all the odds, she falls in love with him in return. But there is a dandified, noble suitor in the offing, and her cold-hearted brother, who acts *in loco parentis* since their father is never there, despises the hero for his poverty and for being the son of a disgraced suicide. One fine spring night there is a ball at the great house; Maud slips out to join her lover in the garden, and her brother surprises them there. Insults: a blow: a duel with pistols in 'the red-ribbed hollow behind the wood': and Maud's brother lies dying on the spot where the hero's father had fallen. As the hero flees, the last thing he hears is Maud's terrible cry as she realizes what has happened. He escapes to Brittany, haunted by his memories of Maud's love and his realization that she cannot possibly now acknowledge it.

> For years, a measureless ill,
> For years, for ever, to part –
> But she, she would love me still;
> And as long, O God, as she
> Have a grain of love for me,
> So long, no doubt, no doubt,
> Shall I nurse in my dark heart,
> However weary, a spark of will
> Not to be trampled out.

Like the mortally wounded Tristan, awaiting Isolde on the same shore, he half thinks that Maud may follow after him:

> Back from the Breton coast,
> Sick of a nameless fear,
> Back to the dark sea-line
> Looking, thinking of all I have lost . . .

But he knows it is over, and grimly tells himself that 'the time is at hand/ When thou shalt more than die'. There follows the lovely song 'O that 'twere possible', in which intolerable recollections of vanished happiness delude the dreams of the insomniac:

> Half the night I waste in sighs, . . .
> In a wakeful doze I sorrow
> For the hand, the lips, the eyes,
> For the meeting of the morrow,
> The delight of happy laughter,
> The delight of low replies.

And this 'deathlike type of pain' drives him into the madness of 'Dead, long dead'. Even in his shallow grave she haunts him: 'she is standing here at my head' (but she throws no flower down). And the image of the garden returns, the red roses turning to blood at the death of its 'keeper', Maud's brother:

> But I know where a garden grows,
> Fairer than aught in the world beside,
> All made up of the lily and rose
> That blow by night, when the season is good,
> To the sound of dancing music and flutes:
> It is only flowers, they had no fruits,
> And I almost fear they are not roses, but blood;
> For the keeper was one, so full of pride,
> He linkt a dead man there to a spectral bride;
> For he, if he had not been a Sultan of brutes,
> Would he have that hole in his side?

'The sound of dancing music and flutes' refers, of course, to the music that 'clash'd in the hall' while the hero was waiting for so long in the dark of the garden for Maud to leave the 'babble and revel and wine' and come out and join him. One might easily suppose that the febrile opening music of Elgar's 'Rondo', which he characterized as 'wild and headstrong with soothing pastoral strains in between and very brilliant',[323] may have taken its cue from the contrast of the wild waltzing within, the balmy garden without, that underlies 'Come into the garden, Maud'. Elgar told Mrs Newmarch that he 'took down the rhythm of the opening bars from some itinerant musicians' on the Piazza of S. Marco in Venice, but that need not disqualify the association which I have proposed. He himself linked the suicidal madness of the hero of *Maud* with the climax of the 'Rondo', and, if we are to believe Sanford Terry, writing about this very Symphony, 'In every movement its form, and above all its climax, were very clearly in his mind – indeed, as he has often told me, it is the *Climax* which invariably he settles first'.[324] If in the climax of the 'Rondo' he was 'reflecting the mood of "Dead, long dead"', to quote Maine, and if the lines 'conveyed a true impression of the emotional significance of this episode'; if Elgar voluntarily 'pointed out' the same poem to Gairdner, saying that 'in the music he represents' its 'horrible' imagery, it is entirely plausible that some of the memories and associations that had reduced Tennyson's hero to a condition of suicidal insanity should be traceable in other parts of the movement.

My purpose is to try and understand Elgar's mental and musical processes, not to chase unprovable programmatic links of the naif Straussian kind that made Elgar so uneasy – at least in public. But where is one to draw the line? For Elgar himself gave many a hint, and no composer was as adept as he was at translating pictorial and emotional images and aspects of personality, both his own and others', into uncannily exact musical analogues. What drew him to *Maud*? Psychologists may care to speculate on the possible link between the dead father in the poem and the father whom Elgar displaced; or point to the fact that, if family disapproval played any part in Helen Weaver's severance from Elgar, it would have operated through her brother Frank (since her parents and stepmother were no longer living). I am content to note that Elgar would have heard in Tennyson's monodrama many sympathetic resonances of his emotional loss and near-madness, his thoughts of suicide, his self-pity and his appeals for help:

> O me, why have they not buried me deep enough?
> Is it kind to have made me a grave so rough,
> Me, that was never a quiet sleeper?
> Maybe I still am but half-dead;
> Then I cannot wholly be dumb;
> I will cry to the steps above my head
> And somebody, surely, some kind heart will come
> To bury me, bury me
> Deeper, ever so little deeper.

Elgar found several kind hearts in the course of his life, and those who really understood him and his art advised him to face his problems and overcome them by transmuting them into musical terms. The hero of *Maud* eventually finds regeneration after personal defeat (and social defeat at the hands of a system that he bitterly criticizes) in the new sense of nobility, national unity and selfless heroism in a worthwhile cause that arose with the onset of the Crimean War; but Elgar could also have concluded, with him, that

> It is better to fight for the good than to rail at the ill;
> I have felt with my native land, I am one with my kind,
> I embrace the purpose of God, and the doom assign'd.

Elgar told Mrs Newmarch that the Rondo 'was sketched on the Piazza of S. Mark, Venice'. The last literary quotation associated with the Second Symphony takes us to another Venetian island, with quite different connotations, and I think explains the strange way in which his talk with Canon Gairdner veered off into a recollection of his experiences as a young man when he provided musical entertainment for the inmates of the Pauper Lunatic Asylum at Powick (from 1877, when he was 20, until 1884).[325] Michael Kennedy has drawn attention to a letter that he wrote to Mrs Frances Colvin on 1 February 1911, just after he had started to put the slow movement into its final shape. Presumably excusing himself for not visiting the Colvins, he said 'I am too busy with the "Spirit of Delight" symphony', and went on to add three lines from another poem by Shelley, *Julian and Maddalo: a conversation*, substituting 'notes' for Shelley's 'words':[326]

> I do but hide
> Under these notes, like embers, every spark
> *Of that which has consumed me.*

This was written to the wife of a well-known scholar who was also a valued friend of Elgar's: Sidney Colvin would have known its context well, even if he had not been a noted biographer of nineteenth-century poets. The 'conversation' is between two friends who are Shelley (Julian) and Byron (Count Maddalo), lightly disguised. They meet in Venice, ride on the Lido and travel about the Lagoon by gondola, disputing about free will, progress and religious faith. Julian maintains that man can improve his lot by his own efforts without recourse to religion; Maddalo, that he will ever be a frail victim of circumstance. He instances the sad condition of a man he knows, once wealthy and genteel and a sensitive musician, an idealist like Julian, who has lost everything and whose mind has given way under the stress of sorrow. Pitying him, Maddalo has installed him in a lunatic asylum on an island in the Lagoon (this would be San Clemente), where he is looked after in some comfort. They visit the 'Maniac', whose music brings some relief to the sufferings of the other madmen (a curious parallel with Elgar's work at Powick Asylum, though he said of it that 'I fear my tunes did little to ameliorate the condition of the unfortunate inmates').[327] Unaware of his visitors, the Maniac talks disjointedly about his wrongs and his misery in a long monologue, mainly addressed to the woman who has abandoned him, which occupies two-thirds of the poem. Its substance is said to be based partly on the madness of Tasso – the poet of the epigraph to the *Enigma Variations* – and partly on Shelley's own relationship with his first wife. Its pathos makes the philosophizing of the two friends seem arid and shallow. The Maniac sits near a piano, his head 'leaning on a music book' and 'his lips . . . pressed against a folded leaf',

> As one who wrought from his own fervid heart
> The eloquence of passion . . .
> [He] spoke – sometimes as one who wrote and thought
> His words might move some heart that heeded not
> If sent to distant lands . . .

He moves disconnectedly between reproach, self-pity, grief, and a cold despair; he begins by lamenting that he was unable to confide the cause of his sorrow to anyone, even to those closest to him, a pretence that he hated; it brings him to thoughts of death, perhaps suicide:

> 'Month after month', he cried, 'to bear this load . . .
> And not to speak my grief – O not to dare
> To give a human voice to my despair,
> But live and move, and wretched thing! smile on
> As if I never went aside to groan,
> And wear this mask of falsehood even to those
> Who are most dear – not for my own repose –
> Alas no scorn or pain or hate could be
> So heavy as that falsehood is to me –

> But that I cannot bear more altered faces
> Than needs must be . . .

>   Would the dust
> Were covered in upon by body now!
> That the life ceased to toil within my brow!
> And then these thoughts would at the least be fled;
> Let us not fear such pain can vex the dead.
> 'What Power delights to torture us? I know
> That to myself I do not wholly owe
> What now I suffer . . .

– how near we are to Elgar gritting his teeth and for years swallowing back his secret grief or railing against destiny! No wonder the Maniac and the hero of *Maud* in his madness made him think of his years at Powick, years which coincided almost exactly with his association with Helen Weaver.[328]

Whoever the woman was who wronged Shelley's hero, she had, and still has, a feeling heart (in fact she eventually returns, but when he has partly recovered she leaves him again – though the end of the poem is none too informative). He pauses in his diatribe, therefore, and decides not to send her what he has written:

> O Thou, my spirit's mate,
> Who, for thou art compassionate and wise,
> Wouldst pity me from thy most gentle eyes
> If this sad writing thou shouldst ever see –
> My secret groans must be unheard by thee;
> Thou wouldst weep tears bitter as blood to know
> Thy lost friend's incommunicable woe.

He imagines her death, which horrifies him. He curses the sexual urge that brought them together, and even wishes, in a startling passage, that he had castrated himself. The punishment he now endures, 'to make that love the fuel/Of the mind's hell', would be harsh for a cruel or unfeeling man; how much worse for him, an artist sensitive to other's wrongs,

> Me – who am a nerve o'er which do creep
> The else unfelt oppressions of this earth . . .

> I live to show
> How much men bear and die not!

He thinks of the guilt that she will feel when he is dead. Because he still loves her, the thought of her remorse keeps him from suicide, and in his closing speech (from which Elgar chose the lines that he sent to Mrs Colvin) he resolves to accuse her no further. The bitter words that he has written are simply a way of externalizing his feelings, now burned away to ash, and he will destroy them before death destroys him:

> Alas, love!
> Fear me not . . . against thee I would not move

A finger in despite. Do I not live
That thou mayst have less bitter cause to grieve?
I give thee tears for scorn and love for hate;
And that thy lot may be less desolate
Than his on whom thou tramplest, I refrain
From that sweet sleep which medicines all pain.
Then, when thou speakest of me, never say
He could forgive not. Here I cast away
All human passions, all revenge, all pride;
I think, speak, act no ill; I do but hide
Under these words, like embers, every spark
Of that which has consumed me – quick and dark
The grave is yawning . . . as its roof shall cover
My limbs with dust and worms under and over,
So let Oblivion hide this grief . . . the air
Closes upon my accents, as despair
Upon my heart – let death upon despair!

In a cancelled passage, printed with the poem by Mary Shelley, the Maniac had invoked the image of his music:

Perhaps the only comfort which remains
Is the unheeded clanking of my chains,
The which I make, and call it melody.

Julian comments on the Maniac's artistic gift:

For the wild language of his grief was high,
Such as in measure were called poetry,
And I remember one remark which then
Maddalo made. He said: 'Most wretched men
'Are cradled into poetry by wrong,
'They learn in suffering what they teach in song.'

The powerful images of this poem must have struck home time and again as Elgar read it. He did not need to destroy the record of his experiences, since he had transmuted them into the enigmatic medium of music. In sending Mrs Colvin her private epigraph, did he mean her to infer from its context that the Second Symphony might be his last important utterance? He wrote nothing on so large a scale again; in the personal catalogue that he kept of his compositions, after entering the Cello Concerto – a work so intimate that one wonders whether it was initially conceived as a sonata – he added the inscription 'R.I.P.', and thereafter let Oblivion hide his grief.[329] It was to be the last statement of that characteristic cycle which he defined as 'a man's attitude to life'.[330]

Plans for libretti; choice of texts for songs and partsongs

I have omitted from this discussion many works to which Elgar did not attach epigraphs or literary quotations, and others of programmatic or literary interest which have been or are about to be competently treated by others.[331] I have made only cursory observations on Elgar's methods in setting words to music: his growing care certainly reflects the growth of his literary sensibilities, but it is a rather special aspect of the question which I propose to examine in a separate study of his songs and partsongs[332] There are however a number of points that deserve mention before I close.

First there are various larger projects that he abandoned, and two subjects that he recommended to Ivor Atkins, which help to fill out the picture of his reading and may also be of biographical interest. Dr Percy Young will no doubt review Elgar's many abortive ideas for operatic treatment when he comes to edit the sketches of *The Spanish Lady* for the Elgar Complete Edition; to the long list of rejections should be added Bunyan's *Pilgrim's Progress* (1928),[333] anticipating Vaughan Williams, and W. S. Gilbert's *Fallen Fairies* (conceived before 1900, eventually performed in 1909 with music by Edward German).[334] On the other hand we should remove from the list Tennyson's *Enoch Arden* (whose timescale would seem in any case to preclude dramatization): a sketch-fragment headed 'Touchsto[ne]' suggests that the true source of 'Arden Opera in three acts', for which no other music seems to exist, must in fact have been Shakespeare's *As you like it.*[335] Presumably the 'idea . . . for a new combination of orchestra, acting, and pictures' that Newman attributed to Elgar in his Birmingham lecture of 8 November 1907[336] must relate to some kind of mime: it may refer to *Rabelais*, or more likely the 'pantomime-ballet' on Boccaccio's *Decameron*, discussed in 1902, whose 'plague tableaux tragic and comic' were never written: was the low comedy perhaps, like that of *Rabelais*, too vulgar for Alice Elgar's taste?[337] But there are yet other titles among Elgar's sketches which might fill the bill: the seventeenth-century Samuel Butler's *Hudibras*[338] is unlikely to have emerged as a vocal work, though Lewis Carroll's *Jabberwocky*[339] would have; and what was the mysterious *Columbia*[340] – a Columbiad for the American market, a piece for British Columbia, or one on St Columba? A project of 1910 for a ballet on the screen scene in Sheridan's *The School for Scandal*,[341] presumably as an interlude in Beerbohm Tree's production, reminds us of two separate passages in Maine's *Life* which, put together, suggest that Elgar contributed not music but words to Tree's 1909 production of *Beethoven* (no doubt speeches about inspiration or the process of composition, but I have not yet run to earth a text of the play).[342]

Among the projects for vocal concert works, one can easily see how Berlioz' love of pastiche might have appealed to Elgar's and tempted him to imitate *L'enfance du Christ* with a 'Flight into Egypt', for which a set of titles survives from 1897.[343] It would not be surprising if Elgar had himself considered writing a piece based on the despair and ultimate salvation of Job, a subject which he recommended to Richard Strauss in 1902;[344] again, it was left to Vaughan Williams to answer the challenge. Of plans for setting two poems by Jean Ingelow (1820–97), tiny fragments remain of 'The high tide on the coast of Lincolnshire' (1871), probably first sketched around 1892;[345] the well-known story of the mother and children drowned seems to have been planned for chorus and smallish orchestra; Elgar offered it to the Festivals of Middlesbrough and Norwich, but abandoned it in 1902.[346] In January 1898 he suggested to Novellos that he might compose 'a work for Ladies' voices' on Ingelow's *Persephone* (1862), for which, however, no music is known.[347] It is easy to see why Elgar should have been attracted to its finely-handled theme of a maiden abducted to the underworld, the consequent mourning and withering of Nature, and Persephone's return, strangely altered, as a goddess; but in 1902 he was already planning his oratorio trilogy, and by the time he later resumed the cyclic theme of loss and regeneration, he had discovered how to shape such ideas into wordless instrumental works.

In 1928 Elgar made proposals through Ivor Atkins for the 1929 Three Choirs Festival, meeting in Worcester, that he should compose a setting of Shelley, either *Adonais* or *The daemon of the world*. According to Mr Wulstan Atkins, Elgar 'seemed to have regained his interest in composing' and 'had volunteered to write a new work'.[348] I think it rather more likely that Ivor Atkins had importuned Elgar to do so, but that the composer was secretly unwilling yet anxious not to hurt his friend's feelings by an outright refusal. It is impossible to believe that Elgar seriously expected the cathedral authorities to permit these texts to be sung in their church, even in edited form. Both poems, as the Dean, Dr Moore Ede, inevitably pointed out, are 'frankly pagan'. *The daemon of the world* is replete with Lucretian atheism; it represents all that Shelley dared openly to publish of his revolutionary *Queen Mab*, and he did not bother to purge it of such anti-clerical references as 'The fanes of Fear and Falsehood', 'Mitres . . . and scrolls of mystic wickedness', 'The works of faith and slavery' and 'the bigot's hell-torch', 'with blasphemy for prayer': this was a deliberate red rag for the Anglican bull. *Adonais*, a funeral elegy without benefit of church ritual, also alludes to religions which 'lie buried in the ravage they have wrought', and to Milton's persecution in his old age, whom 'his country's pride,/ The priest, the slave, and the liberticide,/Trampled and mocked with many a loathèd rite'.

'The daemon' reminds us of the demons that Elgar inked in on two postcards of Worcester Cathedral in October 1902,[349] when he had just been forced to endure a version of *The Dream of Gerontius* performed at a Three Choirs Festival with excisions snipped out from Newman's text by Canon T. L. Claughton and the then Dean, Dr R. W. Forrest, and formally approved by Bishop Gore.[350] Elgar's demons are all pointing to a house near the cathedral labelled 'Former abode of Bowdler', that is the Precentor, the Rev. E. Vine Hall, who in 1896 had successfully objected to a 'blasphemous' quatrain in *The Light of Life*,[351] and whom Elgar suspected, perhaps wrongly, of fomenting the present trouble. Nearer the time of the Shelley episode, in 1926, his memory of that resentment and his dislike of clerical censoriousness would have been sharpened by his controversy with Canon T. A. Lacey in *The Worcester Daily Times* (March 15–17), who thought Wagner's morals and music distressingly 'sensuous' and objected to a proposal to perform excerpts from *Parsifal* in the Cathedral. All in all, the Shelley suggestion of 1928 has a strong flavour of 'jape'. It occurs, of course, at a time when Elgar is thought to have lost his faith: however he used Shelley's poems, he may well have taken their critical content seriously.

In 1908, when his friend Atkins had been invited to compose a new work for the Worcester Festival but could not think of a subject, Elgar came up with two suggestions, poems by Tennyson and Browning.[352] Their emotional qualities and musical potential must have caught his imagination; even if he had not intended to make settings of his own, he must at least have tested their suitability on himself before passing them on to Atkins. The first was the episode of Jephthah's daughter from Tennyson's *A dream of fair women*, to be set for soprano or contralto solo and chorus. The story from *Judges*, Chap.11, familiar from Handel's magnificent oratorio and similar to that of Mozart's *Idomeneo*, concerns a general whose doubt that the Lord will grant him victory in battle leads him to vow that he will sacrifice to God, if successful, the first living thing that comes from his house to meet him on his return: and it is his daughter (unnamed), who sweetly and stoically accepts her fate. Tennyson's poem, like its model, Chaucer's *The legend of good women*, is cast in the form of a medieval dream-vision. It tells of eight women famous in myth and history, most of them heroic figures who have endured death; all unhappy. Elgar suggests that Atkins should start with stanza 4: 'Beauty and anguish walking hand in hand / The downward slope to death'. The first of the women bears a name fateful to Elgar, Helen (of Troy): 'Where'er I came,' she says, 'I brought calamity'; and she is immediately cursed by Iphigenia, whose death she helped to bring about – another sacrificial victim killed by a father's hand. Helen replies:

> 'I would the white cold heavy-plunging foam,
>   Whirl'd by the wind, had roll'd me deep below,
>   Then when I left my home.'

Cleopatra supervenes, and then Jephthah's daughter, whose seventeen stanzas form the centrepiece and the longest section of the poem. There follow briefer references to Rosamond (Henry II's mistress), Margaret Roper (Thomas More's daughter), Joan of Arc and Eleanor of Castile. Elgar responded to the lush imagery of Tennyson's prologue, depicting the poet falling asleep amid the forest flowers, among which burns the 'red anemone': he commends stanzas 13–20 for use as a prelude, especially 16 and 17. The touching story of Jephthah's daughter, the virgin who goes to a willing death, occupies stanzas 45–61; wondering at the beauty and majesty of her song, the poet imagines himself listening outside some great cathedral at the open door,

> Hearing the holy organ rolling waves
> Of sound on roof and floor
> Within, and anthem sung . . .

– almost an invitation to let her song be heard at the Worcester Festival! Elgar the artist would have sympathized with the fine ending of the poem, though he told Atkins that it 'is not practical for your purpose':

> As when a soul laments, which hath been blest,
>   Desiring what is mingled with past years,
> In yearnings that can never be exprest
> By signs or groans or tears; [sighs
> Because all words, tho' cull'd with choicest art,
>   Failing to give the bitter of the sweet,
> Wither beneath the palate, and the heart
>   Faints, faded by its heat.

The other candidate for Atkins' attention was Browning's magnificent *Saul* (1845–55), again a subject superbly treated by Handel. It is impossible to imagine how Browning's fifteen-syllabled anapaestic couplets could be set to music as they stand: here it must have been the situation and the complex of emotion and idea that appealed to Elgar. The golden-haired young musician David is very like Callicles, save that he narrates the whole story himself, and must also directly confront the would-be suicide whom he restores to life and hope. The gigantic figure of Saul lurks in his darkened tent, dumb, motionless, mad, locked in a trance of black despair. David has been summoned to soothe his mind with minstrelsy and lead him back to his true self. How can he 'save and redeem and restore him, maintain at the height' the perfection of his kingliness and valour?

> Interpose at the difficult minute, snatch Saul the mistake,
> Saul the failure, the ruin he seems now – and bid him awake
> From the dream, the probation, the prelude, to find himself set
> Clear and safe in new light and new life . . .

The sequence of David's songs and thought and of Saul's reactions (though he does not speak) is too long and complex to analyze here. In the end, David is exalted into a state of mystical fervour. He casts away his harp and, realizing that he loves Saul enough to die in order to save him, discovers the true nature of divine love and sees a vision of Christ. God's love must 'fill infinitude wholly', and

> As thy Love is discovered almighty, almighty be proved
> Thy power, that exists with and for it, of being Beloved!

Anyone who wishes to understand Elgar's own struggle to escape from despair, from fear of madness and thoughts of suicide into renewed faith and a life of effective artistic activity, anyone looking for a commentary (besides the music of the First Symphony) on what Elgar meant by the phrase 'a great charity (love) and massive hope in the future' in his letter to Walford Davies of 13 November 1908,[353] would be well advised to read the powerful poem that had been in his mind nine months before, Browning's *Saul.* When he wrote to Atkins in March, he had just spent a wasted winter unable to work in Rome; yet thoughts of the new symphony, which he began to put on paper only after his return to Hereford in June, must even then have been labouring for utterance inside him.

I must end by discussing a couple of issues arising from Elgar's songs, partsongs and related sketch material. Critics have adduced these, in particular the songs (and aspects of the solo vocal line in larger works), to suggest that in two respects Elgar's literary sense was far less highly developed than that of Parry or Stanford:[354] he stands accused of lapses in taste in his choice of poems for setting, and of a deficient ear for English prosody in his manner of setting them. On the face of it, there is some justice in these observations. Elgar certainly bestowed his talents on a number of poems that would not have found a place in Parry's *English Lyrics*; and I have already mentioned examples of his 'poor' prosody, at least when judged by prevailing standards of naturalistic diction and the belief that stressed syllables should fall on metrically strong beats (both questionable assumptions, as Stravinsky has demonstrated).

'Poor' prosody is in fact extremely rare in the mature Elgar, and in the sketches for *The Dream of Gerontius* one may trace through the great number of improvements in the solo lines how Elgar taught himself the principles of 'good' musical diction. That is not to say that he thought them paramount. He shrewdly criticized Parry's finicky word-setting in a letter to Jaeger of 1908,[355] and elsewhere comments on the unwillingness of many hymn-writers to remember that their words are to be sung to a strophic tune which imposes certain limitations of rhythm, phrasing and cadence: an ill-placed *enjambement* or the substitution of a trochee for an iamb can easily make nonsense of a melody.[356] Elgar knew that musical considerations of line, phrase and what he called 'breath' must at times take precedence over the claims of 'just accent'. He would have preferred Dowland's ayres to those of Henry Lawes or Campian, Schubert's Goethe-settings to Zelter's (unlike Goethe himself), and Brahms' *Lieder* to Wolf's. A further consideration arises from a piece of advice that he gave Atkins in relation to the new projects for composition that we have just been discussing; at first sight it seems very odd: 'Set to work on your new thing at once. Don't wait for words'.[357] Yet this was to be a vocal composition.

One of the ways in which it is possible to compose without 'waiting for the words' is the Wagnerian method of devising a symphonic texture out of a brief but telling musical motive, over which a vocal line may then be fitted (though that is by no means the whole story). Elgar had certainly mastered this technique; but he was also, like the Wagner of Siegmund's 'Winterstürme' or Wotan's Farewell, a supreme tunesmith. Sometimes the tune came to him before the words, or might be adapted to quite different words, and there is growing evidence that Elgar used the technique of 'parody', fitting new text to an existing tune, more often than we had suspected. Dr Moore has pointed out that the first 'Millwheel Song', to a poem by Alice Elgar, vanished into *King Olaf*: this and a second song in the sketches were both provided with new text.[358] In 1889, since it seemed unlikely that Andrew Lang would grant copyright permission for the use of 'My love dwelt in a northern land', Mrs Elgar provided a clever parody as a substitute.[359] A. C. Benson obliged with new words for 'Speak, my heart' when it turned out that the original text by 'Adrian Ross' (which is still unknown) was not available; Benson twice made parodies for the Trio tune from the *Pomp and Circumstance March No. 1*, and Alice Elgar did the same for that of No.4.[360] Dr Young's *Alice Elgar* enables us to follow the process by which the existing music for two choral works, *From the Bavarian Highlands* and *A Christmas greeting*, was afterwards fitted with text.[361] Elgar made a little song out of the 'Welsh Tune' in the *Introduction and Allegro for Strings* and presented the MS to Alice for texting, with the title 'For the Bag Poet' (but no words survive).[362] The term 'Bag Poet' is unknown to the *O.E.D.*, but evidently means a poet in one's bag, or household verse-manufacturer. On the title-page of the MS orchestral score of *Sea Pictures*, 'C.A.E.', who wrote the text for 'In haven', is described in a pencil annotation as 'Bag poet'.[363] That is not because the text is slightly altered from her earlier 'Lute Song' to the same music, but because the 'Lute Song' is itself a second attempt to provide words for the tune. In the first known sketch of the music, we find the ominous name 'Lang', a vocal line whose rhythm, at first different, is gradually approximated to that of the 'Lute Song', and at the foot of the page two drafts of a mawkish first shot at providing a parody.[364] Presumably Lang had again forbidden the use of one of his poems, or was thought likely to do so. I have not yet managed to identify the original text among Andrew Lang's hundreds of poems and translations, many never collected; but it must have been something like his translation of Du Bellay's *Hymn to the winds*,[365] doubtless with an additional final syllable:

> To you, troop so fleet
> That with winged wandering feet
> Thro' the wide world pass . . .

Ex.6 gives the three early forms of the melody, with variants numbered 1, 2 and 3 in their likely chronological order, fitting the parody text and its variants to the notes. I have corrected two irrational changes of octave (since this was a sketch for a 'song acc[ompanimen]t', Elgar had fitted in the vocal part at whatever pitches happened to be left free).

Ex. 6

x: extra bar for
orchestra inserted.
y: *f* for *e* in error.

The habit of parody, the re-use of music conceived independently (sometimes for other contexts), and the fitting of a vocal line to a movement imagined principally in orchestral terms (such as the 'Angel's Farewell' in *The Dream of Gerontius*), are factors peculiar to Elgar among English composers of his time. Sometimes, as with 'In Haven', the result is a certain stiffness in the relationship between words and music, but that is in the first place the poet's fault; while I would not always wish to excuse this feature of Elgar's solo vocal music, since the ultimate responsibility rests with the composer, I hope at least that I have helped to explain it. Examples of 'poor' prosody (and cases become very rare after *c.*1900) are often attributable more to the method of composition than to any gross defect in Elgar's ear for English diction.

In his choice of texts for setting, too, although there are certainly lapses which might offend genteel taste, it is hardly justifiable to use them to argue that his literary taste was generally coarse or deficient. A man known to be largely self-educated was of course an easy target, but it is extraordinary that so broad a charge could have been levelled against the composer of the oratorios and the partsongs. Objective criticism must try and see Elgar whole. What we have to explain in Elgar's selection of literary texts is the surprising coexistence of an unquestionably refined and discriminating taste with an equally unquestionable acceptance of less demanding standards in works intended for a more popular market. It is precisely the same paradox, as we have seen, that two interviewers commented upon, perhaps prompted by the Elgars themselves, in discussing his library (though apparently without realizing what they were saying): his was a taste both 'catholic and fastidious'. Elgar may have become, by self-education, a cultural aristocrat, but he never forgot that he was a man of the people. He did not, in the end, sell his Dickens . . .

A comprehensive study of the poems that Elgar set to music or thought of setting, and of the ways in which he came by them, supports this view of the paradox of his tastes, and throws further light on his reading-habits and cultural aspirations in general. I cannot however do more than summarize here, with a certain amount of supportive detail. As usual with Elgar, there is a complex of interlocking factors at work, and the situation is further bedevilled by changes in literary and intellectual fashion following World

War I. The root of the matter lies in his early taste, formed at his mother's knee, for what we would regard as simple-minded, moralistic, often sentimental poetry, usually written in song-like stanzas but monotonous and unsophisticated in rhythm, such as the lyrics of Longfellow, Procter or Hemans. This was a popular taste, already regarded as naïve by fashionable opinion, but enduring longer in the provinces. Even at the time when the infant Edward was hearing 'Speak gently'[366] from his mother, Lewis Carroll was preparing to satirize it in *Alice's Adventures in Wonderland* (1865) as 'Speak roughly to your little boy'. There was also a tradition of popular songs painting the adventuresome life of the soldier or sailor, a tradition extending back to Charles Dibdin and beyond, recruiting-songs judged necessary in the centuries before conscription (for which indeed the state rewarded Dibdin). Elgar's acquisition of higher literary sensibilities, traceable from about 1900 onwards in the texts he set and in his manner of setting them, superimposed a much more sophisticated taste upon his early inclinations; but it did not extinguish them.[367] He remained loyal to his literary favourites, just as he remained loyal to friends and relations whom his wife refused to visit. Though in his major works he achieved international stature, he continued to provide music for the whole nation and prided himself on his knowledge of popular taste. Even so, long before the period of masterly partsongs on texts by Byron, Shelley or Rossetti's translation of Cavalcanti, we find him setting Waller and Wyatt and sketching music for Herrick.[368]

It is easy to forget that he was a professional composer in the sense that almost the whole of his income came from his compositions, which was not the case with Parry or Stanford. But it would be wrong to suggest that he lowered his sights because of that. Though he at one point denied that he was a song-writer,[369] he wrote much better pieces than were generally to be heard in a Victorian drawing-room. A song that has always been commended as excellent of its kind is his limpid setting of Barry Pain's 'The Shepherd's Song', which dates from 1892. He found this in a volume of half-humorous, half-serious commentaries on art and society entitled *In a Canadian canoe: the nine Muses minus one* (London, 1891, p.99). The verses are there presented as an example of a superior kind of song, and we may be fairly sure that Elgar was consciously responding to the challenge. It is sung by the flute-playing Euterpe, patroness of Music itself.

'I like music at night,' said Erato. 'At night it has a speaking voice, and one understands it better . . . but it must not be a drawing-room song. They are called drawing-room songs because they are whistled in the street. No, my song must be good. There mustn't be any –

"Love me! love me forever!
Till the years shall porse awye;
Beside the flowin' river

> You 'ear the words I sye.
> Love me! love me forever!
>   Love, tho' the world grows cold,
> Till no more we roam, and they call us 'ome
> And there's tew more lambs in the fold."

That sort of thing couldn't possibly make anybody love anybody, you know . . . '

This parodies, with deadly accuracy, one popular style that Elgar had very decidedly put behind him, that of the Christy Minstrels songs for which he had been required to write symphonies and accompaniments as a young man in Worcester.[370] There ensues a discussion of real love-music, Chopin's eleventh Nocturne, and then:

'Euterpe shall sing to us now. I don't mind a song that can be sung in a drawing-room – it's the drawing-room song that I hate . . . ' [Here Euterpe sings 'The shepherd's song'.] 'Dear Euterpe,' said Erato, 'you must have been thinking of Sicily.'

Songs like this one, or Elgar's setting of Arthur Salmon's 'Pleading' (so despised by Dunhill), have survived in the repertoire because, even though they do not give us the inmost Elgar, they are sincerely imagined and well and honestly composed. And this was at a time when there was virtually no English tradition of *Lieder*-singing: ballad-concerts were very much commoner than the dignified recitals that we are now accustomed to. That probably helps to explain why Elgar orchestrated so many of the subtler songs that were dearest to him: it was not simply because he disliked the pianoforte, but because the songs could then be performed in the more exalted surroundings of an orchestral concert, before a more sophisticated and discerning audience. For such songs he demanded 'singers with brains', of the kind whose absence had made for difficulties in the early performances of the oratorios. As well as musicality and a lovely sound, he required from them a high level of general intelligence and a subtle response to words, as his Birmingham lectures made clear. His more private views on singing and on vocal composition are amusingly encapsulated in an almost complete setting of an anonymous early Italian Ballata translated by Rossetti (in which Elgar transposed the 'But' and the 'For' in lines 4–5):[371]

Of True and False Singing

A little wild bird sometimes at my ear
Sings his own little verses very clear:
Others sing louder that I do not hear.

But singing loudly is not singing well;
  For ever by the song that's soft and low
The master-singer's voice is plain to tell.
  Few have it, and yet all are masters now,

> And each of them can trill out what he calls
> His ballads, canzonets, and madrigals.

> The world with masters is so cover'd o'er,
> There is no room for pupils any more.

After the music, which pokes boisterous fun at academic contrapuntality, stands the direction: 'Spoken "But!"'. If he had completed and published his *jeu d'esprit*, he would have caused considerable annoyance to Novellos' conservative advisers such as J. E. West.

In spite of his higher aspirations, Elgar also thought it his duty to compose or arrange well-made popular songs for the medium of the ballad-concert, particularly at the upper end of the market, where singers such as Clara Butt could command the accompaniment of an orchestra in a large hall. His boastful remark to Troyte Griffith that 'I write the folk songs of this country'[372] would have annoyed the worthy conservationists, antiquarians and revivalists of the English Folk Dance and Song Society; but in terms of the urbanized England of his time it was perfectly true. He provided popular music on a broad front, quite deliberately, from his early café-tunes to marches, patriotic songs for ballad-concerts and war-songs (even arranging one for boys, with bugles and drums); at first despising the quality of much military band music, he moved on to make successful attempts to improve its standards and widen the repertory of this most popular medium; he understood the potential of recorded music, too. The search for suitable texts for all this led him to poets like Kipling, Cammaerts and Binyon, though also to many mere versifiers whose efforts were commissioned or suggested to him by publishers; but he was sometimes moved to write poems of this kind himself.[373] In the change of taste that followed World War I, progressive opinion came to despise militarism, imperialism and the darker side of nationalism, so that most of Elgar's music composed for this domain lapsed into oblivion, was condemned unheard and is still awaiting objective assessment. But his musical persona as a man of action (like his carefully-cultivated military appearance) was always an important part of his image of himself; the weedy lad, later a sedentary composer writing in his study, evidently needed – like the hero of *Maud* – to feel kinship with his nation's fighting men, whether the imaginative excursion took him to the chronicles of Froissart or to the Boer War, the Western Front and the North Sea.[374] Elgar's popular vein, of course, extended far beyond military and nationalistic music, and enabled him to write the enchanting *Starlight Express*. He enjoyed light revues and certain dance-music; to the literature documenting this unlikely taste may be added the following, from Osbert Sitwell's *Noble Essences* (London, 1950):[375] Bernard Shaw is described as 'telling us of Sir Edward Elgar and how the famous English composer had liked to play, over and over again, the gramophone records made by Cicely Courtneidge and Jack Hulbert, alleging that in them he found the secret of the perfect use of rhythm'.

Elgar's interest in popular music, and his determination to provide it, must have helped to bring on his head the charge – which he revelled in – that his language was 'not quite free from vulgarity' (Dent) and, alas, the adjective 'velgar' (Tovey, Toye).[376] It is likely that a purely literary judgement of the large quantity of indifferent verse that Elgar set to music played some part in this. If one accepts a statement such as W. H. Reed's,[377] that Elgar 'read all the modern writers of poetry with interest', without pausing to assess Reed's qualifications, and then goes on to consider as literature the texts that Elgar used for his popular music, it is easy to picture him uncritically wading through volume after volume of third-rate poetry and deriving from it the same pleasure that he obtained from reading Shakespeare, Donne or Browning. Such an impression might be strengthened by the fact that he rarely set the finest poetry, sensibly observing to Mrs Vera Hockman that it had a music of its own that got in the way;[378] though when he did, there is no doubting the sensitivity of his response. But he evidently wished to reach out to an audience who did not understand such an exalted use of language, yet could appreciate (as he did) the demotic verse of Kipling or the simpler tastes of his own childhood. He understood what was needed from a national laureate, and once noted approvingly of Elizabeth I's use of state ceremonial, 'popular feeling exactly observed'.[379]

A study of the routes, where known, by which the texts of his songs and partsongs came into his hands, in fact suggests, curiously enough, that his reading among the English poets may not have been so wide as we had thought. He knew his Shakespeare very well, and the great nineteenth-century poets. He had a scholarly interest, as opposed to a musical one, in Grierson's edition of Donne, a poet then thought obscure, and in other poets, and dramatists too, of the late sixteenth and the seventeenth century; his scholarly and 'applied' interests came together when late in life he acquired Gifford's edition of Jonson and started to hunt through it after suitable verses for arias and ensembles in *The Spanish Lady*.[380] If a book by a lesser poet was presented to him, perhaps that of a sympathetic collaborator like A. C. Benson, or if a volume caught his eye because its contents or some aspect of the poet's life chimed with his own experience, then he would read it carefully and make notes. But the evidence of the songs and partsongs, such as it is, points to serendipity rather than system, as with his other reading. While he liked anything quaint or curious, he did not seek it out by elaborate exploration.

To find verses suitable for setting he often relied on others. Publishers such as Arthur Boosey and Alfred Littleton sent him single copies of poems, sometimes whole books (even, once, a Shelley),[381] though he often rejected their suggestions. Alice Elgar left her own poems lying about with comments such as 'Words free!' or 'In case my Beloved might like it';[382] but she also made suggestions and copied poems by others for him. 'Just you write me those two short songs,' wrote Arthur Boosey in 1902, '– Mrs. Elgar will find you some words'.[383] How many she found, and how many Elgar discovered for himself, we cannot know; but a large number (33) came either from pre-selected anthologies, such as the still untraced *Sea Poems* from which Elgar sketched Longfellow's 'Seaweed' and possibly also the as yet anonymous 'Sea mist',[384] or from literary magazines where most of the contents were prose, such as *Temple Bar, The Century Magazine* and (after Lady Elgar's death) *Country Life* and *Punch*. A careful study of variants and accidentals shows that a number of Elgar's texts, such as for example A. L. Gordon's 'A song of autumn' and 'The swimmer' came to Elgar not directly from a collected volume of the poet's works, but at second hand, mediated either by the editor of some journal or anthology, or by the MS of a publisher, Alice, or some friend.[385] Certain friends are known to have sent Elgar poems, such as Dr Buck, Canon Gorton (T. E. Brown's 'Weary wind of the West'), Lord Frederick Hamilton, probably Gervase Elwes and Mrs E. L. Anderson.[386] Several poets sent volumes of verse: Benson, Binyon, F. H. (not F. E.) Fortey, Gilbert Parker, Arthur Salmon, probably Mrs Rosa Newmarch and the Australian Arthur Maquarie;[387] their presentation copies sometimes contain markings which suggest (as do related musical sketches) that Elgar might have made more settings of their verse than he actually completed. It remains a puzzle where he found two poems, not available in collected editions, by the little-known poets Bishop Henry King and Simon Wastell.[388] These too must have come from journals or anthologies, like the single stanza, 'It is not growing like a tree', from Jonson's *A Pindaric ode to the immortal memory and friendship of that noble pair, Sir Lucias Carey and Sir H. Morison* which Elgar probably found excerpted by Quiller-Couch as No.194 of *The Oxford book of English verse* (1900): Elgar's sketch (for SATB) spells 'sear' as 'sere', and presumably dates from the days before he bought his complete Jonson.[389] The pretension to recondite research, suggested by the naming of the anthology 'Wit and Drollery (1661)' on the title-page of 'The Wanderer', is not borne out by a sketch in the Birthplace Library (MS 113); this shows Elgar drafting his own first stanza beneath the reference 'I Dis p. 316', which has led both Dr Roger Savage and myself to trace its intermediate source in Isaac D'Israeli's *Curiosities of Literature*, a collection of short historical and critical enquiries of the out-of-the-way kind that Elgar loved to read.[390] Similarly, it was not in the obscure publications of the 'Spasmodic' Scottish poets Alexander Smith and Gerald Massey – much as we might like to imagine Elgar hunting down the books of these self-educated poets, both poor men – that the composer came across the texts for his partsongs 'The Herald' and the unfinished 'No star looks down'. He found both texts excerpted in an Everyman anthology, itself a selection, of reviews by George Gilfillan:[391] this gives us 1909 as a *terminus a quo* for the date of both settings. One must of course give credit to Elgar for noticing the musical potential of the passages creamed off by Gilfillan; but one may be forgiven for wondering whether Elgar was not at times more interested in the history and criticism of poetry, in opinions and information, rather than in the poetry itself – at least where minor poets were concerned.

Concluding observations

Elgar's use of literature was complex and multifarious, and my attempt to discuss it in a reasonably analytical and critical manner has turned into a very long essay, crammed with footnotes in a manner that would have pleased its subject. Its length is in part due to the difficulty of 'placing' literary references in relation to Elgar's life and of trying to suggest what inner meaning they held for him, particularly those connected with his music; there are many uncertainties and obscurities here, and I will confess that I love to offer up a suggestive analogy, or to chase a speculative hare until it vanishes and then continue circling in order to try and pick up a fresh scent – a method which is intended to provide hypotheses to be confirmed or denied by future research. I have also thought it worth while to spend time discussing the intellectual background provided by authors such as Cardinal Newman or Ruskin whom I cannot prove that Elgar studied in detail, though it is very likely. It would be wrong to conclude from the range of authors mentioned, however, that Elgar was massively and systematically well-read: that would have made my task easier; the difficulty stems not from the universality and depth of his reading, but from its randomness. I have not discussed his 'researches' in chemistry and microscopy, but they have the appearance of dabblings on the practical margins of science. No doubt they are unusual and laudable. He may have modelled himself on the example of Goethe; but Goethe, though some of his findings were false, had mastered the contemporary literature on botany, optics and anatomy, whereas there appears to be no evidence that Elgar was seriously interested in the great achievements and controversies of natural science in the Victorian age. He seems also to have had little interest in philosophy or in recent developments in historical writing; he apparently preferred the more concrete minutiae of local history and topography, but this was a conversational ploy rather than a scientific skill.

My subject, though, has been his engagement with literature. Here, omitting from consideration for the moment his professional search for subjects and texts for musical treatment, we find the usual motivations which impel all who love to read: delight in language, in story, in the record of human personality, the pleasure of familiarity with ever re-readable classics, an element of escapism, the need of a restless sensibility to occupy itself during otherwise idle and unproductive hours, the desire to achieve the cultural norms of those around one, the special enjoyment of filling the memory with topics for reference and conversation between like-minded devotees. In Elgar's case there was justifiable pride in his achievement, but also a continuing resentment, not so much that he lacked educational advantages, but that this formal deficiency caused others to look down on him: this produced in him a mixture of robust self-assurance and anxious neurasthenia that we may also trace in his musical language. A relevant passage from the newspaper report of his speech when the Freedom of Worcester was bestowed upon his old friend Hubert Leicester (6 April 1932) has never been reprinted in detail:[392]

> What was done for us? Scarcely anything. Hubert Leicester and myself only had three years at a preparatory school. Think of that . . . I will tell you this: That on the whole of my musical and general education only £60 was spent . . . We must not forget that home influences were at work to make us, if I may say so, the men we are. Somehow we won through. That is owing simply to the home influence, not to any help from scholarships or anything like that, but simply by having the desire to do as well as we could.

There is certainly pride here, almost an advertisement for the self-help of Samuel Smiles and the survival of the fittest; but there is also some resentment. That insecurity, combined with a native love of the quaint and out-of-the-way, led Elgar to pursue a number of unfrequented paths in literature and other forms of learning, and to develop notions of scholarship; here, though his ambitions were sometimes justified, he trod a dangerous track where honest pretension sometimes became pretence.

This aspect of Elgar makes an interesting psychological study; but although his reading turned him into a marvellous writer of letters, we have to remember that we are studying a composer and not a Man of Letters, however important that image was to him. Tracing the development of Elgar's poetic predilections, surveying both the verse that he liked and the verse that he set, seems to show that his simpler, early tastes were not forgotten or abandoned even after he had acquired a much more sophisticated approach; this helps us to a better understanding of his aims and methods in providing popular music alongside his more complex masterpieces. More important for an understanding of the latter, though, is the study of the epigraphs and literary quotations that he associated with them, of texts that he marked or annotated in his books, and of poems that he considered setting to music, for which we have many incomplete sketches. In individual cases it must remain a matter for speculation how far he expected a quotation or allusion or the choice of a poem for setting to invoke in the reader's mind the whole context from which a passage was taken, or wider knowledge of a poet's life and beliefs; but the general drift of the evidence shows, among other interesting matter, an unmistakable preoccupation with themes closely identifiable with his own situation and emotional difficulties, out of which he made his finest music: the loss of loved ones through death or parting, the fear of madness and even suicide, and regeneration through the hope offered by religion and by a renewal of positive and fruitful artistic activity.

Sensitized by the loss of two brothers in childhood – an experience too early for him to have learned to face it with adult comprehension – he reacted to the loss of his first love, Helen Weaver, by hugging his grief to him so that it dominated the whole of his subsequent emotional life and inner view of the world. The need to give it expression made him into a great composer, which is perhaps enough for us but was not enough for him. He was impelled to confide his sorrow to close friends, some of them women (one of whom to some extent took Helen Weaver's place in his affections); they appear either to have been sworn to secrecy, or to have been so touched by Elgar's private grief that they decided not to reveal the matter to others, at least, in Ivor Atkins' case, until fifty years after Elgar's death. It does not take much thought to imagine what 'Elgar's distressing remark', made on his deathbed to Ernest Newman, may have been. It consisted 'of only five words' (like the five dots of the Violin Concerto dedication?). Newman thought that to disclose the secret 'would lend itself too easily to the crudest of misinterpretations', and later said of the mysterious five words that 'the scope they would give to a "reading" of him is infinite, so I am determined to keep them to myself: they are too tragic for the ear of the mob'.[393] Now that the essentials of the secret are out, it seems unlikely that many will share that view. I hope that my attempts in the preceding pages to link various literary aspects of Elgar's life and music to this central grief will not seem 'crude', though some of them are admittedly unproven and hypothetical. Such speculations are not strictly necessary to an understanding of Elgar's greatness as a composer, and he achieved worldwide recognition decades before much of the material that has now come before the public was known about. In reading his comments to intimates, however, one must conclude from all kinds of private hints that he himself thought that his friends' understanding of his music would be deepened by such private revelations as he afforded them. Though certainty often remains out of reach, we may surely take the same line today.

I end with a passage from an essay by A. C. Benson on 'Art', written for *The Cornhill Magazine* in 1905–6. Benson was, like Elgar, a sensitive melancholic; he would have recognized in Elgar, whom he came to know closely in the years just before writing his essay, not only a fellow-sufferer, but the greatest artist he had ever been close to; his comments on the potential curse of the artistic temperament must surely owe something to his observation of the composer. After discussing the 'outward' role of technique, with its danger of academicism, and the 'inward' power of perception, which without hard work remains amateurish in expression, he continues:[394]

Very rarely one sees the outward and the inward power perfectly combined, but then we get the humble, hopeful artist who lives for and in his work; he is humble because he cannot reach the perfection for which he strives; he is hopeful because he gets nearer to it day by day. But, speaking generally, the temperament is not one that brings steady happiness; it brings with it some moments of rapture, when some bright dream is being realized; but it brings with it also moments of deep depression, when dreams are silent, and the weary brain fears that the light is quenched. There are, indeed, instances of the equable disposition being found in connection with the artistic temper; such were Reynolds, Handel, Wordsworth. But the annals of art are crowded with the figures of those who have had to bear the doom of art, and have been denied the tranquil spirit.

Envoi

This study was originally intended for *Elgar Studies* (Scolar Press, 1990), edited by Raymond Monk, and was completed long ago. A demanding new post and other claims upon my time have prevented me from revising it to take account of such important new publications as Dr Jerrold Northrop Moore's *Edward Elgar: the Windflower Letters* (Oxford, 1989) and *Edward Elgar: Letters of a Lifetime* (Oxford, 1990); the latter handsomely fulfils the hope expressed in my article on p. 255 and in n. 308, but does not require me to amplify my remarks. I regret that I have not had time to up-date references to Michael Kennedy's *Portrait of Elgar,* which are to the second edition, not the third. Geoffrey Hodgkins' *Providence and Art* (London: Elgar Society, n.d.) usefully fills out my comment on Elgar's sacred works, Cora Weaver's *The Thirteenth Enigma* (London, 1988) valuably supplements and corrects our information about Helen Weaver. My comments on the birth of her daughter Joyce (p. 218f), which I had tentatively placed in 1898, need revision with the discovery, which I had made independently, that she was born on 16 Feb. 1893: some other event or crisis, perhaps the long-delayed news that Helen was a mother, perhaps the final resolve to put his emotional difficulties into his music, must explain the mysterious date 18 Feb. 1898 in the *Variations* score. Cora Weaver further reveals that Helen had borne a son, Kenneth, on 7 July 1891 (killed in the Great War on 3 July 1916); the knowledge that Helen had two children, a boy and a girl, considerably reinforces my remarks about *Dream Children* on p. 242.

The British Library's kindly agreement to unstick the various paste-overs and leaves in the *King Olaf* sketches allow me to emend p. 273 and n. 358 on p. 322: the second song is not Alice Elgar's second 'Millwheel Song', still lost, but a setting of 'Tossed in doubts', the Muleteer's Serenade from Cervantes' *Don Quixote* (I, xliii, translation unidentified). My reason for attributing the lost 'The Wave' to Longfellow/Tiedge rather than Alice is that Elgar ticked the title and altered the unsingable word 'muddy' to the slightly better 'earthey' [sic] in his Chandos Classics edition of Longfellow (1887, Birthplace Library); but Gil Vicente's Muleteer (not marked in the volume) must now bow out in favour of Cervantes'. Again on p. 273, and at n. 360 on p. 323, I have been able to identify Adrian Ross's poem, which has a unique metrical scheme, as 'White blossom, pink blossom' from Act II of *A Country Girl* (1902); it was published in 1903 as 'May, June and July' by its original composer, Lionel Monckton, who obviously had prior claim to the use of the words. This and other songs (and many fragments edited by myself) will shortly appear in Dr Geoffrey Bush's collection of the songs in the *Elgar Complete Edition.*

Elgar loved footnotes, and I must perhaps apologize to the reader for my 'jape' in reflecting his taste by putting so much material into the footnotes, though most of it is secondary to the main argument.

Brian Trowell
Oxford, June 1992

Appendix 1: Elgar and E. J. Dent

I give here the text (with translation) of E. J. Dent's comments about Elgar on p.938 of his essay 'Engländer' in the section 'Die Moderne (seit 1880)' of *Handbuch der Musikgeschichte*, ed. Guido Adler (Frankfurt-am-Main, 1924), pp.934–48; reprinted verbatim in second edition, 2 vols. (Berlin: Wilmersdorf, 1930), ii, pp.1044–57.

Elgar trat später als die andern ins Musikleben ein und überraschte die Zuhörer durch den ungewöhnlichen Glanz seiner Orchestration und die glühende Empfindung seiner Musik. Wie Mackenzie, war er Violinspieler von Beruf und studierte Liszts Werke, welche den konservativen akademischen Musiken ein Greuel waren. Er war überdies Katholik und mehr oder weniger Autodidakt, der wenig von den literarischen Bildung Parrys und Stanfords hatte. Im Jahre 1890 zog er zuerst die Aufmerksamkeit auf sich, eine Kantate "Caractacus" wurde im Jahre 1898 in Leeds aufgeführt, and im Jahre 1900 veröffentlichte er den "Traum des Gerontius", eine Komposition über Kardinal Newmans halbdramatisches Gedicht über Tod und Fegefeuer. Darauf folgten noch zwei Oratorien, "Die Apostel" und "Das Königreich". Für englische Ohren ist Elgars Musik allzu gefühlvoll und nicht ganz frei von Vulgarität. Seine Orchesterwerke, Variationen, zwei Symphonien, Konzerte für Violine und Violoncell und verschiedene Ouvertüren sind lebhaft in der Farbe, doch pomphaft im Stile und mit einer gesuchten Ritterlichkeit des Ausdrucks. Sein schönstes Orchesterwerk ist das symphonische Gedicht "Falstaff", das jedoch durch allzu enges Anlehnen an das Programm geschwächt wird, aber auf jeden Fall ein Werk von grosser Originalität und Kraft ist. Seine Kammermusik (Violinsonate, Streichquartett und Klavierquintett) ist trocken und akademisch.

Elgar entered musical life later than the others and surprised his hearers by the unusual splendour of his orchestration and the ardent sensibility of his music. Like Mackenzie he was a professional violinist and studied the works of Liszt, which were an abomination to conservative academic musicians. He was moreover a Catholic and more or less a self-taught man who had little of the literary education of Parry and Stanford. He first attracted attention in 1890; in 1898 his cantata *Caractacus* was performed in Leeds, and in 1900 he produced his *Dream of Gerontius*, a composition on Cardinal Newman's poem about death and purgatory. This was followed by two more oratorios, *The Apostles* and *The Kingdom*. To English ears Elgar's music is over-emotional and not entirely free from vulgarity. His orchestral works, variations, two symphonies, concertos for violin and cello and various overtures, are lively in colour, but pompous in style, and with an affectation of the chivalresque in their utterance.* His most beautiful orchestral work is the symphonic poem *Falstaff*, which, although weakened by an excessively close dependence on its programme, is certainly a work of great originality and power. His chamber music (a violin sonata, string quartet and piano quintet) is dry and academic.

[* Literally 'and with a sought-after knightliness' (not 'nobility'); perhaps intended as a feline attack on Elgar's supposed hunger for honours.]

Appendix 2: Elgar and Canon Gairdner

Canon W. H. T. Gairdner's account of 'one of the happiest afternoons of his life', when he was present at the first run-through of Elgar's Piano Quintet at Severn House, 'brand-new from the composer's hand and played in his own home', is to be found in a letter reprinted on pp.122f. of Constance E. Padwick's *Temple Gairdner of Cairo* (London: S.P.C.K., 1929). The interpretation of the work may well owe something to discussion with the composer; Constance Padwick notes that 'Sir Edward Elgar, who had, he says, "a very great esteem for Canon Gairdner", kindly allows the reproduction of the description written at the time'. Since Gairdner does not mention the Violin Sonata or the String Quartet, which were played with the Quintet on 7 March 1919 to invited friends including Arthur Bliss and the Bernard Shaws, and since he heard the Quintet played two-and-a-half times, his letter may possibly have been describing an earlier occasion (see Moore, op. cit., p.738).

'The scene in the fine music-room was very picturesque. The grand piano on the oak floor. The dim light, and the fire burning silently and fitfully in the deeply recessed fireplace with its ingle-nooks, in one of which sat Elgar's rather elf-like daughter. That fire-vignette had almost an air of illusion about it – it reminded me of the fireside scene in *Valkyrie*, Act I – you know how curiously unconcerned, and therefore illusory, homely fire seems on a stage when the impossible fantastic is being played. A fit setting then to the weird quintet. I heard it twice clean through and part of a third time that afternoon, and got to know it really well. It is glorious. The second subject of the first Allegro is one of the most haunting Elgar ever wrote – I found myself quite unconsciously using it as a prayer at my orisons that night.

'The first movement begins with some pianissimo mutterings, like souls turning from side to side in mortal discomfort, weird chords, very eerie, with terrible appealing broken utterances from the first violin. "Spirits in pain." An inferno scene – not so much in hell as in an earthy Tartarus of some evil spell. The beautiful slow movement is clearly the redemption scene. And the finale is the resurrection of those damned ones, not to a heavenly Paradise, but rather to a second chance of a blessed, healthy, sane life in a restored world. It is most moving . . . I don't think that chamber-music ever could have been heard under more exquisite conditions.'

Constance Padwick adds a comment from Gairdner's friend Brother Douglas Downe, perhaps the addressee of the letter just quoted: 'I never knew that music could be so spiritual and sacramental until I heard his interpretation of some passages of Elgar. He showed me for the first time in my life that music may be the language of Heaven'.

Gairdner was a fine musician, learned in Arab music and in Egyptian and

Syrian hymnology, a composer and an expert pianist and chamber-organist (playing both instruments simultaneously!) whose domestic recitals to his friends in Cairo made up for the lack of orchestral concerts there. He liked Vaughan Williams and Holst, but 'his musical intimacies . . . were closest of all with the music of Wagner and Elgar' (ib., p.118; see also I. Smith, *To Islam I go*, Eagle Books, No.17, London and Edinburgh, House Press, 1939, p.17; and Alfred Nielsen, *William Temple Gairdner, en Muhammedanermissionaer, Copenhagen*, 1931, pp.5f, reprinted from *Nordisk Missions-Tidsskrift*). Chap.7 (pp.109–25) of Padwick, op. cit., gives a full picture of his musical proclivities, which led him frequently to 'demonstrate' music to his friends (pp.110f.): 'After dinner at a visit to the Clergy House in Khartoum on a Sunday evening, Gairdner sat down at the villainous piano – all pianos were villainous in the Sudan – and played to three of us the piano transcription [by Karg-Elert] of Elgar's Second Symphony. Suddenly he stopped, repeated a phrase and said, "Voilà la femme! Here she enters just like a serpent in the grass – the notes, even, have the sinuous appearance of a serpent. Elgar drives her out backwards at the end of the movement"'.

His comments on Elgar's achievement in *The Apostles* are unusually perceptive (p.121, June 1904): he found it 'new and great'. 'What strikes one is his grasp on the *whole* and the wonderful spirituality of that whole. Elgar seems to me to be tapping a new spring in art – dramatizing the oratorio. What can be more dramatic than the Magdala-storm section? The *absence* of the stage enables him to disregard necessities introduced by time and space, and, grouping together events ideally connected, though in time and space sundered, to suggest a novel and most powerful dramatic situation.'

He brings evidence about the unfinished oratorio, whose completion he longed for (ibid., pp.121f.): 'and when in 1919 Sir Edward Elgar told him something of the outline of this conclusion he was eagerness itself: " . . . The work is to close with the unspeakably touching close of the Revelation, 'Even so, come, Lord Jesus!' Merely to see Elgar's setting of that it will be worth while to pray for the completion of the work"'. His comments (he was an Anglican) on a London performance of *The Dream of Gerontius* in 1919 give one an excellent idea of the response that Elgar hoped for from the broad church that he addressed, and help the agnostic or atheist to understand the religious effect of Elgar's music (p.122): 'I can't say much: it overpowered me. I should have liked to sit in perfect silence for half an hour after it, . . . but the Albert Hall audience behaved extremely badly. The Kyrie and Intercession music in Part I shook me like an aspen. I had just come from seeing X. [X was in deep mental trouble.] It seemed suddenly to me as if not only we, I, but the choir, all spiritual powers in earth and heaven were praying for him, and the thought broke me up, yet inspired and calmed as well'. It is easy to see why Elgar should have made a friend of this remarkable man.

Appendix 3: Elgar, Ben Jonson and Joan Elwes

It is well known that from 1932 onwards Elgar raided Ben Jonson's poems and plays for additional verses to put into *The Spanish Lady*. One is not, therefore, surprised to see the poet's name attached to an unfinished soprano song in the Elgar Birthplace Library MS 82A, which is described in the useful typescript checklist of MSS as 'to words by Ben Jonson'. The sketch, dated 11 November 1930, is an elaboration of an earlier version, copied without the words as MS 111, which bears the date '21st Oct. 1930'and also in MS 80. Closer examination of MS 82A reveals that the words of this passionate and curiously old-fashioned song are not by Jonson: the many improvements and corrections allow us to deduce that they were written by Elgar himself. I give the text below, printing the emendations in italic beneath the words or lines that they were intended to replace:

> I gave my heart unto my love
>   As we passed across the dark mysterious forest vast
>   *rode   along   deep   ?mountain pass*
> The daylight faded, and above
>   As the sunset flamed down to gild the past
>   *Clouds of darkness circles, gathered to amass* [circled?]
>
> Oh, my love! Oh, my life, dost thou remember?
> My beloved, dost [deleted] that dark December?
>   My
>   *heart with rapture oerflow'd*   [not in Elgar's hand?]
>   My very inmost soul awaken'd
>   *was quick[en'd?]*
> We leaned against each other in the moonlight
> Darkness came upon us, oh, lovely night.
>   *fell around*
>
>   We were lost then but ah! awaking!   [omit 'then'?]
>   *at*
> Our hearts and souls were all aflame
> As the forest deep enfolded close[r came]
>   *along the mountain pass our true love came*
>   *we   lovers*

The song is headed 'XTC[E]', which must mean 'Ecstasy', and ends with the mock-Italian phrase 'Fine del songo' and the date. Below this Elgar has written, at some later time, and in a box, the name 'B Jonson', which is plainly intended to refer to nine mysterious words that follow, in the form of a quotation, after which he adds 'for the above beautiful tune?':

"Allevial eld and pervious epic/sheaves washed every second – ?" . . .

Elgar does not usually write gibberish, still less attribute it to Ben Jonson. Thinking, like Le Sage's wise student, that 'there is certainly some mystery here', I examined the inscription more closely, though without benefit of ultra-violet light, which may yet reveal more. Some of the letters had been written over erasures (indicated by italics below). The quotation marks were half-erased: the first pair were placed over the second letter of the first word and the closing pair over the question mark, showing that the original, deleted first word had had two or three letters added to its beginning, and that the question mark had been put in later. The 'i' of 'pervious' was a later insertion. There was a dot, as of an erased 'i', over the 'as' of 'washed'. Thus:

> *Alle*vial eeld and *perv*i*ous* *epic*
> *shea*ves wa*she*d every second – ? . . .

'Allevial' must have read 'Jovial' (the 'J' is discernible), and 'pervious' must have read 'nervous'; but that does not get us very far. For whom had he composed the song? It is in fact the only solo song that Elgar is known to have written (as opposed to unison songs or songs with chorus refrain) since *The Starlight Express* of 1915, except for one, 'It isnae me', which sets a Scottish poem by Sally Holmes. This was taken from *Country Life* for 14 June 1930 (vol.lxvii, No.1743, p.862b) and was first performed by its dedicatee, the Scottish soprano Joan Elwes, in Dumfries in the following October (Kennedy, op. cit., p.357). That was the very month in which Elgar first sketched 'I gave my heart'. As yet I know little about Joan Elwes, who may have been related to the famous tenor and Catholic exponent of Gerontius, Gervase Elwes, but was not his daughter. Dr Moore describes her as 'the young soprano . . . whose voice he [Elgar] had liked at Three Choirs Festivals' (op. cit., p.788); this must in part repose on a letter of 15 September 1927 that he prints elsewhere, in which Elgar commended her singing, along with compositions of Granville Bantock, to Osmond Williams of The Gramophone Company; Dr Moore describes them as 'two well-known musicians whom he had met again at Hereford' (Ibid., *Elgar on record*, op. cit., p.75). Elgar thought her 'a soprano who should be allowed to make more records: she sings *without* tremolo & the specimens I heard seemed to me to be quite successful; personally I should be glad if it might be found possible to adopt both suggestions' (to engage both her and Bantock).

The likelihood that Elgar wrote his song for Joan Elwes enables me to offer a reconstruction of the original 'quotation' at the end of 'I gave my heart unto my love'. It was evidently an acrostic (though not copied as one), but with a message of its own:

"Jovial
Old
And
Nervous
EE's
Leaves
Wither
Every
Second"

'Jovial' must have its true meaning of 'like Jove', since the song appears to reflect an actual or wished-for amour. The inscription, if I have 'had wit enough to discover its meaning', reminds us sadly of the epigrams on love in old age that Elgar had marked in the Greek Anthology (see above, p.208ff). He did not complete the song, and scored through his inscription in pencil with the words 'no good'.

Dr Moore has shown, in his sensitive treatment of Elgar's relationship with Mrs Vera Hockman, that the lonely composer's quest for feminine understanding and consolation in his old age – for he was still passionate and susceptible – must be regarded with sympathy. While we hear of less dignified escapades (see Kennedy, op. cit., pp.296f.: Lady Elgar was still living), we must assume that he was seeking, and sometimes found, more tender and lasting rewards. Just as Vera Hockman inspired a theme in the Third Symphony (evidently made out of four of the letters of her name, EAH[=B]A, vErA HockmAn, but transposed: see Moore, *Edward Elgar*, op. cit., p.800), so Joan Elwes appears to have inspired two songs. Elgar needed a White Goddess in order to compose, and his attempts to find her should inspire compassion; no doubt he felt, though, like Yeats in his seventies, that he was at times an unwilling victim of the forces inside him:

THE SPUR

You think it horrible that lust and rage
Should dance attention upon my old age;
They were not such a plague when I was young;
What else have I to spur me into song?

Appendix 4: Elgar and Jeremy Bentham

Since completing my article, I have been informed by Dr Cyprian P. Blamires, who is engaged in editing the *Collected Works of Jeremy Bentham* for the Bentham Project at University College, London, that he has managed to locate the quotations from the distinguished philosopher and juridical theorist mentioned above on p.204. They are taken from a very obscure place, the *Draught of a work for the organization of the judicial establishment in France: with critical observations on the draught proposed by the National Assembly Committee, in the form of a perpetual commentary*, printed in vol.iv of the Bowring edition of Bentham's *Works*, where they are to be found on pp.397b and 398a of Chap.8, Sec.vi, 'Of sleeping laws'. In his Birmingham lecture, Elgar likens the hoary rules of academic harmony and counterpoint teaching – a code learned by all students which, however, the composer may break without fear of penalty – to laws which remain as Acts of Parliament or statutes but which are largely forgotten and never invoked. It is an excellent parallel; but the interesting point is that Bentham's comments occur in the middle of an attack upon religious intolerance. Elgar's year of legal studies, when he says he came across the passage, was spent in the office of a Catholic solicitor, William Allen, who was something of a singer and 'not only a member of the Catholic congregation [of St George's Church, Worcester] but their solicitor as well', so Dr Moore informs us (op. cit., p.55). I am not sure how long Catholics continued to fear the threat of disabilities under 'sleeping' laws after their official emancipation in the late 1820s, which owed much to Bentham's advocacy; but we can now understand why Elgar should have read Bentham, whom he would have regarded as a hero, and chose to quote him from his professorial *cathedra*. I have suggested that Catholics present on that same occasion (13 December 1905) may have known the context of Elgar's reference to Macaulay's New Zealander, which alludes to the indestructibility of the Catholic Church (see p.205 above and n.117, the end of which I would now phrase more strongly). How might they have reacted to the paragraph leading into the first of Elgar's quotations? –

> Of the condition of him whose curse, I had almost said whose crime, it is to live under such laws, what is to be said? It is neither more nor less than slavery . . . Law, the only power that gives security to others, is the very thing that takes it away from him. His destiny is to live his life long with a halter about his neck; and his safety depends upon his never meeting with that man whom wantonness or malice can have induced to pull it . . .

The context of Elgar's second quotation describes the silent tyranny endured by a Catholic or Protestant dissenter who has to live under disabling laws, even though they are not invoked (Elgar cites the passage italicized):

. . . Silent anxiety and inward humiliation do not meet the eye, and draw little attention, although they fill up the measure of a whole life.

Of this base and malignant policy an example would scarcely be to be found, were it not for religious hatred, of all hatred the bitterest and the blindest. *Debarred by the infidelity of the age from that most exquisite of repasts, the blood of heretics*, it subsists as it can upon the idea of secret sufferings – sad remnant of the luxury of better times.

Bentham continues his irony, deriding the fears of the Establishment in a magisterial footnote:

Seventy thousand catholic dissenters, added to two hundred thousand presbyterians and other protestant dissenters, are to join in first subduing and then oppressing, eight millions of church of England men. So irrational are the principles of these heretics, that their prevalence is the greatest calamity that can befall the nation. So rational are they at the same time, as well as so concordant among themselves, that they want nothing but fair play and the liberty of being heard upon equal terms, to gain the majority of churchmen, and make them either catholics, or presbyterians, or independents, or quakers, or all at once. To prevent a catastrophe thus horrible and thus imminent, the whole body of these heretics are to be kept in a state of slavery, collectively and individually, with regard to the whole body of the orthodox . . . Upon such terms, and upon such terms only, the church is safe.

Reading this gives us a very telling impression of the attitude, if no longer the legal disabilities, with which a poor young Catholic in a country town such as Elgar's Worcester would have had to contend, and helps to explain the chip on the outsider's shoulder. It may have been because he did not wish his own experience to be visited on the heads of the Northern Irish Protestants by the grant of Irish home rule, which would have made them a minority in a predominantly Catholic state, that Elgar decided in the end to sign his friend John Arkwright's public declaration of protest in 1914 (see Young, op. cit., pp.169f; Moore, op. cit., p.664). Bentham's reminder that Nonconformist dissenters suffered under the same oppression as Catholics may illuminate the bond of respect and understanding that evidently existed between the Catholic Elgar and the Nonconformist choirs of the Midlands. Finally, the passages from Bentham are unlikely to have been excerpted for student use in some legal primer: William Allen must himself have drawn them to Elgar's attention and evidently played a valued part in the lad's intellectual development. This suggests that Elgar's year of legal study was not a period of dusty routine: it was, after all, the only higher education that he received. Allen was a respected friend as well as a mentor, and when he died early in 1887 Elgar sketched the offertory 'Pie Jesu' in his memory (see Moore, op. cit., pp.118, 363: it later became the *Ave verum corpus*, Op.2). Elgar kept all his life the translation of Thomas à Kempis that the solicitor's family gave him at this time, and it is still in the Birthplace Library, marked 'From Miss Allen. This book belonged to W.A. dec.d E.E.'. In 1902, fifteen years later, he visited Allen's grave, which he found in a state of dilapidation

(Maine, *Life*, op. cit., pp.115f.; Moore, op. cit., p.370, dating the occasion): did he see to it that the fallen tombstone was mended or replaced?

It is remarkable what a variety of considerations derive from the tracing of a single reference.

I wish to thank the British Library and the trustees of the Elgar Birthplace for permission to publish material in their collections, and for the unfailing courtesy and efficiency of their staff.

Notes

1.   This essay has its origins in a paper that I read to the Elgar Society nine years ago as the first A. T. Shaw Memorial Lecture. My purpose then was not to review the whole matter of Elgar's involvement with literature, although I did mildly question one or two received views and advanced a little new material. I said very little about the texts that Elgar set to music. Though invited to publish the paper, I felt that it needed more research and greater breadth, particularly in view of the spate of valuable new books about Elgar that Dr Jerrold Northrop Moore and others have been giving us. A study of Elgar's general use of quotations and allusions, besides those which relate to his music, and consideration of all the evidence about his reading seemed necessary. I also wished to investigate the sources and original contexts of the words that he chose for musical setting; this latter task has led on to the discovery and identification of over eighty sketches, all fragmentary, for projected songs and partsongs, many of them not previously mentioned in the literature. I can here present no more than a selection from my researches, but I must thank the Elgar Society and its former chairman, Mr Michael Pope, for honouring me with their invitation to commemorate the work and personality of A. T. Shaw, and for giving me the first impulse into such a fascinating domain.

2.   Michael Kennedy (1968, rev. 1982, 1987). *Portrait of Elgar*, O.U.P. Jerrold Northrop Moore (1984). *Edward Elgar: a Creative Life*, O.U.P.

3.   I did not read Michael De-la-Noy's *Elgar: the man* (1983, London) until my own work was well advanced. His findings touch mine at several points, and he adduces some valuable new material; my interest, however, lies more in explaining and in exploring motivations than in debunking, and in examining and assessing the problems of historiography that the Elgar literature raises.

4.   Philip Radcliffe (1976). *E. J. Dent: a centenary memoir*, Cambridge, pp.17ff. He suggests that certain of Dent's remarks were intended to be two-edged, and that he was in fact criticizing the 'English ears' who found Elgar's music vulgar (since Dent used to inveigh against the Englishman's 'ultra-respectable fear of vulgarity') as well as the 'conservative academic musicians' who abhorred Liszt (since Dent 'was always a staunch upholder of Liszt', with whom he had associated Elgar). Dent had a personality every bit as paradoxical as Elgar's, and Radcliffe may well be right: if so, Dent was very ill-advised to attempt irony in the German language and in the pages of a learned encyclopedia.

5.   op. cit., pp.789f. Appendix 1 gives Dent's remarks in full.

6. Basil Maine (1933) *Elgar: his life and works*, 2 vols., London, *Works*, p.277: 'both first and second editions'.

7. Lawrence Haward (1956). *Edward J. Dent: a bibliography*, Cambridge See also *Music Review*, vii (1946), p.242 et seq., p.8, no.90.

8. According to Lewis Foreman, who prints the full text of the Open Letter and Shaw's postscript in *From Parry to Britten: British Music in letters 1900–1945* (1987) London, pp.147f.

9. See William H. Reed (1936). *Elgar as I knew him*, London, p.107, and E. Wulstan Atkins (1984). *The Elgar-Atkins Friendship*, Newton Abbot, pp.77f. Note also the Liszt score mentioned in n.52 below.

10. See Francis Toye (1949). *For what we have received: an autobiography*, London, pp.65f. On Dent aiding Toye's impertinent musical criticism, see p.83; for other references to Elgar see pp.83, 89, 194 and especially 207 (a weekend with Elgar and Shaw, and Elgar's admiration of Puccini).

11. Ernest Newman, in 'A fingerpost for criticism', an article of 1922 reprinted in *More essays from the world of music* (1958) London, cites a criticism by Dent in the *Nation* reporting on the performance of an Elgar symphony in Prague and describing the composer as '*the Pope of music* [my italics], the man of ripe experience, the conservative who as gone through the school of Liszt's technique, and there fixes, more or less, the boundaries of music' (p.165). In another article, Newman must be alluding to Dent among the 'professors' who 'have not forgiven him [Elgar] to this day' (ibid., p.214; article of 1932).

12. The Rowe Library, King's College, Cambridge, has some of Dent's papers.

13. So far as I have been able to ascertain, Dent never commented in public on this matter.

14. George Bernard Shaw, 'Edward Elgar', *Music & Letters* i, no.1, conveniently reprinted in *An Elgar Companion*, ed. by Christopher Redwood, Ashbourne, 1982, where see p.249. Gerald Cumberland (pseud. of C. F. Kenyon), *Set down in malice*, London, 1919; the extract on Elgar is reprinted in *An Elgar Companion*, op. cit., where see pp.134ff. Cumberland, who was a friend of and librettist to Havergal Brian, held left-wing views; but he greatly admired Elgar's music and his reports on his personality and opinions, though at times decidedly astringent, seem honest and accurate. See above, pp.196ff.

15. See above, pp.192f.

16. See the drafts of his Birmingham lectures in Percy M. Young, ed. (1968). *A future for English music and other lectures*, London, p.xvi and *passim*; Percy M. Young (1955 rev. ed. 1973). *Elgar O.M.*, London, p.230; MS draft of Elgar's note on *The Music Makers*, British Library Add. MS. 47908, ff.87–9.

17. Percy M. Young, ed. (1965). *Letters to Nimrod: Edward Elgar to August Jaeger, 1897–1908*, London, p.271; 'I say! that "Vision" of Parry's is *fine stuff* & the poem is literature'. Also, writing to Kilburn, 'the poem (his own & sui generis) is a splendid thing': Ibid. (1956). *Letters of Edward Elgar and other writings*, London, p.176.

18. Maine, op. cit., *Life*, p.259; *Works*, p.278. Elgar would not have allowed the perpetuation of any disparagement of Parry, and in March 1920 wrote to *Music & Letters* to correct an erroneous assertion about him by Shaw. We must regret that he never redeemed his promise to write an account of Parry's advice and encouragement to him (see *An Elgar Companion*, op. cit., p.250 for a reprint).

19. Maine, op. cit., p.273.

20. Kennedy, op. cit., p.317.

21. London, reprinted 1973. See Preface, and p.151.

22. The Master Musicians, London.

23. ibid., Chap.18; see p.175.

24. London; revised and expanded, 1973. Diana M. McVeagh's *Edward Elgar* (London, 1955), so excellent on the music and its techniques, does not take up this particular challenge.

25. For these see n.17.

26. Ed. by H. A. Chambers, London, pp.55–64.

27. ibid., p.60; one might add two further hitherto unnoticed letters to the *Times Literary Supplement*, Elgar's own song-texts (of which *Owls* is worthy of Walter De La Mare), and his most beautiful piece of writing, intended for children to read as a preface to a collection of piano pieces, but not published until Dr Moore rescued it (op. cit., pp.24f.).

28. Young, op. cit., pp.56f., and for ensuing passages quoted.

29. On pp.249–255; it is a great pity that much of Elgar's library has been sold: one hopes that a catalogue or card-index may have survived.

30. On p.251.

31. *Letters of Edward Elgar*, op. cit., p.232: to Sidney Colvin; see also the notes about the Anthology, evidently jotted down during a conversation with Colvin, in British Library Add. MS. 63162, ff.34 and 35, including 'See Athenaeus', 'Harmodus and Aristogeiton' [*sic*] and 'NB there is an early M.S. in the small museum at Leicester' – a piece of information of no use to Elgar, save to surprise people with.

32. *Elgar O.M.*, op. cit., all on p.250.

33. ibid., p.254.

34. ibid., p.255.

35. Moore, op. cit., pp.290f.

36. See the Chapman and Hall edition (1904) 3 vols., London, p.20; the only complete English translation of *Levana* then available, by 'A.H.', reads quite differently.

37. *Letters of Edward Elgar*, op. cit., p.xix. But Elgar's footnoted epistle to Griffith, mentioned immediately afterwards, was plainly a 'jape'.

38. *A future for English music*, op. cit., pp.xvi, xix.

39. ibid., pp.118f.; they are marked in Elgar's copy, now in the Birthplace Library, the second edition (1888, London).

40. ibid., pp.47, 156f.; in Mew's Book (1903, London), Elgar has also underlined the italicized words in this passage from Thomas Burnet: 'Whatever you determine within yourself about the eternity of punishment, you certainly ought to preach the common doctrine of hell-fire to the people, *especially to those of the lower rank*' (p.320).

41. *A future . . .* , p.249.

42. See Bohn edition (1910) 3 vols., London, i, p.233. The point is not trivial, for this is the only one of the great nineteenth-century histories that Elgar ever alludes to in the literature that I have searched.

43. *A future . . .* , p.180.

44. He seems to have owned remarkably few himself, if the selection in the Elgar Birthplace library is anything to go by; but he ordered a number for the Birmingham students (see *A future . . .* , pp.71f.).

45. See op. cit., Index, under *Elgar: Literary tastes*.

46. 'Elgar at Craeg Lea', interview with Rudolph de Cordova, *The Strand Magazine* (May 1904) reprinted in *An Elgar Companion*, op. cit., pp.115–124; see p.116.

47. Reginald Nettel's observations in *Ordeal by music* (1945) London, p.75, are

germane here; Nettel was a working man, and both this book and *Music in the Five Towns* (1944), London, are essential to an understanding of Elgar's Midland culture.

48.   Two poems by Alice Elgar – her best, in fact – give an honest and exact account of her relationship with Elgar at the time of marriage and at some later date, when he had begun to grow away from her (if indeed the second poem refers to Elgar, which seems likely). They survive in the Birthplace Library, but have never yet been published, no doubt for family reasons.

(i)   No.3 of a set of three Sonnets

Bring me thy tired heart and let it lie*   [*originally 'rest'
All burdened as it is upon my breast
And win perchance some soothing in such rest.
New hope may light those eyes, dear, bye and bye,
And smiles may come to lips more used to sigh.
My pulses quicken at thy least behest[;]
My touch scarce quickens* thine, and pain, thy guest,   [*orig. 'hastens'
Still clouds thy brow while doubts thy joy outvie,
But all, for thy sake all, I will forget
Nor loving, wish thee* other than thou art,   [*orig. 'thou'
Though deep the gloom, Love yet may lift the pall.
I am content, and e'en forswear regret
That in past brighter days I had no part.
Thou giv'st me what thou canst, I give thee all.

(ii)   [Untitled]

Thy love doth fade, too like a winter sun;
    I watch it grow as cold;
    The summer's joy is done,
Although its radiant hours seemed scarce begun,
    Dark night must it enfold.

Deceive anew* and smile as if no part   [*orig. began 'Be happy'
    Were thine in my lost life;
    Leave me my wasted heart
And buy new joys from out the world's gay mart;
    Leave me the bitter strife.

Neither poem is dated; the second is copied on white paper, not the usual blue of the earlier poems, and was included in a list sent to a prospective publisher; Dr Young says that it was sent 'before leaving Malvern', that is before June 1904; but the list includes '*Something afar*', the MS of which is dated Nov. 16th, 1904 (Percy M. Young, *Alice Elgar: Enigma of a Victorian lady*, London, 1978, pp.154f.).

49.   For Bennett and Sassoon see, besides references in Moore, Kennedy and De-la-Noy: *The Journals of Arnold Bennett*, ed. by Newman Flower, London, ii (1932), p.280 (an agreeable dinner party in Nov. 1920); iii (1933), p.43 (Elgar's complaints of poverty and his bedside 'tea-machine', May 1924); p.220 (Schuster's concert at Bray, 'Homage to Elgar', in June 1927, at which Elgar countered praise with 'The silences are good, anyhow'); p.259 (Bennett not impressed by 'The Dream of Gerontius', April 1928); see also *Arnold Bennett's letters to his nephew*, with a preface by Frank Swinnerton, London (1936) p.300 (reporting Elgar contrasting the original reception of the 'Enigma

Variations', 'when it was called silly' with current opinion of its 'profound psychological import' (in June 1930): Elgar was now 'rather a silly and disgruntled old man', and Bennett had tired of 'his affectations' as early as 1922); for Sassoon, whom De-la-Noy also invokes, see *Siegfried Sassoon Diaries 1915–1918*, ed. by Rupert Hart-Davies, London (1983) p.124 (the Violin Concerto: Elgar 'always moves me deeply, because his is the melody of an average Englishman (and I suppose I am more or less the same)', with poem, never collected, but revised in *Siegfried's Journey 1916–1920*, London (1945) p.44 (with account of a dream inspired by the concerto); Id., *Diaries 1920–22*, ed. Hart-Davies, London (1981) p.69 (Elgar and Muriel Foster at Schuster's, with comment on Frank and Adela Schuster, June 1921); p.73; p.79 (Elgar's rudeness to Schuster: 'There is no doubt that Elgar is a very self-centred and inconsiderate man . . . "Selfish, conceited old brute!" I thought . . . I suppose he is very "English" – always pretending and disguising his feelings'); p.81 (envy of Elgar's achievements and continued activity); p.89 (after hearing *Gerontius*: 'a great composer. His sense of form is flawless; he never lets one down in his constructive power, although in detail he may occasionally be derivative or commonplace'); Ibid., *Diaries 1923–1925*, ed. Hart-Davies, London (1985), various entries, including p.152 (the 'other Elgar': 'just a type of club bore'); Ibid., *Collected poems*, London, 1947, pp.127–129 (satirical poem 'Afterthoughts on the Opening of the British Empire Exhibition': mention of Elgar conducting at Wembley).

50.   *Sir Edward Elgar* (1904) London, pp.33f.; also in *An Elgar Companion*, op. cit., p.113.

51.   F. G. Edwards, 'Edward Elgar', *The Musical Times*, October 1900, reprinted in *An Elgar Companion*, op. cit., pp.35–49.

52.   Jerrold Northrop Moore, ed. (1987). *Elgar and his publishers: letters of a creative life*, 2 vols., Oxford, pp.235–40. It is puzzling that Dr Moore has omitted to record the following cuts and alterations, mainly relating to the family music business in Worcester, and referred to in Alice Elgar's third paragraph on p.239. Using Dr Moore's system of reference, these are as follows (passages cut are bracketed, and additions are in italic): 641/ii: 'started a music-selling business *of his own* [C. A. E.'s hand] (which, under the name of 'Elgar Brothers', continues to flourish to this day). Mr Frank Elgar, the composer's younger brother, (now at the head of the business,) . . . Mr Elgar, Senior, was, however, much more of a musician than a (music-seller) *business man* . . . (He had a large tuning collection for miles around the 'faithful city') . . . '; 644/i: 'He also arranged accompaniments for Christy minstrel songs, at the (official) remuneration . . . This (Asylum) experience . . . '; 646/i: Mr Elgar married the only daughter of the late Major-General Sir Henry Gee Roberts, *K.C.B.*, (who greatly distinguished himself under Sir Charles Napier at Sind and elsewhere in India. He) *a very distinguished Indian officer and who* received the thanks of Parliament . . . [C. A. E.'s hand, as also the following]; 646/i: 'has resided at Malvern. *Where on the production of King Olaf in 1896 at the Hanley Festival appreciation and fame at length came to him.*'; in the passage about the Liszt score returned by a stranger, [Moore, op. cit., p.238]. Elgar has added 'who turned out to be Mr. Main, a local professor' [not used]; 648/i: 'Pictures of every school *[and] literature* – especially (those) *that* of the last century – have a strong fascination for him' [C. A. E.'s hand]. Elgar seems to have loved Dickens all his life, since in June 1933 he was 'extolling Dickens and Montaigne', in Florio's translation, no doubt, to Delius (Gaisberg's account, in Jerrold Northrop Moore (1974). *Elgar on record: the composer and*

the gramophone, London, p.204). This would lead one to question how far he was expressing his wife's views rather than his own when he wrote to Buck in December 1891 about selling the very books that he evidently drew to Edwards' attention five years later: 'We don't admire Dickens enough to want to keep them & have thought of selling 'em & changing them into other literature' (*Letters of Edward Elgar*, op. cit., p.54). He appears to have resisted gentrification and kept them, just as he held on all his life to the scruffy paperback copies of Artemus Ward (another vulgar taste, as we shall see) that are still in the Birthplace Library.

53.   Sir Richard Baker (1568–1645), *The chronicle of the kings of England*, 1643; continued by Edward Phillips, Milton's royalist nephew.

54.   Michael Drayton (1563–1631), Poly-Olbion (not 'Polyalbion'), 1612 and 1622.

55.   Her letter is in the British Library Egerton MS 3090, ff.35–8.

56.   Reprinted in *An Elgar Companion*, op. cit., pp.115–124.

57.   British Library Add. MS. 47904A, f.23v. Elgar makes nine mistakes in twenty-three words. The letter as sent – still not faultless – was printed by Volbach's son Walter in *Musical Opinion* for July 1937 and has been reprinted in *The Elgar Society Journal* (Sept.1988, p.6).

58.   His French exercises survive in the Birthplace library, but he stopped less than a third of the way through M. D. Berlitz, *Deuxième livre pour l'enseignement des langues modernes: Partie française pour adultes* (1907); thinking of Saint-Saens' Le Rouet d'Omphale, he christened Hercules *'le roué d'Omphale'*, but spoils the effect by mis-spelling 'une petite paranomasie' (*Letters of Edward Elgar*, op. cit., p.128, to Griffith); correspondence with Pitt in the British Library Egerton MS 3303, f.116, suggesting improvements entered into the score (ibid., Add. MS. 52529).

59.   See ibid., Add. MS. 63160, f.11v, where he copies out a dictum of Galuppi as 'vagghezza, chiarezza e buono modulazione' (it should be 'vaghezza', 'buona'); Add. 63161, f.15v. names 'Cina da Pistoia' (it should be 'Cino'); Elgar even had trouble at first in spelling his characteristic term 'nobilemente', which he writes as 'nobilmente' in ibid., Add. MS. 49973B, f.4v, and in the first sketch for 'Nimrod'; letter to Schuster in *Letters of Edward Elgar*, op. cit., p.128.

60.   op. cit., p.119; Ralph Holinshed and others, *Chronicles of Englande, Scotlande, and Irelande* (1577; new ed. 1586 by J. Hooker and J. Stow). De-la-Noy, op. cit., p.13, says that the Elgars possessed no 'stable-loft' after moving from Broadheath: a rented one perhaps, since Mr Elgar senior rode a horse?

61.   Buckley, op. cit., pp.5f.

62.   *Life*, op. cit., p.10.

63.   *Life*, op. cit., p.9; see Moore, *Edward Elgar*, op. cit., p.67 ('1874' in note 18); ibid., for the factory girl.

64.   Buckley, op. cit., p.40.

65.   ibid., p.41.

66.   *Letters of Edward Elgar*, op. cit., pp.229f.

67.   Buckley, op. cit., pp.76, 84.

68.   ibid., p.38.

69.   ibid., pp.5f. The fact that Anne Elgar read classical authors *in translation* evidently became garbled by double hearsay when Sassoon reported Schuster in 1922 as saying that she 'used to sit up half the night reading Greek and Latin with him [Elgar] when a boy'; Michael De-la-Noy rightly felt that this stretched credulity too far (op. cit., p.28), but overlooked the passage in Buckley.

70.   'I often think that the present generation of music-lovers owes more to Sir Edward Elgar, Ernest Newman and Sir Henry J. Wood than to any twenty, or

even fifty, other men. They are in a very great measure responsible for our musical renaissance of the last twenty-five years. Sir Edward Elgar gave our musical life dignity when it stood in need of that quality; he was both an example and a rallying-point for our younger men; and the speedy recognition of his genius on the Continent, and more particularly by Germany, helped us to realise that in him we had a figure destined for immortality' (Gerald Cumberland, *Written in friendship: a book of reminiscences*, London, 1923, p.235; see also p.173). Not relevant here, but too curious to omit, is the statement on p.234 that 'Ernest Newman once told me that Elgar used to wince when he heard his First Symphony conducted by Richter – to whom it was dedicated!'

71.   15 January 1906, conveniently reprinted in *An Elgar Companion*, op. cit., pp.125–130; for Cumberland's later account of the same interview, see ibid., first complete paragraph on p.131 to end of first complete paragraph on p.135.

72.   *A future for English music*, op. cit., p.93; the lecture had been delivered on 1 November 1905, less than two months before the interview.

73.   ibid., p.89.

74.   The passage (ibid., pp.91, 93) is taken from Kingsley's essay 'Alexander Smith and Alexander Pope', in *Fraser's Magazine*, October 1853, pp.464f., reprinted in vol.xx of *The Works of Charles Kingsley*, London, 1880, pp.94–96; neither source agrees exactly with Elgar's version, but both give 'prose-run-mad, diffuse, unfinished, unmusical, to which' (five lines from the end of the first citation), which the editor has wrongly attempted to re-cast.

75.   Elgar seems also to have admired Newbolt, since he gave Carice a copy of his *Collected poems 1897–1907* (London, n.d.) as a Christmas present in 1910 (now in the Birthplace Library); it was Stanford, however, who set Newbolt to music in *Songs of the Sea* (1904) and *Songs of the Fleet* (1910). In 1897, Elgar had thought of shaping the stories of Caractacus, St Augustine, and others like King Canute into 'perhaps a series of illustrative movements for orchestra with 'Mottoes' from English history', for the Leeds Festival (Moore, *Edward Elgar*, op. cit., p.229, citing a letter to Kilburn). He later passed on the 'Canute' idea to Edward German. As late as 1901, perhaps later, we find him copying headings for a three-movement work of this kind, with a wave-like theme sketched for Canute, on f.2v of British Library Add. MS. 63154: 'II Childe Rowland to the dark tower came/I Canute/III Arethusa'. These had appeared earlier in ibid., Add. MS. 49973B (f.53), where the 'w' of 'Rowland' is underlined, presumably to show that it refers not to Browning but to the ballad mentioned in *King Lear*; '(Arcadia Mixture)' is appended to 'Arethusa', presumably to show that a further motto from Milton's *Arcades* (hardly Sydney's *Arcadia*) is to be added to lines from Shelley's [?] *Arethusa*. Moore plausibly suggests that the 'Pomp and Circumstance' marches also derive from the 'Mottoes' idea (op. cit., p.339; see also ibid., *Elgar and his publishers*, (1987), Oxford, p.63).

76.   Elgar slightly misquotes Diogenes Teufelsdröckh's phrase 'weltering . . . like an Egyptian pitcher of tamed vipers, each struggling to get its head above the others' from *Sartor Resartus*, bk.i, ch.iii, in 'English Executants' (*A future for English music*, op. cit., p.143); Carlyle's chapter ends with a reference to the 'buried soul' from Lesage's *Gil Blas*. A letter of 1918 shows Elgar re-reading *Past and Present* 'or rather I only read "Past" I cant stand Plugson etc' (*Letters of Edward Elgar*, op. cit., p.244; the editor's bracketed query after 'Plugson' may be removed, for Plugson, 'of the respected Firm of Plugson, Hunks and

Company, in St. Dolly Undershot', is Carlyle's embodiment of the money-grubbing captain of industry).

77.   This rests, admittedly, on one vague reference in a letter to Canon Gorton of 1903, though it is an interesting one in relation to *The Apostles*: 'To my mind *Judas*' crime & sin was *despair* (Ibsen etc. etc.)'. What was he thinking of – *John Gabriel Borkman*? (ibid., p.121).

78.   See Moore, *Edward Elgar*, op. cit., p.642, for a telling passage on poverty copied out with underlinings by Elgar from *The Fourth Generation*.

79.   By 1885: see De-la-Noy, op. cit., p.47.

80.   See the reprint in *An Elgar Companion*, op. cit., pp.130–136; p.81 for this and the next citation; for Lady Elgar, pp.131f.

81.   See for example Rosa Burley and Frank C. Carruthers (1972). *Edward Elgar: the record of a friendship*. London, p.99: 'I have always remembered the glow with which Edward told me of a meeting at Bettws-y-Coed at Mr Rodewald's house with Ernest Newman. The talk had turned on, among other subjects, Caroline poetry and it made a deep impression. For once Edward felt that he had been fully and sympathetically understood'. See also *Letters to Nimrod*, op. cit., p.87: 'I can't tell you how much good your letter has done me: I do dearly like to be *understood*'.

82.   Ernest Newman (1906). *Elgar*, The Music of the Masters, London: see pp.184f.; Kennedy (op. cit.) and Young (*Elgar, O.M.*) misdate this book. Elgar, like many others who worried about the autonomy of music when associated with literary ideas, never managed to resolve this vexed question, and at one point went so far as to ask Jaeger to remove a reference to Strauss's programme music from his analytical essay on *In the South*: 'S. puts music in a very low position when he suggests it must hang on to some commonplace absurdity for it's [sic] very life' (*Letters to Nimrod*, op. cit., p.238: 1904). Today we might say that music and literature are both symbolic arts, and that programme music does not so much directly interpret the words on which it appears to be based, but rather goes beyond them to the substratum of events and feelings which they also symbolize: the two arts operate in parallel, not in series.

83.   Moore, *Edward Elgar*, op. cit., pp.649f., quotes part of the report, published on the following day; for Cumberland's later account, see reprint in *An Elgar Companion*, op. cit., second complete paragraph on p.135 to end. Dr Moore omits a piece of literary criticism by Elgar, interesting in that it associates 'Falstaff' with Rabelais: Gargantua and Pantagruel might have trod the boards at Covent Garden in a grotesque Elgarian ballet, had not Lady Elgar scotched the idea (according to a note by Troyte Griffith now in the Elgar Birthplace Library): 'In the latter play [*The Merry Wives of Windsor*] we see Falstaff almost solely as a buffoon, but, in all probability, much of 'The Merry Wives of Windsor' did not come from Shakespeare's pen at all. As he is pictured in the two historical dramas I have named [*Henry IV*, Parts 1 and 2], he appears to me one of the greatest characters ever created – as great as anything in Rabelais'.

84.   See *Letters of Edward Elgar*, op. cit., p.239 (1918).

85.   Even in his first interview Cumberland exercises some care: Elgar has 'a nature that is at once extremely wide in its outlook on life, and enthusiastically studious *in certain directions*' [my italics].

86.   'The Music Maker', in *Edward Elgar: centenary sketches*, op. cit., p.37.

87.   Burley and Carruthers, op. cit., p.66.

88.   Issues for 10 August 1922 (on Swift in Bury St.) and 2 August 1923, headed 'Poluphloisboisterous'. The latter might well have seemed pretentious to

Elgar's Use of Literature 303

Greek scholars, particularly in Cambridge . . .

89.   These may be seen in some notes on Greek modes in the Shed Book, British Library Add. MS. 63146, ff.5v–6.
90.   See *Elgar, O.M.*, op. cit., p.219, fn.2.
91.   Interview in *The World*, 22 October 1912, reprinted in *An Elgar Companion*, op. cit., pp.137ff.
92.   August, 1916, reprinted ibid., pp.140–6. Scholes, of course, was an exceptionally learned man.
93.   'In 1930 John Murray tried hard to extract an autobiography from Elgar', but in vain (see *Elgar, O.M.*, op. cit., pp.251f.).
94.   Quoted from *My own trumpet* in De-la-Noy, op. cit., p.50, fn.3. It is to Newman, a university-educated man of remarkably broad culture, that we owe the most judicious assessment of Elgar's intellectual abilities: 'his emotions were under the control, for purposes of art, of a powerful and critical mind. He was a man of great knowledge, of wide and curious reading in matters that lay rather off the beaten track, such as heraldry, that have a note of their own, even if it be only one of quaintness' ('Elgar: some aspects of the man in his music', *The Sunday Times*, 25 February 1934, reprinted in *An Elgar Companion*, op. cit., where see p.156). Note that he admires Elgar's 'powerful and critical mind' for its ability to channel his emotional energies into music, and how carefully he defines the nature of Elgar's 'wide and curious reading'.
95.   See n.49 above.
96.   *Letters of Edward Elgar*, op. cit., p.223, and Dr Young's notes on p.222.
97.   Two are reprinted in *Letters of Edward Elgar*, op. cit., pp.253–8 and 270ff.; for the others, see fn.89 above. Bruce Richmond, founder and editor of the *TLS*, was a friend of Elgar's (see *Elgar, O.M.*, op. cit., p.219).
98.   *The Gramophone*, June 1957, reprinted in *An Elgar Companion*, op. cit., pp.158f.
99.   Pierre Bayle, *Dictionnaire historique et critique*, 1695–7, enlarged 1702; first English translation 1710, which Elgar possessed: why then did he not use the English title in his letter?
100. Atkins, op. cit., p.270. Like his letters to Griffith, Elgar's correspondence with Atkins is full of literary allusions; unlike Griffith, Atkins resembled Elgar in that he was an autodidact who had not enjoyed a university education. He hero-worshipped his older friend, who sometimes set him literary conundrums as in his letter in imitation of Sir Richard Burton's translation of *The Arabian Nights*, which Bantock had evidently shown him: see ibid., p.122, where however it is not made clear that Burton is the 'Knight' in 'The Thousand and One Nights and a Knight' (one of the book's titles is 'The Thousand Nights and a Night'). The two correspondents called themselves Firapeel and Reynart after the Leopard and the Fox in Caxton's *Reynard the Fox*, which they both possessed in its original spelling as recently published in E. Arber's series, *English reprints*; their letters sometimes merrily parody Caxton's and other literary styles. See ibid., pp.64, 66 and *passim*. Atkins sympathetically understood Elgar's need for intellectual reassurance. Thanking Elgar for his 'Hymn of Faith' libretto in 1905, he wrote, 'you really are a brilliant man: the best intellect I know'; eight years later, after studying the annotated score of *Falstaff* that Elgar had sent him, he ended his letter 'I *do like* the picture it gives of Reynart the *English scholar*. This aspect seizes me greatly. Bless you, you are a cultured mortal!' (ibid., pp.129, 249).
101. *Letters of Edward Elgar*, op. cit., pp.214f.
102. 1905. The short libretto has been assembled with great ingenuity from at least

a dozen different places in the Bible, yet reads as a continuous whole.

103. Noyes did not publish this occasional verse, and there is no libretto in the British Library, but the error is obvious.

104. Thomas Toke Lynch (1856). *The Rivulet.* London, 2nd ed. (1868), pp.24f.

105. Adam Lindsay Gordon (1876). *Bush ballads and galloping rhymes.* Melbourne, pp.12–16. Gordon also wrote 'See! girt with tempest', not 'So, girt', perhaps altered by Elgar to avoid confusion with 'Sea'. A third case is also hard to decide: the accent marked on 'under', at 'strong winds treading the swift waves under / The flying rollers with frothy feet' might suggest that Elgar had in mind the correct wording, which also makes much better sense: 'strong winds treading the swift waves sunder / The flying rollers'. But all the sketches have 'under', which actually appears in Marcus Clarke's posthumous edition, *Poems of the late Adam Lindsay Gordon,* [1887], London, pp.137–40. The consecutive sibilants in 'waves sunder' would be hard to sing. We may also note here that in copying lines from Cino da Pistoia's Sonnet X (to Guido Cavalcanti) from D. G. Rossetti's *The early Italian poets* (1861, London, p.393), Elgar mistranscribed 'Though the world reach alone the coarser sense' as 'Though this would reach above the coarser sense', in British Library Add. MS. 63161, f.15v. See p.210.

106. He evidently kept a commonplace-book or file in which he gathered passages that caught his fancy, for in a letter to Griffith of 1918 he says, about a disappointing book, 'From it I have extracted only two bits', which he does not go on to quote (*Letters of Edward Elgar,* op. cit., p.237). Moore prints several extracts from poems or books copied on to loose sheets; one also finds references and quotations scribbled on to blank leaves in his musical sketches (see my article 'Elgar's marginalia' in *The Musical Times,* March 1984, pp.139–43). Elgar knew that he relied too heavily on quotations and wrote to Griffith 'too much quotation of course in the preamble [to his *Falstaff* essay] but I had to do it hurriedly' (*Letters of Edward Elgar,* op. cit., pp.212f.).

107. *The fountain,* op.71, no.2, a setting of lines from vv.6–7 of Henry Vaughan's 'Regeneration', in *Silex scintillans* i (1650). Foreword reprinted in *Letters of Edward Elgar,* op. cit., pp.303–5.

108. Milton, Sonnet xi, line 11; Keats, last line of sonnet 'On first looking into Chapman's Homer'.

109. Novello's Music Primers: Educational Series, no.91, London. n.d.; also in *The Musical Times,* August 1920.

110. See Thomas Gray. *Poems, letters and essays.* Everyman ed. (1912): London, p.250; to Horace Walpole.

111. 'Ode to the Athenian Society'; for poem and letter, see *The Poems of Jonathan Swift* (1937) ed. Harold Williams, i, Oxford, pp.13–25.

112. *Letters to Nimrod,* op. cit., (1898) p.22.

113. ibid., (1899) p.64.

114. A *future for English music,* op. cit.

115. Elgar collected unusual words but did not always get them right, as we have seen. He treated Atkins to 'cacoturient', which should presumably have been 'cacaturient', 'desiring to go to stool', as my brother suggests (Atkins, op. cit., p.293); Colvin was honoured with 'crispiculant' (deckle-edged: *Letters of Edward Elgar,* op. cit., p.229).

116. *Westminster Review,* new series xlii, October 1872, p.318; *Studies of the Greek poets* (1873–6), London, 2 vols., i, p.164; the later editions of 1877–9 and 1893 do not help; nor does Percy L. Babington's *Bibliography of the writings of John Addington Symonds* (1925).

117. *Edinburgh Review*, October 1840; collected in *Miscellaneous Essays*. I doubt if Elgar's audience were any more familiar with Macaulay's Antipodean than we are today. This is an example of the entirely irrelevant use of quotation: could it possibly have been a coded message for any fellow-Catholics present who were in the know?

118. From *Essays, First Series*, 1841: see *The complete essays and other writings of Ralph Waldo Emerson*, (1940), ed. by Brooks Atkinson, The Modern Library (Random House): New York, pp.295f. The passage is not marked in the Birthplace Library copy of *Essays, Representative men, Society and solitude*, (1886), 2nd ed., London, p.73a; but there are ticks pencilled against certain names in a list of 'favourites' in the essay on 'Books', p.254b, marking Froissart's *Chronicles*, Cervantes, Rabelais, Izaak Walton, Evelyn, Sterne, Lamb and De Quincey.

119. A few minor observations nevertheless deserve mention. Elgar's mention of 'Jack Wilton' in a letter to Griffith of 1917 has nothing to do with Defoe's Jonathan Wild, but alludes to the hero of Thomas Nashe's *The Unfortunate Traveller*, 1594 (*Letters of Edward Elgar*, op. cit., p.233). The first anthologist of Shakespeare, hanged for forgery, was the Revd William Dodd (*The Beauties of Shakespeare*, 1752), whom Elgar probably came across in Boswell's *Life of Johnson* (letter to Colvin, 1917, ibid., p.234). The poem by Kirke White suggested for setting by Jaeger and rejected by Elgar in 1905 must have been 'O give me music': its final couplet is incomplete, which explains Elgar's comment that 'the last two lines . . . had better be omitted' (*Letters to Nimrod*, op. cit., p.253: see *The poetical works and remains of Henry Kirke White*, (1837), London, p.76). The quotation from Homer (not Virgil, *pace* Rosa Burley) with which the Cambridge Public Orator concluded his account of Elgar at the honorary degree ceremony in 1900 refers to the bard Phemius, spared by Ulysses in Book xxii of *The Odyssey*; the usual translation, given in an interview in *The Sketch* (7 October 1903: see Jerrold Northrop Moore, *Elgar: a life in photographs* (1972), London, p.[45]), seems to have been adapted from Pope's version by Elgar himself, since the Orator spoke it in the original Greek. Pope has: 'Self-taught I sing; by Heaven, and Heaven alone,/ The genuine seeds of poesy are sown', altered to 'Self-taught I sing; 'tis Heaven, and Heaven alone,/Inspires my song with music all its own'; Moore translates the final phrase as 'with promise all its own' on p.337. One would give much to know exactly how Elgar, after the ceremony, 'criticised the Public Orator's Latin much to that great person's astonishment and amusement' – for Elgar's Latin must have been of a very elementary and monkish variety (see Moore, *Edward Elgar*, op. cit., p.338).

120. For Colvin and Griffith, see *Letters of Edward Elgar*, op. cit., pp.229f. and passim; for Atkins, *The Elgar-Atkins friendship*, op. cit., *passim*, and see n.100 above.

121. Edited twice, first by Percy M. Young in *Letters to Nimrod*, op. cit., with a few in *Letters of Edward Elgar*, op. cit.; all, with Jaeger's replies, are in Moore, *Elgar and his publishers*, op. cit.

122. See Mrs Richard Powell (1937). *Edward Elgar: memories of a Variation*, London, second ed., revised and enlarged, ibid. (1947).

123. Cited from London ed. (1888) by Routledge; two editions are in the Birthplace Library, one by Routledge (London, 1865) and another, undated, bound with *Artemus Ward his travels*.

124. Applied to Handel's 'Water Music' in Powell, op. cit., (1947), p.66.

125. Young, *Alice Elgar*, op. cit., pp.112, 143.

126. Everyman edition (1924) London, p.353.
127. See Alice Elgar's brave and realistic sonnet in fn.48 above.
128. 5 vols., London; for his criticism of Paton's translation, see his letter to Colvin of August 1917 in *Letters of Edward Elgar*, op. cit., p.232; also *Elgar, O.M.*, op. cit., p.251. It is curious that in sketching the grandiose music for 'Feasting I watch', op.45, no.5, translated from Marcus Argentarius by Richard Garnett, he added the note '*not* good stuff, this' (British Library Add. MS. 63153, f.22v).
129. See n.59 and 105.
130. In *Poems and Ballads* (1866), first series.
131. *Edward Elgar*, op. cit., p.753. I have not seen the sheet, and cannot say whether the inscription was written at the same time as the verses.
132. 'Elgar: some aspects of the man in his music', *The Sunday Times*, 25 February 1934; reprinted in *An Elgar Companion*, op. cit., where see p.156.
133. Cited in Kennedy (1982). *Portrait of Elgar*, p.273.
134. *A Future for English music*, op. cit., p.xix.
135. Cited in Moore, *Edward Elgar*, op. cit., p.103; the cedillas are omitted in *Elgar, O.M.*, op. cit., p.55.
136. See Newman, *Elgar*, op. cit., p.128; Elgar was well versed in Scott's other novels too, and perhaps knew that Sullivan was even then at work on *Ivanhoe* (1891).
137. See *The Poetical Works of John Keats* (1939), ed. H.W. Garrod, Oxford, pp.21f.
138. Kennedy, op. cit., (1982), p.285.
139. Reproduced on p.[33] of Atkins, op. cit.; Elgar gave the copy of the MS score with the picture on the front page to Ivor Atkins to commemorate their first meeting in 1890 at the first performance. It is now on loan at the Elgar Birthplace. The MS score with no picture from which the printed full score was published was given by Elgar to the Worcester Cathedral Music Library. This copy has also now been placed in the Birthplace Library.
140. *Letters to Nimrod*, op. cit., p.126.
141. *Alice Elgar*, op. cit., pp.107, 103; also 35.
142. *Elgar and his publishers*, op. cit., p.43; *The Musical Times*, January 1897.
143. See Everyman edition, London, n.d., vol.ii, p.66.
144. ibid., p.7.
145. *Caractacus*, op.35, ed. by R. Anderson and J. N. Moore (1985), Elgar Complete Edition, vol.5, Novello: London, pp.v–vi, xvi, xxii note 4.
146. *Letters of Edward Elgar*, op. cit., pp.117f.
147. Had Elgar left the theme or 'Enigma' in what I believe must have been its original key, E minor (a favourite key, which he used in order to depict himself, 'a man's life', in the Cello Concerto), all who knew him would have spotted his very serious 'jape' immediately. If, in a work where most of the 'subjects' are identified by initials, the forward-looking, confident Elgar of the Finale is E. D. U., the lonely, desolate Elgar of the Enigma must be E. E., an octave E which he often employed as a rebus in later life. Why else should he have signed two letters to Dorabella with the Enigma theme? Why else should he have expected her, 'of all people' to twig the secret – for she had penetrated the mystery of 'E. D. U.', is the first to record the fact that Elgar was known as 'E.E.', and must have used these initials constantly in conversation until she opted for 'H.E.' (His Excellency). Jaeger alludes to the secret when he calls Elgar 'the octave' in a letter of 7 November 1899 (*Elgar and his publishers*, op. cit., p.148), saying:

'I'll try hard for the octave's sake . . . you SPHINX!!'

Ex. 7

(surely an allusion to the 'sphinxes' in Schumann's 'Carnaval'), and referring to Elgar on 18 September 1900 as 'that wretch of a *teazer* yclept E.E.!' (ibid., p.234); to which Elgar played up, varying his signature to show the octave on 21 May 1900 as E and to show no less than six octaves on [?] August 8 1899:

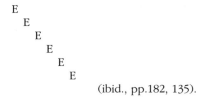

(ibid., pp.182, 135).

Jaeger must have chortled inwardly when, after refusing to reveal the secret to Dorabella, he added: 'the dear E.E. did make me promise not to tell you' (Powell, op. cit., (1947), p.28). The octave EE, played as an inverted pedal on a plangent violin (Elgar's instrument), and in the repeated semibreves which the rests in the Enigma theme invite, makes unusual but perfectly good Elgarian invertible two-part counterpoint with the Enigma theme over its bass; if it is 'for fuga', as the first sketch suggests, the combination will then repeat in the dominant, as the absence of an inked final B natural at the end of the sketch suggests (see music example 8):

Ex. 8

Other evidence confirms that there are two themes, minor and major, for the *Variations*, and the Enigma, which occupies the first page of the full score and is marked off with a double barline, is the first. E major (*pace* Bruckner) would have been an awkward orchestral key for the faster major passages and variations; but Elgar may have changed it deliberately. If the second theme is also played in E (major), its first two bars also have an octave EE in the bass, while its second two have a B, or in Elgar's cryptological use of German note-names, an H (for Helen?). Variation XIII, transposed into E major, would begin E, H, and the Finale EHE HEH EHE HEH EHE (twice): before dismissing this as idle fancy, see HEEC (Harriet Cohen unmistakably embracing EE) in *Letters of Edward Elgar*, op. cit., p.312, and also facing plate. There is much more to say about this aspect of the *Variations*, but that must await a later article.

148. A study of the rhymes employed by Tasso in G. Coen, *Rimario della Gerusalemme Liberata di Torquato Tasso* (1878) reveals that the poet, although he employed the form 'veggio' for 'vedo', always uses 'chiedo, richiedo' for 'chieggio, richieggio'; the altered version is thus unlikely to be his.

149. *Godfrey of Bulloign, or The Recovery of Jerusalem* (1600). Tasso's stanza runs:

> Colei Sofronia, Olindo egli s'appella,
> > D'una cittade entrambi, e d'una fede.
> Ei che modesto è sì, com' essa è bella,
> > Brama assai, poco spera, e nulla chiede;
> Nè sa scoprirsi, o non ardisce: ed ella
> > O lo sprezza, o nol vede, o non s'avvede.
> Così finora il misero ha servito
> > O non visto, o mal noto, o mal gradito.

150. November issue, vol.33, p.546. Elgar's rediscovery of these volumes from the early 1870s at his sister Pollie's in Stoke Prior '– very very amusing to read now & took me back to boyhood's *daze* – is described in a letter to Griffith of September 1916 (*Letters of Edward Elgar*, op. cit., p.222; see also p.233). The text of his early and unpublished *Rondeau*, 'If she love me', by 'R.C.G.', is taken from *Temple Bar*, December 1878, vol.54, p.572.

151. 'Tasso's life and genius', in *Stories from the Italian poets* (1846), London; see p.384.

152. 'She is a most angelic person & I should like to please her – there are few who deserve pleasing' (*Letters to Nimrod*, op. cit., p.44, March 24 [1899]). In 1898 Lady Mary was 29 years old, 'a lively intelligent creature, who, like her fellow 'variant' Winifred Norbury (according to the latter's niece) 'could keep him [Elgar] in order and make him work as well as amuse him . . . I believe she [Mrs Elgar] made these friendships with other women [including Florence Norbury and Dora Penny] – all young and attractive – who could do the parts she couldn't always manage': see Moore, *Edward Elgar*, op. cit., p.241, citing a letter of 1948 from Mrs Gertrude Sutcliffe (a Norbury niece) to Dr Roger Fiske.

153. This version is given in Kennedy (1982), op. cit., p.253.

154. British Library Add. MS. 47908, ff.87, 98.

155. Reference to Tasso's original will show that the next line neither fits the music nor makes sense on its own (see fn.149).

156. See Elgar's letters of 27 June and 30 June 1899, in *Elgar and his publishers*, op. cit., pp.127–9; the shorter original ending has its adherents, and Donald Tovey evidently found the revised coda too magniloquent.

157. *Edward Elgar*, op. cit., p.270.

158. Kennedy, op. cit., pp.31f., 97; Moore, *Edward Elgar*, op. cit., pp.96–8, 100–4 and see index; most valuably, Atkins, op. cit., pp.477–80: I have borrowed from all three, but have gratefully corrected my account from Dr K. E. L. Simmons' work (see n.161 and Envoi, p. 284).

159. Newman: see Kennedy, loc.cit., and also p.330. Burley and Carruthers, op. cit., pp.125–7.

160. *Letters of Edward Elgar*, op. cit., p.20; the letter was misdated (August for October). The phrase 'her lungs are affected I hear' seems to relate Helen Weaver's disease to her mother's consumption; perhaps Ivor Atkins' mention of 'asthma' in fact refers to this, though his informant was Elgar himself,

whose continuing contact with the Weaver family was Miss Weaver's brother Frank, a leading amateur violinist in Worcester.

161. As established by Dr K. E. L. Simmons, who has generously allowed me to read and profit from his excellent unpublished article 'The Weavers of Worcester: a preliminary history', as revised at 27 June 1988.

162. The sketch of the Violin Concerto that he presented to Alice Stuart Wortley and her husband, on the other hand, is (as she noted) 'signed and purposely antedated Feb. 7 1910' (Elgar Birthplace Library): here again it was the date of the initial impulse to compose the first movement that Elgar recorded. We may note here that Elgar appears to have used a quotation to record the loss of another lady once close to him, in British Library Add. MS. 63161 (f.17); in an entry probably dating from 1909, he has twice copied (and altered) an unattributed quotation that recalls the 'Song of Songs', adding '*Holloway/powyke*', which must refer to Miss Holloway, the pianist in the Asylum band, to whom he had dedicated one or two early pieces. It runs (deletions are given in brackets):

> "(At) In the time of the singing birds she was (dumb,) silent,
> (with) at the coming of the buds she was taken away"

163. *Letters to Nimrod*, op. cit., p.48.

164. She might also have mentioned Senta's ballad in *The Flying Dutchman* or, more appropriately, Beethoven's 'Lebewohl' sonata, or dozens of eighteenth-century cadential phrases; but this unjustifiable multiplication serves only to darken counsel. More to the point, she says (op. cit., p.125) that the quotation 'bore no reference to the liner and the sea voyage which were afterwards associated with this variation', meaning Lady Mary's voyage, and later suggests that 'at sea' was intended in a figurative sense; but she quotes the phrase 'at sea' from hearsay only, and seems not to have known of Helen Weaver's earlier voyage.

165. See n.163 above; and p.xix of the *Variations* in the Elgar Complete Edition.

166. Goethe: 'Geschwinde! Geschwinde!/Es teilt sich die Welle,/Es naht sich die Ferne,/Schon seh' ich das Land!': 'Quick! Quick!/We cleave the billows,/The distance grows nearer,/Already I see the land!' Goethe's poems *Meeres Stille* and *Glückliche Fahrt* date from 1795.

167. See the new edition cited above, pp.xvi–xvii.

168. op. cit., p.vii; Elgar originally wrote 'mood' for 'intention' (Elgar Birthplace Library, MS no.722).

169. Or vice-versa; but Dorabella's Intermezzo, of which she was so proud, may well antedate her first meeting with Elgar by seven or eight years. It is a true Intermezzo: it has almost nothing to do with the surrounding argument and contains 'only a trace' of the Theme (see Elgar's comment to Dora Penny in Powell, op. cit., (1947), p.15, note 1); it is designed to afford contrast and relief, and was at one point placed earlier in the sequence of movements, nearer the middle as no.VIII; one of Elgar's lists in the sketches makes this clear. He even proposed it (and it alone, at first) for separate publication. Its incipit appears, foreshortened to three notes, a rest and a barline, as the third movement – entitled 'Intermezzo' and in its proper key, though the signature is lacking – of a Suite in G for strings. This was the first of two such works that he was then planning (British Library Add. MS. 49974D, f.33). The first and second movements evidently existed in some form, for they were used as the Woodland Interlude in *Caractacus* and the opening section of the *Sérénade* (or *Intermezzo*) *Mauresque*, which argues that the Intermezzo had also been

sketched: no incipit is entered for the fourth movement, a finale. Elgar deleted the Intermezzo, adding the word 'No' and presumably deciding to save it up – to good purpose, if so. The tiny incipit, given as (1) below, corresponds to the triplet that he originally entered in his Table of incipits for the Variations, given as (2); this he later altered to (3), changing it yet again in the piano fair copy and the published version:

Ex. 9

170.   op. cit., p.xviii. We may also note here that the editors have omitted from consideration a source that contains corrections, namely the autograph fair copy of the piano arrangement of the *Variations*, which is in the Memorial Library of Music at Stanford University in California (MS No.298); as long ago as 1965, Emanuel Winternitz included a leaf from it – the opening of Variation XIII, as it happens – in his *Musical Autographs from Monteverdi to Hindemith* (2 vols., New York; plate 157 in vol.ii); the same library also possesses Elgar's fair copy of the violin-and-piano version of 'Liebesgruss' ('Salut d'Amour'), which describes this version as the 'original', 'Op.6', dedicated 'à X X X' and dated 'July 1888', all in Elgar's hand (MS No.295). It would also be useful to note here that the mysterious annotation '13ieme' referred to by the editors on p.xvii should in fact read 'Biz' (with a long 'z'), and refers to 'Ysobel'. The editors have not recorded that the same annotation is scribbled in pencil at the foot of the Table on f.6 of the sketches. This gives us a clue to Elgar's perversion of her forename: obviously, seeing her come into his study with a sheaf of proofs and interrupting some favourite non-musical pursuit, he must have exclaimed, Spooneristically, 'Biz! Oh 'ell!' Also of interest is the heading '2 secys' scribbled on the sketch for Variation VIII (W.N.), for it explains the long sequences of doubled sixths or thirds: the movement was at first intended as a double portrait of the joint secretaries of the Worcestershire Philharmonic Society, with Martina Hyde accompanying Winifred Norbury everywhere and making her laugh with her evidently droll wit at fig.31 (like Rosalind and Celia: 'And wheresoe'er we went, like Juno's swans,/Still we went coupled and inseparable').

171.   'Suddenly there opened an immense horizon of friendship and love and longing . . . this penultimate music took its composer too far from his innocent friendship and simple regret at Lady Mary Lygon's departure. He deleted her initials . . . ' (*Edward Elgar*, op. cit., p.264). It is not clear whether Dr Moore thinks that Lady Mary herself was the focal point of this immense horizon – Goethe's 'ungeheure Weite'? – or whether it was the memories of Helen Weaver's departure in 1885.

172.   op. cit., p.126.

173.   *Edward Elgar*, op. cit., p.265.

174.   From the redundant D flat in the first bar of Ex.4 we may deduce that Elgar originally wrote a crotchet rest between the two crotchets and forgot to

remove the second D flat when he added the two semiquavers; the up-beat group emphasizes the connection with the triumphantly self-assertive version of the same rhythm that cadences upward at fig.64.

175. *Elgar*, op. cit., p.157.

176. See *My friends pictured within*, Novello: London, n.d.; the Elgar Complete Edition, vol.27, op. cit. gives the draft notes on pp.vi–vii, but not the sometimes revealing deleted words and passages.

177. This important feature of the *Variations* is not always noticed. All now agree that Elgar is the lonely artist of the Theme, and Elgar wrote to F. G. Edwards not only to say that he had 'sketched "portraits" of my friends', but also that 'in each Variation I have "looked at" the theme *through* the personality (as it were) of another Johnny' (see Moore, *Elgar and his publishers*, op. cit., p.108; also his letter to Jaeger, ibid., p.95, in which the 'Grecian ghost' comes from Dryden's *Alexander's Feast*). He was not pleased with some of the advice – to lower his sights – that he received from his friends after *Caractacus*, at a time of great personal crisis: hence the mildly satirical tone of some of the portraits.

178. This Variation, above all, qualifies for the description 'an incident known only to two people' (in Elgar's comments for the first programme note by C. A. Barry): a further reason why Elgar could not explain its nature in public. We know that the portrait of Nimrod also reflects a long personal talk about Beethoven and the way he turned his tormented life into powerful art: Jaeger's variation would have resembled Lady Mary's even more if Elgar had carried out his original intention, as annotated in the first sketch, to introduce the Theme itself, 'mesto', in C minor (perhaps in the form used in *The Music Makers?*) as a short interlude. This may have given Elgar the idea for his use of the Mendelssohn theme in Variation XIII.

179. Atkins, op. cit., pp.465f.; Burley, op. cit., p.127.

180. Article in *The Sunday Times*, 18 November 1956, cited in Kennedy, op. cit., pp.96f.

181. See Kennedy, op. cit., p.123, citing Newman's article in *The Sunday Times*, 23 October, 1955.

182. *Letters to Nimrod*, op. cit., p.9. It was in writing *Caractacus* that he stumbled on both the bass to the Enigma theme and the second theme in the major. The former, which he must have realized had a strong affinity with the passacaglia of Brahms' Fourth Symphony, makes triple invertible counterpoint (of the 'Meistersinger' variety) with the Enigma theme and the octave pedal and, since it is a fugato, obligingly moves to the dominant minor (see music example 10); in *Caractacus* it is the first theme heard, is introduced beneath a tonic pedal, and would presumably have formed the basis for the Prelude originally planned; Elgar may have mused ironically on the words, since he felt that at least some of the 'comrades' (friends pictured within) had let him down; the divergent bass progression B:B flat:A in bar 4 occurs in 'Nimrod'. The words of music example 11 would also have affected him ironically if he were thinking of the past, but evoked from him a tune that was much too good for the single statement in *Caractacus*.

183. *Elgar and his publishers*, op. cit., pp.67f.

184. Moore, *Edward Elgar*, p.249.

185. See Moore, *Edward Elgar*, op. cit., p.340, note 167; W. W. Skeat's edition for Clarendon Press Series, Oxford, 7th edition, 1893.

186. ibid., p.341.

187. See pp.192ff

188. *The Cambridge University Reporter*, 27 November 1900, p.265.

Ex. 10

* *Caractacus*, vocal score, p. 11, fig. 13, transposed and note-values doubled.

Ex. 11

* *Caractacus*, vocal score, p. 182, fig. 48.

189.   Moore, *Elgar and his publishers*, op. cit., p.265.
190.   ibid., p.273. I suspect that the cryptic 'I read it in 2d Toobe night and morning' should really be 'in ye Toobe' (with a medieval 'thorn', imitating Langland's orthography).
191.   Facsimile in Moore, *Elgar: a life in photographs*, op. cit., p.36.
192.   *The Daily Telegraph*, 22 June 1901, cited in Moore, *Edward Elgar*, op. cit., p.349.
193.   British Library Add. MS. 63154, f.48v, headed 'Cockaigne No.2 *City of defl night*'.
194.   ibid., f.49v, marked 'begin (Cockaigne no II, *deleted*) The [Last] Judgement'; the idea is treated in diminution on f.49, marked 'cry'. This was the theme, by then destined for the Third Symphony, that the dying composer thrust into W. H. Reed's hand, saying 'with tears streaming down his cheeks . . . "Billy, this is the end."' It is given in fascimile as Ex.23 on p.223 of Reed, *Elgar as I knew him*, op. cit.; see also p.179.
195.   See the introductory memoir by Bertram Dobell in his edition of *The poetical works of James Thomson*, 2 vols, London, 1895.
196.   Section XIV.
197.   There are many sketches for 'Callicles', first intended as a scena for bass (Plunket Greene?) and orchestra, later for mezzo-soprano (Muriel Foster); he worked on it from c.1905 or earlier to 1927. Was 'Callicles' in fact the 'beautiful

Scena from Greek Anthology – beautiful idea' that Elgar was thinking about in July 1917? – for no poem in the Anthology really answers to this description (see Young, *Elgar, O.M.*, op. cit., p.186, footnote 1, quoting Lady Elgar's diary).

198. See Everyman edition of *The poems of Matthew Arnold, 1840 to 1866*, London, 1908, pp.4f.

199. Letter to Gorton of 17 July 1903: see Young, *Letters of Edward Elgar*, op. cit., p.121; the previous letter describes Judas' scena as 'a bitter, lonely soliloquy'.

200. See p.187.

201. Michel de Montaigne, Essais, Paris, Garnier-Flammarion, 1969, ii, p.219. Montaigne does not adapt or translate the Latin (see Moore, op. cit., p.317), and the very accurate translation is entirely Florio's.

202. Letter to Kilburn of 29 March 1898, cited in Moore, op. cit., p.234: 'it "flows on somehow" like the other best of me'.

203. Atkins, op. cit., p.289, a letter of 23 September 1918: 'it's the best of me'.

204. *Sesame and Lilies*, 4th edn., 1867, p.20 (see Moore, op. cit., p.323).

205. See above, n.77.

206. See n.204 above. The same lecture contrasts the harshness shown to petty thieves with the leniency shown to bankrupts and failed bankers, condemns the scandal of the Opium Wars, attacks the principle of inherited wealth (pointing out that you cannot have that 'great production', the English gentleman, 'but by sacrifice of much contributed life'), and tells the Church of England to stop chasing after rituals and the trappings of the theatrical property-man and learn to 'look after Lazarus on the doorstep'; and much else besides.

207. *A future for English music . . .* , op. cit., p.87 and elsewhere.

208. See p.197.

209. He completed only three, 'The Rapid Stream' and 'The Woodland Stream' in 1932, 'When Swallows Fly' in 1933; Maine, *Works*, op. cit., p.254, reports that there were to have been twenty-four, all to poems by Charles Mackay, and this is borne out by Elgar's copy of his *Poetical Works* (reprint of Chandos Classics edition of 1876), purchased in 1932, in which twenty-one further poems are marked up for setting (Birthplace Library). Three other such songs, composed in 1914(?) were published in the USA and perhaps later on in Canada; these I have not seen, though a sketch for Allingham's 'Windlass Song' is to be found in British Library, Add. MS. 63160 at f.63v, and another, possibly for one of the others, on f.64 (and see Moore, *Elgar and his publishers*, op. cit., p.814).

210. *Letters to Nimrod*, op. cit., p.2 (Bridge's *The flag of England*) and p.110.

211. In *The Queen of the Air* (London, 1869), section 42, Ruskin blasts out of the water the following opinion, cited without the author's name (Mrs Emilia F.S. Pattison) from p.153 of *The Westminster Review* for January 1869: 'This so persuasive art is the only one that has no didactic efficacy, that engenders no emotions save such as are without issue on the side of moral truth, that expresses nothing of God, nothing of reason, nothing of human liberty.'

212. See *A future for English music . . .* , op. cit., pp.150–5, 167–73.

213. Maine, *Life*, op. cit., p.56; Moore, *Edward Elgar*, op. cit., p.120 – but Gordon was hardly a 'high Anglican'.

214. Moore, op. cit., p.90 (1881); according to the index, the 'Fr Bellasis' mentioned on p.290 (1899) was Henry's elder brother Richard; Young (*Elgar, O.M.*, op. cit., pp.84, 88) simply says 'Fr Bellasis' both times, adding that he was a musician.

215. Moore, op. cit., p.296.

216. Young, op. cit., p.88.

217. First and third editions under this title, London, 1864, 1873; second edition as *History of my religious opinions*, ibid., 1865.

218. *Discourses on the scope and nature of university education*, Dublin, 1852; *The scope and nature of university education*, London, 1859; *The idea of a University defined and illustrated*, London, 1873.

219. The Birthplace Library contains two books on Newman presented to Elgar by their authors on publication, presumably in acknowledgement of his special interest: Alexander Whyte's *Newman: an appreciation in two lectures* (New York, 1902) and William Barry, *Newman* (London, 1904). Elgar also set Newman's 'They are at rest' as a memorial elegy for Queen Victoria, performed in January 1910 (from *Lyra Apostolica*, p.62 of 1879 edition; no doubt he noticed that Newman had adapted it from 'Enoch and Elias', *Verses on religious subjects*, Dublin, 1853, p.47). See also n.242 below.

220. I quote the latest text of 1873, here differing only slightly from the earlier versions. See also Chapter xvi of *Loss and gain*, pt. ii (1848).

221. Mary Frances Baker, later Dora Penny's stepmother, had prepared an oratorio text from St Augustine's *Civitas Dei* in 1894, to form the third part of Elgar's trilogy (Moore, *Elgar and his publishers*, op. cit., pp.512f.). Elgar would certainly have read so famous a book as *The confessions of St Augustine* and noted Chapter 33, 'Concerning temptations arising from love of sweet music'; I quote from the anonymous revised translation published in The Ancient and Modern library of Theological Literature, London, 1886, pp.213f.

222. See Moore, *Elgar and his publishers*, op. cit., pp.189 ('rather an Agnostic than anything else') and 191.

223. June 1908: *Letters to Nimrod*, op. cit., p.275.

224. ibid., pp.256f.

225. British Library, Add. MS. 47904B, f.76. Matthias, mentioned in the passage leading up to the chorus in question, was the new apostle chosen to take Judas' place.

226. ibid., pp.218, 262f.

227. Letters of Edward Elgar, op. cit., pp.120f.; Elgar and his publishers, op. cit., pp.463, 500.

228. ibid., p.645.

229. *Apologia pro vita sua*, op. cit., 1873 ed., chapters i–iv.

230. See p.188. I have not found time to explore the significance of Elgar's reading of Renan, who had trained as a priest but left the Catholic church in 1845, becoming an anti-clerical and devoting his life to an attempt to show how intellectuals such as scientists, historians and mythologists might help the masses to find their way back to 'the hidden god'. The plan at least, of the first volumes of his *Histoire des origines du christianisme*, seems to relate to Elgar's scheme for the oratorio trilogy: *Vie de Jésus* (1863), *Les Apôtres* (1868), *Saint Paul* (1869), *L'Antéchrist* (1873).

231. Kennedy, op. cit., p.206.

232. See his valuable essay *Providence and art: a study in Elgar's religious beliefs*, London, Elgar Society, n.d., p.8; the sentence from which I quote was underlined by Elgar in W. H. Pinnock's *An analysis of New Testament history*; but Elgar did not need to be told of the significance to a Catholic of Matthew xvi, 16–19 – what he was noting, surely, was a possible cause of controversy. Hodgkins does not mention Elgar's letter to Randall Davidson.

233. Maine, *Life*, op. cit., p.115.

234. Young, *Elgar, O.M.*, op. cit., p.230. But see Kennedy, op. cit., p.131, which might conceivably suggest that Elgar's letter was a subtle reproof to the Archbishop.

235. 'How I became a socialist', *Justice* (1894) and as pamphlet (1896), here cited from *William Morris: News from Nowhere and Selected writings and designs*, ed. with an introduction by Asa Briggs, London and Harmondsworth, Penguin Books (1962), Penguin Classics reprint (1986), p.36.

236. G.B. Shaw, 'William Morris', *The Daily Chronicle*, 20 April 1899, quoting an unnamed essay of c.1895, here cited from *Pen portraits and reviews*, London (1931), revised Standard Edition (1932), p.203.

237. *A future for English music*, op. cit., p.199; *The Earthly Paradise* (1868–70), introductory poem and 'L'Envoi'. Elgar actually set to music six lines by Morris as a song with refrain written in 1916 for Gervase Elwes and the 'Fight for Right' movement (a patriotic, anti-German association); they are taken from the newly-awakened Brynhild's advice to Sigurd in Book ii (Regin) of *The story of Sigurd the Volsung and the fall of the Niblungs* (1876) and condemn the notion that one may do evil that good may ensue: the gods are not dead, and the idealist must fight for the right.

> When thou hearest the fool rejoicing, and he saith, 'It is over and past,
> And the wrong was better than right, and hate turns into love at the last,
> And we strove for nothing at all, and the Gods are fallen asleep;
> For so good is the world a growing that the evil good shall reap:'
> Then loosen thy sword in the scabbard and settle the helm on thine head,
> For men betrayed are mighty, and great are the wrongfully dead.

238. *Letters to Nimrod*, op. cit., pp.109f.; Kennedy, op. cit., p.261.

239. *Letters of Edward Elgar*, op. cit., p.187. Moore (op. cit., p.537) prints an extract from one of the otherwise unpublished letters to Newman that Elgar enclosed with his note: doubtless their influence was at work in Newman's review (*The Birmingham Daily Post*, 4 December 1908, cited in Moore, op. cit., p.546), which says that 'The work has profited by all his varied experience of life' and speaks of the 'tempered philosophical strength' of the first and last movements, a quality which 'suggests Gerontius with a difference – a Gerontius who instead of dying has continued to live and is all the better for the agony of spirit he has been through'.

240. *Letters to Nimrod*, op. cit., p.262.

241. Bodleian Library, Oxford, MS Mus. b. 32.

242. Information gratefully received from Mr Raymond Monk, who owns the score. (He also possesses Elgar's copy of Burns, '*full* of markings and comment', and Frederic Chapman's small edition of a selection of J. H. Newman's poetry (London, 1905), dedicated by Chapman to Elgar, in which the composer has noted on the flyleaf 'page 103 (Einstein)', referring to the words 'That Space is a name, and that Time is a dream', underlined in the poem 'Reverie on a journey: to my mother' (private letter of 1 August 1988)).

243. On p.88. Elgar would also have noticed 'The tidings to Olaf' on pp.124–37; the two are also in *Poems* (London, 1904), ii, pp.234–6 and 268–73, and on 277–83 an Ode on the coronation of King Edward VII; Elgar would also have appreciated the lovely 'A windflower' in Carman's *Low tide on Grand Pré* (London, 1893), p.19.

244. op. cit., p.172. Moore, op. cit., p.339 also notes, of the Trio tune, 'perhaps it sounds his own "Recessional" '.

245. Moore, op. cit., p.338.

246. Dr Moore, however, does not miss this (op. cit., p.352).

247. op. cit., p.289.

248. Elgar, op. cit., p.150.

249. J.B.L. Warren, 3rd Lord de Tabley, also used the pseudonyms 'George F. Preston' and 'William Lancaster' in publishing some of his poetry.

250. op. cit., p.159.

251. op. cit., p.213.

252. ibid., p.161; but see note 277 below.

253. op. cit., p.363.

254. *Poems and essays of Charles Lamb*, The Chandos Classics, London n.d. [before 1892], Sonnets II–IV, pp.5f.; for dating, see *The letters of Charles Lamb*, Everyman edition (reprinting text of W. Macdonald from Lamb's *Works*, 1903) (1909), pp.4–5.

255. *The letters*, op. cit., pp.47f.

256. 'Written a year after the events (September 1797)', *Poems and essays*, op. cit., p.23.

257. ibid., p.25.

258. Atkins, op. cit., p.251: 'But the birth of a New Year is of an interest too wide to be pretermitted by king or cobbler'.

259. The italics are Elgar's. The essay continues, curiously enough, with a reference to the passage in Virgil where Elgar had found his epigraph for another and sterner dream, that of Gerontius: ' . . . and must wait upon the tedious shores of Lethe millions of ages before we have existence and a name'. See above, p.228. Elgar again used Lamb's phrase 'what might have been' in describing another perfect miniature 'dream-picture' that muses tenderly and regretfully on lost youth, Falstaff's dream of his days as 'page to the Duke of Norfolk' (*Falstaff, The Musical Times*, 1 September, 1913; see Novello reprint, n.d., pp.11f.).

260. See n.161 above.

261. Moore, op. cit., p.363.

262. Moore, *Elgar and his publishers*, op. cit., pp.673f. Elgar noted the origin of some of the music on f.66v of British Library Add. MS. 47903 as 'Song [deleted] Sorrowful Child's Suite'.

263. op. cit., p.247.

264. See above, p.213

265. For Elgar's pride, see *Letters of Edward Elgar*, op. cit., p.139 (it would indeed have gone better in Italian); Newman, *Elgar*, op. cit., pp.123f., condemns the 'Procrustean' prosody.

266. *Letters of Edward Elgar*, op. cit., p.201; Dr Moore (*Edward Elgar*, op. cit., p.587) gives the reading I follow, slightly different in the use of brackets and underlinings, but omitting the Spanish.

267. Moore, loc. cit.

268. *Works*, op. cit., p.141.

269. op. cit., p.480.

270. Elgar Birthplace Library.

271. Diana M. McVeagh, *Edward Elgar: his life and music* (London (1955), p.53) was the first to take up Newman's article in *The Sunday Times*, 21 May 1939; see also Kennedy, op. cit., p.234. Moore, op. cit., p.587, opines that the dots 'might stand for numbers of names, or for one'; Young, op. cit., p.335, suggests 'not one specific soul, but a composite spirit'. In this, arguing from his musical examples 45 and 46, he would include Adela Schuster; but his Ex.46, transcribed from British Library Add. MS. 63161, f.8v (but omitting

Elgar's improvements) was designed for a quite different work entitled 'The Soul', based on Sir John Davies' 'Of the soul of man; and the immortality thereof', the second part of his famous philosophical poem *Nosce teipsum* (1599); Elgar copies stanzas 4 and 5 around the music, and also quoted them, with stanza 6, in a letter to Miss Schuster of 11 June 1932, when he sent her the sketch of '25 years ago' (*Letters of Edward Elgar*, op. cit., pp.309f.); this would place the original in 1907. See also British Library Add. MSS. 63157, f.18v (a torn copy of the same music) and 63162, among the 'Crown of India' sketches, ff.3v ('Nosce teipsum/Davies/ 5 flats § or $\frac{6}{4}$ slow/Very serious indeed/ Nosce teipsum/for this see other book') and f.12 (reversed: 'All this is quite good enough for something/serious/Nosce teipsum'). The work was apparently to have been a symphony, if I read Add. 63161 correctly: 'Sym is about poem'.

272. See fns.266–7; but Dr Young gives four dots after '*the soul of*' in *Elgar, O.M.*, op. cit., p.335, while Kennedy, op. cit., p.234, expands them to five!

273. The correct orthography would be 'el alma de la anémona': the feminine 'alma' takes 'el' because the initial vowel is stressed, Professor Jack Sage informs me, whereas that of 'anémona', being unstressed, does not require 'del' before it.

274. Moore, op. cit., p.586, offers W. E. Henley's *Echoes* (1872–89) as a source, where Elgar may indeed have noted the use of the phrase as an epigraph; Henley seems to have interested Elgar, perhaps because he was born in nearby Gloucester. Kennedy, op. cit., p.233, cites Oliver Wendell Holmes' *The autocrat of the breakfast table*. I have already noted (see fn.76) that Carlyle refers to the passage at the end of Bk.I, Chapter iii of *Sartor resartus*, where he corrects Le Sage's unlikely 'Garcias': 'does not his Soul [Diogenes Teufelsdröckh's] lie enclosed in the remarkable volume, much more truly than Pedro Garcia's did in the buried Bag of Doubloons?'

275. *Letters of Edward Elgar*, op. cit., p.233.

276. See p.201.

277. Her letter of bequest, dated 27 March 1927, is also at the Birthplace; it tells us that the portrait was painted in 1887, when she was twenty-five (it is reproduced in monochrome in Kennedy, op. cit., f.p.160); and that 'Everything is carefully put together in the years from 1905 until the present as given to me', which suggests a concrete date for the beginning of their closer association. Unreferenced material in the following discussion is all from her bequest in the Birthplace Library.

278. It does not seem plausible that Alice Stuart Wortley herself should have doctored the records of an association that she was proud of and wished to place, eventually, in the public domain. MS 57, the opening of *Sospiri* (called 'Absence') has been shorn of its inscription, and on MS 49, a quotation from *The Music Makers*, dated 'May 15 1912/the complete understanding', erasing fluid appears to have been used. Clare Stuart Wortley added to the collection some notes on the Violin Concerto (1940), extracts from her father's diary, and there are two letters from her to Carice Elgar Blake dated 3 and 16 March 1936 whose aim appears to be to record for posterity an entirely 'proper' account of her mother's relationship with Elgar at the time of the Violin Concerto.

279. op. cit., p.569.

280. op. cit., p.568. The theme derives from a prominent new idea in the Finale of the *Variations*, Op.36.

281. See *Elgar as I knew him*, op. cit., p.154.

282. op. cit., p.578 (but the poem is not a sonnet). Elgar also set Watson's best-known poem, *April*, but used it up in *The Spanish Lady* (Young, op. cit., p.372).

283. op. cit., pp.569f., 764.
284. There is also in the Birthplace Library an envelope with dead flowers in it, inscribed in Alice Stuart Wortley's handwriting 'Wild (Roses) Flowers from the hedge surrounding the house where Edward Elgar was born Broadheath Worcestershire picked June 26 1920'. (She must have gone there without Elgar: see Moore, op. cit., p.756).
285. Moore, op. cit., p.699.
286. Elgar Birthplace Library.
287. op. cit., p.558 (but Elgar's copy is dated 'October 1908'); for the work on the Concerto, p.555; on the Symphony, p.556; on p.559 Dr Moore traces thematic relationships between the Songs and the Concerto.
288. As well as the Op.59 Songs, he marked the following two poems for setting: 'Aloes and myrrh' (pp.100ff.), in which the poet promises his dead love to 'Weave you a chaplet of song' (stanzas 2–4 are marked 'omit'); 'The last dream' (p.117), in which the poet dreams a peaceful death (stanza 2 is marked 'omit', after which 'repeat 1 & end', omitting 4). Elgar ticked a poem commemorating the death of W. E. Henley (p.131), but made no note against 'Inside the bar' (pp.123f.), added to 'The Fringes of the Fleet' in 1917.
289. Folio references (and page references to Parker's book) are: f.14, 'The Waking' (p.98); ff.19v–20, 'Twilight', Op.59 no.6 (p.112, 'The Twilight of Love'); ff.42v, 45, 'Oh Soft was the Song', Op.59 no.3 (p.5, 'At Sea'); ff.43v–44, 'Proem' (p.xi); f.44, 'There is an Orchard' (pp.69f.); f.44v, 'Was it Some Golden Star', Op.59 no.5 (p.12).
290. MSS 107, 108, 109 respectively.
291. See Moore, op. cit., p.745.
292. At one point he thought of substituting 'from the Ukraine': see British Library Add. MSS. 58026–8. Perhaps his thoughts were turned to Russia and Eastern Europe by Mrs Rosa Newmarch's translations of Minsky and Maikov, to which he turned in 1914 for Opp.72 and 73: they were published in *Horae amoris* in 1903, and Maikov's 'Love's tempest', Op.73, no.1, is subtitled 'A modern Greek song'.
293. Dr Moore conjectures that the enigmatic place-name 'LEYRISCH-TURASP' appended to 'The river' is an anagram of 'PETRUS HAS[E] LYRIC' (p.571), but anagrams ought to be perfect, and 'Hase' is German for hare, not rabbit (Kaninchen). It might better stand for 'TRULY A.S.'S CIPHER' . . .
294. See Moore, op. cit., pp.561f. The image of the Torch may, however, be a fusion of both Elgar's loves: if he had looked up 'Helena' in the *O.E.D.*, he would have noticed that 'helene' is Greek for 'torch'.
295. See Moore, op. cit., pp.572f. A diary of this tour survives, but I have not yet been able to consult it.
296. See n.132 above.
297. Moore, op. cit., p.536. The page is headed '*Sunday*/21 Augt 1904', which stands between two deletions; the quotation and autograph signature at the foot are dated 1905 (see facsimile of British Library Add.MS 47907A, f.87, in Elgar Complete Edition, vol.30, London, 1981, *Symphony No.1*, edd. J.N. Moore and C. Kent, p.[2]). Arthur Bliss found this theme, and indeed the whole movement, a particular revelation of Elgar's personality: 'whenever I hear the Slow movement . . . I see the man: especially do I see a clear-cut image of him in the final bars' (Moore, op. cit., p.537).
298. ibid., p.610.

299. *A future for English music*, op. cit., p.[98]. Elgar's own notes for this lecture are sketchy: it is a pity that the report from *The Birmingham Post* was not reprinted in full.

300. From Newman's article, like subsequent quotations; reprinted ibid., pp.105f.; see also Newman, *Elgar*, op. cit., Appendix, and fn.82 above. See also *A future* . . . , pp.205, 207 (13 December 1905): 'I still look upon music which exists without any poetic or literary basis as the true foundation of our art . . . absolute music [is] the real staple of our art'; 'the Symphony without a programme is the highest development of art'.

301. The earlier volumes: 4 vols., Berlin, 1904–14.

302. Moore, op. cit., p.473.

303. ibid., p.537.

304. *Letters of Edward Elgar*, op. cit., pp.186f.

305. ibid., p.186; he had just completed the First Symphony.

306. 'I have written out my soul in the [violin] concerto, Sym. II & the Ode & you know it', he wrote to 'Windflower' on 29 August 1912, 'in these three works I have *shewn* myself' (Kennedy, op. cit., p.254).

307. *Elgar and his publishers*, op. cit., pp.741f. (13 April 1911).

308. *Edward Elgar*, op. cit., p.509 (9 May 1911); this too one would like to see published in full.

309. The Spirit of Delight, 'with the joyous and the free', might perhaps shy away from pain, but would it 'scoff' at it? What kind of Pity would 'cut away/Those cruel wings'? Does 'thou lovest' rhyme with 'new leaves dressed'? And surely he would on revision have replaced 'almost' and 'may be', present merely for the rhyme, in stanza 6.

310. Moore, op. cit., p.604.

311. Elgar at some time between 1901 and 1912 planned and partly sketched a set of three songs for women's voices and instruments on poems whose theme is the death and burial of Love, all (like his song *After*) from Philip Bourke Marston's *Song-tide* (1871): I 'Love has turned his face away' (pp.303f.), II *Love lies a-dying*, 'Come in gently, and speak low' (pp.304–6), and III 'Now we stand above Love's grave' (pp.306f.): these may have been the 'ladies' trios' of 1901 (*Elgar and his publishers*, op. cit., pp.303f.); see British Library, Add. MSS. 63154, ff.55v–6 (I); ibid., ff.53v–4 and 47903, f.53v (II); 63154 ff.54v–5 and 63162, f.12 (III). Elgar acquired a secondhand copy of Marston's *Song-tide* (1871) in Birmingham in 1880 (Young, op. cit., p.250); *After* (1895) is also about the death of love; if Elgar composed it with Helen Weaver in mind, one may take, perhaps, a more charitable view of his rudeness when a young singer offered to perform it for him at a soirée in 1904: 'A while 'twas given/To me to have thy love;/Now, like a ghost, alone I move/About a ruined heaven' (see Kennedy, op. cit., p.299 and Moore, op. cit., p.449).

312. British Library Add. MSS. 63159, f.31v (without Poe's name), followed by a lacuna of two leaves torn out, which may have contained more of the setting; also 63160, f.23, textless, among sketches for *The Kingdom* (2 bars after fig.60, v.s., p.58). For the responsible artist as 'the heir of Israfel' see *A future for English Music* p.118.

313. Cited in Moore, *Edward Elgar*, op. cit., p.598, presumably from his letter of 29 January 1911 (see n.314).

314. ibid., p.603.

315. Kennedy, op. cit., p.246.

316. *Works*, op. cit., p.167.

317. McVeagh, op. cit., p.166; Mrs M. D. Gairdner (ed.) gives the letter (undated) on pp.157f., the appreciation on pp.158–73. Mr Raymond Monk now possesses Elgar's presentation copy of the volume.

318. op. cit., p.608.

319. op. cit., p.247.

320. See ns.318 and 319. Moore cites the longer version from Shore's *The orchestra speaks* (London, 1938, p.135), Kennedy the later one from *Sixteen symphonies* (London, 1949, p.329).

321. E. F. Benson, *Final edition: informal autobiography* (London, 1940, posthumously published, pp.141f.); Benson visited Henry James at Rye on the same occasion, whose death on 28 February 1916 provides a limiting date. Only W. H. Reed has ever mentioned the 'Air songs' (*Elgar*, op. cit., p.127); Benson reveals that there were four of them, 'on the subject of flying, air-raids, and travel by air', composed for solo voice, chorus and orchestra and intended to be performed at the Coliseum; but Elgar 'had some disagreement about terms with the management, and bundled them into a drawer, refusing to take any further steps about them'. That is no doubt what Elgar told Benson; but in an undated note at the Birthplace Library, Carice Elgar Blake informed Clare Stuart Wortley that the songs were destroyed because her mother disliked the words.

322. Facsimiles in Elgar Complete Edition, vol.31: *Symphony No.2*, ed. R. Anderson and J. N. Moore (London, 1984), pp.x–xi; see also Moore, *Edward Elgar*, op. cit., pp.421f.

323. In his notes for Mrs Newmarch: see fn.307 above. There is another haunted garden in the background of the partsong 'Evening scene' (1905), a setting of stanzas 31–33 of Coventry Patmore's *The river*, but at the time of composition Elgar did not know that the charming landscape of the river concealed the suicide of a disappointed suitor, for he found the three stanzas that he set excerpted on their own in the anthology *A treasury: The Ancoats brotherhood*, ed. Charles Rowley (Manchester, 1904), p.20; copy at Birthplace Library (not in British Library); see *Letters of Edward Elgar*, op. cit., p.146.

324. Moore, op. cit., p.601 (Terry's visit was on 3 January 1911).

325. Young, op. cit., pp.46f.; at first merely a player, he succeeded to the post of Band Instructor in January 1879.

326. op. cit., p.236; Moore, op. cit., p.605, does not reproduce Elgar's underlining of the last six words.

327. See Moore, *Elgar and his publishers*, op. cit., p.235; but a local newspaper report said that 'those of the unfortunate inmates who were able to be present had not lost the faculty of enjoyment, and they were not the least hearty with their applause' (Young, loc. cit.).

328. The surviving compositions that he associated with Helen Weaver, which presumably document their continuing relationship, are 'Shed No.2', which Elgar annotated 'Nelly Shed' (1878), the *Nelly* Polka (1881) and another Polka, *Helcia* (1883); the Polkas were probably both intended for Powick, since in signing the last-named he described himself as 'composer in ordinary to The W[orcester] C[ity] & C[ounty] L[unatic] A[sylum]' (Moore, op. cit., pp.77, 92, 101). Helen, or Nelly, was actually mis-spelt as 'Hellen' on her birth registration, as Dr Simmons has shown (see fn.161 above).

329. Information kindly supplied by Mr Raymond Monk, who now owns the catalogue.

330. Elgar's reply to Troyte Griffith when he 'asked Elgar once what his Cello Concerto meant' (typescript notes by the latter at Birthplace Library).

331. For example, Dr K. E. L. Simmons' study of *The Starlight Express* in *Elgar Studies* (Aldershot, 1990), and Dr C. J. Kent's work on *Falstaff*.

332. In a paper for the Royal Musical Association, November 1988.

333. Letter to Percy Pitt, 16 May 1928: 'I have given the *pilgrim* a good trial & find it will *not* go as I wish: I fear the want of scenery, view, or whatever, the listeners-in do not get.' (British Library, MS Egerton 3303, f.51). This would have been in the first place a radio opera for the BBC, where Pitt was then Director of Music.

334. See Sir A. C. Mackenzie, *A musician's narrative* (London, 1927), p.204 (other references to Elgar on pp.205, 240); it was offered to Sullivan (d.1900), Messager, Massenet, Liza Lehmann and Mackenzie besides Elgar, 'who gave no reason for refusal'.

335. British Library Add. MSS. 49974C, f.2 ('Arden') and 63154, f.14 ('Touchsto[ne] in E').

336. *A future for English music*, op. cit., p.283.

337. *Decameron*: Moore, op. cit., p.377. Elgar said of *Rabelais*, according to Griffith, that 'It got so far that Covent Garden said they would put it on. But Lady Elgar didn't like it and so [deleted] he gave it up. I asked him years later what had become of "Rabelais". He said "It's been used up."' (Birthplace Library, typescript). *Rabelais* appears to date back as far as *c*.1897, according to Rosa Burley (op. cit., p.101), when Elgar discussed it with Prof. Rapson, Cambridge Professor of Sanskrit and Keeper of Indian coins at the British Museum. (One of Elgar's anthologies, still in the Birthplace Library, was *Fables and proverbs from the Sanskrit being the Hitopadese*, trans. C. Williams, intro. by H. Morley, London, 1885: did he arm himself with it for his dinner with Rapson?)

338. British Library Add. MS. 63154, f.12; 'Hudibras' is deleted and 'Falstaff' added, but the idea was not in the end used in the latter.

339. Identifiable from three words of text, 'brillig & th[e]', of which the first is luckily unique to its inventor; set for solo voice and orchestra (British Library, Add. MS. 63159, f.32). Elgar had earlier rejected Jaeger's suggestion of a mock-heroic cantata on 'The Jabberwock', because it would not sell: 'the English never take to anything of that sort – treated mock-heroically' (*Elgar and his publishers*, op. cit., pp.104f.: letter of 27 January [1899]).

340. British Library Add. MSS. 63154, f.52 (deleted, no music); 63156, ff.12f., with cross-reference to the above, annotated 'Masque' (*Crown of India*) and [?] 'Phalanstery' (a socialist grouping in Fourier), followed by 'Falstaff' material.

341. Tree's idea: letter quoted in Maine, *Life*, op. cit., pp.173f.

342. Ibid., p.173 (Tree's ' "Beethoven" production, in the preparation of which Elgar had given some assistance') and p.207 (Elgar went 'so far as to write part of a play for which . . . he was highly commended by Tree'). The play, heavily altered and adapted from René Fauchois' *Beethoven* (1909), remains unpublished; the English adapter's recollections do not mention Elgar, but he would have been the ideal adviser, and no other production of Tree's would have needed his expertise: 'Beethoven was shown in the act of composing, of thinking out a composition . . . We went to Beethoven's own sketchbooks for our material . . . in which he jotted down germs of musical thought during his solitary walks; erased them; turned them this way and that; until he found the one right way' (L. N. Parker, 'A tribute', in *Herbert Beerbohm Tree . . .* , ed. Max Beerbohm, London, [1920], p.210).

343. Moore, *Edward Elgar*, op. cit., p.225: to his own libretto?

344. Kennedy, op. cit., p.176 (but Rosa Burley, op. cit., p.160, is surely correct in

observing that Strauss would not have been able to identify the English pronunciation of 'Job' with the German name 'Hiob', pronounced 'HEE-op').

345. Its cover, with the title 'The High Tide' and opening bar (?), scored for double woodwind and strings, survive in British Library Add. MS. 57995 as ff.88 and 87v respectively (both reversed) in the draft vocal score of *King Olaf*; the former has a line of text just discernible as 'And all the world was in the sea' (Last line of stanza 16); on f.85 (rev.) is 'Play up "the Brides of Enderby"' and a bell-motif mingling Wagner's *Parsifal* bells with one of Siegfried's themes: the mayor calls for this warning chime at the end of stanza 1. The heading 'Enderby', heavily deleted and replaced by 'Ynys Llochtyn', occurs above themes copied into the beginning (ff.1–2) of Add. MS. 63153, presumably in 1901, and the appearance of the lines 'The waters laid thee at his door' and 'Down drifted to thy dwelling place', from stanza 19 of Ingelow's poem, shows that motives as important in *The Apostles* as 'Light and Life', 'Morning Glory' and 'Fellowship' may have had their origins in *The high tide* (I am indebted to Mr Jeremy Summerly for pointing this out). More may be discovered, since the British Library has kindly agreed to separate certain of the pages pasted together by Elgar in Add. MS. 57995.

346. See Moore, op. cit., pp.169, 355, 367, and *Elgar and his publishers*, op. cit., pp.351f. For Kilburn's unsuccessful request on behalf of the Middlesbrough Festival, see Foreman, *From Parry to Britten*, op. cit., p.14 (June 7 1902): 'I am, when permitted, engaged on mightier stuff'.

347. See Moore, *Elgar and his publishers*, op. cit., p.64.

348. op. cit., p.408.

349. *Letters to Nimrod*, op. cit., facing p.77, and Moore, *Elgar and his publishers*, op. cit., pp.373, 375, identifying the house.

350. The apparently full account in Atkins, op. cit., pp.70ff., does not mention Vine Hall, but Elgar's suspicions are apparent in a letter of [31 July 1903]: see Moore, op. cit., p.463.

351. Moore, op. cit., pp.36–9; Vine Hall was a minor composer, a local music critic and a competent conductor who directed first performances of Elgar works in 1883 and 1888: his differences with the composer were apparently doctrinal, not personal or artistic (see Moore, *Edward Elgar*, op. cit., pp.99, 124, 144, 182).

352. Atkins, op. cit., p.174; in the end, his earlier 'Hymn of Faith' (to a libretto by Elgar) was performed (p.183), so he presumably composed nothing new.

353. See pp.239 and 255.

354. Among many examples, see Newman, *Elgar*, op. cit., pp.119f.; Dunhill, *Sir Edward Elgar*, op. cit., p.188; McVeagh, op. cit., pp.137ff.

355. *Letters to Nimrod*, op. cit., p.273.

356. Ibid., p.153 (about S. Childs Clarke's coronation hymn 'O mightiest of the mighty': 'I never write hymn tunes – they are so ghastly inartistic'); Atkins, op. cit., pp.40f. Elgar altered some of the trochaic beginnings to lines in J. Brownlie's *Hymns of the early Church*, which he evidently considered setting (Birthplace Library copy).

357. Atkins, op. cit., p.174 (letter of 3 March 1908).

358. Moore, op. cit., p.205; the second 'Millwheel Song' is probably the extraneous MS stuck into the same volume (Add. MS. 57995, at f.93v) as a setting, not in the end included in 'King Olaf', of 'She heard in the silence' down to 'lost in the distance' (Epilogue). Or this may be one of the other lost early songs, such as 'The Wave' or 'The Muleteer' (these, by the way, are poems translated by Longfellow from the German of C. A. Tiedge and the Portuguese of Gil Vicente respectively, not poems by Alice Elgar).

359. 'The happy isles', which Elgar thought 'very clever': see Young, *Alice Elgar*, op. cit., pp.103f.

360. 'Ross', a prolific writer of lyrics for musical plays, was Arthur Ropes; there seems to be no surviving sketch for 'Speak, my heart', but it should prove possible to identify the original poem, for the metre is distinctive (see Moore, op. cit., p.439). For 'Land of hope and glory', ibid., pp.365ff. For Alice Elgar's 'The King's way', (not 'Kingsway'), ibid., pp.564f.; Dr Young (*Alice Elgar*, op. cit., p.165) prints what he calls 'an appendage by Elgar' for this, and it is possible that Elgar wrote the words as a model for his wife to follow – but if so, she included them in verse 2 of her poem.

361. op. cit., pp.118–34, 162f.

362. op. cit., facsimile f.p.151; Alice Elgar's 'Reconciliation' (ibid., pp.144f.) looks as if its first four lines may have been written with the melody in mind.

363. British Library, Add. MS. 58005, f.2.

364. ibid., Add. MS. 47902, f.14. Alice Elgar gave her husband Lang's *Grass of Parnassus* (London, 1892), hot from the press, as a birthday present; he altered stanza 4 of 'They hear the sirens for the second time' (p.99), presumably in order to make a love-song out of it: if he asked Lang's permission to use this distortion of the original, that might explain the poet's otherwise inexplicable mistrust of him. The copy is in the Birthplace Library.

> Lang:
>
>> It once had seemed a little thing
>>> To lay our lives down at their feet,
>> That dying we might hear them sing,
>>> And dying see their faces sweet; . . .
>
> Elgar:
>
>> It now but seems a little thing
>>> To lay my life down at thy feet
>> If dying I might hear thee sing
>>> And dying see thy face so sweet.

By 1902, however, now famous, Elgar was permitted to include Lang's 'Changeful beauty' as No.2 of the *Five part-songs from the Greek Anthology*.

365. From *Ballads and lyrics of old France* (London, 1872), p.14.

366. See Moore, op. cit., p.9, citing Lucy Elgar's recollections; for a broadsheet by the S.P.C.K. printing the original poem, see British Library, callmark 1871.e.1.(12) (London, 1851); stanza 2 begins 'Speak gently to your little boy'.

367. It was probably in 1907 that he started an impressive choral setting of Longfellow's unpromisingly titled 'Seaweed' (British Library Add. MS. 63159, ff.34v–35v, where it is surrounded by Arthur Maquarie's 'Love' (1907) and sketches for two songs with poems also taken from his *The dance of olives* (London, 1905), 'I with the young wide Empire in my veins' and 'Nirvana'). His interest in Longfellow even took a scholarly turn: Rosa Burley says that Elgar asked her to spend a fortnight studying the poet and his circle at the British Museum Library in the mid or late 1890s (op. cit., p.88). On his poetic loyalties see Mrs Vera Hockman's statement that 'He never forgot anything he had read and loved' in Moore, op. cit., p.794.

368. Waller: 'The self-banished', a very early unpublished song (MS 69, Birthplace Library). Wyatt: see Moore, op. cit., p.91. Herrick: a wordless sketch for the opening of a partsong marked 'Herrick 42' on f.83v of British Library, Add. MS.

57994 (*King Olaf* sketchbook) can only be 'The wounded Cupid', which appears on p.42 of the Morley's Universal Library edition of the *Hesperides* (London, 1884); there is a sketch for a song, 'The white island' on ff.27v–8 of ibid., Add. MS. 63161, marked 'Herrick p 71 Treasury Sac[red] song', which refers to F. T. Palgrave's anthology *The treasury of sacred song* (Oxford, Clarendon, 1890 edition), bought by Mrs Elgar at Morecambe in 1904 and now in the Birthplace Library. Elgar's early songs also include translations from Froissart and Charles d'Orléans.

369.   Letter to Starmer of 12 August 1921: 'I am not a song writer although a few of such things have achieved some popularity. My best songs are not sung for the reason that they require "*breath*" – the modern singers seem to emulate young terriers and prefer a staccato falsetto bark': it was line that Elgar wanted, not the excessive emphasis on diction common in operetta or cabaret (*Letters of Edward Elgar*, op. cit., p.272).

370.   Examples survive in British Library Add. MS. 63146, such as 'Still I love thee' (f. 2v) and 'Ballad: What shd make thee sad my darling?' (f.19), which form a single item in *The Christy Minstrels second pocket songster* (London, [1880]), p.25.

371.   Poem copied in Alice Elgar's hand on f.iv at the end of British Library, Add. MS. 63161, from D. G. Rossetti, *The early Italian poets* (London, 1861), p.186; the music, sketched for SAATB with divisions, is in ibid., ff.11–11v [?12], and Add. MS. 63157, ff.11v–12.

372.   See Kennedy, op. cit., p.104. His friendship with Lady Mary Lygon and Lucy Broadwood nevertheless led him to support the foundation of the Folk Song Society, as it was then called.

373.   Some poets, like Clifton Bingham who wrote 'Love's old sweet song' as well as Elgar's 'Come, gentle night', made a business of writing for publishers; I count seven texts certainly supplied to Elgar in this way, and the probability of seven more; he may have known Harold Begbie, of 'The Roll Call' (= 'Soldier's Song' or 'War Song', 1914), a journalist interested in early recording techniques (see Moore, *Elgar on record*, London, 1974, p.5). Elgar wrote the words for 'Zut, zut, zut', assuming the persona of a veteran infantryman, under the pseudonym 'Richard Mardon'; but although he was less than candid in manoeuvring for the alleged poet's copyright fee (*Elgar and his publishers*, pp.834–7 gives the whole comedy), I do not think that he was in any way ashamed of the text or that 'Mar-don' means 'mar-gift' as Dr Moore suggests (*Edward Elgar*, op. cit., p.766); it is probably an anagram of 'random'. (We may note here that the surname of another of Elgar's pseudonyms, 'Bernhard Pappenheim', does not in fact mean 'Pope's home', which would be 'Papstheim'; the name appears to derive from two famous generals on opposite sides in the Thirty Years' War, Bernhard Duke of Weimar and Count Pappenheim: see Moore, op. cit., p.62). I do not know if the text survives for Elgar's 'Patriotic Song' or March Tune of 22–23 March 1909, whose anti-German words Arthur Boosey thought too strong or too ephemeral; the MS has the one word 'Wake' repeated at the end, probably a refrain such as 'Wake, O England, wake!' (Young, op. cit., p.147; British Library Add. MS. 63160, f.55v).

374.   In spite of Alice's soldier father, Elgar may have preferred to imagine himself in the role of an admiral rather than that of a general. At the end of a note to Alice Stuart Wortley of 1910, wishing her 'a serene time at the sea', he suddenly adds 'which is mine by birth, adoption & heritage': that plainly implies some naval connection (Moore, op. cit., p.572). The other distin-

guished Elgar of his time was in fact Admiral x.x. Elgar of Kent, some of whose correspondence survives in the British Library.

375. On pp.249f.; I am grateful to Mr Leslie East for drawing my attention to the passage.

376. For Elgar's defence, see *A future for English music*, op. cit., pp.47–9, 155–6; on the tub-thumping chauvinism of the *Caractacus* finale, *Letters to Nimrod*, op. cit., pp.13, 16.

377. See p.186–7.

378. Moore, op. cit., p.280: 'it is better to set the best second-rate poetry to music, for the most immortal verse is music already' (typescript of 1940, Birthplace Library).

379. A note on her Maundy Thursday ceremonies, if I read it correctly, on f.31v of the Violin Concerto short score, now in the Birthplace Library; also 'Queen Mary xtremely popular – entirely clothed in English cloth'.

380. See Young, op. cit., ch.xxiii, and Barry Jackson's account of his collaboration with Elgar in *Music & Letters*, xxiv/1, reprinted in An Elgar companion, op. cit., pp.210–28.

381. References omitted in this summary will be given in my catalogue of texts used or considered by Elgar for musical setting, to be issued in conjunction with the paper mentioned in fn.332 above.

382. Young, *Alice Elgar*, op. cit., pp.113, 145.

383. Moore, *Elgar and his publishers*, op. cit., p.361 (1902).

384. 'Longfellow Sea poems p.168' in British Library, Add. MS. 63159, ff.34v–5v; 'Sea Mist p 501 p [name illegible]' ib., Add. MS. 47903, f.35v.

385. His first taste of Walter De La Mare, for example, undoubtedly came from a poem or poems published in a literary review. British Library Add. MS. 63154 contains on f.64v the note 'p 311/ Open road Peace Prince of sleep'; the music for an incomplete setting of the latter as a song, quite different from the partsong of 1925, is to be found in Add. MS. 63160, f.54, headed 'Prince of sleep (Ramal)'. ('Walter Ramal' was De La Mare's pen-name until 1916.) In collected volumes by De La Mare, from *Songs of childhood* (1902) onwards, the title is always the opening words, 'I met at eve', and Elgar's text of the poem and its punctuation differ slightly from the collected versions. The high page number 311, noted in Add. MS. 63154, can refer only to some journal paginated for the whole year: were 'The open road' and 'Peace' also poems by De La Mare that Elgar considered setting? 'Peace' may have been, for a poem with that title, evidently written during World War I, was eventually collected into *Memory and other poems* in 1938; 'The open road' seems unknown, but it is not by R. L. Stevenson or W. H. Davies.

386. Buck: *Clapham town end* (folksong). Gorton: Moore, *Elgar and his publishers*, op. cit., p.378. Hamilton: Birthplace Library MSS, 'In May Week'. Elwes: Morris' 'Fight for right'. The Australian Mrs Anderson's 'The ballad of brave Hector' was published in *Punch* of 12 April 1922, p.295, but letters with the sketch suggest that she sent Elgar 'The Worcestershire Squire' later on (Birthplace MS 84).

387. Elgar knew Mrs Newmarch through her various musical activities; Arthur Maquarie seems to have lived in Florence, and Mrs Worthington may have been Elgar's intermediary.

388. 'Dry those fair, those crystal eyes'; 'Like to the damask rose'.

389. In British Library Add. MS. 63159, f.40.

390. Moore, *Edward Elgar*, op. cit., p.765, *Elgar and his publishers*, op. cit., p.828. Elgar's eye was evidently caught by D'Israeli's note: 'The last stanza of this

Bedlam song ['With a heart of furious fancies'] contains the seeds of exquisite romance; a stanza worth many an admired poem'.

391.   *A gallery of literary portraits*; Elgar's 'p 69 Gilfilan' [*sic*] shows that he owned the Everyman edition (n.d., Preface 1909), for the Smith text is excerpted on that page; there is no page reference for the Massey, but its sketch is copied directly after the Smith piece, and the fact that its text is also excerpted from a much longer poem on p.95 of Gilfillan makes the identification of source irresistible; sketches are in British Library, Add. MS. 65154, respectively on f.65v–6 and f.66v.

392.   *The Worcestershire Advertiser*, 9 April 1932, alluded to in Young, op. cit., p.249. The speech also tells of his delivering bread to the poor (see above, p.198: 'Alderman Leicester would remember that when they were boys they were permitted to drive a baker's cart through Dolday and they were struck by the insignificance of the dwellings. He thought that germ had grown into the vast improvements which had been made' (presumably initiated or supported by Leicester in his terms of office as Mayor). In the same issue we learn the original occasion for the Mackay songs of 1932–3: at the annual meeting of the Worcester City Schools Music Festival on 7 April 'It was mentioned that Sir Edward Elgar was approached before the last festival [that is before May 1931?] and asked to compose a special song for the occasion. Sir Edward stated that whilst he wished to undertake the composition he wanted to have more time for the consideration of suitable words, and he would see what he could do for the next festival' (that is, May 1933). Stephen S. Moore, the intermediary according to Dr Moore (op. cit., p.797), was involved as secretary of the Worcestershire Association of Music Societies.

393.   See Kennedy, op. cit., p.330 and footnote.

394.   Collected in *From a college window*, and cited from a reprint by Thomas Nelson and Sons, London, n.d., pp.98f.

12 Music in the Air: Elgar and the BBC

Ronald Taylor

The Elgar enthusiast is fortunate today in having available so much information regarding the composer's life and work. We know more of Elgar's background, methods of composition, and the problems he encountered, perhaps, than those who knew him personally. We know more of the antecedents of the composer than he probably knew himself, and almost every aspect of his life has been covered by scholars engaged in music research.

It is, then, curious that there is still an aspect of Elgar's life and work which has escaped any serious study until now. Elgar in the recording studio has, due to the scholarly research of Dr Jerrold Northrop Moore, been covered in minute detail, but that other great twentieth-century music medium, the radio, has been almost totally ignored. For the most part we only learn of the BBC and broadcasting generally when we read of the BBC commission for Elgar to write a Third Symphony. That story has been told fully in several places, and I shall only touch on it lightly here.

Broadcasting, in practical form, began in this country in November 1922, when Elgar was in his sixty-fifth year. He was to live until February 1934, and in that time radio developed from an uncertain experimental start reaching a few thousands, to a national and overseas network, with a sophisticated output of programmes, and even television already advancing through the experimental stages. Elgar, although mid-Victorian by birth, had always shown himself to be interested in many forms of research and development, and his early fascination with the gramophone was an indication of this. We do not know when he first acquired a radio (or 'wireless' as he would have called it) but it is unlikely that he delayed long in acquiring one. He was, after all, within easy receiving distance of the Birmingham station. The request for Elgar to broadcast must surely have come from the young British Broadcasting Company at an early date. The fact that the biographies were of no help to me in this matter prompted my own researches, but had I known of the difficulties and the extent of the work I might well have decided not to proceed. Thinking it to be a matter of simply delving into the archives I innocently went ahead. The fact that it took many years, and that the researches could never be complete, was compensated for by the fascinating material which emerged, not least a complete listing of Elgar's *twenty-eight* broadcasts, and, as a result of the study, I arrived at a completely new understanding of Elgar's popularity during what has usually been regarded as his declining years.

This survey then will restrict itself to the period from 1922, the commencement of British broadcasting, up to the day of Elgar's death in 1934. For a proper appreciation of the survey I shall deal first with the broadcasts which Elgar made during those years, and then proceed to the larger assessment of Elgar's music broadcast *live* in his lifetime. It is necessary to stress live performances for this constituted the great bulk of music broadcast in the years under review – unlike the contemporary system in the U.S.A. – and records made up only a very small proportion of air time. We know that records of Elgar's music *were* broadcast, in addition to the enormous number of items to be dealt with in the second part of my survey, but since most record programme details do not survive I have restricted myself purely to live performance.

To understand the background to broadcasting in the early days of the BBC it is necessary to give a brief account of the setting up of radio throughout the British Isles. Following a period of increasing experiment by a number of private companies, under a watchful government eye, the BBC was formed to control both transmissions and the sale of wireless receivers.

The BBC's licence actually dated from January 1923, but as the studios – such as they were – were ready in several locations before that date, the service began in London on 14 November 1922. Birmingham and Manchester followed the next day. On Christmas Eve 1922 the Newcastle station opened, and 1923 saw the addition of Cardiff, Glasgow, Aberdeen, and Bournemouth as main stations. The last of the major centres, Belfast, was not ready until September 1924. Because of the limited power of even these major stations (this was before the advent of high-power transmitters), a series of small local stations was also built. These were at Sheffield, Plymouth, Edinburgh, Liverpool, Leeds-Bradford, Hull, Nottingham, Stoke-on-Trent, Dundee, and Swansea. All of these opened between November 1923 and December 1924. High-power came into operation from Chelmsford in December 1924, to cover much of the country, until this was replaced by the large Daventry transmitter in July 1925. There was much re-organization in the late 1920s and early 30s, and most of the low-power local stations disappeared with the setting up of the National and Regional networks which are still remembered fondly by many older people. Some idea of the remarkably rapid growth of radio can be judged from the number of Radio Licences issued which ranged from under a quarter of a million at the end of the first year to over two millions at the beginning of 1927. Remembering that each radio was probably listened to by several persons the potential audience for any programme, whether of minority interest or otherwise, was enormous. By the 1930s the number of licence holders had risen to over five millions.

There is no doubt that the earliest programmes, relayed for a very limited period each day, were crude by modern standards. In the same way, early gramophone recordings were crude, but development in radio was even more rapid than that of the gramophone. Technical and artistic development went hand in hand, hours of broadcasting were increased, and despite the opposition of many music and theatre managements radio programmes quickly became accepted and indeed welcomed. A new audience, often far from a concert or recital hall, had been born, or their existence realized for the first time. For the artist it was necessary to learn that the art of successful broadcasting was to realize its intimacy. No longer was the artist performing to a group or large audience. They were performing to each and every listener, and not all performers were able to learn the necessary techniques. This point was well made in an article in the 1928 edition of the BBC Handbook.[1]

Each major station, and some of the minor ones, appointed their own music directors, and the central organization appointed the conductor and composer, Percy Pitt, first as Music Adviser in 1923, and then from 1924, until his retirement in 1930, as Director of Music. At first the local stations had a great deal of autonomy, but this was gradually eroded as the company grew, and a central control of music policy was brought in. We shall see more of the results of this when I come to assess the music of Elgar during the period.

Percy Pitt and Elgar were old friends dating back to the first Elgar Festival at Covent Garden at the beginning of the century. Elgar's contract with HMV naturally had not envisaged such a thing as radio, and a 1923 letter (quoted by Jerrold Northrop Moore in his *Elgar on Record*[2] from HMV to Sir Edward shows how even a company as large as the Gramophone Company did not really know how to treat radio as a competitor. It seems that Elgar was given a free hand and negotiated his appearances directly with the BBC. He was not entirely without advice, however, as Sir Landon Ronald gave him invaluable assistance in his negotiations at various times. By the 1930s Elgar was receiving a fee of £50 for each conducting engagement with the BBC.

Elgar's first broadcast was one in which his contribution was almost overwhelmed by the occasion. 23 April 1924 marked the official opening of the British Empire Exhibition at Wembley. Elgar was shortly to be appointed Master of the King's Music (following the death of Sir Walter Parratt) and of course had to be present. Despite having written a special *Empire March* for the occasion, this was not performed during the opening ceremonies. *Land of Hope and Glory* was the King's preferred choice, and the massed bands and choirs were directed by Elgar, as well as in Parry's *Jerusalem*. Elgar did not enjoy the occasion – the raucousness, and what he saw as vulgarity, did not appeal to him. The BBC was attempting to relay a large open-air event for the first time and success was only partial. HMV also tried to record the event from the BBC's land-line, but due to the imperfections of the acoustic recording process none of the matrices was a success and, regrettably, they were scrapped.

Elgar's first broadcast concert appearance, with the Royal Philharmonic Society's Orchestra, was on 2 May 1924, the venue Central Hall, Westminster. The BBC was conscious of the importance of the occasion, broadcast from the London station with simultaneous broadcasting to other regions, and a special article by Percy Scholes appeared in *Radio Times*. The programme was lengthy by today's standards and included: *Cockaigne* Overture, Cello Concerto (with Beatrice Harrison), *Enigma Variations, Pomp and Circumstance* Marches Nos. 2 and 3, and a special 'new arrangement' of items from the *Wand of Youth* suites 1 and 2. Alas, no note of Elgar's new arrangement survives in the archives and we do not know which items he put together to make the new suite. Elgar did not broadcast again until nearly a year later, on 31 March 1925.

This programme used the BBC Wireless Symphony Orchestra, a forerunner of the BBC Symphony Orchestra. It consisted of a core of contracted players regularly playing for the Company, augmented to full orchestral size by using players from various London orchestras, often from the Covent Garden and Queen's Hall players. Some of these found their way eventually to the fine orchestra founded in 1930 which was composed entirely of contract musicians. For Elgar's second broadcast concert he chose a very full programme: the Handel *Overture in D minor* arrangement, *In the South*, Funeral March from *Grania & Diarmuid, Enigma Variations, Polonia, Sea Pictures*, and Prelude and Angel's Farewell from *The Dream of Gerontius*. The soloist in the vocal items was Astra Desmond. This concert was also heralded by a *Radio Times* article analysing the music, by Percy Scholes. In the previous issue Charles Tristram had also contributed a short article on 'England's Great Composer' which consisted mainly of amusing anecdotes about Elgar.

On Armistice Day, 1925, Elgar again conducted the BBC Wireless Orchestra in a concert which this time included the Adagio from Symphony No.1 (complete symphonies were as yet considered a little risky), Meditation from *Light of Life, Pomp and Circumstance* Marches Nos.1 and 2, and *Spirit of England*. The soloist in the latter was the soprano Dorothy Silk. Two days later a relay from the Eastbourne Festival included Elgar conducting *Polonia* and Astra Desmond singing *Sea Pictures*.

In 1926 the BBC inaugurated a series of National Concerts at the Royal Albert Hall. There were many distinguished musicians who took part, including a number from Europe. The 'National Orchestra' which appeared at each concert consisted of the usual BBC players and the Covent Garden Orchestra. Elgar's concert, again a strenuous one, comprised: *Cockaigne*, the Violin Concerto, *Falstaff*, the larghetto from *Serenade for Strings*, and the Triumphal March from *Caractacus*. The soloist in the Concerto was Albert Sammons. This concert was notable for the fact that it coincided with one of London's worst 'pea-souper' fogs, much of the fog penetrating the hall, and making enjoyment of the concert difficult. Nonetheless it was remarkably well attended, and one of the most successful concerts of the series.

During 1926 Elgar served the BBC in another capacity. The Company announced a music competition for British composers, to cover various types of composition. A distinguished panel of judges included Elgar, Sir Hugh Allen, Sir Landon Ronald, J. B. McEwen, and Colonel Somerville. The BBC expressed a desire to assist 'new music', but in the event the entries were disappointing and the judges reported that they were unable to award any prizes as the entries failed to reach a desired standard. Elgar had taken this competition very seriously and he must have been satisfied, as were all the judges, at the outcome. It is intriguing to speculate on *who* were those budding composers who submitted entries.

On 15 April 1927, Elgar conducted *The Dream of Gerontius* on radio for the first time. The BBC Wireless Chorus, augmented for the occasion, joined the BBC orchestra, with Olga Haley, Steuart Wilson, and Harold Williams the soloists. On 2 June, an Elgar Birthday Concert was arranged in the No.1 Studio at Savoy Hill. The BBC had hoped to arrange a Festival to celebrate Elgar's seventieth Birthday, but plans had to be abandoned. However, Percy Pitt and the BBC were determined that the occasion should be marked in a way that Elgar would remember with pleasure. Elgar was to conduct and 'In a break in one of the rehearsals for it ... Sir Edward was presented by Mr. Pitt with a salver which was a birthday offering from members of the orchestra and his other friends in the BBC. It was given and accepted amid the laughter with which old friends mask their deeper feelings, and the little ceremony was one of the happiest of many which that studio witnessed in the few years of its busy life'.[3] The concert celebrated the birthday in style, was of considerable length, and included Muriel Brunskill and Beatrice Harrison as soloists. The full programme was *Cockaigne, The Music Makers,* Cello Concerto, *Enigma Variations, Sea Pictures, Pomp and Circumstance* March No.2, and the Wireless Chorus performed *My Love Dwelt in a Northern Land* and *As Torrents in Summer*. It was at the conclusion of this concert that Elgar turned to the still live microphone and uttered the only words which he is known to have broadcast 'Good night, everybody. Good night Marco!'.

At the opening of the Three Choirs Festival, on 4 September, in Hereford Cathedral a local relay broadcast the Fanfare (specially composed for the occasion) and the National Anthem. *The Apostles* Prologue was also included in the items conducted by Elgar.

On 11 November 1927 Elgar conducted a broadcast of *Spirit of England*, again with Dorothy Silk, and the programme also included the Meditation from *The Light of Life*. The orchestra was the National Orchestra with the National Chorus. The latter was composed principally of the BBC Wireless Singers, trained by Stanford Robinson.

On 30 March 1928, a BBC concert – one of a series from the People's Palace, in Mile End Road, London – by the National Orchestra was again conducted by Elgar. The programme was the last of the very long ones then in vogue, and consisted of *Froissart, Introduction and Allegro, Wand of Youth* Suites 1 and 2, *Polonia, In the South, Contrasts, Pomp & Circumstance* Marches Nos.2 and 4, scena from *King Olaf* (with Walter Widdop), and the same singer in a passage from *The Light of Life*. The orchestra also played the Meditation from the latter work. A full programme indeed, and something of a strain, surely, for a seventy-year old conductor! Nevertheless, only five days later, on 4 April, Elgar conducted *Gerontius* from London, with the same artists as in the performance broadcast a year earlier.

December 1929, on the 9th of that month, saw an unusual concert from Windsor. The programme was to mark the recovery from a very serious illness of King George V. Part of the concert was to be conducted by Sir Walford Davies, the Choir of St George's Chapel singing a number of traditional pieces. To accommodate the equipment necessary for the broadcast it was not made from the Chapel in the Castle, but was relayed from the Albert Institute, Windsor. Elgar had composed a special *Carol for His Majesty's Happy Recovery* for the occasion, and before that he conducted five part songs: *Weary Wind of the West; Evening Scene; Fly, Singing Bird, Fly; The Snow;* and *The Reveille*. Sir Walford Davies and Sybil Eaton also performed part of the Op.82 Violin Sonata. Thus Elgar's new 'Carol' reached an audience far greater than for any other première of the composer, due to the new medium.

The 30 January 1930 saw the first of five broadcasts which Elgar was to make that year. The occasion was a London concert by the Royal Philharmonic Orchestra, relayed to the whole country from Daventry. The programme, now of more manageable proportions comprised: *In the South*, Symphony No.1, and the Violin Concerto with Albert Sammons as soloist. On 21 March a concert from the Queen's Hall, London, included *Enigma Variations* and the new arrangement of the Cello Concerto for Viola, played by Lionel Tertis. The composer conducted both items.

In February an advertisement for 'Marconiphone' (the radio arm of HMV) had attributed the following words to Sir Edward Elgar: 'There are people who are music-starved – who cannot go to concerts, to recitals, to the opera. Such people *need* a Marconiphone. To be able to hear, in your own home, all the important musical events of the day is the great advantage of wireless...' The last sentence undoubtedly reflected Elgar's view of the benefits which had come from radio, (though he had not always been so well-disposed towards the BBC and its activities[4]) and a year and a half later, in an interview with Herbert Hughes, published in the *Daily Telegraph*, he said: 'You cannot blame the BBC for a decline in concert-going that began before the radio had come into existence'.

On 11 May, Elgar conducted the National Orchestra of Wales (largely a BBC creation) in Cardiff. The broadcast programme included *Wand of Youth* Suite No.1, *Enigma Variations* and *In the South*. In addition Heddle Nash sang *King Olaf heard the Cry, Speak Music* and *In the Dawn*.

A relay from the Three Choirs Festival on 10 September, and broadcast in the Midlands only, included Elgar conducting *In the South*. On 2 October part of a BBC Symphony Orchestra concert was broadcast from London, with Elgar conducting his Second Symphony. The personnel of this orchestra was not the same as that of the newly-formed BBC Symphony Orchestra which was to give its first concert on the 22nd of the month. However, Elgar did conduct the new orchestra on several occasions, but the first broadcast with the orchestra did not take place until the première of the *Nursery Suite* at the Queen's Hall Promenade Concerts on 20 August 1931. Eighteen days later the Midland region heard the work, this time with Elgar conducting the London Symphony Orchestra at the Three Choirs Festival in Gloucester Cathedral. Midland listeners were fortunate on this occasion for the broadcast also included Gustav Holst conducting his *Fugue a la Gigue* and Herbert Howells conducting his *In Green Ways*. Alas for posterity, this was before the days of programme recording and such events can only exist in the memory.

On 1 October a broadcast from the Proms at Queen's Hall featured an all-Elgar evening. Sir Henry Wood conducted the BBC Symphony Orchestra in *Cockaigne*, and the brilliant young cellist Thelma Reiss (who died in September 1991) gave a remarkable performance of the Cello Concerto. Elgar conducted the Second Symphony only as he was now restricting himself to less strenuous engagements.

On 26 May 1932, a Musicians' Benevolent Fund concert was broadcast from the Royal Albert Hall. Elgar's contribution was to conduct the *Pomp and Circumstance* March No.1. The orchestra was composed of the united Royal Philharmonic and BBC Symphony players. On 21 October Elgar honoured a promise to an old friend, E. Godfrey Brown, Music Director of the Belfast station of the BBC, and conductor of the Belfast Philharmonic Society. Brown was an ardent Elgarian, and had performed many Elgar works both on and off the air. Now Elgar conducted a Belfast Philharmonic concert with their Orchestra and Chorus, in *Enigma Variations* and *The Dream of Gerontius*, with Astra Desmond, Steuart Wilson and Victor Harding.

The latter was also a member of the BBC Chorus. The concert was broadcast from the Belfast station.

Six days later, on 27 October, listeners in the North of England only were able to hear Elgar conduct a broadcast of *King Olaf* for the first time. The event took place at Hanley, and was the famed North Staffs Choral Society's tribute to Elgar in his seventy-fifth year. The soloists were Joan Elwes, Frank Titterton and Frank Phillips. Phillips was then a well-known baritone, and was later to gain renewed fame as a wartime radio announcer. It is sad, in retrospect, that this performance was not broadcast nationally. Obviously the powers at the BBC decided that it had insufficient countrywide appeal! However, the BBC was to make handsome amends with the forthcoming Elgar Festival. On Armistice Day 1932 Elgar conducted the BBC Orchestra and Chorus, with Elsie Suddaby, in *For the Fallen* from *Spirit of England*, which was broadcast nationally.

On 30 November the Elgar Festival began at the Queen's Hall. All the programmes were to be broadcast in full. *The Radio Times* had printed a number of introductory articles and tributes, though the coming programmes were overshadowed to some extent by the sad news of the death of Percy Pitt. Handsome programmes had been printed, and a preliminary talk was relayed by Basil Maine. Elgar conducted the BBC Symphony in *Cockaigne*, and the Violin Concerto. Albert Sammons was again the soloist. The concert concluded with the First Symphony under the baton of Sir Landon Ronald.

Other Elgar concerts followed and will be mentioned in the second part of this study, but Elgar was to conduct one more Festival performance. This was on 7 December when he conducted the Second Symphony, again at Queen's Hall. Sir Adrian Boult conducted the other items in the programme: *Introduction and Allegro* and *Enigma Variations*. This concert was also preceded by a talk by Basil Maine.

Despite the retirement in 1930, and the death in 1932, of Percy Pitt, Elgar's relationship with the BBC became an increasingly warm one with the renewal of his friendship with Adrian Boult, who succeeded Pitt as Director of Music, and who was now chief conductor of the newly-formed BBC Symphony Orchestra.

The commissioning by the BBC in 1932 of a Third Symphony, hopefully for the 1933, or at latest the 1934 season, has been written about at length. The original surviving sketches were presented to the BBC by Carice Elgar Blake, and were reproduced in *The Listener* in 1934, with a commentary by W. H. Reed. Reed used them again in his book *Elgar as I Knew Him* (1936). Modern research, principally by Dr Christopher Kent, has revealed more about the sketches, and the whole episode is dealt with fully in Dr Jerrold Northrop Moore's *Elgar, a Creative Life* (O.U.P., 1984).

On 26 January 1933 a Hallé Orchestra concert was broadcast conducted by Elgar. *The Dream of Gerontius* had as soloists Muriel Brunskill, John

Coates and Harold Williams, with the Hallé Chorus. The broadcast came from the Manchester station. Elgar's last broadcast appearance, before his final illness, was relayed from the Proms on the 17 August. Again it was his beloved Second Symphony, with the BBC Symphony Orchestra.

Two concerts had been arranged, with Elgar conducting, for the coming months. The first was at Belfast on 14 October, this time with the BBC Belfast Wireless Symphony Orchestra, and the second had been booked far ahead to 15 February 1934 with the Hallé Orchestra. Both concerts took place – the first with E. Godfrey Brown, and the second with John Barbirolli.

As can be seen, far from ignoring radio, Elgar had performed for the new medium with some regularity. The few who could attend public concerts had the privilege of watching Elgar conduct. Through the 'magic' of radio a new, vast, audience could join in and listen as England's greatest composer crafted yet another performance of his own works.

Elgar's music broadcast live, in his own lifetime

'Nobody wants my music nowadays.' This was the complaint that was heard several times during Elgar's latter years. We now know that this was the cry of a man who often needed reassurance, even if all the facts proved that his music was popular, and that he was appreciated. However, it has generally been accepted that there *was* a falling off of interest in Elgar. Critics were less enthusiastic, and we have tended to accept the view of young musicians and pundits of Elgar's last years that he and his music were outmoded, and that in the world of the 1920s he had no real place. But was that really so? Did these bright young men represent anything but their own prejudices? And do we not tend to accept at face value the pronouncements of critics who often went with what they believed to be the prevailing tide? What REAL evidence is there as to Elgar's popularity with the mass of people. Going to concerts has always been a fairly expensive luxury for the majority, and in the cold economic climate of the 1920s and early 30s it was even more so. Records too, despite the marvellous efforts of HMV, Columbia and the other companies, were proportionately expensive for many people. Radio, then, for the payment of a modest annual fee, plus the cost of an equally modest receiver, was to open the doors of music-making to a new audience nationwide. By noting down each broadcast performance, its origin, and artist, I have found a pattern which indicates that the popularity of Elgar's music, as performed by an incredible number of music artists, was really quite astonishing. It gives the lie to any suggestion that Elgar's music was in decline, and the sheer range of performance right across almost all of the composer's output shows that it was often the critics who were out of touch. One such critic, and yet an admirer of Elgar, F. H. Shera, wrote, in a preface to a little book on Elgar's instrumental works:[5]

> . . . the *Imperial March, The Banner of St George* (1897) and *Caractacus* (1898). Imperialism gave us the *Pomp and Circumstance* Marches and the *Coronation Ode* (1901) . . . The War brought *Carillon, The Spirit of England,* and *The Fringes of the Fleet.* Much of this music (not to mention *The Crown of India* (1912) and the Wembley music of 1924) has been allowed to fade into deserved oblivion, even though *Land of Hope and Glory* is still to be heard on Empire Day . . .

Oblivion? Mr Shera was not the only music critic and writer who obviously considered the wireless to be beneath his notice. Let us just take the works cast into oblivion (and remember that Mr Shera was writing in 1930, less than four years before Elgar's death), and see just how the BBC had treated these works. Each figure represents the number of live broadcast performances in the years from 1922 to February 1934:

Imperial March		65
Banner of St George		10
Caractacus		A few fragments
Pomp and Circumstance Marches:		
	No.2	60
	No.3	15
	No.4	92
Coronation Ode		1
Carillon		29
Spirit of England		6 (and 4 parts)
Fringes of the Fleet		1 (and several parts)
Crown of India		102 (including several parts)

If this was oblivion, then many a composer would be grateful for it! *Caractacus* was one of the few Elgar works not to receive a radio performance. So Mr Shera scores on one! As for *Land of Hope and Glory* which I have paired with *Pomp and Circumstance* No.1, there were so many performances over the years that I decided to ignore these in my researches, on grounds of space, and also discounted *Salut d'Amour.* That charming salon piece was too popular to be of statistical importance.

In the early days of broadcasting each station music director had a wide measure of independence as to the type of music which would be played, and who the artists were to be. Sometimes, especially in those first crucial months, the BBC was glad to accept almost anybody for audition and a fair number of amateurs, or semi-professionals, found their way to the microphone. Later on the amateur gave way almost entirely to professional singers and instrumentalists, though a large number of choirs and choral groups of amateur status, as well as brass and military band combinations, broadcast regularly. But whatever their background the remarkable fact emerges that a very high proportion *chose* to perform Elgar, and obviously his music was in their repertoire, contrary to the received opinion that his popularity was in decline, and therefore as the period drew to a close there would be a reduction in performances of his music. In fact, if anything, it actually increased. Of course, the BBC staff conductors and musicians were directly under the control of music directors and producers, but it would be foolish to pretend that they were nearly all members of an Elgar Appreciation Society. As new faces appeared at the BBC throughout the regions Elgar's music continued to be played, and commented on in talks on the wireless, and articles in *Radio Times*. It was said that an index, now alas apparently lost, of music articles which had appeared in *Radio Times* had more entries for Elgar than for any other composer, including Beethoven! (And that was up to 1932.)

One of the most interesting facts to emerge from my studies is that many of the 'forgotten' or 'neglected' pieces, which we fondly imagine we have rediscovered during the years of long-playing records, were being performed fairly regularly. I have found that over sixty of Elgar's songs were performed, plus many excerpts from the song-cycles, ranging from one performance to (in the case of *Pleading*) nearly 200! *The Empire March* received no less than twenty-one playings after its first broadcast in August 1924. *Polonia*, always considered a rarity, achieved seven performances. The very early *Romance* for violin, Opus 1, reached eleven, *Sursum Corda* an astonishing forty-one, *The Light of Life* four performances, and *King Olaf* eight. The *Romance* for bassoon & orchestra, which one writer a few years ago assured us had been forgotten since its early performances in 1911, was played four times, and even the *Grania and Diarmid* incidental music of 1901 received eight performances. And one performance of *Une Voix dans le Desert*.

What then, of possible performances, was NOT played or sung? Very little, as it happens. *Bizarrerie*, Op.13; *The Black Knight*, Op.25; *Te Deum and Benedictus*, Op.34; a complete *Caractacus*, Op.35; *Le Drapeau Belge*, Op.79; the orchestral version of *The Severn Suite*; the *Arthur* music; the 1932 *Sonatina*; the *Offertoire* for violin & piano; and the arrangement of Chopin's *Funeral March* – none of these seems to have been broadcast. But, everything else was, at least once, and some a great many times. There were a number of the songs not broadcast, but Elgar wrote over eighty of these, and as I have already said, some sixty were performed, some of them many times over. In fact, on *most* days of the year, once the BBC stations were all opened, it was inevitable that on at least one of the stations Elgar's music was being played. I doubt if this could be claimed for any other composer. Omitting *Pomp and Circumstance* March No.1 (or *Land of Hope and Glory*) and *Salut d'Amour*, there were over 5,100 performances.

In the confines of a study such as this it is impossible to list each and every item, but I hope one day that it may be possible to publish a complete listing. Until then the Appendix to this article must suffice to give just the total number of broadcasts of each item. However, it is instructive and, I believe, important to consider a few of the Elgar interpretations chronologically.

Various names recur as the years go on, some disappearing early on as a new generation of conductors and interpreters took over, others remaining with the BBC through Elgar's remaining lifetime. Names such as Herbert Carruthers, an organist who became Director and Music Director of the Glasgow Station, Warwick Braithwaite, Music Director at Cardiff, E. Godfrey Brown at Belfast (previously mentioned), Frederick Brown at Liverpool, T. H. Morrison, previously with the Queen's Hall and other orchestras, and appointed Music Director at Manchester, Joseph Lewis, first at Birmingham, then transferred to London, Dan Godfrey, Jr., Music Director in the early Manchester days, and then moved to London, Capt. W. A. Featherstone, a military bandsman at Bournemouth who became Music Director at the Bournemouth station, and who conducted numerous Elgar works until the local orchestra disappeared in the late 1920s' reorganization. There were, of course, many others, but they must mostly wait until the full listing can be published.

We are fortunate in that the Marconi Co. experimental broadcast archives largely survive in the BBC Archives at Caversham. The only Elgar item that I could discover was a mid-September (date not certain) 1922 broadcast from Marconi House to a hospital. It was the song *Pipes of Pan*, sung by a Mr Rex Faithful, baritone. Mr Faithful changed his surname to Palmer and became one of the first radio singers, a Children's Hour 'Uncle', and Director of the London station. Three days after the official opening on 14 November the London station played a Duo-Art Pianola Roll of *Pomp and Circumstance* No.1, and this was repeated on 23 November. On 25 November came a further performance, but this time by the 'Orchestra'. It is doubtful if the orchestra consisted of more than nine players in the cramped studio conditions of the time. Between then and the end of the year there were seven short Elgar items. The first Elgar piece I have traced from the provinces was from Manchester on 10 January 1923 when a Mr S. J. Nightingale sang *Pleading*. In the months that followed there were many Elgar songs and a lesser number of instrumental works. In August, a performance of the Violin Sonata by Jo Lamb (violin) and Eric Fogg (piano) in Manchester, was to have been preceded by a 'short chat on the Sonata by Mr Fogg'. Unfortunately, the chat was cancelled, or it would have rated as the first broadcast talk on Elgar. In September the same station 'orchestra' (again a small body of players) performed 'Melody' by the composer. What was this, I wonder? It was not the only error which the programme supervisors were to make when describing what had been or was to be broadcast.

In September 1923 the RAF Band visited first the London studio, and a few days later Glasgow. On each occasion they played Elgar's music, and in Glasgow on 4 October the station orchestra boldly tackled the *Crown of*

India suite. On Armistice Day of that year Joseph Lewis and the Birmingham studio 'Repertory Company and Orchestra' gave the first radio performance of *Banner of St George*. In October Dan Godfrey, Jr. had conducted the *Enigma Variations* at Manchester, with an augmented orchestra, and, not to be outdone London responded with a performance by their orchestra, under Maurice Besly, in November. The number of Elgar songs and instrumental works was increasing steadily and several choral works had been heard from around the country.

In 1924 broadcasting, especially where music was concerned, began to leap ahead. Studios were improved and more performers coaxed to the microphone, and since September 1923 the *Radio Times* had appeared to inform people as to the programmes available. The enterprising Dan Godfrey, Jr. conducted *Sea Pictures* in its entirety, with the augmented orchestra and local contralto Rachel Hunt, in Manchester in February. From London a broadcast was taken by most stations, when a concert was relayed from Central Hall. This was of the Royal Albert Hall Orchestra, under Sir Landon Ronald, playing Elgar's Second Symphony, one of the first symphonies ever broadcast, and, according to the *Radio Times* was 'by special request of a large number of Broadcasting Listeners'.

The list of Elgar performances was growing apace, many 'first broadcast performances' had already taken place by mid-summer of 1924, among them a complete *Gerontius* at Manchester. Dan Godfrey, Jr. again responsible, with Rachel Hunt, John Perry, and Lee Thistlethwaite, together with the grandly-titled 'Station Opera Co.' The enterprising Aberdeen station put on an Elgar Night, and in the interval broadcast the first talk on the composer, given by a local organist Albert Adams. A rather odd broadcast in October of that year was when Arthur Wilkes sang the 'Sanctus Fortis' from *Gerontius* with the accompaniment provided by the organ of the Piccadilly Picture Theatre, Manchester! As the new smaller stations opened during the year, and the major Belfast station, opening concerts and ceremonies almost always included an Elgar item. Indeed at Stoke-on-Trent no less than three Elgar pieces were performed. The distinguished conductor Felix Weingartner was heard directing a performance of the *Enigma Variations* in a concert with the Scottish Orchestra from St Andrew's Hall, Glasgow, in November.

The following January saw another European maestro, again not usually connected with Elgar, when Ernest Ansermet conducted Albert Sammons in a performance of the Violin Concerto relayed from Covent Garden.

The new music director at Aberdeen, Arthur Collingwood, inaugurated 'An Hour with Elgar' from his station, and several other Elgar evenings were heard during the year from other stations.

The first broadcast of *King Olaf* came from Newcastle in March. The conductor was the Northumbrian composer W. G. Whittaker, and the artists were Elsie Suddaby, John Adams and E. J. Potts. A famous north country choir, the Newcastle & Gateshead Choral Union, with their orchestra, provided the main resources. What a pity that in those days it was only heard in the local area.

Glasgow presented a very unusual performance, the first on radio, of *The Music Makers*. According to the BBC 'with the composer's approval the contralto part was transferred for baritone voice'. The singer was Herbert Heyner, and H. A. Carruthers conducted the augmented station orchestra and chorus. In June came the only broadcast I have traced of the *Coronation Ode,* from the lively Aberdeen station. Scottish singers, and the local station choir and orchestra combined under Arthur Collingwood's baton. At the beginning of the month Belfast had honoured Elgar's birthday with a special concert. Unfortunately I have been unable to trace which items were played on this occasion. Elgar's music was being played with increasing frequency during the year, and the range of his works was being extended as the capacity of the studios, and the increased use of outside broadcasting, gave new opportunities to producers.

In November the young BBC faced its first state occasion – something for which it was to become famous throughout the succeeding years. Queen Alexandra died on 20 November, and it was not until the previous day that the radio authorities in London were warned that the Queen Mother was unlikely to survive for many hours. There was nothing in the BBC's licence to indicate what they should do at such times as national mourning or crisis, and a decision had to be made. What was done set a precedent which still maintains. An article in *Radio Times* for 4 December 1925, which from its style I surmise was written by John Reith himself, is worth quoting for it has its place in the Elgar story:

> The evening of November 21st was given to a special programme of choral and orchestral works – broad and noble music in harmony with the mood of the day. The outstanding items were the Adagio Movement of Elgar's First Symphony, 'Meditation' from the same composer's *Lux Christi*, and two movements of the *Pathètique* Symphony of Tchaikovsky. It was not easy to improvise such a programme at a day's notice. All the orchestral works named normally call for large orchestras, which are not to be had without long pre-arrangement. The mood of the day unmistakably demanded music that was grand as well as solemn, and it is to be regretted that certain critics, who have complained of the abandonment of the usual light Saturday programme, were not present in our Head Office to feel the atmosphere in which the special service and the special programme were born. It is worth recording that certain provincial stations, to which permission had been given to retain so much of their pre-arranged programmes as was not incompatible with the spirit of the day, voluntarily elected to take the London Programme.

Thus it can be seen that Elgar's music was a first choice for such an occasion – a position it still largely holds. The London orchestra was probably conducted by either Percy Pitt or Dan Godfrey, Jr., though the archives are unclear on the point. It may have been a shared occasion.

1926 was to be the last year of the old British Broadcasting Company – at the end of the year the granting of a Charter would see the birth of the Corporation. As if in anticipation of that change the year saw some radio highlights – the number of licence holders continued to rise and there was an air of confidence about the programmes generally. Elgar was, as ever, to the fore, and in March, in addition to the normal run of smaller works, came a remarkable trio. On 11 March from Manchester a broadcast from the Free Trade Hall of a Hallé Concert, with the orchestra and chorus, under Hamilton Harty, of *The Apostles*. The soloists were Dorothy Silk, Muriel Brunskill, Herbert Heyner, Walter Glynne, Dennis Noble, and Norman Allin. Part One only was broadcast. Seven days later from Birmingham came a complete *Gerontius*, under Joseph Lewis, with the station orchestra and chorus augmented by the Wolverhampton Music Society, the solo performers being Mary Foster, Frank Mullings and Joseph Farrington.

Not to be outdone E. Godfrey Brown at Belfast presented *King Olaf* two days later. For good measure he also gave the *Enigma Variations* in the same programme. The soloists in *Olaf* were Stiles Allen, Tudor Davies and Harold Williams, with the Belfast Philharmonic Society's chorus and orchestra. E. Godfrey Brown also gave a talk on the *Variations* during the interval. In April John Barbirolli's name appears for the first time, conducting Elgar's *Elegy* for strings with the Chenil Orchestra. In September Sir Ivor Atkins conducted the Belfast Station Symphony Orchestra in a relay from that city of the *Enigma Variations* and the transcription of Handel's *Overture in D minor*. In October Albert Coates conducted a BBC National Concert, from the Royal Albert Hall, and included the *Enigma Variations*. Another first broadcast performance this year was a complete *Light of Life* from Cardiff on 19 December. Three weeks before this they had broadcast *The Dream of Gerontius*. The soloists this time, under the baton of Warwick Braithwaite, were Dorothy Silk, Edith Furmedge, Tom Pickering, and Stuart Robertson. Braithwaite was unswerving in his allegiance to Elgar's music and in his years at Cardiff brought many Elgar performances to Wales, both before the microphone and in the concert hall.

The birth of the Corporation at the BBC was to herald many changes, and a number of the small provincial stations were to lose their identity. The larger stations were to be reformed and the music organization concentrated in fewer centres. Station orchestras in the smaller centres were downgraded to octets and similar chamber music size, and more reliance was placed on non-house orchestras, especially light orchestras. There were a large number of these at the time, and the majority survived into the 1930s.

Much of Elgar's music fitted in well with the programmes of these light orchestras, many of which were based in theatres, cinemas and hotels. For the remaining years of this survey almost all of Elgar's lighter pieces were regularly performed, as well as the small number of new pieces which Elgar composed during the period. Orchestras and individual performers were quick to take up any new piece coming from the composer.

In 1927, an unusual, if minor, performance took place on 20 January. Steuart Wilson sang the solo part in *For the Fallen*, normally sung by a soprano. Another performance of *King Olaf* appeared, this time from Glasgow, under H. A. Carruthers, with Mavis Bennett, Parry Jones and Roy Henderson. To make up for the broadcast the previous year of Part 1 of *The Apostles*, Part 2 was broadcast but from Wales this time, and also relayed in London. The Newport Choral Society, under Arthur Sims, imported a number of soloists, some from the operatic stage, to fill the solo roles: Ida Cooper, Gladys Palmer, Sidney Pointer, Walter Saull, Frederick Woodhouse and Herbert Heyner. Although the Wembley Exhibition of 1924 (repeated in 1925) was well behind us, Elgar's music for the occasion was still being performed fairly regularly. Both the *Pageant of Empire* songs and the *Empire March* had a number of performances during the year. A special Empire Day Concert from London in May, conducted by John Ansell, included four Elgar items.

A short extract from the Hereford Three Choirs Festival was broadcast from Daventry on 4 September, when, Sir Percy Hull conducting, the choirs and the London Symphony Orchestra were heard in part of *The Apostles*. An indication of the amount of Elgar's music being played on radio at this time, is shown by the fact that in October 1927 on only seven days were we without an Elgar item. On many days there were numerous choices to be made from the various stations of the BBC. An interesting programme from Birmingham in December was of excerpts from Oratorios composed for the Birmingham Festivals. This programme was the idea of Joseph Lewis and six excerpts from *Gerontius* were included, the tenor part being sung by Geoffrey Dams.

1928 saw an increase, if this were possible, in Elgar's contribution, and there was no question of neglect, though other living composers might well have felt neglected by comparison! Of the larger works, *The Light of Life* was heard twice early in the year, from Cardiff and from Birmingham, the second performance having for soprano the charmingly named Fifine de la Cote. Another major broadcast was relayed from Manchester – a Hallé performance of *The Kingdom*, under Harty, with Dorothy Silk, Muriel Brunskill, John Coates and Harold Williams. St George's Day saw another performance of *Banner of St George*, now a regular fixture for the day.

During this year the BBC-sponsored National Orchestra of Wales began its all too brief life. For several years it maintained a high standard and endeavoured to establish itself as the Welsh Orchestra. The BBC was generous with money, and gave much publicity and air-time to the concerts. However, the times were not propitious and an appeal for funds to enable the orchestra to continue, made in 1931 (not the best of economic times) failed completely and a reluctant BBC had to withdraw. The final concert was broadcast from Cardiff on 7 October 1931. In the intervening years though its chief conductor, Warwick Braithwaite, had brought a great variety of music to the Principality, and often performed Elgar's music. Much of this was broadcast, though these programmes were not always available outside Wales.

Promenade Concert relays usually included some Elgar, and Sir Henry Wood never let a season go by without a generous helping of the composer's music. Adrian Boult, then conductor of the City of Birmingham Orchestra first conducted Elgar for a broadcast in October when he directed a performance of the Handel Overture transcription. This work, first heard in 1925, was a favourite with broadcasters and was performed twenty-nine times during the period to 1934. During this time there were many broadcasts by choirs and choral societies, the favourite Elgar piece being *Feasting I Watch*. This must have seemed like a choral signature tune to listeners for it achieved a remarkable ninety-four performances during the years. Singers still programmed Elgar regularly, their favourite songs being *Pleading* and *Shepherd's Song*. But even obscure songs by the composer found their champions, and some singers regularly repeated the same favourite Elgar pieces from their repertoire. Bands – military and brass – played on the radio regularly. Elgar's music, especially arrangements of works not composed with bands in mind, was often performed. To show how important music had become to radio the BBC's music library at the Savoy Hill headquarters had grown to 8,500 items in November 1928, compared with 200 in December 1922. It eventually claimed to be the largest music library in the world.

1929 had an interesting item early in the year – William Primrose was soloist in the Violin Concerto in a concert from the Birmingham studio. The orchestra was conducted by Joseph Lewis. Primrose was still a violinist at this time, and his great career as a viola player lay ahead. Another unusual item was on 17 March when Elgar's setting of Psalm 48, Op.67, was given, but in Welsh! The only large-scale work during the next few months was a relay of *The Kingdom* from Belfast Cathedral. There were, however, numerous performances of a wide range of Elgar's compositions. In the autumn *The Light of Life* was given from Birmingham, under Joseph Lewis once more, and *King Olaf* was produced in the Belfast studios, with the first movement of the First Symphony in the same programme. The latter was on 8 October. From London on that same day could be heard the Second Symphony played by the BBC Orchestra under Sir Landon Ronald. In the weeks before that the First Symphony had been heard from Birmingham, under Malcolm Sargent, and the Cello Concerto from Manchester, under the station Music Director T. H. Morrison, with Kathleen Moorhouse as soloist. On 15 November Daventry broadcast the only radio performance of the wartime piece by Elgar *Une Voix dans le Desert.* Gladys Ward sang with the Midland Octet! A curious performance it would seem, to score such a work for octet when the studio orchestra was, presumably, available.

March 1930 saw the introduction of National and Regional programmes, bringing a new era of planning to radio. It had the advantage of relaying many programmes to a wider audience, but mostly restricted local programmes to those of local interest. However, this did not stem the Elgar flow in any way. Singers continued to perform his songs, and particular favourites, as in several years past, were those from *Sea Pictures.* Organists, both classical and popular, were a stand-by of programmes, and there were many playings of the Organ Sonata No.1, or at least a movement from it, as well as organ arrangements of a number of items originally scored for other instruments. Surprisingly, there had never been a broadcast of the Piano Quintet. When it came on 16 June it was not by a professional group but by Kathleen Mapple (piano) and students at the Guildhall School of Music. At a Hallé Concert, broadcast on the 18 June, listeners heard an unusual *Gerontius.* Olga Haley, who was to have sung the Angel, was replaced by Margaret Balfour. At the last moment she too was indisposed, and the only way the performance could continue was if the baritone Harold Williams took over the role of the Angel, as well as the Priest and the Angel of the Agony! He did, and the performance went ahead. Was this unique? On 24 September a talk on Elgar by Adrian Boult was advertised. Alas, the script does not survive in the archives, and when an enquiry was made of Sir Adrian some years ago he had no recollection of the occasion.

The BBC had taken to broadcasting a concert from the Brass Band Festivals held yearly at Crystal Palace. This year Elgar had provided *The Severn Suite* as the test piece. Following the Winner's Concert on 28 September, there followed nine performances of the suite between then and Elgar's death. No performance of Elgar's version for orchestra can be traced, however.

There was no slackening of interest and performance of Elgar's work in 1931 and there were as many entries as ever in the list of works given. A new Elgar work was the *Pomp and Circumstance* March No.5, the first broadcast performance of which was heard on 19 March. It was by the Shepherd's Bush Pavilion Orchestra, conducted by Louis Levy. Levy was to become famous as a film music arranger and director, and his recordings with his 'Gaumont-British Symphony' sold in large numbers. Levy was noted for his orchestral arrangements and it would be interesting to know what he made of Elgar's latest March. The *Nursery Suite,* dedicated to the two Princesses, was first heard this year, and it was immediately taken up by some of the broadcasting orchestras. There were to be twenty radio performances in the next two and a half years. *Gerontius* was relayed from Worcester Cathedral in March, Enid Cruikshank, Steuart Wilson and Harold

Williams being the principals, and Sir Ivor Atkins the conductor. On the same day (3 March) as this relay to the Midlands, the West region was hearing a performance of *King Olaf* from Swansea. Miriam Licette, Heddle Nash and William Barrand were principals, with the National Orchestra of Wales and the Swansea Orpheus Choral Society. Lionel Rowlands conducted.

Later in the month E. Godfrey Brown presented another performance of *Gerontius* from Belfast, and two days later the National programme relayed the concert celebrating the sixtieth anniversary of the Royal Albert Hall. Among the items was the *Enigma Variations* conducted by Boult. This was one of a number of performances of the *Variations* that year. A popular piece with light orchestras and larger forces alike was the charming minuet from the *Beau Brummel* music, which Elgar had composed in 1928.

Although I have mentioned Elgar's own performances of the new *Nursery Suite* previously, the indefatigable Mr Brown of Belfast managed to get in the first performance of the new suite after Elgar's own. This was on 1 September with the Belfast Studio Orchestra. There were, of course, the usual relays of Elgar performances from the Promenade Concerts, including an all-Elgar night. His music appeared sometimes in unlikely settings. The Faraday Commemoration Meeting at Queen's Hall was partly given over to a concert. The BBC Symphony Orchestra, under Sir Henry Wood, included 'Dorabella' in the programme. The last concert of the National Orchestra of Wales, already referred to, took place in October. Warwick Braithwaite included the Cello Concerto in the programme, played by Ronald Harding. Another interesting sidenote to the Elgar story came on 13 October, when the North stations broadcast Gustav Holst conducting Elgar's arrangement of the National Anthem, with the Huddersfield Select String Orchestra.

Right at the end of the year came a broadcast which has often intrigued me. There had been several performances of the *Nursery Suite*, but on 30 December Quentin Maclean, organist of the Trocadero, Elephant & Castle, London, gave the full suite on the organ. Maclean was one of the finest organists around at that time, and had played at the Queen's Hall. I have not traced an organ arrangement available then, so did Maclean arrange it for the Trocadero's large cinema organ himself? If so, does his arrangement survive?

1932 marked the year of Elgar's seventy-fifth birthday, and also it was to be a vital one for the BBC. Broadcasting House, specially built in Portland Place, would mark a new era in radio. But Savoy Hill had seen the growing up of the BBC, and there was nostalgia for the old studios. The last night at Savoy Hill on 14 May included the Wireless Male Voice Choir, under Stanford Robinson, singing Elgar's *Feasting I Watch*. Three days later from the comfortable new BBC studios the Catterall Quartet performed the String Quartet, and a few days later the BBC Orchestra played the two *Chansons*, under the baton of Victor Hely-Hutchinson. The latter would eventually be music director of the BBC, but now he was a conductor of the orchestra, especially in the lighter repertoire. The orchestra now comprised 115 players, which could be used in sections, according to the dictates of the music. Additionally the BBC set up a Theatre Orchestra of some twenty-four players, as well as the now well-established Wireless Military Band of thirty-six. All of these organizations were to play a great deal of Elgar in the next two years; they, and everyone else it seems, for the amount of his music performed on the radio was, if anything, more than usual. Vocal music in particular seemed to attract performers, and many choral groups gave Elgar partsongs. There were, perhaps, fewer of the major orchestral works than usual, but this could be explained by the fact that the Elgar Festival was due at the end of the year. However, there were some major events, including the Violin Concerto from Bournemouth, with Albert Voorsanger (violin) and the Municipal Orchestra under Sir Dan Godfrey. There were also Elgar's own broadcasts during the year. On 30 November came the long-awaited Festival, which has already been mentioned when dealing with Elgar's own broadcasts, including a chamber music concert featuring the Violin Sonata (played by Arthur Catterall and William Murdoch) and the Piano Quintet (played by Murdoch and the Catterall String Quartet). This was one occasion when the public could buy tickets for the new concert hall in Broadcasting House.

The month also included the First Symphony, by the City of Birmingham Orchestra (under its new conductor Leslie Heward), a performance of the same work from the Belfast Orchestra, under Sir Henry Wood, and *Falstaff* by the BBC Orchestra, under Adrian Boult. On 14 December *The Kingdom* was given a Festival performance under Boult, with the BBC Symphony Orchestra, Chorus, Ladies Chorus, Elsie Suddaby, Muriel Brunskill, Walter Widdop and Arthur Cranmer. On 30 December the year ended with a flourish when the *Cockaigne* Overture was performed by Leslie Heward and the Birmingham Orchestra.

In March 1933 the Vienna Philharmonic Orchestra's concert, relayed from that city, conducted by a visiting Adrian Boult, played the *Introduction and Allegro*. It would have been interesting if a recording had been made of this occasion, but despite the BBC's experiments with the Blattnerphone (an early form of tape-recorder) few music items were recorded at this time, and even fewer kept for posterity. Also during the month of March there was a Memorial Concert for Percy Pitt. The strings of the BBC Orchestra, under John Barbirolli, played the *Elegy*, a moving tribute to one of Elgar's very good friends, and a man who had done much for the BBC from its earliest days. Also during the month, in addition to many short works, there was the Violin Concerto, and two performances of *Enigma Variations*. One of the latter was conducted by Boult, the other by Sir Dan Godfrey. There were also several performances of the late (1932) pieces *Serenade* and *Adieu*. These had been arranged for Elgar by Henry Geehl.

The last Elgar première to be given on the radio was the choral song *The Woodland Stream*, sung by the Worcester Massed Elementary School Choirs. This was relayed by the Midlands station from the Worcester Schools Festival on 18 May. On 27 May Elgar's setting of the 29th Psalm was included in the Festival of Music at Coventry Cathedral. The massed choirs were conducted by the organist of the Cathedral, Dr Harold Rhodes. Rhodes was a frequent broadcaster, and often included Elgar's music in his many recitals. On 31 May he played the second radio performance of the Organ Sonata No.2, the first presentation having been given by Herbert Westerby from Belfast Cathedral, on 5 May. There were to be four more performances of the new work before Elgar's death. The first recording had been made on 6 April by Herbert Dawson.

There were relays from the Proms, including *Sea Pictures* sung by Margaret Balfour, and Albert Sammons in the Violin Concerto. The concert in Belfast, which Elgar would have conducted had he not been taken seriously ill, was conducted by E. Godfrey Brown on 14 October. The Belfast Wireless Symphony Orchestra played the Prelude from *The Kingdom, Cockaigne*, the First Symphony, and Rispah Goodacre sang two of his songs, and two excerpts from *Sea Pictures*. A similar concert was heard from Birmingham on 19 October, with the City Orchestra and Leslie Heward, playing the Prelude and Angel's Farewell from *Gerontius, Falstaff* and the Cello Concerto. Margaret Balfour also sang two songs, as well as her role as the Angel. The solo cello was played by Harry Stainer. In November the cellist Gregor Piatigorsky was heard in the Concerto, with the BBC Symphony Orchestra, conducted by Beecham. On 1 December Sir Granville Bantock introduced a record programme on Elgar in his series 'Development of the Orchestra'. Barbirolli conducted the Scottish Orchestra in the Handel Overture transcription two days later, and on 22 December eight items were given from *The Starlight Express*. The music from Elgar's children's play had been to some extent neglected on the radio and the performance was warmly welcomed. The artists were Alice Moxon and Stuart Robertson, with a section of the BBC Orchestra, under Joseph Lewis. The last months of the year had produced a veritable flurry of Elgar performances – were they trying to cheer the composer as he lay in the nursing home? Certainly Elgar was not forgotten, from the humblest singer, given their first chance on radio, to the professional symphony orchestra.

1934 dawned with almost daily performances of Elgar. *Cockaigne, Sea Pictures, Dream Children*, the Piano Quintet, String Quartet, *Bavarian Dances, Sevillana* and songs – all in the space of eight days! Sir Landon Ronald conducted the First Symphony on 10 January, and *Froissart* was given, under H. Foster Clark's baton, on 15 January. On 15 February the concert which should have been conducted by the composer – he was

President of the Hallé Society – was given by John Barbirolli. Albert Sammons again performed the Violin Concerto, and the orchestra played *Froissart, Enigma Variations* and *Cockaigne.*

Each day contained an item from Elgar's large output over a long life, and on the morning of 23 February there was one more piece scheduled. It was *Salut d'Amour,* relayed from the Imperial Hydro Hotel at Blackpool, conducted by the hotel's popular orchestra leader Laddie Clarke. There was a gentle irony in the evening programme to be heard in the North region. It was to be Delius's *Songs of Farewell,* by the Huddersfield Choral Society, under Albert Coates. The London station was to broadcast a concert of contemporary music, including the 20-year old Benjamin Britten's *A Boy was Born.*

It fell to Sir Landon Ronald, a friend of many years, to pay tribute to the composer in a special evening programme from London:

> . . . I have lost in Edward Elgar one of the truest friends of my life. For him I had a love and admiration which amounted to hero-worship. England has lost a very great man, the like of whom we musicians will not know again in this generation – and in saying England I might well add Europe, and, perhaps, the world. To the outside world he was elusive, reserved, and shy, but in the intimate circle he was full of affection and warmth. He was a highly cultured man apart from his music: he had a great knowledge of such diverse subjects as Greek literature, chemistry, poetry and even horse-racing, which he professed to love . . . He was full of enthusiasm up to a few months ago for the new symphony he was writing for the BBC. We shall never be able to hear it because there are only sketches of the principal themes, and not any of it is scored for orchestra. It is a tragedy that Fate decreed that he should not live to finish it . . .

The programme closed with the orchestra. Fred Smith, a noted critic and partner in the record company Rimington Van Wyck Ltd, wrote in 1936, when reviewing a recording of the *Enigma:*

> One of these days HMV must give us Sir Landon Ronald's performance of the Variations. No one of us who heard his performance of the 9th Variation (Nimrod) on the night of Elgar's death can forget its tragic beauty. In a life devoted to music I have experienced nothing more moving than that.

The tributes from the BBC were not quite over. In the BBC's journal *The Listener* Sir Granville Bantock paid a fulsome tribute in a long article:

> We were old friends, of close upon forty years, as he feelingly reminded me when I last saw him, and as I bade him, though we knew it not at the time, what was to be our last farewell. He was cheerful as ever, and we talked of the old days, our hopes, ambitions, and reminiscences. Then we listened to a new proof record of the glorious slow movement from his Quintet for Piano and Strings, which he declared to be the best he had written. He followed the music, and the fine performance of the artists, with evident satisfaction, and expressed his appreciation of the merit of the recording. It left an impression that I shall always remember with emotion and gratitude . . .
>
> His lovable personality, his warm-hearted sympathy and generosity, his affectionate nature – these are all memories that will be cherished gratefully by

those whose privilege it was to know him, apart from the debt that the nation owes to a great and supreme artist . . .

The BBC's other journal *World Radio* had an article by Basil Maine, a journalist and musician with considerable knowledge of Elgar. His obituary[6] was particularly valuable for the passages dealing with the unfinished Third Symphony.

Finally, the BBC broadcast the Memorial Concert held at the Royal Albert Hall on 24 March, the benefits from which went to the Musicians' Benevolent Fund. Adrian Boult and Landon Ronald were the principal conductors in a tribute from the music world to a great composer.

Epilogue

In 1923 that great music educator Percy Scholes likened the spread of radio to the invention of printing. The early history of broadcasting is a fascinating study, and those wishing a fuller background both to the structure of radio in the United Kingdom, and incidentally the development of music broadcasting, should study the considerable literature that has appeared since the 1920s. Essential are the works of Professor Asa Briggs where many of the matters referred to briefly above are covered in detail.[7]

Before radio knowledge of the world of music was so much less than today that it is hard to imagine. Much of music in its many forms was unknown to a wide audience. Elgar was right to speak of people being 'music-starved', but by the end of his life, thanks to the wireless – whether a humble crystal-set or a princely radiogram – a great many people were able to take part in a feast. Elgar's music was provided in generous quantities, and it was not simply because musicians enjoyed performing his works. It was also because Elgar struck a chord with listeners – the BBC would hardly (even in Reithian times) have persisted in giving us so much of his music for some eleven years if the listeners had not wanted it. The BBC received many thousands of letters each year, as well as those directed to their journals. The fact that the presentation of Elgar's music never declined in his lifetime proves that the listener did indeed 'want his music nowadays'.

Notes

1. Oxford University Press, 1974, p.47.
2. BBC Handbook, 1928, p.91.
3. Notes in the BBC Elgar Festival Programmes, 1932.
4. Burton-Page, Piers. 'Goodnight Marco!' Address to the London Branch of the Elgar Society, December 1990. Unpublished.
5. Shera, F.H. (1931). *Elgar's Instrumental Works*. Oxford University Press.

6. Maine, Basil. Reprinted in the *Elgar Society Journal* 1 (1), 1979.
7. Briggs, Asa (1961–65). *History of Broadcasting in the United Kingdom*, vols 1 & 2. Oxford University Press.
    idem. (1984). *The BBC – the First Fifty Years.* Oxford University Press.

Author's note

Unfortunately, my study is not complete, despite a long search. I would like to thank all those people who have supplied information, or answered questions over a number of years. I acknowledge with gratitude the assistance of the staff of the BBC Library, then housed in the Langham, and the staff at BBC Archives Centre, Caversham. My thanks too for assistance at the Westminster Public Library, Charing Cross Road, and the British Library Newspaper Library at Colindale. The incompleteness of the survey is no fault of theirs, as part of the picture is missing. Certain archives from the early period of broadcasting cannot be traced. The BBC Archives began on a voluntary basis in 1933, and certain important items were not lodged at Caversham. The most serious loss is that from Birmingham, where the original 'Programmes as Broadcast' books are missing for all the years up to 1933. Our only information for these years has been culled from the *Radio Times* of the period. Since that journal did not appear until nearly a year after the start of transmissions it will be seen that I have not been able to check many months of programmes. It is known that a book existed in 1937, at Birmingham, known as the 'Manager's Book' giving details of the first days of the station, but this book is lost today. Similarly, the details are missing for the early months of Cardiff, Newcastle, and Aberdeen, and the first three months of the Bournemouth station. If anyone has information that would help in tracing the missing books or papers the writer would be pleased to know of it, as, no doubt, would the BBC Archivist. It is also remarkable that a volume of *Radio Times* cannot be traced! Despite checking with the regional offices of the BBC, and with the British Library and National Library of Scotland, the Northern Editions of the magazine for September to December 1926 have not been located. Southern editions abound, but the writer would dearly like to trace the Northern copies for that period.

First broadcast performances of Elgar's Music Nov. 1922 to Feb. 1934.

The list is in opus number order, works without opus number following. Works not performed, lost or not available for performance at the time are omitted. Songs are listed separately; those songs with opus numbers are also in the first list. Date of first broadcast traced follows the short title, with the total number of performances known in brackets.

Opus

1	Romance for violin	30.11.22	(11)
1a.	Wand of Youth, no.1	17.1.24	(51)
1b.	Wand of Youth, no.2	30.9.23	(116)
2.	Church Motets	16.12.23	(8)
3.	Cantique	16.11.28	(1)
4.	Idylle, Pastorelle & Virelai	23.7.25	(4)
5.	A Soldier's Song (War Song)	27.7.24	(11)
7.	Sevillana	23.3.24	(39)
10.	Three Pieces; Mazurka, Serenade		
	Mauresque, Contrasts	9.1.25	(25, 17, 25)
11.	Sursum Corda	27.3.24	(41)
12.	Salut d'Amour	2.12.22	Many
13.	Mot d'Amour	1.3.23	(16)
15.	Chanson de Matin	27.2.24	(112)
	Chanson de Nuit	22.12.22	(121)
16.	Shepherd's Song	10.2.24	(182)
	Through the Long Days	12.10.24	(16)
	Rondel	17.8.24	(19)
17.	La Capricieuse	19.3.23	(72)
18.	O Happy Eyes	18.6.23	(23)
	Love	30.3.24	(6)
19.	Froissart Overture	3.8.24	(16)
20.	Serenade for Strings	10.4.24	(104)
21.	Minuet	24.5.23	(32)
23.	Spanish Serenade (Stars of a Summer Night)	24.6.24	(9)
26.	The Snow	28.5.24	(35)
	Fly, Singing Bird	13.11.23	(15)
27.	Songs from the Bavarian Highlands	16.2.25	(26)
28.	Organ Sonata no.1	30.3.24	(48, including parts)
29.	Light of Life	19.12.26	(4)
30.	King Olaf	25.3.25	(8)
31.	After	12.5.24	(19)
32.	Imperial March	11.11.23	(65)
33.	Banner of St. George	11.11.23	(10)
35.	Caractacus		Fragments only
36.	Enigma Variations	24.10.23	(69)
37.	Sea Pictures	20.9.23	(256, many incomplete)
38.	Dream of Gerontius	21.4.24	(14)

39.	Pomp and Circumstance Marches,	No.1	25.11.22	Many

39.	Pomp and Circumstance Marches,	No.1	25.11.22	Many
		No.2	10.3.23	(60)
		No.3	2.5.24	(15)
		No.4	31.10.23	(92)
		No.5	19.3.31	(22)
40.	Cockaigne Overture		8.7.23	(85)
41.	In the Dawn		31.8.24	(42)
	Speak, Music		12.7.23	(34)
42.	Grania & Diarmid incidental music		8.12.24	(8)
43.	Dream Children		1.10.23	(43)
44.	Coronation Ode		4.6.25	(1)
45.	Partsongs from the Greek Anthology		30.3.23	See song list
47.	Introduction & Allegro		19.7.25	(36)
48.	Pleading		13.11.23	(192)
49.	The Apostles		10.3.27	(1 & 5 parts)
50.	In the South		2.4.24	(19)
51.	The Kingdom		1.3.28	(3 & 9 parts)
53.	There is Sweet Music		29.2.32	(1)
	O Wild West Wind		27.3.26	(3)
	Owls		28.6.28	(1)
54.	The Reveille		2.2.25	(12)
55.	Symphony no.1		8.9.27	(13 & 3 parts)
56.	Angelus		26.12.24	(10)
57.	Go Song of Mine		10.12.25	(10)
58.	Elegy		14.9.24	(13)
59.	O Soft was the Song		21.3.23	(45)
	Was It Some Golden Star		22.5.25	(2)
	Twilight		11.2.26	(1)
60.	The Torch		22.7.24	(9)
	The River		5.6.23	(21)
61.	Violin Concerto		15.1.25	(24 & 6 parts)
62.	Romance for Bassoon & Orchestra		1.5.25	(4)
63.	Symphony no.2		7.3.24	(12)
64.	O Hearken Thou		13.10.29	(1)
65.	Coronation March		13.5.24	(2)
66.	Crown of India Suite		4.10.23	(102 including parts)
67.	Great is the Lord (Psalm 48)		17.3.29	(1)
68.	Falstaff		25.11.26	(16)
69.	The Music makers		20.5.25	(5)
70.	Sospiri		20.7.24	(8)
71.	The Shower		16.3.24	(9)
72.	Death on the Hills		12.4.30	(4)
73.	Love's Tempest		25.10.32	(2)
	Serenade		31.5.23	(15)
74.	Give unto the Lord (Psalm 29)		22.8.26	(2)
75.	Carillon		6.5.24	(29)
76.	Polonia		31.3.25	(7)
77.	Une Voix dans le Desert		15.11.29	(1)
78.	Starlight Express – excerpts		27.11.24	(12 parts)
80.	Spirit of England		11.11.24	(6 including 4 parts)

82.	Violin Sonata	23.8.23	(27 including 3 parts)
83.	String Quartet	17.7.24	(12)
84.	Piano Quintet	16.6.30	(5)
85.	Cello Concerto	2.5.24	(19)
86.	Fantasy & Fugue (Bach)	14.9.24 (Fugue 10.8.24)	(23)
87.	Severn Suite (Brass Band)	?28.9.30	(9)
87a.	Organ Sonata no.2	5.5.33	(6)
	Gavotte in A, 1886	21.9.24	(5)
	Serenade Lyrique, 1899	5.2.23	(38)
	May Song, 1901	1.5.25	(24)
	Carissima, 1914	24.4.24	(63)
	Rosemary, 1914	13.2.25	(30)
	Empire March, 1924	18.8.24	(21)
	Beau Brummel-minuet, 1928	20.4.29	(32)
	Nursery Suite, 1931	20.8.31	(20)
	Adieu, 1932	7.2.33	(16)
	Serenade, 1932	7.2.33	(20
	Overture in D minor (Handel)	22.2.25	(29)
	God save the King, arrangement	26.11.25	(6)
	Petite Reine (Beraud)	2.3.25	(1)
	Three Bavarian Dances	9.8.23	(215 including parts)
	Viola Concerto	20.3.30	(4)
	O Salutaris Hostia	7.10.28	(4)
	Ecce Sacerdos	7.3.26	(1)

Songs

After	13.5.24	(19)
After Many a Dusty Mile	11.12.23	(29)
Angelus	26.12.24	(10)
Arabian Serenade	3.5.28	(1)
As Torrents in Summer (King Olaf)	7.2.24	(51)
Carol for the King's Recovery	9.12.29	(1)
Chariots of the Lord	11.11.23	(4)
Come Gentle Night	9.9.23	(8)
Death on the Hills	12.4.30	(4)
Evening Scene	24.3.26	(7)
Feasting I Watch	5.8.23	(94)
Fly, Singing Bird	13.11.23	(15)
Go Song of Mine	10.12.25	(10)
The Herald	29.12.27	(8)
How Calmly the Evening	24.1.26	(8)
In Moonlight	5.4.25	(8)
In the Dawn	11.9.23	(42)
Inside the Bar	20.2.23	(3)
Is She Not Passing Fair?	10.10.24	(29)

It's oh to be a Wild Wind	12.6.23	(45)
King's Way	13.5.24	(1)
Like to the Damask Rose	31.1.23	(132)
Love	30.3.24	(6)
Love's Tempest	25.10.32	(2)
Marching Song (Follow the Colours)	12.9.27	(3)
My Love Dwelt in a Northern Land	19.3.24	(35)
O Happy eyes	12.6.23	(23)
O Soft was the Song	21.3.23	(45)
O Wild West Wind	27.3.26	(3)
Owls	28.6.28	(1)
Pansies	19.11.24	(8)
Pipes of Pan	Mid-Sept, 1922	(86)
Pleading	10.1.23	(192)
Poet's Life	28.7.23	(40)
Prince of Sleep	2.7.26	(10)
Queen Mary's Song	13.5.24	(30)
Reveille	2.2.25	(12)
The River	5.6.23	(21)
Rondel	17.8.24	(19)
Serenade	31.5.23	(15)
Shepherd's Song	20.12.22	(182)
The Shower	16.3.24	(9)
The Snow	28.5.24	(35)
Soldier's Song (A War Song)	27.7.24	(11)
Song of Autumn	28.5.23	(29)
Spanish Serenade (Stars of a Summer Night)	24.6.24	(9)
Speak Music	12.7.23	(34)
There are Seven that pull the Thread	12.9.27	(2)
There is Sweet Music	29.2.32	(1)
Through the Long Days	12.10.24	(16)
The Torch	22.7.24	(9)
Twilight	11.2.26	(1)
The Wanderer	10.9.24	(32)
Was It Some Golden Star?	22.5.25	(2)
Weary Wind of the West	11.12.23	(26)
Whether I find Thee	1.1.25	(12)
Woodland Stream	18.5.33	(1)
Yea Cast Me from the Heights	17.8.24	(8)
Zut, Zut, Zut	27.7.25	(19)

Sea Pictures Complete,	?20.9.23	Def.15.2.24	
Sea Slumber Song		5.9.23	
In Haven		3.12.22	
Sabbath Morning at Sea		28.10.23	(256 complete
Where Corals Lie		8.8.23	or in part)
The Swimmer		30.6.24	

Pageant of Empire Complete	7.11.24	
Shakespeare's Kingdom	29.6.25	
The Islands	24.5.28	
The Blue Mountains	21.10.24	(23 complete
The Heart of Canada	1.7.26	or in part)

Sailing Westward	21.10.24	
Merchant Adventurers	8.2.27	
Immortal Legions	11.11.24	(2)
Fringes of the Fleet	25.2 23	(1 & parts)

Index

Elgar, Sir Edward (Music index)